Eyes on the Stars and Feet on the Ground

Eyes on the Stars and Feet on the Ground

The Foreign Policy of Theodore Roosevelt

Howard Jones

Edited by Donald A. Rakestraw

ROWMAN & LITTLEFIELD
Lanham • Boulder • New York • London

Rowman & Littlefield
Bloomsbury Publishing Inc, 1385 Broadway, New York, NY 10018, USA
Bloomsbury Publishing Plc, 50 Bedford Square, London, WC1B 3DP, UK
Bloomsbury Publishing Ireland, 29 Earlsfort Terrace, Dublin 2, D02 AY28, Ireland
www.rowman.com

British Library Cataloguing in Publication Information available

Library of Congress Cataloging-in-Publication Data

Names: Jones, Howard, 1940–2022, author. | Rakestraw, Donald A. (Donald Allen),
    1952– editor.
Title: Eyes on the stars and feet on the ground : the foreign policy of Theodore
    Roosevelt / by Howard Jones, edited by Donald A. Rakestraw.
Description: Lanham: Rowman & Littlefield, [2025] | Includes bibliographical
    references and index.
Identifiers: LCCN 2024052593 (print) | LCCN 2024052594 (ebook) |
    ISBN 9798881801892 (cloth) | ISBN 9798881801915 (epub)
Subjects: LCSH: Roosevelt, Theodore, 1858–1919. | United States—Foreign
    relations—1901–1909. | United States—Politics and government—1901–1909.
Classification: LCC E756 .J66 2025 (print) | LCC E756 (ebook) | DDC 973.91/1—dc23/
    eng/20241209
LC record available at https://lccn.loc.gov/2024052593
LC ebook record available at https://lccn.loc.gov/2024052594

For product safety related questions contact productsafety@bloomsbury.com.

∞™ The paper used in this publication meets the minimum requirements of American
National Standard for Information Sciences—Permanence of Paper for Printed Library
Materials, ANSI/NISO Z39.48-1992.

In memory of my wife and dearest friend, Mary Ann . . . who I hope would have approved my treatment of her favorite character in America's history.
—Howard Jones, 2022

In memory of my dear friend and mentor, Howard Jones . . . who I hope would have approved my completion of his treatment of Theodore Roosevelt.
—Donald A. Rakestraw, 2024

Contents

Foreword

Howard Jones (1939–2022)

Howard Jones devoted his career to the teaching and study of the history of American foreign relations—a career that produced over a dozen books (many award winning) and a generation of teacher-scholars eager to adopt his example. When he died in March 2022, he was working on what he knew would be his last book, a much-needed and broadly accessible work that chronicles President Theodore Roosevelt's leadership as America's chief diplomat. Fading under the assault of a terminal illness, Jones eventually accepted that he would not see the manuscript through to publication. As with all of his work since I had the good fortune of studying with him in the 1980s, he routinely discussed the project with me, sending drafts of each chapter. My inbox still contains first drafts, rewrites, revisions, and questions to ponder about everything from Roosevelt's beliefs about a racial hierarchy to the reliability of the president's reflections on particular episodes. In the autumn of 2021, Howard acknowledged there was a good chance the book's completion would fall to me. When he died the following spring, his family asked me to speak at the memorial service, after which his daughter, Shari Prentice, gave me every scrap of paper, every book, every printed version or draft of the manuscript, two computers, and any digital storage device that might contain files related to the "TR book." This she did to honor her father's wishes and to assist me in fulfilling my promise to adopt the project and see that this final title joined the other spines on the impressive Jones shelf.

Howard Jones's purpose in writing a book on Theodore Roosevelt's foreign policy was twofold. First, he wanted to produce a work useful to both the specialist and the student of U.S. diplomatic history. While the long-established standards on the subject, Howard K. Beale's *Theodore Roosevelt and America's Rise to World Power* (1956) and Frederick Marks III's *Velvet on Iron: The Diplomacy of Theodore Roosevelt* (1979), remain essential resources, they are framed around a collection of lectures (Beale) and essays (Marks). In contrast, *Eyes on the Stars and Feet on the Ground* is designed to carry the narrative of Roosevelt's diplomacy during his time at the helm of the nation's foreign policy. As such, Jones examines every angle of the byzantine process that resulted in the Panama Canal, a Roosevelt achievement that most would label epic but one to which Beale devotes scant attention. He also develops, in vintage Jones prose, Roosevelt's decisive efforts to secure the Western Hemisphere against European exploitation; to broker peace in the Russo-Japanese War, earning him the Nobel Peace Prize; to extend, in large measure as a hedge against conflict, the respect due to the Japanese people and nation; to project American might through a modern navy; to advance the critical Anglo-American rapprochement; and to secure for the United States a seat at the table and a respected voice in all major international matters. Jones has achieved this purpose by skillfully interweaving all significant international episodes addressed by Roosevelt during his presidency.

The book's second purpose derived from Jones's desire to produce a narrative that would be accessible to a broad readership and one that would mitigate the simplistic image of Roosevelt as the cartoonish figure who strode across the landscape wielding a big stick and clubbing all who dared oppose him. Those who have read his books would agree that Jones had an ability to develop his subject in a way that, at times, lifted the two-dimensional figure from the page, often inviting a surprising level of empathy. About his most recent book, *My Lai: Vietnam, 1968, and the Descent into Darkness*, I wrote in an essay for the Peace History Society that "no one could engage it without sinking into the darkness and suffering as if sharing a palpable, almost tangible, experience with the words on the page." His intention to bring this same vibrancy to the Roosevelt book was evident in how he first crafted it; and, although he wrestled with whether to recast it after some early editorial resistance, I have chosen to honor his original purpose, most pronounced with the inclusion of the Prologue. This decision has been embraced by readers of the manuscript with an affirming "yes, this is Jones." I should note that Howard did not intend to dilute his purpose with excessive Roosevelt biography, but he did feel it essential for the reader to appreciate how the attributes and characteristics formed in Roosevelt's early years and the personal tragedies he endured contributed to how he piloted the ship of state into international waters. Jones also has achieved this goal in the pages that follow, making this a book to be enjoyed by a readership beyond the academy.

Howard Jones trained with Robert H. Ferrell at Indiana University and never abandoned his commitment to the "Ferrell Method," one that he passed on to me and numerous others. This method involved dogged research, copious notetaking, writing, rewriting, editing, and rewriting again; and then, a bit of marinating before submission. Howard always had future projects underway while completing existing ones, and he left behind yellowed pages of notes from his research on the TR book, collected years before drafting the first chapter.

It has been my task to complete the last few steps of the method, but with a foundation, a direction, and an understanding passed down to me of how those steps should be taken. The task has, nevertheless, been a laborious one, with numerous episodes of my calling for clarification from a voice that had sadly gone silent. My mission, in some ways, has been to divine as best I could Howard's intentions while resisting the intrusion of my own voice. When we co-authored *Prologue to Manifest Destiny* in the late 1990s, we were told by the editor that he could not distinguish where my words ended and Howard's began—one of the most satisfying compliments of my career. My hope is that this remains so in this effort. I must add, however, that I bear responsibility for any shortcomings in this work and adapt for my role Howard's humble words from his widely acclaimed *Mutiny on the Amistad*: "Whatever good qualities this work may have" belong to my mentor and dear friend Howard Jones; "the inadequacies I jealously claim as my own."

—Donald A. Rakestraw
March 28, 2024

Acknowledgments

While a challenge with any book, for a posthumously published work it is especially difficult to find a starting point for acknowledging all who had a hand in its completion. In truth, there are two sets of people to recognize—the names Howard Jones noted (some on the back of a dog-eared envelope) that he wanted included and those of friends, colleagues, and former Jones students who assisted me in picking up the baton and getting the project to the finish line.

For his part, Professor Jones wished to acknowledge the late George Herring, who, sadly, only survived Howard by a few months. Dr. Herring read an early draft of the manuscript and offered valuable insights on how it might be improved. Having found his report in Howard's files, I see evidence that his remarks and suggestions were considered in subsequent versions. As a peer in the field, Howard regularly expressed his admiration for Professor Herring's contributions to the history of U.S. foreign relations. A number of other prominent historians (some, anonymous readers) also voiced their approval of the Roosevelt project, understanding the significant contribution this work would make to both the Roosevelt literature and the history of U.S. foreign relations. Of these, I wish to extend special appreciation to Don Doyle, not only for his support of Howard but for the continued encouragement he offered to me after Howard's passing. Among others on Howard's list are Pete Maslowski, who encouraged and followed his work throughout their decades of friendship; Robert May, with whom Howard maintained a strong bond over the course of their careers; Jim Jones, for his steadfast support; and Michael Stedman, a former student with whom Professor Jones nurtured a treasured relationship across several decades.

Howard Jones often mentioned how grateful he was to have had the support of his colleagues and friends at the University of Alabama, especially those with whom he shared the halls of ten Hoor over his long tenure there. On the list he left, Howard highlighted colleagues who joined him in "The Sages" lunch group—Lawrence Kohl, Michael Mendle, and George Rable, all faithful companions to the end.

Although Howard did not leave details of his appreciation for the hard work of staff at libraries and archives, I here take the liberty to thank them on his behalf, knowing that he has a history of generously acknowledging their importance to his work. Along with the Library of Congress, the Gorgas Library, and the National Archives, he frequently lauded the work of the Theodore Roosevelt Center at Dickinson State University. In the area of research venues, Howard provided only two names, Lauren Tubbs, who during the development of the Roosevelt project served as Circulation Librarian at the University of Alabama's Gorgas Library, and Phillip Hays, Head of Government Information Services and Interlibrary Loan Coordinator at Winthrop University's Dacus Library. Both Tubbs and Hays proved valuable conduits for essential sources. My sincere apologies if I have missed anyone whom Howard may have intended to acknowledge but whose name did not make it to my desk.

.Finally, Howard never failed to thank his family for giving him the wonderful life he enjoyed as a husband, father, grandfather, and great-grandfather. His precious great-granddaughters, Annie Elizabeth Skelton and Leleigh-Ann James Skelton, whom he doted over excessively during the last years of his life while working on the Roosevelt book, were set to be joined by great-grandson, John Maddux Skelton. Had Howard lived to meet him, "Maddie," too, would have enjoyed the affection of his "Poppy." One cannot help but imagine Howard channeling the playful antics of Roosevelt in his interactions with these three. Howard's grandchildren, Timothy Skelton, Lauren Prentice, and Ashley Brown, were the apples of his eye, as were the mother of his great-grandchildren, Kari Skelton and his daughters Debbie Brown and Shari Prentice. Howard, as always, would have concluded with his enduring gratitude to the love of his life, Mary Ann, who preceded him in death in 2017 and who had encouraged him to write this book. Of the members of the family, no one was more dedicated to seeing this book completed than his daughter Shari. She tragically passed away before its publication, but I wish to honor her memory with my sincere gratitude for her love and perseverance. Without her efforts, this book would not have been possible.

A few months before his death, Professor Jones engaged in a Zoom visit with a group of his former students; and, one last time, we enjoyed seeing him command the virtual space in much the same way he had commanded the classroom. All of those on the call thanked him for his contributions to their successful careers (many in academia), and several later supported my completion of the Roosevelt book. I wish to express special thanks to Carol

Jackson Adams, Ryan Floyd, Paul Grass, and Dan Pierce for investing their valuable time in the improvement of this work. Among my own students, a few deserve mention for their persistent interest in my projects, especially this one. Nicole Holbert Morrow, as a student intern at Winthrop, edited my essay for the Peace History Society and continued to follow the project afterward. Christopher Goodwin and Marlana Mayton Goodwin—who met in my office as students and later married—have left me with countless images of friendship and support, as has my favorite "Russian," Vladimir Markarov. Lastly, I would like to thank my dear friend and former graduate student, Cory Andrews, for his reliable encouragement over the years as well as for his excellent work on Roosevelt's Alaska boundary controversy in my graduate seminar at Wadham College, Oxford "last century." Also contributing to sections of this book are my good friends and colleagues Anastatia Sims and Charles Thomas, joined by the gifted editorial eye of my brother-in-law, Westbrook Finlayson, Jr.

Here, I set aside special appreciation from me and the spirit of Howard Jones for my good friend and colleague Vernon Egger who invested a tremendous amount of time in reading and editing every word of the manuscript from preface to bibliography. Having read, reread, and edited the work numerous times, I was amazed at how much he found in need of additional edits and recasting for clarity. It is no exaggeration to say that his thorough reading has greatly improved *Eyes on the Stars and Feet on the Ground*.

I am also grateful to my former dean at Winthrop University, Takita Sumter, and the current chair of history at Winthrop, Greg Bell, for kindly providing support and workspace for this project. My good friend and colleague at Winthrop, Ginger Williams, knew Howard and his work on Roosevelt and offered continual encouragement for my efforts to complete the book. Further, the exceptional staff of Winthrop University's Dacus Library, especially Nancy White and Phillip Hays, deserve credit for effectively keeping my desk covered with every source needed. I would be remiss if I did not also express gratitude to the staff at the Library of Congress for their continued efforts to provide efficient access to their holdings and to the staff at the Thomas Cooper Library at the University of South Carolina for their gracious accommodation.

Of course, getting the project from manuscript to the shelf required the efforts of a capable publishing team. Jon Sisk, Senior Executive Acquisitions Editor for the press, was instantly enthusiastic about the opportunity to publish Howard Jones's last title and maintained that enthusiasm from start to finish. I also would like to express my gratitude to Executive Editor Ashley Dodge for stepping in after Jon's retirement to see the book through the critical last phase of production. In the trenches, no one was more important than Jon's Assistant Editor, Mikayla Lindsay, who patiently endured my back and forth over any nit I sought to pick. She has been a wonder to work with. I also wish to acknowledge the cover design efforts of Kathi Ha. With Mikayla as go between and me on holiday in Scotland, she somehow managed to get it "exactly right." For navigating my efforts through the final production stages with a very capable copyediting team, I am forever indebted to Associate Production Editor Lynn Zelem and Project Manager Dilip Shanmugasundaram. They kept the coal dry and the ship steaming to port.

Finally, this book owes more gratitude than is possible to convey to the members of the "core manuscript team"—my fellow follower of all things Howard Jones, Paul Grass (whose name was among those listed on Howard's envelope), and my wonderful dean *emerita* and wife, Jennie F. Rakestraw. Our part in the Roosevelt project literally began around the kitchen table with the three of us sifting through every version of the manuscript as well as scraps of chapters included in the numerous files provided by Shari. It was here that the struggle began over determining how Howard would have envisioned the final approach and how best to honor his wishes to produce a seamless, comprehensive, highly readable and enjoyable treatment of Theodore Roosevelt's foreign policy. Going forward from "the table," every question I had over every verb to apply was taken up by both before circling back to me for deliberation. In the end, I lost count of how many times they each read and commented on every version of every chapter, from initial drafts to page proofs. I am convinced that without their labors (for Howard), I would not have survived the process. My words are not adequate to express how important they were to this project.

And, as ever, I offer special acknowledgment to my family—to my daughters Charity Wait Rakestraw and Foster Rakestraw Hays, who have been a constant encouragement, and to my grandchildren, Tom and Finlay, for their welcomed distractions. Although I mentioned my wife, Jennie, in her professional capacity above, I would also like to express my love and appreciation here for persevering through all of my late hours at the desk while dealing with and overcoming her own challenges—you are a support beyond words.

—Donald A. Rakestraw
Fort Mill, South Carolina
Fall, 2024

Preface

Look at Roosevelt's face: it is all there, even that wistful conflict between his brain and his temperament . . . an optimist who saw things as they ought to be, wrestling with a realist who knew things as they were.

—Owen Wister
1913

Be practical as well as generous in your ideals. Keep your eyes on the stars, but remember to keep your feet on the ground.

—President Theodore Roosevelt
May 24, 1904

At the Sorbonne in Paris in early 1910, Theodore Roosevelt spoke about the responsibilities of citizenship in a republic and the importance of leaders with character, which he defined as "force and courage" and a "good faith and sense of honor" in dealing with all citizens. "It is not the critic who counts," he declared. "The credit belongs to the man who tries and fails over and over in seeking "a worthy cause." He knows, at best, "the triumph of high achievement," and, at worst, "he fails while daring greatly, so that his place shall never be with those cold and timid souls who know neither victory nor defeat."[1]

The following study of the 26th president's foreign policy begins with an account of how the young Roosevelt developed into the man quoted above. At its heart is the evolution of a sickly child born in 1858 into a president whose firm hand piloted the U.S. ship of state into the so-called "American Century." My primary goal is to provide a single-volume treatment of

Theodore Roosevelt's foreign policy that chronicles the major episodes he addressed during his nearly two terms in office. By offering a glimpse into Roosevelt's life before the White House, I also have sought to provide a broader understanding of how and why he addressed foreign policy as he did. This approach will hopefully appeal to the general reader as well as to students and specialists in the field of U.S. foreign relations.

As the United States entered the late nineteenth-century period of territorial expansion known as "New Manifest Destiny," Roosevelt emerged as the country's first architect of twentieth-century foreign policy and a staunch advocate of American exceptionalism—a characteristic he rooted as much in the will of backwoodsmen who conquered the frontier as in the oft-cited "city upon a hill" vision of the Puritans.[2] To reach this pinnacle in life, Roosevelt had to overcome a series of personal hardships and tragedies that molded his character. His many personal misfortunes encouraged the development of what historian Doris Kearns Goodwin terms the essential feature of an effective leader: an empathy that enabled him to set aside his own problems to understand, sympathize, and care for the weak, the downtrodden, and the aggrieved.[3]

Roosevelt matured during his presidency at a pivotal inflection point in America's history—a time of massive industrial, commercial, and technological expansion, both at home and abroad. In foreign affairs, a dangerous new world had materialized in which the Great Powers of Britain, France, Germany, Japan, and Russia competed so ardently for naval bases and colonies that they engaged in an arms race that shaped the histories of several areas of the world, including the Western Hemisphere. Roosevelt welcomed the opportunity to help resolve these global issues despite congressional and popular opposition to foreign entanglements.

He understood that isolation no longer guaranteed the security afforded by two oceans. With the advent of faster and larger steam battleships, the Atlantic and the Pacific did not provide natural protective shields as they had in the past but had become instead avenues for foreign adventure in the hemisphere. To defend the United States, he called for an enlarged and improved navy and an active involvement in this volatile international system—not through alliances, he determined, but through unilateral action guided by America's best interests.

Roosevelt's new approach posed severe challenges, especially given the growing number of imperial nations that had penetrated the Latin American markets and that sought naval bases in the Caribbean, South America, Asia, and the Pacific. The United States was also a power in terms of population, resources, and territory and had to act out of self-interest in resisting foreign encroachments in the Western Hemisphere and other areas of national concern. It could also claim membership in the imperial club in 1898 with the annexation of Hawaii and the victorious war with Spain that led to America's first colonies of Puerto Rico and the Philippines, the acquisition of Guam and other small islands in the Pacific, and the establishment of a protectorate over Cuba. According to historian George C. Herring, "The internationalization of America and the Americanization of the world was under way by 1900."[4]

I

The late 1890s and early 1900s were an exciting and optimistic time for Americans. Among many changes, prosperity had returned after the Depression of 1893; Americans were proud of and emboldened by their triumph over Spain in 1898; optimism had spread over the possibility of global commerce tying the rival nations together; revolutions in Russia and China perhaps pointed to a further spread of civilization; and women's rights gained traction.[5]

Not by coincidence did the new era become synonymous with the robust, magnetic, colorful, and charismatic personality of President Theodore Roosevelt. Five feet, eight inches tall, thick necked, broad chested, and a solid 200 pounds in weight at one point, he relished life to the utmost and made no secret of his joy in holding the highest office in the land. The "poorest way to face life is to face it with a sneer," he asserted. Roosevelt became the central figure in a decade of domestic and foreign policy challenges that was enlivened by photos of dignitaries and families, cartoons in the press and magazines caricaturing the president and other leaders, and the advent of stardom brought about by the burgeoning motion picture industry.[6]

"No one could accuse *me* of having a charming personality," Roosevelt once remarked. Contemporary historian Henry Adams might have agreed: "Theodore is never sober, only he is drunk with himself and not with rum." Roosevelt's presence, according to another observer, "so crowds the room that the walls are worn thin and threatened to burst outward." If you go to the White House, "you shake hands with Roosevelt and hear him talk—and then go home to wring the personality out of your clothes." Roosevelt's friend, journalist William Allen White, declared that he "sounded in my heart the first trumpet of the new time that was to be." And Woodrow Wilson, no friend of Roosevelt's, admitted to being "charmed by his personality. There is a sweetness about him that is very compelling. You can't resist the man."[7]

Roosevelt also had a sense of humor, including the capacity to laugh at himself. Joseph B. Bishop, a journalist, friend, and authorized biographer of the president, regularly collected cartoons from the press and took them to the White House for Roosevelt and his family to see. "It is very curious," Roosevelt once observed. "Ever since I have been in the Presidency I have been pictured constantly as a huge creature with enormous clenched teeth, a big spiked club, and a belt full of pistols—a blustering, roaring swashbuckler type of ruffian, and yet," he mused, "all the time I have been growing in popularity. I don't understand it at all."

Bishop thought cartoonists liked him and his good nature. Rarely did their caricatures contain a cutting message. Roosevelt had some of them framed and put in his bookcases, both in the White House and in his home at Oyster Bay in New York.[8]

Roosevelt thrived on being the focal point of everything. Two of his children, Kermit and Alice, agreed that their father always wanted to be "the bride at every wedding and the corpse at every funeral." Henry James was blunt in characterizing Roosevelt. James, a distinguished novelist who focused on genteel subjects and manners, privately pronounced Roosevelt "a dangerous and ominous jingo" and "the mere monstrous embodiment of unprecedented resounding noise." Henry Adams, a patrician from that long-standing Boston Brahmin family, asserted that Roosevelt possessed "that singular primitive quality that belongs to ultimate matter—the quality that medieval theology assigned to God—he was pure act."[9]

Roosevelt welcomed every challenge before him, including a perilous ride in one of the navy's six new submarines, *The Plunger*. In August 1905, after a morning at home spent cabling the conferees at the Portsmouth (New Hampshire) peace negotiations over the Russo-Japanese War, the president stunned Americans by wriggling through an eighteen-inch opening in the tower of the submarine during a rainstorm and taking a fifty-minute test dive to the bottom of Long Island Sound. After exploring the entire vessel, he accepted the commander's invitation to take the controls and put it through several maneuvers before surfacing—albeit by accident—stern first. Roosevelt squeezed out of the hatch, calling this "a splendid day's fun." As commander in chief, he could have defended his action as an effort to keep up-to-date on the submarine's potential; instead, he explained that "I did not like to have the officers and enlisted men think I wanted them to try things I was reluctant to try myself."[10]

When the *New York Times* learned of this incident, it expressed regret that the more the president risked his life by such foolish ventures, the more his popularity soared. The submarine was dangerous, but he joined the expedition with a "boyish delight." One disgruntled politician groaned, "Whatever hurts him helps him." The paper admonished him for ignoring his responsibility for millions of Americans by going underwater in "some new-fangled, submersible, collapsible, and otherwise dangerous device."[11]

The *Times* had no doubt of Roosevelt's secret desire to participate in another innovation of the time: to fly in that "yellow sausage" over Manhattan, which threatened "instant and terrible death" to its pilot. "It is most fortunate that the aerial machine in question will hold but one, because if it held two the President would insist upon being the other." These "stunts" were "well enough for Theodore Roosevelt," but not for the president of the United States.[12]

Five years later, the flying machine could carry two, one of whom was Roosevelt, now in his post-White House years. When he and his entourage attended an air meet arranged by Wilbur and Orville Wright in St. Louis on October 11, 1910, an aviator working for them, Archibald Hoxsey, invited the former president to fly with him. "No, thank you. There are enough high-fliers up there already." But within seconds, he changed his mind and climbed aboard the box-kite "flying machine." Asked by the press about his four-minute flight experience, he replied, "Bully!"[13]

Not every American reacted positively to Roosevelt. He had a dark side, according to more than a few contemporaries. He could be rude by keeping guests waiting while he played with his children, or, when involved in what he considered to be a boring conversation, pulling out something from his pocket to read or abruptly retiring for the evening. He could also be vengeful toward those who seemingly wronged him or the country. "Roosevelt lies and curses in a most disgusting way," according to George Newett, the editor of a small weekly newspaper in Ishpeming, Michigan, in October 1912. He "gets drunk too and all his intimates know it." Roosevelt filed a libel suit, and the result was a May 1913 trial in a county courthouse in Marquette that drew national and international attention. Newett failed to provide evidence for his charges, and Roosevelt turned down a handsome compensation to settle for "nominal damages" of six cents.[14]

On a national level, critics then and now frown upon the late nineteenth-century emphasis on colonial rivalries, imperialism, and white supremacy doctrines that heavily influenced the thinking and policies of many Americans—including Roosevelt. Anglo-American cooperation he considered essential to civilizing the so-called backward peoples in the world by spreading Anglo-Saxon (more precisely, "English-speaking") principles of government. Who could resist the infusion of republican ideals? At the time, it did not seem to matter that this so-called progressive argument often rested on race or color, or followed the dictates of efficiency in production and living standards.

No one could question Roosevelt's courage in confronting every problem before him. Life was a series of battles, he declared, each followed by victory or defeat, only to see another challenge emerge. "There were all kinds of things of which I was afraid at first, ranging from grizzly bears to 'mean' horses and gun-fighting; but by acting as if I was not afraid I gradually ceased to be afraid."[15] His charge on horseback while under fire and leading the "Rough Riders" against the Spanish in the Cuban jungle is the type of story from which legends are made. Perhaps he played a role on the public stage, but he chose that role and stayed with it from the time he built his body as a young child to the time he lost his youngest son Quentin in the Great War and considered his life over.

Roosevelt described his life as a race. As a young boy, he loved horseback riding, hunting, hiking, climbing, swimming, and exploring for wildlife in the woods. In the White House, he enjoyed all the same pleasures while adding tennis, boxing, wrestling, and the game of single-stick, where dignitaries in the White House exchanged whopping blows with sticks that hurt both players despite helmets and heavy padding. The young president relished the dare of big-game hunting in the American West, Africa, and South America. On the hunt and in everyday life, he declared, "black care rarely sits behind a rider whose pace is fast enough."[16]

He never tired of strenuous activities, and in his adult life, both at Sagamore Hill in New York and in the White House, Roosevelt displayed such boisterous behavior that the First Lady often had to bring him under control. At home in Oyster Bay, he played outdoor games with the children of three families of Roosevelts—sixteen cousins, most of whom loved the challenge of the "obstacle walk," which required players to move "point to point" by going "over or through" but "never around" the barn, a precipice, a boulder, a river, or anything else in the way of victory. Similarly, Roosevelt as president led foreign leaders on hikes, regardless of weather, through the wilderness of Rock Creek Park that required following a straight path through rough land, hills, trees, and sometimes icy water. On one occasion, a guest "was doubtful as to his ability to get over" the creek, so, Roosevelt conceded, "I was afraid to let him" make the attempt. "For I did not want a guest to drown on one of my walks."[17]

It is no exaggeration to say that Roosevelt approached the challenges of his presidency the same way he followed the rules of the obstacle walk.[18]

Through it all, he kept his sense of humor, on one occasion laughing as he refused an umbrella when speaking in a rainstorm at a Fourth of July celebration in Oyster Bay that no more than five persons left until he was through. And he always had time for not only the "plain folks" he met but for his children, whether a pillow fight with Quentin and Archie in the evening or reading to them for a half hour before bed.[19]

As a supporter of Progressive reform, Roosevelt decried the so-called loose living of smoking, drinking, and other forms of misbehavior that violated the Victorian social order—made real to him while president when his daughter Alice, at eighteen years of age, modeled this inappropriate lifestyle to such an extent that the press labeled her "Alice in Wonderland." When longtime friend and author Owen Wister was in Roosevelt's White House office and she burst in and out three times, he finally asked, "Theodore, isn't there anything you can do to control Alice?" "Dan," replied the president (Wister's nickname from college days), "I can do one of two things. I can be President of the United States, or I can control Alice. I cannot possibly do both."[20]

His office, Roosevelt nonetheless declared, furnished "a pulpit of an unusual character from which to preach." For America to be great, he told the Interfaith Committee on Marriage and Divorce, we must save "our own national soul."[21]

II

Much of our story necessarily covers familiar events and yet will, I hope, establish connections between them and an aggressive foreign policy led by a president who attempted to secure the Atlantic and Pacific worlds from imperial nations by building peace based on a balance of power on a global scale.

Roosevelt did not formulate and execute his foreign policy by rigid adherence to either idealism or realism alone. Wister called Roosevelt "an optimist who saw things as they ought to be, wrestling with a realist who knew things as they were." Roosevelt sought to strike a balance between the two, knowing he could succeed only by seeking a foundation of "realizable ideals" in both private and public life.[22]

"When America's history is written," Roosevelt declared in the Earl Lecture Series of 1911 at Pacific Theological Seminary in Berkeley, California, "the mere acquisition of wealth itself" will mean nothing. There is nothing wrong with enjoying life and amassing wealth, but with that wealth comes the moral obligation to serve "the rest of mankind." Money is "a means to an end," he declared, and "if you make it the end instead of a means you do little good to yourself and are a curse to everybody else." Roosevelt often quoted Abraham Lincoln in asserting that there is in every person "a deal of human nature" that requires helping those in need. As president, Roosevelt expanded on this principle by seeking to enlighten the less fortunate peoples of the world in an effort to establish order and stability and thereby discourage war between opposing colonizing powers.[23]

For Roosevelt, the character of a leader should be a model for the people he leads. Worthy nations must have a "lofty ideal" that can be "measurably attained." More than anything in public and private life, Roosevelt valued personal character. "If I wished to accomplish anything for the country," he wrote in his *Autobiography*, "my business was to combine decency and efficiency; to be a thoroughly practical man of high ideals who did his best to reduce those ideals to actual practice." The "cardinal sin against the people in a democracy" was to "play the demagogue for purposes of self-interest."[24]

The protection of America's ideals, the president told Congress, requires adherence to the law. "No man is above the law and no man is below it; nor do we ask any man's permission when we require him to obey it. Obedience to the law is demanded as a right; not asked as a favor."[25]

Inscribed on a plaque near Roosevelt's gravesite at Oyster Bay are the words that express the essence of his philosophy: "Keep your eyes on the stars and keep your feet on the ground." When he chose not to run for reelection in 1908, he boasted that his administration had combined ideals and realism to take a leading role in maintaining peace during his tumultuous seven and a half years in the White House.[26]

The pages that follow will explore that assertion by highlighting the path to peace that he began to develop shortly before becoming president in the fall of 1901 and that he attempted to follow throughout his tenure in the White House.

In taking on this project, I decided to let Theodore Roosevelt speak for himself in every important instance. Rather than tell an oft-related story based on public actions and public criticisms of his presidency in foreign affairs, I have allowed him to explain his objectives and defend their importance in protecting America's interests and security. On occasion, Roosevelt's words are reflections on events and tend, some have argued, to inflate his performance. Even if so, his perspective as "the bride at every wedding and the corpse at every funeral" offers insight into his actions as America's chief diplomatist.[27]

Despite his efforts to confine his many acerbic remarks to confidential correspondence, Roosevelt knew as a historian that he must leave a written record of his discourse as indispensable to our understanding of the nation's history. Fortunately for future generations, he dictated his thoughts—sometimes on two topics at once to two stenographers—leaving a record rich in detail and critical to research. His vast legacy of private correspondence (estimated by his private secretaries to be 150,000 letters during his public career alone); his extensive publication list of almost forty books and countless articles, essays, and speeches; his lengthy and meaningful messages to Congress; his numerous letters to his children; his exhaustive and invaluable *Autobiography*; the massive online digital collection of Roosevelt materials at the Theodore Roosevelt Center at Dickinson State University in North Dakota—all these define Roosevelt better than any scholar's scrutiny. They consistently show his understanding that the greatness of a leader rests on serving the greater good rather than the lesser self.[28]

To think this way requires a leader who understands the steps necessary to develop a great nation, a vision of where that leader wants to take the people, and personal qualities essential to the mission—a lofty goal of hope; a personal education, both in academics and wisdom gained from experience;

a commitment to honor and truth in public service; a depth of character and compassion; an understanding of human nature and its needs; a willingness to listen to and follow the advice of others; a loyalty to the Constitution and the rule of law; and, just as important, an empathy gained from personal experiences that helps a leader identify with fellow Americans suffering from grief, pain, or personal hardship. The standard is high: An effective leader must be aspirational, honest, empathetic, and trustworthy.

Few would suggest that Roosevelt embodied all the features listed above. It is the reader's task to judge his leadership by "hearing" him explain his thoughts behind every important decision and analyzing the results. "In foreign affairs," Roosevelt wrote in his *Autobiography*, "the principle from which we never deviated was to have the Nation behave toward other nations precisely as a strong, honorable, and upright man behaves in dealing with his fellow-men."[29]

It was not a great leap for Roosevelt to argue that the same rules of civility governing an individual's behavior should apply to nations as well. Both citizens and their country must have good character and respect for the law to succeed.

Roosevelt once claimed that he was not impressed with himself. "I have only a second-rate brain," he told Wister, "but I think I have a capacity for action." When Wister, years afterward told Lord Bryce of this conversation, the renowned British writer dismissed the modesty. Roosevelt "didn't do justice to himself there, you know. He had a brain that could always go straight to the pith of any matter. That is a mental power of the first rank."[30]

Too often we attribute Roosevelt's actions more to impulse and show than to reason and knowledge. Many of these judgments rest on the jokes, cartoons, and criticisms appearing in his enemies' public statements and writings, the press, and other public venues. Yet, we know from his letters and other writings that he thought out his decisions after extensive reading in newspapers, magazines, and books, his own research, as well as a willingness to take advice from experts. "If Congress," he declared to President Jacob G. Schurman of Cornell University, "will give me a certain amount of freedom and a certain amount of time, I believe I can do much better than by any action taken out of hand."[31]

Roosevelt wanted to be known as a decent, fair, and knowledgeable leader committed to honesty, zeal, and perseverance in public service. "No man can lead a public career really worth leading, no man can act with rugged independence in serious crises, nor strike at great abuses, nor afford to make powerful and unscrupulous foes, if he is himself vulnerable in his private character."[32] He understood that there was more to life than personal gain—that fealty to country was more important than either his political party or himself.

Throughout his political career, Roosevelt told his son Kermit in 1915, he tried "to make the necessary working compromise" between what he wanted to do and what he had to do, "between the ideal and the practical." He warned, "If a man does not have an ideal and try to live up to it, then he becomes a mean, base and sordid creature, no matter how successful."[33]

Statesmen, Roosevelt wrote in his *Autobiography*, "need more than anything else to know human nature, to know the needs of the human soul." They acquire this wisdom and knowledge not only from personal experience, but from reading poetry and novels, history and government, science and philosophy. And read he did—often more than a book a day, and sometimes before breakfast.[34]

Roosevelt knew that bluffing and making empty threats could undermine credibility, which he considered the essential attribute of a successful person, leader, or nation. A leader must control the tenor of his public statements to avoid inciting followers to violence. He told a friend, "I do not believe in the officers of high rank continually using language which is certain to make the less intelligent or more brutal of their subordinates commit occasional outrages."[35]

Roosevelt understood the power and public responsibility inherent to the presidency. He recalled a cartoon of the time assuring justice to all Americans. Titled "His Favorite Author," the cartoon "pictured an old fellow with chin whiskers, a farmer, in his shirt-sleeves, with his boots off, sitting before the fire, reading the President's Message." This "old fellow," Roosevelt wrote, was always on his mind as he governed. Probably a veteran of the Civil War, the man had doubtless "worked hard ever since he left the army; he had been a good husband and father; he had brought up his boys and girls to work; he did not wish to do injustice to anyone else, but he wanted justice done to himself and to others like him." Roosevelt emphasized his fundamental duty as a president: "I was bound to secure that justice for him if it lay in my power to do so."[36]

⌒∞⌒

Before turning to Roosevelt's foreign policy, it is essential to understand the man by winding the clock back for a glimpse into the struggles he experienced from birth to early adulthood. These events, some of them intimate tragedies, shaped his character, guided his attempts to "civilize" others at home and abroad, and taught him the meaning of empathy so crucial to his life and to his presidency.

Prologue

An Obstacle Walk from "black care" to the White House

It's not in the still calm of life, or the repose of a pacific station, that great characters are formed . . . the habits of a vigorous mind are formed in contending with difficulties.

—Abigail Adams
1780

The chief factor in any given man's success or failure must be that man's own character.

—Theodore Roosevelt
June 28, 1913

In his *Autobiography* of 1913, Theodore Roosevelt wrote: "When I left the Presidency, I finished seven and a half years of administration, during which not one shot had been fired against a foreign foe. We were at absolute peace," he boasted, "and there was no nation in the world with whom a war cloud threatened, no nation in the world whom we had wronged, or from whom we had anything to fear."[1]

Roosevelt's assessment of his foreign policy is a mixture of truth and hyperbole. True, the United States did not fire a shot against a foreign enemy during his tenure as president; nor did a single American soldier die in a foreign war. But at the turn of the twentieth century and early in his presidency, a large number of uniformed Americans perished while putting down a tragic and bloody insurrection led by Emilio Aguinaldo in the Philippines, thousands of miles away in Southeast Asia.[2]

1

If Roosevelt's nearly eight-year tenure in office was one of peace, it was nonetheless a dangerous time. Running through this tense period were many international issues that later combined to cause two world wars. More immediate was the possibility of war with Germany. In South America, Roosevelt's threatened use of military force to stop Germany's blockade of Venezuela and possible occupation of territory led Berlin's strategists to draw up contingency plans for an invasion of the United States, with one of the prime avenues of entry at Long Island. We are left with the image of German soldiers marching by the president's home at Sagamore Hill en route to New York City.[3]

Roosevelt did not shrink from these problems; he took the lead in attempting to resolve them and promote global order by "civilizing" less fortunate peoples. In nearly every instance, he played an integral role in defusing explosive situations in Latin America, Europe, and Asia, always insisting that the United States had not wronged any nation. But not all contemporary leaders agreed with this claim. Colombians and Canadians could certainly make a contrary case, and none of the Great Powers achieved all their imperial objectives, often blaming Roosevelt for their failures.

And yet, Roosevelt never had to exercise his constitutional powers as commander in chief of the nation's armed forces at war, and there was no international conflict during his time in office that required U.S. intervention. An acceptance of Roosevelt as that reckless and blustering "damned cowboy" (as party boss Mark Hanna described him) seems at odds with this record. To reconcile the persona with the man requires a consideration of his formative years and an understanding of how factors from that period informed and influenced his views on and implementation of foreign policy.

I

Many contemporaries and historians have agreed that Theodore Roosevelt reveled in the spotlight and enjoyed what he called "the vigor of life." The roots of his strenuous lifestyle lay in his youth when he defied recurring health problems by building a body ravaged by asthma and other illnesses to such an extent that he could later go mountain climbing in the Alps. As a cowboy in the Dakota Badlands, he maintained two ranches, herded cattle, hunted buffalo, wolves, and grizzly bears, and in one instance read Leo Tolstoy's *Anna Karenina* in French while single handedly escorting three thieves to justice.

Roosevelt was a dedicated public servant with a range of experiences that helped qualify him for the presidency: New York state assemblyman who, at twenty-three years of age, became the first leading political figure to advocate national health care; U.S. civil service commissioner who greatly extended the merit system; New York City police commissioner who reformed the force after seeing the problems firsthand by prowling the streets at night; assistant secretary of the navy who persistently called for naval preparedness; legendary hero of the "Rough Riders" who, in the Spanish-American War, left his seriously ill second wife to volunteer for military service; governor of New York who introduced numerous progressive reform bills; and vice president before President William McKinley's assassination.[4]

Nothing on the above résumé would have been in his life's forecast after his birth in New York on October 27, 1858. Afflicted with numerous childhood maladies, the young Roosevelt was so stricken with asthma that to breathe, his father, Theodore Senior, often took him on carriage rides in the night to force cool air into his lungs. At other times, his father picked him up from the bed at night where he sat gasping for air and walked him around the room until he found relief. Theodore Senior, a wealthy businessman and philanthropist, had a gymnasium constructed on the back porch of his home where his young son worked out on a regular basis; and, with his father's approval, young Theodore took up boxing for self-defense after an encounter with two boys on a stagecoach. Unfortunately for the young man, he was nearsighted and could not wear his glasses while fighting and suffered a raking more times than he cared to admit. Years later, while in the White House, he gave up both boxing and wrestling for a year's flirtation with jujitsu after a blow in a boxing match that ultimately left him blind in his left eye.[5]

His father, regarded by the younger Roosevelt as "the best man I ever knew," was of Old Dutch Knickerbocker stock, a committed man of faith in the Dutch Reformed Church who practiced Christianity every day, and a "strong Lincoln Republican." Father taught his four children—brothers Theodore (Teedie) and Elliott, and two girls, Anna (Bamie) and Corinne (Conie)—the differences between right and wrong while urging them to exemplify "strength and courage," combined with "gentleness, tenderness, and great unselfishness." Years later, Roosevelt publicly asserted that his father would not "tolerate in us children selfishness or cruelty, idleness, cowardice, or untruthfulness." He "was the only man of whom I was ever really afraid." But it was not a "wrong fear," because "he was entirely just, and we children adored him."[6]

Roosevelt never forgot his father's emphasis on the importance of decency and respect for others. Decency was not a sign of weakness but of manliness if practiced toward everyone. "You can be just as decent as you wish," he counseled his son, "provided you are prepared to fight." To a friend, Roosevelt wrote that Father "most wisely refused to coddle me, and made me feel that I must force myself to hold my own with other boys and [be] prepared to do the rough work of the world." He combined the "courage and will and energy of the strongest man with the tenderness, cleanness and purity of a woman." Never did he put this into words, "but he certainly gave me the feeling that I was always to be both decent and manly, and that if I were manly nobody would laugh at my being decent."[7]

To the Pulitzer Prize-winning novelist, Hamlin Garland, Roosevelt later expressed what he learned at home. "Brutality by a man to a woman, by a grown person to a little child, by anything strong toward anything good and helpless, makes my blood literally boil."[8]

Theodore Senior enjoyed life, duty, and public service almost as much as his marriage to Martha Bulloch (Mittie), years afterward remembered by her son as "a sweet, gracious, beautiful Southern woman." A Presbyterian (leaving Teedie and his siblings to reconcile the two religious beliefs in the home), Mittie was raised on a Roswell, Georgia, plantation and, despite marrying a Yankee, remained "unreconstructed" her entire life. Teedie and Bamie often listened to their mother's loving stories about life on the plantation and came away hating slavery. One evening, while saying his prayer in front of her, Teedie asked God to grant a Union victory by helping its armies "grind the Southern troops to powder." Mittie laughed but made clear that this would not happen again without her telling his father.[9]

The young Theodore perhaps acquired his love for history at home—from the differing opinions of the Civil War expressed by Unionist Theodore Senior and Confederate Mittie. His father was an active member of the Union League; his mother spoke wistfully of the South and kept close watch on its progress in the war. Father hired a substitute to avoid serving in the war, leaving a rare but lasting negative impression on the boy.[10]

In defending his decision not to enlist in the Union army, Theodore Senior agonized over splitting the family over the war and chose instead to do charity work for the families of Union soldiers. On Mittie's side of the family, her half-brother James Bulloch served as the Confederacy's chief secret agent during the war, contracting with British shipbuilding firms in Liverpool and Birkenhead to construct several vessels, including the CSS *Alabama*, a commerce raider that for two years wreaked havoc on Union shipping. Mittie's brother, Irvine, was a midshipman on that vessel and famously fired its last shot in a battle with the Union Navy's *Kearsarge* off the coast of Cherbourg, France, in 1864.[11] It was James (Uncle Jim), however, who influenced Roosevelt the most. The two connected on their writing endeavors with Roosevelt consulting Bulloch on his book, *The Naval War of 1812,* and taking credit for persuading Bulloch to record his Civil War experiences in *The Secret Service of the Confederate States in Europe.*[12]

The young Theodore learned from his father the importance of family and marriage that he carried throughout life. "I left college and entered the big world owing more than I can express to the training I had received, especially in my own home." In an article for *The Sewanee Review* in 1894, he wrote that "The highest ideal of the family is attainable only where the father and mother stand to each other as lovers and friends, with equal rights." And in his *Autobiography*, he looked back to those experiences and declared that the relationship between a man and a woman "stands at the base of the whole social structure." The law must put "women on a footing of complete and entire equal rights with man—including the right to vote, the right to hold and use property, and the right to enter any profession she desires on the same terms as the man." If her "work is as valuable as that of a man it should be paid as highly."[13]

In academic matters, Roosevelt (who learned to read French, German, Italian, and Latin) was home-schooled by private tutors (partly because of continued asthma attacks) and was well read in all manner of subjects, including the classics. The young Theodore grew up in a cosmopolitan family setting that emphasized extensive reading, writing, and international travel, all helping him develop a broad and learned view of life. On one occasion, Roosevelt wrote his father about time spent perusing the 38,000 books in the Academy Library in Philadelphia.[14]

While Theodore was on the second of two year-long trips abroad (the first as a ten-year-old in Europe and later as a teenager in the Holy Land, the Middle East, and Africa), he wrote his aunt that he and his family were on the Nile River for more than a month and that he had never enjoyed himself as much—particularly his bird collecting and, at moonlight, gazing at the ruins of the Temple and the columns at Karnak. The thousands of years of history, he mused, raised philosophical questions incapable of answering until after "The Great Sleep."[15]

Roosevelt entered Harvard in 1876, where he studied a range of subjects, including science, history, geography, mathematics, Greek, and the laissez-faire doctrine of free trade—the last emphasizing self-interest, which he regarded as the antithesis of the benevolent behavior toward the less fortunate taught by his father. At one point, Roosevelt wrote home that within the past week, he had read from Horace, Homer, and Socrates. He avoided debating classes because they placed no emphasis on "getting a speaker to think rightly, but on getting him to talk glibly on the side to which he is assigned, without regard either to what his convictions are or to what they ought to be."[16]

More than from his textbooks, Roosevelt later claimed, he learned from the popular magazine, *Our Young Folks*, that impeccable character was essential to success. No one could become a responsible citizen without having an inner core of morality based on "self-reliance, energy, courage, the power of insisting on his own rights and the sympathy that makes him regardful of the rights of others."[17]

As Theodore began college, his father offered this advice: "Take care of your morals first, your health next and finally your studies." If we can believe the young man's private diaries, his thoughts about finding a wife seemed less complicated because, he declared, "Thank Heaven, I am at least perfectly pure." When later engaged, he once more "thanked Heaven" that he could tell his fiancée "everything I have ever done." His college friends were "honorable and rigidly virtuous, and with plenty of common sense." In referring to his father's advice, he wrote that with God's help, "I shall try to lead such a life as *he* [father] would have wished, and to do nothing I would have been ashamed to confess to him."[18]

At Harvard, Roosevelt was on both the boxing and wrestling teams while maintaining grades deserving of a Phi Beta Kappa key. He had been in Germany when he wrote his father (after receiving boxing gloves as a gift) about what fun it was to box. But he admitted, "If you offered rewards for bloody noses, you would spend a fortune on me alone."[19]

Roosevelt's interest in history continued to grow during his undergraduate years at Harvard. Outside his required curriculum of study, he wrote two chapters of what became his first book, *The Naval War of 1812*. "Those chapters," he later remarked, "were so dry that they would have made a dictionary seem light reading by comparison." His modesty was unwarranted. After its publication in 1882 (two years after graduation), this seminal study appealed to naval strategists and historians both inside and outside the United States then and to the present day. It also went through eight editions as required reading in several American colleges and established his credentials as a historian who, in 1912, became president of the American Historical Association. He continued to be a prolific reader and author all his life, including writing almost forty books, three of them based on his living as a cowboy for nearly three years in the Dakota Badlands.[20]

A year into his studies at Harvard, Roosevelt, not yet twenty years old, suffered the loss of his father to cancer on February 9, 1878. It was like a "hideous dream," he confided to a friend, in which that "part of my life had been taken away." At times "when I fully realize my loss I feel as if I should go wild." Father "was everything to me; father, companion, friend . . . and so deeply religious." That last quality of his father may have had the greatest impact on the young Roosevelt. Amid his first month of grief, he wrote in his diary how thankful he was that class work left him little time to think of his loss. Without it, "I believe I should almost go crazy. But I think I can really and humbly say 'Thy will be done.'"[21]

Perhaps a Sunday sermon that summer of 1878 helped the young man accept his loss and adopt a principle that he followed throughout his life. "I was much struck with one remark," he recorded in his journal. "Christianity gives us, on this earth, rest *in* trouble, not *from* trouble." Only "my faith in the Lord Jesus Christ could have carried me through this, my terrible time of trial and sorrow." Several months later, he asserted in his diary that "my duty is clear—to study well and live like a brave Christian gentleman."[22]

As an adult, his mind often drifted back to his childhood days when he repeatedly felt a crushing sensation in his chest from asthma attacks, and his father lifted him from the bed and walked him around the room night after night. "Oh how my heart pains me when I think that I never was able to do anything for him in his last illness!" The day he died was "the blackest day of my life." Yet, Roosevelt admitted to a close friend, mine was "a purely selfish sorrow, for it was best that Father's terrible sufferings should end."[23]

Throughout much of that year, Roosevelt chastised himself for failing to meet his father's expectations of him. Just after the burial, Roosevelt wrote in his diary, "With the help of my God, I will try to lead such a life as he would have wished." In July, he confided to his diary that "I often feel badly that such a wonderful man as Father should have had a son of so little worth as I am." During a Sunday church service, he reflected "sadly on how little use I am, or ever shall be in the world, not through lack of perseverance and good intentions, but through sheer inability I realize more and more every day that I am as much inferior to Father morally and mentally as physically." One winter evening at Harvard, he lamented his perceived unworthiness with "How I wish I could ever do something to keep up his name." "Fortunately," Roosevelt biographer Carleton Putnam determined, "the burden was lighter than the spur." The path forward, the young Theodore committed to his journal, lay in strength drawn from faith and a desire to "Trust in the Lord, and do good!"[24]

II

Roosevelt's grief over the loss of his father helped to mold his image of the woman he might someday marry. In the spring of 1878, he had written in his diary that "no one but my wife, if ever I marry, will ever be able to take his place. I so wonder who my wife will be! A rare and raidiant [*sic*] maiden I hope; one who will be as sweet, pure and innocent as she is wise."[25]

In the autumn of his third year at Harvard, Roosevelt met that woman and entered a defining period of his life. He was at the Boston home of his friend, Dick Saltonstall, when he met Dick's sister Rose and their cousin Alice Hathaway Lee, the latter a striking young lady from a prominent banking family living next door in the affluent village of Chestnut Hill, six miles from Harvard. To his cousin John, Roosevelt later described that moment when Alice first walked toward him through the garden gate between the twenty yards of grass separating the two mansions. "As long as I live, I shall never forget how sweetly she looked, and how prettily she greeted me."[26]

Roosevelt treasured his time with Rose and "especially pretty Alice," whom he frequently visited in her home. "I first saw her on October 18, 1878," he wrote in his diary, "and loved her as soon as I saw her sweet, very young face." After celebrating the Thanksgiving holidays at Chestnut Hill, he described "pretty Alice Lee" as "one of the sweetest, most ladylike girls I have ever met." More than a year later, his ardor had not cooled. In his diary he wrote, "It was a real case of love at first sight—and my first love too."[27]

Seventeen years old and at five feet seven, only one inch shorter than Theodore, Alice was a statuesque and golden-haired beauty. Often dressed in white brocade attire and wearing her hair in large and popular "water-curls" framing eyes that drifted between pale or misty blue and pearly gray, she was, to Roosevelt, "a star of heaven . . . my pearl, and my pure flower." Known as "Sunshine" because of her cheery disposition, she enjoyed outdoor activities such as hiking, tennis, boating, and archery. His growing acceptance of his father's death, his good home and family, his popularity and high grades at Harvard, and now—Alice; little wonder that he recorded in his diary of late 1878 that "these are the golden years of my life."[28]

The courtship was nonetheless rocky, given that Alice was coquettish around young men, the very image of a refined and soft-spoken young lady who, by the Victorian standards of the day, dutifully (and yet coyly) recoiled from straightforward advances. She was often taken aback by Theodore's boisterous behavior—accompanying him to a boxing match to see him thoroughly beaten; joining him on the dance floor where, according to Rose, he "danced just as you-d [*sic*] expect him to dance if you knew him—he hopped"; and shuddering over his excited and high-pitched voice as he told her ghost stories at home or graphically described hunting bears and wolves to her wide-eyed, five-year-old brother. But "Teddy" would not be deterred by her real or feigned resistance to his entreaties.[29]

He proposed to Alice in June 1879 without getting an answer. Sleeplessness and despair only made him more resolute. As a guest at Alice's "coming-out" party, he watched as she flirted with the young men gathering around her amid a cascade of rosebuds. Theodore was still steaming days later when, at Harvard's Hasty Pudding Club, he pointed to Alice on the other side of the room and exclaimed to a friend nearby, "See that girl? I am going to marry her. She won't have me, but I am going to have *her!*"[30]

A contemporary familiar with the Roosevelt family remarked that Theodore, like his father, "almost always got what he wanted."[31]

And that he did. "After much pleading" and going "nearly crazy," he admitted, she promised her hand in marriage on January 25, 1880, eight months after his proposal. "I am so happy that I dare not trust my own happiness," he shared with his diary that night. "The aim of my whole life shall be to make her happy, and to shield her and guard her from every trial; and, oh, how I shall cherish my sweet queen!" A day or two later, his emotions remained high. "I do not believe any man loved [a] woman more than I love her."[32]

But Teddy soon learned that with love often comes jealousy, sometimes so intense that it followed him as much as he followed Alice during their betrothal period. In the succeeding months, according to a member of her family, he bristled every time a young man talked with her; and more than once he warned of a duel if a rival suitor tried to woo her away. In one instance, he ordered a set of dueling pistols from France and caused a public row at customs when trying to bring them into the country. Fortunately for everyone involved, he never needed them.[33]

On October 27, 1880, on his twenty-second birthday and four months after graduating from Harvard with honors in Natural History and Political Economy, Roosevelt married nineteen-year-old Alice. Two months later, he admitted to his diary: "I never can understand how I won her!"[34]

After two weeks at Mittie's summer home in Oyster Bay, the couple relocated to her house in New York City, joining Elliott, Corinne, and Bamie, who were already living there with their widowed mother. Theodore had enrolled in law school at Columbia University that fall, walking fifty blocks each morning to classes at the Manhattan campus.[35]

Roosevelt's life took a new direction a year later in September 1881 after he and Alice returned home from a five-month delayed honeymoon in Europe. Law had not interested him, but politics and writing did. Consequently, he dropped out of law school after the first year to begin a career in public service. That autumn, he was elected to the state legislature of New York, and the young couple moved to the capital city of Albany. Five months later, in 1882, at the age of twenty-three, he published *The Naval War of 1812*, the book he had begun two years earlier while an undergraduate at Harvard. In the summer of 1883, they learned that Alice was pregnant, leading them to move from Albany into a house close to his mother's home in Manhattan. As the expected delivery day of mid-February 1884 approached, Alice settled into an apartment on the third floor of her mother-in-law's house.[36]

But the euphoria abruptly ended that February when tragedy struck twice in rapid succession. Roosevelt received a telegram while in Albany on February 13, informing him that Alice had given birth to a healthy girl on the previous evening of February 12; but as he prepared to leave the state house for the five-hour train trip home, he received a second telegram leaving the impression that something had gone wrong. Doubtless, his fears grew during the long and slow-moving train ride down from Albany in the midst of what the *New York Times* called "suicidal weather," a two-week period of "raw and chilly air" along with a dense and steady rain and fog that suggested "death and decay in the dampness that fills the world." The following day, February 14, he must have remembered, marked the fourth anniversary of his announced engagement with Alice.[37]

A little before midnight, Roosevelt arrived home, noting a single light glowing from the third-floor window as he rang the bell. His brother Elliott threw open the door, declaring, "There is a curse on this house. Mother is dying and Alice is dying too."[38]

Anxiously expecting to see his wife and new child, he first found his mother deathly ill from what was later determined to be typhoid fever.[39]

More terrible news awaited him as he hurried upstairs. In the past few hours, the young mother had become severely weak and insensible from what was later diagnosed as a lethal kidney infection known as Bright's disease. Alice had declined so quickly that she was semi-comatose and barely knew he was there, even though he held her in his arms on the bed all through the night as if to prevent her from leaving him. Just before 3 a.m., he had to rush downstairs upon hearing that his mother had passed away. Standing alongside the bed with his sister Corinne and brother Elliott, Theodore alluded to their father's death in that same room six years earlier by agreeing with Elliott: "There *is* a curse on this house."[40]

At 2 p.m., about twelve hours later on that darkest of Valentine's days, Alice also died.[41]

"The light has gone out of my life," Roosevelt wrote in his diary that night, the words appearing below a large X he had drawn to mark the day of Alice's passing.[42]

Two days later, after a double funeral service in the Fifth Avenue Presbyterian Church in New York on the below-freezing day of February 16, both Roosevelt's mother and his wife were buried in Greenwood Cemetery. A day or so afterward, he wrote in his diary for that day, "For joy or for sorrow my life has now been lived out."[43]

Months later, he wrote a tribute for Alice and his mother that a publishing house privately printed in 1884. "By a strange and terrible fate," Roosevelt wrote of Alice, "death came to her." Of his mother, he wrote that "keeping her freshness and beauty to the end . . . she died, in the fulness of our time."[44]

Roosevelt's initial response to grief was to destroy everything that reminded him of Alice—correspondence, photographs, scrapbooks, and souvenirs. Never speak her name again, nor allow anyone to do so in his presence. No one was to call him "Teddy" again. He would bury himself in work, letting the fatigue dull the pain. If Roosevelt believed that no words could express his love for Alice, perhaps one of his earliest biographers, Carleton Putnam, came closest in saying, "Roosevelt's silence paid Alice Lee the highest tribute possible."[45]

In the week following the funerals, Roosevelt seems to have followed the advice of a political rival in New York, Lucas Van Allen, who had prayed in the Assembly that his colleague would have the strength "to work bravely in the darkness." To a friend, Roosevelt confided that "there is nothing left for me except" to strive to live my life "as not to dishonor the memory of those I loved who have gone before me." At one point he declared, "I shall go mad if I were not employed." Admittedly, he wrote reformer and journalist Carl Schurz, "I have not lived long, yet the keenness of joy and the bitterness of sorrow are now behind me; but at least I can live so as not to dishonor the memory of the dead whom I so loved." He later confided to another friend, "It was a grim and evil fate, but I have never believed it did any good to flinch or yield for any blow, nor does it lighten the blow to cease from working."[46]

The year before, in September 1883, Roosevelt had taken a trip West to relax from the demands of political life. On the morning of September 7, he arrived at Little Missouri, a small settlement in the Dakota Badlands where he bought his first ranch. Now, broken in spirit by this double tragedy, he arranged with his older sister Bamie to take care of infant Alice, and in early June 1884, went West to seek inner peace in the solitude of the Dakotas. There he continued his reading and writing while living the rigorous life of a cowboy and hoping to find "enough excitement and fatigue to prevent over much thought" about the past. His daughter, he later told his close friend in the West, William Sewall, "would be just as well off without me." But "you have your child to live for," Sewall reminded him. "Her aunt," Theodore replied, "can take care of her a good deal better than I can." Another friend, William Merrifield, had also recently become a widower and assured him that time would ease the pain. Roosevelt shot back, "Don't talk to me about time will make a difference—time can never change me in that respect."[47]

A little over a week after his arrival, Roosevelt set out to fulfill a "boyish ambition"—a two- or three-day hunting trip alone on the prairie to test his survival skills "without a guide." After packing a few essentials—including a book—he and his horse, Manitou, made their way south along the river and up through the buttes before crossing the plateaus in the prairie. "Nowhere, not even at sea, does a man feel more lonely than when riding over the far-reaching, seemingly never-ending plains," themselves fascinating by "their very vastness and their melancholy monotony." All he could see was flat land broken only by mild slopes created by the runoff from creeks. "Nowhere else does one seem so far off from all mankind."[48]

On returning to his ranch about five days later, he wrote his sister Bamie that the trip was better than he could have hoped. He had killed two antelopes while at constant risk of wolves, Indians, and horse thieves, along with a bout with quicksand and two days of cold and hard rain. Yet, he had not disappointed himself: He could make life-determining decisions in grueling circumstances. "I felt as absolutely free as a man could feel. As you know, I do not mind loneliness; and I enjoyed the trip to the utmost."[49]

Roosevelt quickened his pace of life, making several trips home over the next two years to meet legislative responsibilities, sometimes staying for lengthy periods with Bamie and his daughter—whom he called "Baby Lee," "little Lee," or "Sister," rather than her namesake. He returned home for good in 1886, always remaining close with his daughter and yet true to his determination never to speak to her about her mother. It comes as no surprise that he did not mention Alice in his *Autobiography*.[50]

Almost three years passed before Roosevelt appeared to have come to terms with Alice's death. Rather than allow life's struggles to define him in a weak or negative light, he regenerated his resolve to make his life meaningful. No one "can hope to escape sorrow and anxiety," he wrote years afterward. "But life is a great adventure, and the worst of all fears is the fear of living."[51]

Through it all, Roosevelt maintained an outward calm that reflected his father's admonition that "weakness is the greatest of crimes." As he attempted to reconstruct his life, he returned to his plans to build a huge house in New York on Cove Neck, the highest point of ninety-five acres of richly forested land that overlooked Oyster Bay along with Cold Spring Harbor and Long Island Sound. He and Alice had worked with the architects in designing the house they called Leeholm. Her death in 1884 did not stop him from going ahead with its construction. In March of that same year, workers began the project and finished the house in 1885, whereupon Roosevelt renamed it Sagamore Hill in commemoration of the Native American Sagamore (chieftain) Mohannis, who had held meetings there with his warriors two and a half centuries earlier.[52]

In retrospect, the following events in Roosevelt's life seemed to take on the appearance of a preordained love story. Biographer Edmund Morris asserts that Roosevelt was "as prudish as a dowager" and loved only two women in his life—Alice and Edith, the latter a childhood friend and neighbor in New York. According to almost everyone in those early years, Edith Kermit Carow, or "Edie," would marry Theodore. But in the summer of 1878, just before he left for college, they had a falling out that Roosevelt later attributed to mutual hot tempers. Then, in the first semester of his third year at Harvard, he met Alice. Edie had been hurt badly by Theodore's marriage to Alice and, even though she grudgingly attended the wedding, swore never to marry unless it was to Teedie, the only man she had ever loved.[53]

For more than a year after Alice's death, Theodore and Edith did not see each other. Then, in October of 1885, by happenstance—or perhaps through a bit of Bamie manipulation—the two met on the stairs inside the front door of her house. Everything that had kept them apart instantly disappeared. Edith no longer saw the familiar adolescent boy; before her now stood a tanned and ruggedly attractive young man. On the other side of the stairway stood the "sweet little flirt" he wrote about in his diary more than six years earlier, her dark sapphire eyes now those of an irresistible woman. Again smitten, Roosevelt agonized over a sense of betrayal of Alice, ridden with guilt stemming from his Victorian belief that marriage was for life and beyond. As he wrote Bamie, a second marriage showed "weakness in a man's character."[54]

Roosevelt and Edith nonetheless overcame their hesitations to meet, and just one month later, on November 17, 1885, they became engaged—secretly, to ward off rumors of his violating social norms by marrying too soon after Alice's death. A year later, he informed friends that he was leaving for England to marry Edith. In December, with Roosevelt's English friend Cecil Spring Rice as best man, he and Edith married in London. After a four-month honeymoon in Europe, the couple returned to the United States to settle in at Sagamore Hill with young Alice, to whom they would eventually add five more children of their own.[55]

Roosevelt's crucible of grief taught him empathy and compassion for others; it also strengthened his commitment to a life of character, work, and public service that his father had modeled. Roosevelt's experiences with personal crises helped him understand and care about the needs of others. There was no time for self-pity. No excuse for incompetence. No denying of responsibility for one's actions. Years later, he maintained that the "chief factor in any given man's success or failure must be that man's own character."[56] From his father, he learned that leaders with character, moral standards, a wide range of experiences, and a good education were more likely to see the bigger picture of right and wrong and to make decisions on behalf of the common good.

Nearly broken by the deaths of three loved ones in a short period of time, he was perhaps honed for a public life based on perseverance, independent judgment, and honesty. "The only safe rule is to promise little, and faithfully to keep every promise." He also refused to treat politics as a career and tried to hold each office as if it was his last one.[57] After his personal ordeal, what political pressures could be strong enough to intimidate him into abandoning his constitutional, legal, and moral principles in exchange for private gain or political survival?

Anxiety over his own early death impelled him to accomplish as much as possible as quickly as possible. His father had passed away at the age of forty-six and his mother at forty-nine, leading him to fear that he too would die young. In March 1880, while at Harvard, he developed heart trouble that he kept from everyone, including Alice. His doctor told him to take nitroglycerin pills and to reduce his physical activities. The former he did; the latter he did not. Instead, he challenged his heart by increasing his regimen of exercise.[58]

Roosevelt was aware of prevalent medical theory—that degenerative ill-nesses were inherited. His brother Elliott had fainting spells, perhaps related to opiate use and alcoholism that led him to suicide in 1894; his sister Corinne had asthma; and his older sister Bamie had debilitating spinal problems. "I appreciate perfectly the exceedingly short nature of my tenure," he wrote historian Francis Parkman in mid-1889. "I much prefer to really accomplish something good in public life, no matter at what cost of enmity from even my political friends than to enjoy a longer term of service, fettered by endless fear, always trying to compromise, and doing nothing in the end."[59]

Shortly afterward, Roosevelt counseled his friend from the West, William Merrifield, about the importance of character in political life as he prepared to run for a legislative seat in North Dakota. Do what is morally correct regardless of political or personal allegiances or consequences. Avoid any questionable act that might become public to friends and enemies. Vote your conscience and not from fear of what others in politics, the press, or the street might say. Do not make decisions based on your reelection or a continued career in politics. "Never get the political bee in your bonnet."[60]

Roosevelt's time on the frontier had taught him resilience, independence, and the capacity to connect and cooperate with people of different back-grounds. Only a person's merit counted. To William Sewall, Roosevelt wrote, "I acknowledge no man as my superior, except for his own worth, or as my inferior, except for his own demerit." He was sustained by his religious faith, which emphasized good works in helping his neighbor "both in soul and body." In the Badlands, he attested in his book, *Ranch Life and the Hunting Trail*, the cowboy so often met death that he dealt with it as he did "many other evils, with quiet, uncomplaining fortitude." He later declared, "I felt a great admiration for men who were fearless and who could hold their own in the world, and I had a great desire to be like them."[61]

In the West also, Roosevelt continued his lifelong struggle for physical strength. Gone was the "slender" and "anemic-looking" body, weak and sickly from asthma and stomach problems; in its place stood what Sewall called a "husky" and hardened young man at 150 pounds of "clear, muscle, and grit" with a strong neck, broad shoulders, and a solid chest who backed away from no one. During his vice-presidential campaign in 1900, he declared from the rear of a train stopped in the capital city of Bismarck, North Dakota: "I had studied a lot about men and things before I saw you fellows, but it was only when I came here that I began to know anything or measure men rightly." A hundred miles later in Medora, in the area of the two ranches he once owned, Roosevelt told a gathering of cowboys and ranchers that "here the romance of my life began."[62]

"I never would have been President," Roosevelt declared in a public address at the Carnegie Library at Fargo College in September 1910, "if it had not been for my experiences here in North Dakota." If his tenure in office had any value, it "depended largely upon the fact that I knew and sympathized with our people as you can only know and sympathize with those with whom you have worked and with whom you have lived." Before a crowd in Sioux Falls, South Dakota, that same week, he declared that his time spent with ranch men on the frontier was "the most important educational asset of all my life." In listening to their long discussions at evening time, "I first came to understand that the Lord made the earth for all of us and not for a chosen few." It was "a mighty good thing to know men, not from looking at them, but from having been one of them." When you have lived and worked with them, "you do not have to wonder how they feel, because you feel it yourself." In short, he understood these people because "I think the same way."[63]

III

In several ways, Roosevelt's worldview reflected the changes taking place across the nation in the late nineteenth century. From the 1870s through the 1890s, the United States had expanded its political and economic role in international affairs. Many Americans had become disciples of British writer Rudyard Kipling, who believed it the "White Man's Burden" to help less-fortunate peoples of the world. Other Americans applied Charles Darwin's biological teachings of natural selection and Herbert Spencer's "survival of the fittest" to society in a theory of rugged individualism called "Social Darwinism." Roosevelt favored his friend Kipling's proactive ideas over those of Darwin and Spencer and applied them both in national and global terms. In accordance with his father's commitment to the missionary impulse of the Social Gospel, those with wealth bore the responsibility of helping struggling peoples, regardless of race.[64]

Roosevelt's paternalistic attitude toward the so-called backward peoples of the world derived from the principles of *noblesse oblige* stressed and practiced by his father. Backward peoples were not backward by nature, the younger Roosevelt declared; anyone of any race could progress with proper guidance. In the name of progressive reform, he and others of wealth had an obligation to spread civilization as a rationale for economic and territorial expansion so integral to order and stability. "Peace cannot be had until the civilized nations have expanded in some shape over the barbarous nations."[65]

Roosevelt's ideas were consistent with a major theme of late nineteenth-century America—that the roots of U.S. expansion lay in the belief that Americans were a people favored by God. From the time the Puritans called their new home in Massachusetts Bay a "city upon a hill," Americans considered themselves engaged in a godly mission to spread an "Empire of Liberty"—as demonstrated by their justification of the Louisiana Purchase in 1803. During the 1840s, this doctrine of redemption, along with the search for land, drove Americans west and led to the acquisitions of territory that fleshed out the continental borders of the United States in the name of "Manifest Destiny." A half-century later, that wave of thinking resurfaced when "New Manifest Destiny" became the basis for American expansion beyond the continent—into Latin America, the Caribbean, the Pacific, and the Orient.[66]

Roosevelt supported the ideas of his friend and historian Frederick Jackson Turner, who argued that American migration west had reached the Pacific by the 1890s, closing the frontier and ending the period of free land. A question remained that Turner did not answer but Roosevelt did: with the passing of the American frontier, what happens to "American energy," which was "continually demanding a wider field for its exercise?"[67]

Roosevelt responded to Turner, privately, with an allusion to U.S. expansion beyond the Pacific shores and to East Asia: "I think you have struck some first class ideas and have put into definite shape a good deal of thought which has been floating around rather loosely."[68]

Roosevelt denied that American annexation was an imperial or military action and cited the Louisiana Purchase and other expansionist policies as illustrative of his argument. "The simple truth is that there is nothing even remotely resembling 'imperialism' or 'militarism' involved in the present development of that policy of expansion which has been part of the history of America from the day when she became a nation." American expansion beyond the North American continent was a continuation of past Anglo-Saxon expansion.[69]

Roosevelt's foreign policy vision aligned with what has become known as American "exceptionalism"—in its simplest (perhaps, crudest) form, that the nation was divinely appointed and that its expansion was more than justified; it was ordained by God for the cause of civilization. It is arguable that his long-held religious beliefs and regular church attendance by the entire family at the Oyster Bay Christ Episcopal Church helped to provide a moral base for his thinking. We know he emphasized the strenuous life, decency, and hard work as the foundation of a great nation with a godly vision. Perhaps Chicago humorist Finley Peter Dunne's newspaper creation, Mr. Dooley, best expressed the spirit of American expansion in his gruff Irish brogue: "We're a gr-reat people. We ar-re that. An' th' best iv it is, we know we ar-re."[70]

When war broke out with Spain in April 1898, Roosevelt resigned as assistant secretary of the navy to accept a commission as lieutenant colonel in the army and ordered a khaki uniform tailor-made by Brooks Brothers in New York. To assemble his fighting force, he recruited college friends from Harvard; cowboys from the West; and a smattering of Native Americans,

Jews, Irish, Italians, and Scandinavians—a voluntary band of 5,000 men who went to Cuba and became known to the press as "Roosevelt's Rough Riders." Even as Roosevelt prepared for war, he was worried about a manuscript he had promised to deliver. In late January 1898, he had expressed concern to his publisher but added, "I believe that this summer I shall be able to break the back of the next two volumes of *The Winning of the West* or at least of the next volume." One can visualize him during a lull in the fighting, working at a makeshift desk in the jungle to meet his deadline.[71]

In his most memorable moment, he led the charge up Kettle Hill and San Juan Hill near Santiago while on horseback, thrusting himself not only into a rain of bullets but into military lore and the national limelight. It was "a bully fight at Santiago," Roosevelt wrote his brother-in-law, Douglas Robinson. "I would rather have led that charge and earned my colonelcy than served three terms in the United States Senate. It makes me feel as though I could now leave something to my children which will serve as an apology for my having existed."[72]

Three months after the war began, the United States defeated Spain and liberated Cuba, emerging as a rising power with Theodore Roosevelt as its mythic national hero. Although Spain was an Old World power in decline, its concession of colonial holdings to the victor enhanced the U.S. position among nations and therefore had global repercussions. How proud Americans were to see their flag waving on shores as far away as the Philippines and as close to home as Puerto Rico (an "unincorporated territory"). Furthermore, Hawaii and several other Pacific islands had become American stepping-stones to the seemingly unlimited economic and religious proselytizing potential of China, which Secretary of State John Hay had recently declared a U.S. interest by proclaiming the "Open Door" policy.[73]

Hawaii, the Philippines, Puerto Rico, Guam, Wake Island, Johnston Island, Palmyra Island, and American Samoa—all fell into U.S. hands in the wake of "New Manifest Destiny," an expansionist fever that in the late nineteenth century spread beyond continental shores and threatened to take on epidemic proportions following the war with Spain in 1898. Even Cuba, though freed from Spanish rule, remained only quasi-independent since it could do little or nothing in either domestic or foreign affairs without the approval of its new American protector. Who could stop this rising new colossus from spreading its strategic and commercial influence into those long-held colonial spheres of Britain, Germany, Russia, Japan, France, and the Netherlands?

Soon after Roosevelt (who now preferred to be called either "Colonel Roosevelt" or "The Colonel") returned home from the war, he won election as progressive governor of New York, but he had already become a legend in his own time, which meant that the only position befitting his nationwide popularity was the presidency. Frightening warrior that he appeared to be, more than a few Old Guard stalwarts in the Republican Party attempted to bury the icon of the Spanish war in the political graveyard of the vice presidency.

New York senator and boss of the state's Republican Party, Thomas C. Platt, led the campaign to recruit Roosevelt as vice-presidential candidate for McKinley's second term by emphasizing his attraction among western Americans. But Roosevelt's friends opposed his accepting the nomination, warning that he could not accomplish anything important in that position. Edith likewise considered the vice presidency "a useless and empty possession," writing her sister that her husband would be "like the bridegroom at a wedding, no one even sees or thinks of him." Edith doubtless shared her feelings with him, as well as with the family, for she had become outspoken and even sharp tongued on political and public issues. Roosevelt had early learned to respect his wife's opinion. To his friend and French ambassador to the United States, Jules Jusserand, he remarked that "people think I have a good-natured wife, but she has a humor which is more tyrannical than half the tempestuous women of Shakespeare."[74]

Roosevelt agreed with the overall negative assessment of the vice presidency, writing Platt that "I would be simply a presiding officer and that I should find it a bore." As governor, "I can achieve something, but as Vice-President I should achieve nothing." Less than a week later, he remained emphatically opposed. "The more I have thought over it," he wrote Platt, "the more I have felt that I would a great deal rather be anything, say professor of history, than Vice-President." To his closest friend, Henry Cabot Lodge (whom he called "old trump"), he confided that "big corporation men" and insurance companies wanted him out of the governor's office in New York by hoping to "kick me upstairs."[75]

However, Roosevelt soon changed his position. From the first mention of the vice-presidential possibility, Lodge had urged him to accept the office as a step toward succeeding McKinley as president in 1904. Roosevelt was interested in running for president at that time and realized he must not fall from public favor in the interim. Politics, he knew, offered no long-range guarantee on the popularity of heroism. Reelection as governor in 1900 would keep him in the public eye only until 1902, and the president refused to consider him for the lone cabinet position he would accept—secretary of war. The only way to stay in the limelight was to become vice president. "I have never known a hurrah endure for five years," he wrote Lodge. By design, Roosevelt left the impression at the Republican convention in June 1900 that he had bowed to its cries of "We want Teddy!"[76]

Republican Party chair Mark Hanna of New York joined other Roosevelt opponents in fearing that his rapid rise to the second-highest rung of the political ladder would come without incurring debts to those controlling the party. The senator detested Roosevelt and, as a close friend of McKinley, tried to convince him to choose another running mate. When the president left the decision to the convention, Hanna became apoplectic, warning his colleagues that Roosevelt's nomination would be a calamity for the country. "Don't any of you realize that there's only one life between this madman and the Presidency?" When he failed to dissuade Roosevelt's supporters, Hanna dutifully approved the nomination but with a strong caveat: "The best we can do is pray fervently for the continued health of the President."[77]

Less than a year after McKinley's reelection, Vice President Roosevelt delivered a speech on the importance of an activist foreign policy before a large and exuberant crowd (including members of the "Roosevelt Rough Rider" clubs) at the Minnesota State Fair on September 2, 1901. Shouts of support came from all sides. "Hello, Teddy!" "Hurrah for the next president!" One city official ran up and shook Roosevelt's hand. "The next time you go to Washington," he asserted, "you had better wipe out that word 'vice'!"

Roosevelt's remarks drew "tremendous applause," according to the press. The United States had a duty to help keep "a self-respecting peace" in the world. "We believe with all our heart and soul in the greatness of this country," but our "first duty" is at home—to maintain "decency and righteousness in all political, social and civic matters." The "whole duty" of every American, he emphasized, is to follow the "old commonplace virtues" that are the bedrock of the nation. The United States "must not shrink from playing its part among the great nations."

In the words of West Africa's "old proverb," he declared: "Speak softly and carry a big stick—you will go far." Avoid "self-glorification" and "loose-tongued denunciation of other peoples." Treat foreign powers with courtesy and respect, always matching words with deeds. "We can best get justice by doing justice." Civilization rests on law and order and the end of barbarism in the world. If we "raise others, we raise ourselves."[78]

The words read like a campaign speech for 1904. Hanna's worst fear had become evident: Roosevelt would be his own man.[79]

IV

Four days later, on September 6, 1901, President William McKinley was shot while attending a reception at the Pan-American Exposition in Buffalo. Leon Czolgosz, a twenty-eight-year-old anarchist, fired two shots from a revolver point blank into the president's stomach, embedding one of the bullets too deeply to extract.

The days afterward were chaotic. The vice president was at a political rally when he learned of the shooting but that the president was in recovery.

Assured that he did not need to come to Buffalo, Roosevelt joined his family on a hiking trip in the Adirondacks. On September 13, he and a small party headed up the slopes to the highest peak of Mount Marcy, while his wife and family went to Avalanche Lake. As Edith and the children were en route to their destination, a messenger rushed past them and toward the mountain, making her wonder if he had a message for her husband.

Roosevelt and his group were having lunch when the messenger burst upon them. "When I saw the runner," he recalled, "I instinctively knew he had bad news, the worst news in the world." He carried a telegram from Elihu Root, the secretary of war:

THE PRESIDENT APPEARS TO BE DYING AND MEMBERS OF THE
CABINET IN BUFFALO THINK YOU SHOULD LOSE NO TIME COMING[80]

McKinley had rapidly declined from gangrene caused by the bullet that remained inside him.

Roosevelt immediately descended the mountain and made his way through pouring rain to join Edith for supper in the hotel as he awaited further instructions. He had sent a messenger to the nearest phone—in the clubhouse ten miles away—to pick up any further messages. Just before midnight, three hours after retiring, they were awakened by the messenger banging on the cottage door with a batch of telegrams telling him that the president's condition had worsened and to come to Buffalo immediately. A special train would await him at North Creek (thirty-five miles away) to take him to Buffalo.

In the midst of frenzied preparations, compounded by young son Archie bawling that someone would shoot his father, the vice president turned his attention to the arduous trip. More than 400 miles of treacherous trails and railroads lay between him and Buffalo. A string of carriage rides down the perilous mountainside and through the misty darkness preceded the train trip, with the driver dodging fallen trees, huge boulders, and near slides off the road into the bogs far below while Roosevelt sat beside him holding a lantern.

The vice president prepared to board the train at North Creek at 5:22 a.m. on September 14 when, amid locals gathered around, his secretary handed him a telegram from Secretary of State John Hay in Washington. Without saying a word, Roosevelt opened the envelope and read the message:

THE PRESIDENT DIED AT TWO-FIFTEEN THIS MORNING[81]

Roosevelt tucked the paper into his pocket and boarded the train to Buffalo, where in a few hours his friend Ansley Wilcox picked him up in a carriage where he was conveyed with a small cavalry escort to meet with Mrs. McKinley to express his condolences. He also telegraphed Edith to take the family and return to Oyster Bay and prepare for the move to Washington. Federal Judge John R. Hazel had joined the small group in the Wilcox Mansion and—with no Bible available—swore in Roosevelt as president. Elihu Root was so overcome with emotion that he could not speak for nearly three minutes before gathering himself and inviting Roosevelt to take the oath of office. Root and other cabinet members broke down at the end of the ceremony.[82]

Roosevelt accompanied Mrs. McKinley and the president's casket on the thirteen-hour train trip to Washington, where his body would lie in state in the East Room of the Executive Mansion. Edith, in the meantime, had to find living space for two parents and six children in just four bedrooms.[83]

Roosevelt became president forty-three days shy of his 43rd birthday, the youngest person to hold that office. From Norway, Henry Adams, a professor of medieval history at Harvard and an undergraduate acquaintance of Roosevelt, immediately reacted to the news with the shock befitting a member of Boston's Brahmin class. "So Teddy is President! Is not that stupendous! Before such a career as that, I have no observations to make."[84]

McKinley's assassination likewise stunned Hanna and his Republican cohort, not only because of their friendship with the president but also because of their concern about his successor. Perhaps they were aware of the prophetic words of Roosevelt's friend and Wild West star Buffalo Bill Cody, who was on the vice president's campaign trail and gave a brief speech from the rear platform of his railroad car in Kansas that ended with a warning: "A cyclone from the West had come; no wonder the rats hunted their cellars!" On the funeral train for the slain president, Hanna groaned aloud about his conversation with McKinley after he selected "that wild man" as vice president. "I asked him if he realized what would happen if he should die. Now look—that damned cowboy is President of the United States!"[85]

Seated in the same car as Hanna was Herman Kohlsaat, publisher of the *Chicago Times Herald,* who, like Hanna, had been a close friend of McKinley. He tried to calm Hanna, assuring him that Roosevelt had not wanted to be "shot into the Presidency."[86] But Hanna would not be consoled.

Kohlsaat went to Roosevelt's private car and asked about his relationship with Hanna but found little hope for mollification in the new president's response. "Hanna treats me like a boy. He calls me 'Teddy.'" Kohlsaat warned that his presidency would have little chance for success without Hanna's help. He controlled the Republican Party and as leader in the Senate could choke off any bills that came to his desk.

"What can I do about it? Give him complete control of the patronage?"

"Hanna would resent any such suggestion," Kohlsaat replied, adding that McKinley's death had virtually destroyed the senator.

Perhaps, he suggested, invite Hanna to a private dinner in your car. Tell him you need his help. Ask for his friendship. Say, for instance, "Old man, I want you to be my friend. I know you cannot give me the love and affection you gave McKinley, but I want you to give me just as much as you can. I need you. Will you be my friend?" Put your hands on the table, palms up. "If he puts his hands in yours, you can bet on him for life."

"All right, I'll try it."

A short time afterward, Kohlsaat saw the waiter ask Hanna something and, after a brief hesitation, he nodded. He then rose and approached Kohlsaat. "That damned cowboy wants me to take supper with him, alone. Damn him!"

"Mark," Kohlsaat declared, "you are acting like a child. Go and meet him half-way."

Almost two hours later, Hanna returned from Roosevelt's car, first stopping at Kohlsaat's seat to smile and remark, "He's a pretty good little cuss, after all!" Recounting their conversation, he declared that Roosevelt put his hands on the table, palms up, and asked for help and friendship.

"What did you do, Mark!"

"Putting my hands in his I said: 'I will be your friend on two conditions: first, that you carry out McKinley's policies, as you promised.'

Roosevelt answered: 'All right, I will.'

Second, that you quit calling me 'old man.' If you don't, I'll call you 'Teddy.' "All right. You call me 'Teddy' and I'll call you 'old man.'""[87]

Kohlsaat's strategy had worked.

Hanna and his friends nonetheless had reason to worry; and their uneasiness would have been stronger had they been privy to Roosevelt's correspondence of the past few years. In 1889, he expressed his feelings about Germany. "Frankly I do'n't [sic] know that I should be sorry to see a bit of a spar with Germany," he wrote his British friend, Cecil Spring Rice. "The burning of New York and a few other sea coast cities would be a good object lesson on the need of an adequate system of coast defences." Seven years later, he wrote privately, "If it wasn't wrong, I should say that personally I would rather welcome a foreign war." A war with Spain "would result at once in getting a proper Navy." And in 1898, his pronouncements had become more aggressive: "In strict confidence," he wrote, "I should welcome almost any war, for I think this country needs one."[88]

The Civil War had receded more than three decades into the past, and yet the mention of war still brought up the image of a romantic adventure to many late nineteenth-century Americans. Roosevelt and Lodge appeared to be proponents of this mindset when they collaborated on a book titled, *Hero Tales from American History*, in which nearly every one of their heroes was a warrior. [89]

Roosevelt became a public advocate of imperialism and colonialism as the path to world power. "The most ultimately righteous of all wars," he explained in one of his volumes on the West, "is a war with savages, though it is apt to be also the most terrible and inhuman. The rude, fierce settler who drives the savage from the land lays all civilized mankind under debt to him." That settler and others like him have "laid deep the foundations for the future greatness of a mighty people."[90] Reckless and rash, these attitudes required tempering before taking the helm of the republic.

The maturation of Roosevelt from a young, outspoken, and self-acclaimed warrior into a statesman and diplomat had not run its course by the time he became president. Perhaps his secretary of state, John Hay, was overly optimistic in observing that youth was "a curable disease." Or, maybe, Spring Rice was accurate in saying, "You must always remember that the President is about six." Most likely, the enormity of the executive office had not yet sobered Roosevelt. But it is certain that the shock and speed of recent events hurried the process. Roosevelt was irritated with humorist Finley Peter Dunne for remarking that the nation's new president had reached that office not on his merits but "through the cemetery."[91]

Roosevelt knew he had to prove himself. The weight of the world might not have fallen on his shoulders, largely because Americans remained predominantly insular in thought; but, nonetheless, the future of an advancing nation and its place in that world, indeed, fell to a leader who was anxious to accept a new and more active role in foreign affairs.

Roosevelt embraced the opportunity. As a realist tempered by idealism, and as an idealist tempered by reality, his chief objective in foreign relations was to safeguard national honor and the national interest by transforming the United States into a major advocate of peace on a global scale. National prestige born of military strength and the honoring of agreements, he insisted, were the bases of power and essential for winning international respect. Effective diplomacy derived from a blend of power and credibility, guided by a trustworthy leader who inspired loyalty and possessed character, courage, and a commitment to morality and the greater good.

Roosevelt quickly realized that his elevation to the presidency would be more challenging and far reaching than he could have imagined. As a forceful personality, he aroused strong feelings, both favorable and unfavorable. His call for a "Square Deal" in domestic policy emphasized fairness in affairs of state as well. But not all Americans agreed. Businessmen railed at his trust-busting activities. Conservatives complained about his violations of "customary" behavior—especially those involving Blacks.

As vice president, Roosevelt had wanted to meet with African American leader Booker T. Washington to discuss federal appointments in the South, but McKinley's assassination had delayed their talks until the new president could make arrangements to meet. Just a month after taking office, he invited Washington to join him and the First Lady for dinner at the Executive Mansion.[92]

Washington, Roosevelt wrote friend John Strachey, was "one of the most distinguished, and without exception the most useful, of the men of the

South." He had proposed the "Atlanta Compromise" in 1895 by which Blacks would forgo demands for political reforms in exchange for educational and economic help. But the new president was also aware of the racial divide encouraged by the post-Civil War's "Jim Crow" laws of discrimination aimed at resolving the "Negro problem."[93]

Many white Americans reacted to the news of the dinner by denouncing the new president with racial epithets worthy of the worst in society. It must be remembered that the simple act of having an African American dine with the first family was seen as provocative—particularly in a climate that had witnessed Black lynchings rise to nearly a hundred a year. A disgruntled Georgian telegrammed the president two days after the dinner, "You have made mistake. He who dines with Negro, we think no better. To compel his wife is worse." The "sole importance" of the incident, Roosevelt privately told Lodge, was to expose "the continued existence of that combination of Bourbon intellect and intolerant truculence of spirit through much of the South, which brought on the Civil War."[94]

Roosevelt privately remarked that he was "astounded" by the reaction to the incident. "I never thought one way or the other about it, so far as outside effect was concerned." He admitted to Black Reconstruction leader and novelist Albion W. Tourgée that he had not been able "to think out any solution of the terrible problem offered by the presence of the negro on this continent."[95]

Roosevelt defaulted to an approach based on what he had learned about the importance of merit in the Dakota Badlands. The "only wise and honorable and Christian thing to do," he wrote Tourgée shortly afterward, "is to treat each black man and each white man strictly on his merits as a man, giving him no more and no less than he shows himself worthy to have."[96]

Early in his presidency, Roosevelt found himself in the awkward position of attempting to apply racial hierarchy inherent in exceptionalism and Anglo-Saxon and Teutonic (Germanic) traditions to "civilize" less fortunate peoples without alienating Black supporters at home along with the Japanese in Asia. Using his standards of merit regarding black and white relations, he criticized the Chinese while praising the Japanese. The Chinese were weak and backward, incapable of resisting nations seeking commercial dominance within their borders. The Japanese, Roosevelt declared to Spring Rice, were "quite as remarkable industrially as in warfare" and would soon become "a great civilized power of a formidable type." And by the same measures of civility and competence, he criticized the Russians for their brutal treatment of Jewish peoples and their inept performance in war. Yet neither the Chinese nor the Russians posed a danger to the United States. Central to Roosevelt's thinking throughout his time in office was Japan's potential threat to American interests in the Philippines, Hawaii, the Pacific, and China.[97]

V

When Roosevelt approached his first evening in the Executive Mansion, the confluence of domestic racial issues with foreign policy previewed above could not have been further from his mind. The White House echoed with sad emptiness, an atmosphere that troubled Roosevelt more, perhaps, than any previous resident. He did not relish the thought of dining alone on his first night, but Edith and the children had remained at Sagamore Hill as she arranged the move to Washington. Fortunately, his sisters, Corinne and Bamie, both lived in Washington and agreed to bring their husbands to join the new president in a small celebration dinner. Also present in spirit were "the hero of his boyhood and manhood, Abraham Lincoln"[98] in the portrait over the fireplace and Roosevelt's father in memory—both inspiring him to act as they would have done.

As the family sat around the table, Theodore asked, "Do you realize that this is the birthday of our father, September 22? I realized it as I signed various papers all day long, and I feel that it is a good omen." Pausing, he added, "I feel as if my father's hand were on my shoulder, and as if there were a special blessing over the life I am to lead here."[99]

Theodore Senior was more than a parent to his son; he was the quintessential father figure. To a friend, Roosevelt declared that he "thought of Father all the time" in the early days of the presidency. He told Corinne many times that as president, "he never took any serious step or made any vital decision for his country without thinking first what position his father would have taken on the question."[100]

Roosevelt recognized the need to unify Americans behind the republican principles of Lincoln rather than see the citizenry drift into what the Founding Fathers had denounced as factions capable of tearing the nation apart. According to his friend Owen Wister, Roosevelt refused "to allow the United States to be ruled by [an] organized minority against the interests of the whole people."[101]

As president, he relied on the expertise of numerous people, both inside and outside the government. In his cabinet, he built an impressive team of advisers that included John Hay as secretary of state and Elihu Root as secretary of war and later secretary of state. Hay was amazed by Roosevelt's "amiability and open-mindedness" in accepting advice; Root considered him "the most advisable man I ever knew." Among those he consulted outside his administration were historians, college presidents, journalists, and friends from all walks of life. "Of course I can't know all about everything," he told a friend. "I never take any important steps at all without consulting everybody available who I hope will help me by telling me what they think and why they think it."[102]

⌒◯⌒

As America's chief diplomat and commander in chief of the armed forces, Roosevelt agreed with President George Washington that peace came through strength. "In time of peace," Assistant Secretary of the Navy Roosevelt told cadets in 1897 at the U.S. Naval Academy, "it is necessary to prepare for war."[103] In foreign relations (as in domestic matters), idealism must often give way to compromise—but never at the expense of morality, honor, or national interests. He also emphasized the importance of maintaining the Anglo-American rapprochement as a check on the expansionist designs of Germany and Japan. In doing so, he became the first president to confront the national, imperial, ethnic, and racial rivalries in Europe and Asia that led to the Great War.

Roosevelt's lodestar was Alfred T. Mahan, who considered a strong navy vital to world power status. As a young captain in the U.S. Navy, Mahan in 1890 published his internationally acclaimed work, *The Influence of Sea Power upon History, 1660–1783,* which brought world fame to this forty-six-year-old instructor at the Naval War College in Annapolis, Maryland. Mahan argued that for the United States to become a maritime and commercial leader, as well as to solidify its security and maintain world peace, it must have a two-ocean navy bolstered by coaling stations or naval bases strung across the Pacific Ocean. Most important, it must construct an isthmian canal to link the Atlantic Ocean with the Pacific, enabling the United States to safeguard itself and the Western Hemisphere from outside threats.[104]

Ironically, Mahan's work had its greatest initial impact overseas, where its translation into Japanese and German helped shape the imperial direction of these two rising powers. The British likewise adopted its precepts, but it was not until the early 1900s that Mahan's ideas provided a strategic rationale for the United States to enlarge its navy as a basis for taking a leading role in international affairs.[105]

At this critical moment in America's history, Theodore Roosevelt assumed the presidency. The new frontier, he believed, was the Pacific Ocean, which lapped onto the distant shores of East Asia. But also important was Europe. For both economic and national security reasons, the United States had to help build a global balance of power that promoted stability and peace by spreading the principles of civilization to all areas of the world. As an individual and as a public servant, he was eager to expand the U.S. role in foreign affairs—starting with securing the Americas.

Chapter 1

Securing the "American" Hemisphere

[Every step in building the Panama Canal] was taken with the utmost care, was carried out with the highest, finest, and nicest standards of public and governmental ethics.

—Theodore Roosevelt
October 7, 1911

At every turn of my steps it seemed as if I were accompanied by a protecting divinity.

—Phillipe Bunau-Varilla
1913

On February 15, 1898, the American warship *Maine* blew up in Havana harbor, causing a crisis with Spain over Cuba that led the McKinley administration to dispatch the battleship *Oregon* to the Caribbean. Rear Admiral Charles Edgar Clark, its commanding officer, received orders to join the North Atlantic Squadron in the troubled waters. But "McKinley's Bulldog," as the *Oregon* was known, was in the North Pacific, in Bremerton, Washington, more than 14,000 miles away. With U.S. interests in Latin America and perhaps the entire southern half of the hemisphere hanging in the balance, the ship rushed to San Francisco to make final preparations for the voyage. Would the Germans, long interested in penetrating this potential commercial and strategic mecca below the United States, take advantage of the tense situation to fulfill long-desired objectives? The British had repeatedly tried to block American commercial and territorial expansion both into Canada and into the South American republics. Would they likewise exploit U.S. vulnerabilities to outmaneuver both the Americans and the Germans?

27

As the *Oregon* plied its way down the Pacific coast, along the Isthmus of Central America connecting the two American continents, down the South American coast and around Cape Horn, through the perilous Strait of Magellan, up the Atlantic side of that same continent, and, finally, into Key West—more than three months after the *Maine* had gone to the bottom—Clark must have rejoiced at news received from the Philippines. On May 1, Commodore George Dewey had led his force to victory over the Spanish fleet in Manila Bay—a triumph at the outset of America's war with Spain made sweeter by the presence of Clark's son-in-law serving in Dewey's squadron.

In the short run, the *Oregon* arrived in Cuban waters in time to participate in America's victory at the Battle of Santiago on July 3, 1898—more than four months after leaving the North Pacific. In the long run, the McKinley administration grasped the wisdom of U.S. Navy Captain Alfred T. Mahan's admonition to cut a canal through the Isthmus to permit the establishment of a two-ocean navy that would facilitate faster inter-oceanic passage and help to secure American interests in the Western Hemisphere. No lesson could have been clearer after the *Oregon*'s arduous sixty-eight-day journey from the North Pacific to the mid-Atlantic.

The voyage of the *Oregon,* the annexation of Hawaii in July 1898, the acquisition of Puerto Rico, Guam, and the Philippines by the Treaty of Paris ending the Spanish-American War the following December, and the establishment of an American protectorate over Cuba afterward all underlined the necessity of an isthmian canal, preferably through Nicaragua but possibly through Panama farther south. There were, however, a number of obstacles to pursuing such a project, most immediately the competing British and German interests in the Western Hemisphere.

I

Years after his presidency, Theodore Roosevelt publicly boasted that every step in building the Panama Canal "was taken with the utmost care, was carried out with the highest, finest, and nicest standards of public and governmental ethics." The United States "has many honorable chapters in its history, but no more honorable chapter than that which tells of the way in which our right to dig the Panama Canal was secured." A flamboyant and outspoken French contemporary, Philippe Bunau-Varilla, less idealistically declared that "Never did Passion more cynically challenge Reason" in defense of "Truth, Justice, and the National Interest."[1]

What is the truth behind these events in Panama?

The foundations for an isthmian canal trace far back in history. The search for a waterway through the North American continent provided the impetus for sixteenth-century European explorers searching for the fabled Strait of Anian as a link in the mythical Northwest Passage that would accomplish Christopher Columbus's mission of reaching the East by sailing west. In the early 1800s, President Thomas Jefferson sent explorers Meriwether Lewis and William Clark to the upper regions of the newly acquired Louisiana Territory beyond the Mississippi River west, always with an eye on finding a water passage to the Pacific coast. That effort also a failure, it seemed the most practical routes lay south of the United States—Panama, Darien, Nicaragua, or the narrow waistline of Mexico known as Tehuantepec.

American interest in a canal began in the early nineteenth century when Secretary of State Henry Clay considered a proposal in 1825 from the Federal Republic of Central America for the joint construction of a canal through Nicaragua. The following year, he instructed the newly appointed American delegates to the Panama Congress to discuss the matter with the stipulations that no country take on the project by itself and that the ensuing canal would be open to all toll-paying nations. But U.S. plans for the Panama meeting ended in a fiasco. Andrew Jackson's followers in Congress, still embittered over his defeat in the presidential election of 1824, embarrassed the victorious John Quincy Adams administration by delaying approval of the Panama delegates for so long that the conference adjourned without American participation.

A decade later, the Martin Van Buren administration tried again. In 1835, a Senate resolution called on private business to finance the building of a canal under the government's protection. The president sent a secret agent, John F. Stevens, who surveyed the area and submitted a report calling for a passage through Nicaragua. But his cost estimate of $35 million proved prohibitive.

In the following decade, U.S. attention turned farther south to the Isthmus of Panama, a poverty-stricken possession of New Granada (later Colombia). In 1846, the U.S. chargé in the capital of Bogotá in New Granada, Benjamin Bidlack, viewed the British presence as a threat to American interests. Acting without instructions, he negotiated a treaty that aimed to block any outside power—that is, Britain—from seizing Panama and to open the way for a U.S. route through that narrow piece of land connecting the two American continents. The terms of the Treaty of 1846 (or Bidlack Treaty), however, were incompatible, virtually allowing the two interested parties to choose which part of the agreement to enforce. In exchange for free commercial passage through the Isthmus, the United States guaranteed Panama's neutrality while also assuring New Granada's sovereignty over the Isthmus. The U.S. Senate nonetheless agreed with Bidlack's warnings and approved the treaty, seemingly leaving Britain as the only barrier to building a canal.[2]

British economic interests in Latin America rivaled those of the United States, meaning that the Crown could not permit a U.S. monopoly over any canal through the Americas. The result was the Clayton-Bulwer Treaty of 1850, whereby the two English-speaking nations agreed to cooperate in building an isthmian canal. Neither nation was to fortify or exert absolute control over the canal, nor could either one "occupy," "colonize," or establish "dominion" status over Central America. In signing this agreement, the British abandoned their hope to dominate Central America, in part because of their uneasy alliance with the Mosquito Indians, but also because of the U.S. victory in the Mexican War of 1846–1848 and the acquisition of what became known as the American Southwest. And yet, for the moment, the United States could neither unilaterally build a canal nor maintain total control.[3]

In fact, that "moment" would extend through the remainder of the century. Before the ink had dried on Clayton-Bulwer, domestic stress over slavery and its status in the newly acquired territory infected wounds that festered throughout the 1850s, culminating in the Civil War and Reconstruction and putting canal plans on hold for nearly a half century.

The Spanish-American War of 1898 revived U.S. interest in an isthmian canal. When an insurgent uprising against Spanish rule broke out that year in Cuba and an explosion sank the *Maine*, the United States moved to protect its interests in the Caribbean by dispatching a naval vessel to the troubled area. But, as we have seen, the *Oregon* was in the Pacific Northwest and did not reach Cuba for more than four months. A waterway through the Central American Isthmus would cut the distance by two-thirds.

The United States emerged from its triumphant three-month war with Spain as a power in both the Pacific and the Caribbean and, for both economic and strategic reasons, needed a canal to connect the Pacific with the Atlantic and lay the basis for a two-ocean navy. Mahan's blueprint for expanding U.S. naval power seemed to materialize in real time. The wartime annexation of Hawaii in July 1898 opened commercial and national security opportunities in the Pacific and Asia. Guam and other islands in the Pacific offered the potential for coaling stations or naval bases, while the Philippines would give the United States its first overseas colony, pointing the way to the vast economic markets of China and the necessity of building a navy capable of safeguarding America's interests both at home and abroad. An isthmian canal would facilitate all these objectives.

In early 1900, Britain's ongoing war with the Boers in South Africa (1899–1902) afforded the United States an opportunity to escape the restrictive provisions of the Clayton-Bulwer Treaty and take a major step toward constructing a canal. The British had stood virtually alone in their war and faced a host of unfriendly countries on the European continent that forced an accommodation with the United States. In Washington, President William McKinley seized the moment and directed his secretary of state, John Hay, to push for a canal agreement with the London government. A congressional bill favored a

Nicaraguan passageway because the country was closer to the United States and had natural waterways that would reduce construction costs. In February 1900, the two Atlantic nations negotiated the Hay-Pauncefote Treaty, which authorized the United States to build, own, and maintain the neutrality of an isthmian canal but, in accordance with the Clayton-Bulwer Treaty, without fortifying it. Still, a neutral canal appealed to many Americans, making the treaty appear certain to pass the U.S. Senate.

But 1900 was a presidential election year, and New York governor Theodore Roosevelt, who had become a national figure after the war with Spain, denounced the prohibition against fortifying a canal. Concerned about European involvement in the Caribbean, he challenged the administration in Washington to explain the value of building a canal without having the right to defend it. As he privately complained to his friend Mahan, "I do not see why we should dig the canal if we are not to fortify it so as to insure its being used for ourselves and against our foes in time of war." In a statement issued by his office, the governor declared, "I most earnestly hope that the pending treaty . . . will not be ratified unless amended so as to provide that the canal, when built, shall be wholly under the control of the United States, alike in peace and war."[4]

Roosevelt argued that the American need for exclusive control of the canal rested on the principles of the Monroe Doctrine in protecting the Western Hemisphere from European involvement. In a personal letter to Hay, the governor warned, "If we invite foreign powers to a joint ownership, a joint guarantee, of what so vitally concerns us but a little way from our borders, how can we possibly object to similar joint action say in Southern Brazil, or Argentina, where our interests are so much less evident?". If Germany and France gained any rights over an isthmian canal, Roosevelt asked his longtime friend in England, Cecil Spring Rice, what would stop them from partitioning South America?[5]

Roosevelt, now vice president after McKinley's reelection victory in November 1900, agreed with the bulk of senators who feared that any concession of control over the Isthmus would virtually invite European powers into the hemisphere. The U.S. Senate, he asserted to the British military attaché in Washington, Arthur Hamilton Lee, should abrogate the Clayton-Bulwer Treaty of 1850, which permitted only a "qualified intervention" in Central American affairs.[6]

It was becoming clear, at least privately, that Roosevelt's chief concern over an isthmian canal was Germany, not Britain. He warned his best friend and confidant, Henry Cabot Lodge, that Kaiser Wilhelm II might exploit the U.S. failure to build up its navy that year by becoming more aggressive in the West Indies or South America and thus challenge the Monroe Doctrine. The Germans, according to Roosevelt, thought the tension between the United

States and Britain over the Clayton-Bulwer Treaty would lead the British to stand aside if a fight broke out between the Americans and the Germans. For that reason, the Germans would support the British in the event of an Anglo-American dispute over that treaty and might themselves attempt to build a canal. Certainly, he must have calculated, the United States could not raise an army that approached the troop strength of Germany.[7]

In view of the German threat, Roosevelt told Lodge, the United States should emphasize to the British that the two Atlantic nations must remain friendly and negotiate a treaty guaranteeing mutual self-respect and the right of the United States to build a canal. "If this is impossible," he declared, "I would then abrogate the Clayton-Bulwer treaty anyhow."[8]

Above all, the vice president declared, the United States must not alienate Britain, particularly since Germany might soon pose a threat to American interests. Either the U.S. abrogation of the Clayton-Bulwer Treaty or an attempt to build a canal on its own could drive Britain and Germany together. If the United States abrogated the treaty, it must continue expanding the navy and army. Reason indicated that it would not be in Britain's interest to side with Germany against the United States. In fact, Roosevelt chided, it would be "the utmost folly"; the British lion would have its "paws burned, while the nuts would go to Germany." Yet in the past two years, he cautioned, both British and American leaders had committed the "wildest follies." The "old frontier principles" must guide policy: "Don't bluster, don't flourish your revolver and never draw unless you intend to shoot."[9]

Lodge was skeptical of a German danger. Admittedly, the kaiser at times seemed "wild enough to do anything." Lodge reminded Roosevelt that Mahan had warned against trying to keep all of South America free from European involvement; the areas in the northern half of the hemisphere were more than enough for the United States to protect. The American army was fairly well prepared, but Lodge, like Roosevelt, believed that the United States must build up its navy as the chief means for discouraging a German attack.[10]

Lodge also played down Roosevelt's concern about Germany supporting Britain if the United States abrogated the Clayton-Bulwer Treaty. Lodge did not believe the Germans wanted trouble at this time. Nor did he consider it likely that the British would go to war over the canal. Germany was preoccupied with China; Britain was "too exhausted by the African war."[11]

Roosevelt was not comfortable with this call for restraint, asserting that he was wary of any policy that could encourage Germany or any other European country to seek territory in South America. He wanted to maintain good relations with Germany because he had "a hearty and genuine liking for the Germans both individually and as a nation." But he knew that neither personal nor national friendships could determine foreign policy. The United States, Roosevelt maintained, had no interest in acquiring territory in South

America, but the nation *did* have an interest in keeping others out, and he was prepared to block any European leader from either taking territory or establishing a protectorate over any of these countries.[12]

The vice president dismissed the idea of neutralizing the canal and insisted that the United States control that passageway for national security reasons. He made clear to friend and British diplomat Arthur Lee in Washington that he opposed his suggestion that any canal should be "always neutral, and open to the commerce of the world." He emphasized that "it would be criminal in this nation to allow the canal to be used against it in time of war, or not to use the canal in its own interest during such a crisis." He nonetheless conceded that this stricture did not apply to Britain; its navy, he thought, would seize the canal in the event of war with the United States regardless of treaty stipulations. If the United States went to war with any European power, an assurance of the canal's neutrality would allow an enemy force to transit the passageway.[13]

Roosevelt's views on America's role beyond its borders rested on the inherent right of self-defense. To New York attorney Frederic René Coudert, Roosevelt denied any interest in controlling people capable of self-government unless they wanted "to go in with us—and not necessarily even then." Except for fortifying an isthmian canal or securing a naval station, "I hope it will not become our duty to take a foot of soil south of us." Yet, such an acquisition might become necessary to preserve U.S. security. Roosevelt assured German ambassador Theodor von Holleben that the United States did not want to take territory from South America and did not seek commercial advantages over European nations. He supported the Monroe Doctrine and strongly objected to any power gaining new territory in the Americas.[14]

Roosevelt again stressed the necessity of military readiness. To Captain Albert Key of the U.S. Navy, Roosevelt declared that he did not want to strike anyone unless there was no choice, "but never under any conceivable circumstances to strike unless one is prepared to strike hard."[15]

Then, on September 14, 1901, McKinley died from an assassin's bullet fired eight days earlier, and Roosevelt took the oath as president.

II

President Roosevelt's worldview became evident at the beginning of his administration when he declared his intention to follow the fair and equal trade principles of the Open Door in China and South America. He recognized that the growing danger in China caused by imperial rivalries could affect U.S. economic and security interests. It was also important to America's welfare that the United States help the Latin American countries develop industries and commerce as integral to improving their economies. He told his longtime friend in Germany, Hermann Speck von Sternburg ("Speck," as he called him), that he did not want the United States or any other nation to seize territory in the two regions but to encourage their people to follow an Open Door policy as essential to the area's stability.[16]

The first test of the Roosevelt administration's foreign policy came with the canal issue.

As the new president wanted, the Senate did not approve the Hay-Pauncefote Treaty in its present form and drafted amendments permitting the United States to fortify the canal. At first, the British government balked at any revisions in the pact, but it changed its policy largely because of the ongoing Boer War in South Africa and the talk in the United States of another Anglo-American war. Furthermore, the British saw great economic and political advantages in promoting what historians later called the "great rapprochement" with the United States.[17]

Roosevelt argued that the two English-speaking peoples needed each other in a world becoming increasingly hostile to their common interests. Britain's war in South Africa was draining the Crown's treasury, both in human and economic terms, and its relations with Germany had deteriorated so badly that war seemed certain. Roosevelt understood that in building a canal, the United States would be in a position to safeguard the Western Hemisphere (and British holdings) by blocking German involvement.

The result was the second Hay-Pauncefote Treaty of November 1901. With Roosevelt now president, the new administration negotiated a pact that authorized the United States to construct, control, and defend the canal. The treaty makers circumvented the issue of fortification by saying nothing about the subject. The United States thus removed the Clayton-Bulwer Treaty's restriction by a tacit understanding that saved face for both nations: the British for not relinquishing the point and the Americans for not claiming it. The British could now transfer much of their West Indian naval squadron to other trouble spots, thereby conceding U.S. supremacy in the Caribbean and chief responsibility for protecting the Western Hemisphere.

The only question remaining was the location of a canal. Would it run through Panama or Nicaragua? As in most historical events, this one has a rich and complex background that helped to shape Roosevelt's decisions.

The story begins in the late nineteenth century when French entrepreneur Ferdinand de Lesseps attempted to build a canal through Panama. Having masterminded the completion of the Suez Canal in Egypt in 1869, the talented and resourceful adventurer soon afterward turned to Panama. By now in his mid-seventies and in good health, he secured concessionary rights to the area from Colombia that took effect in 1878 and would expire in October 1904. Three years after the clock started, excavators from the Compagnie Universelle du Canal Interocéanique de Panama prepared to break ground.[18]

The first obstacle to de Lesseps's project appeared before the digging began. President Rutherford B. Hayes declared in a special message to Congress in March 1880 that Colombia's concessions had violated the Treaty of 1846 (or Bidlack Treaty), which guaranteed the United States a right of way through the Isthmus in exchange for its agreement to maintain the neutrality of the area. Declaring that U.S. policy stipulated "a canal under American control," he could not permit the French company to construct a canal "between our Atlantic and our Pacific shores, and virtually a part of the coastline of the United States." As a warning, he ordered warships to the coastal region. The bluff did not work. Neither the canal company nor Colombia aborted the project.[19]

Not long after the digging was under way, a fatal engineering flaw became evident in de Lesseps's plans. As in Suez, he intended to build a sea-level canal. But unlike Egypt, the water levels on the two ends of the projected Panama Canal were not equal (the Pacific is deeper than the Atlantic), resulting in enormous mudslides caused by digging and heavy annual rainfall. Five to six feet of rain deluged Panama City on the Pacific side of the Isthmus every year, creating mountains of mud that buried workers and equipment. To add to the frustration, the mud left a thick residue of orange rust on the machinery and tools along with endless colonies of mold and mildew that covered the workers' shoes and everything else in their spongy path. As if by providential veto, an earthquake shook the area in 1882, followed by a massive wave of deaths due to yellow fever.[20]

The future of a Panama canal depended on de Lesseps's ability to reduce the number of catastrophic mud and rock slides while keeping his workers healthy. In suffocating temperatures that ranged from 100 to 130 degrees at the lowest dig of the Culebra Cut, his team clawed its way nine miles through a mountain, hauling the dirt away with forty-three steam shovels, more than a hundred locomotives, and 2,000 flat rail cars. But torrential rains left horrendous slides in their wake—one covering nearly fifty acres of land as rivers swelled to forty feet in a single day. All the while, the deadly fever continued its merciless assault.[21]

A decade after beginning the project, the company had dug less than half of what the schedule had called for in six years. Half of 50,000 workers had died from what became known as the "black vomit," which made death so certain that French workers wrote their wills before departing for Panama and arrived with coffins among their belongings. The city of Colón on the Caribbean side of Panama was, according to one report, a foul hole [that], by comparison, the ghettoes of White Russia, the slums of Toulon, Naples, and old Stamboul . . . deserve prizes for cleanliness. There are neither sewers nor street cleaners. . . . toilets are quite unknown, all the rubbish is thrown into the swamps or onto rubbish heaps. Toads splash in the liquid muck . . . rats infest the solid filth . . . snakes hunt both toads and rats; clouds of mosquitoes swarm into the homes.

The primitive wilds of the Isthmus did not buckle under to the marvels of modernity.[22]

De Lesseps gave up on the project in 1889. His reputation had vanished along with his wealth as French courts uncovered a string of bribes and fraudulent practices used in raising financial support for the canal that sent his son to jail. All that was left in Panama were the remains of a huge construction company now mired in the mud and muck that made up much of the Isthmus during the long rainy season.

French owners of the New Panama Canal Company took over de Lesseps's equipment and his Colombian concessions, hoping the United States would buy them and resume the Panama project. The U.S. decision depended on the recommendation of the Isthmian Canal Commission in Washington, a collection of engineers chaired by Admiral John G. Walker and appointed by President McKinley in 1897 to determine the most feasible location for an isthmian canal. Nicaragua remained its choice in 1899. But William Nelson Cromwell, the legal counsel for the New Panama Canal Company, did not consider the matter closed. A prominent New York City attorney with an expertise in railroads and corporations, he claimed to have been instrumental in establishing the Walker Commission and set out to persuade its members to favor Panama.[23]

The commission should begin its work in Paris, Cromwell convinced Admiral Walker, where they would have the assistance of the New Panama Canal Company in providing materials and office space over a five-week period. Two years later, four of the seven commissioners still leaned toward Nicaragua for the site of a canal; the other three supported Panama. Cromwell remained optimistic at a stockholders' meeting of the New Panama Canal Company just before Christmas of 1901 in Paris.[24]

Prospects looked good for Panama. Two times—in the preliminary report in November 1900 and in its final report a year later—Walker Commission members expressed concern about the shallow waters of Nicaragua's rivers and showed a preference for Panama, which offered lower building and maintenance costs and a shorter distance from sea to sea. Nevertheless, the commission as a whole stood firm for Nicaragua, primarily because of what its members considered an exorbitant selling price that rested on the French canal company's estimated worth of the Colombian concessions—more than

$109 million. A realistic figure, according to the commission, was $40 million. Perhaps to put pressure on Colombia, Secretary of State Hay opened negotiations with Nicaragua and neighboring Costa Rica for canal rights.[25]

The French company's stockholders panicked and, after a brawl broke out on December 21, 1901, required the police to restore order. Amid the chaos, Cromwell convinced the New Panama Canal Company to lower its asking price by more than half, from $109 million to $40 million.[26]

The scene then shifted to Washington, where it was now January 1902 and Roosevelt as president quietly leaned toward Panama. Though initially appearing neutral on the canal site, he had recently become uncertain about Nicaragua. On December 10, he received a letter from an engineer on the Walker Commission, George S. Morison (a friend of Cromwell's), who argued that recent technological advances made Panama the better choice. Another consideration also weighed on the president's mind. Early on the morning of January 4, the New Panama Canal Company informed the Walker Commission of the huge drop in the concession price. At noon, Walker told the State Department of this development, and it delivered the news to the White House moments afterward.[27]

Less than a week later, on January 9, the House of Representatives, unaware of the price change and perhaps interpreting the president's silence as support for Nicaragua, took the lead. It overwhelmingly approved the Hepburn Bill favoring Nicaragua by a vote of 308-2—a project strongly supported by Democratic Senator John Tyler Morgan of Alabama and all the Gulf States.[28]

Morgan had won the first round of the battle in Congress and now intended to close the deal in the Senate. As chair of the Committee on Interoceanic Canals, he was a formidable proponent of a Nicaraguan canal that benefited southern interests. His main rival for commercial connections between the oceans was the transcontinental railroad running some distance north and completed in 1869. Mobile and New Orleans would profit the most from a canal through Nicaragua, which was closer to the United States than Panama and meant lower costs for transporting merchandise to Latin America and the Pacific Coast.[29]

Morgan's optimism faded on the morning of January 16, when, at a meeting of the Senate canal committee, Mark Hanna of Ohio shocked him by calling for a delay in implementing the House bill on Nicaragua until the Walker Commission could consider a new Panama offer.

"It is not worth waiting for," declared Morgan.

"Well, the President thinks it is worth waiting for," replied Hanna.

"What do you mean by that?"

"I mean that the President has asked Admiral Walker to call the Canal Commission together so it can make a supplemental report for him, which he intends to send to Congress."

"Don't believe anything of the kind," asserted Morgan.

"Suppose you ask the President."[30]

And that he intended to do.[31]

But before Morgan could make it to the White House, Hanna telephoned the president, alerting him that Morgan was on his way and was livid over the turn in the Nicaraguan situation.[32]

We do not know the substance of their conversation, but one can imagine Roosevelt attempting to calm his visitor by explaining that the new French offer made it incumbent on the Walker Commission to "reconsider" its support for Nicaragua. What the president surely did not explain was that earlier that morning he had directed Walker to talk with the French company's representative and had also arranged to meet with each of the nine commission members in the afternoon to hear their views. Morison's December arguments in favor of Panama and the lower price for the concessions had convinced the president that Panama was a better choice than Nicaragua.[33]

That Thursday afternoon of January 16, the president met with each member of the commission, asking them to work together in preparing a supplementary report based on the reduced price offered by the New Panama Canal Company. Roosevelt knew the transcontinental railroad lobby would take advantage of a split commission vote to ramp up opposition to any isthmian canal. Despite the House rejection of the new offer, he directed the commission to revisit the matter and return a "unanimous" recommendation "not later than tomorrow evening."[34]

At the quickly assembled commission meeting, only one member opposed Panama, but he soon changed his vote after a private conversation with the president. Lewis Haupt, a civil engineering professor from the University of Pennsylvania, claimed that Roosevelt called him to the White House and "persuaded" him to drop his dissent and sign the report. Haupt agreed to do so, insisting that the reasons for changing his vote appear in the minutes of the commission meeting. He later told this story to Earl Harding, a journalist from the *New York World* who had spent two years in Panama investigating the background of the canal.[35]

Haupt later publicly declared that he had yielded to the president's fears that failure to achieve unanimity in the commission's recommendation might result in no canal. In Haupt's article published in the *North American Review* of July 1902, he alleged that he favored Nicaragua but signed the supplemental report because of Roosevelt's warning that a divided vote would jeopardize hopes for a canal. For Haupt, the question was "Panama or nothing." A canal was vital to the "general good" of the United States and the world, and he did not want to be the "sole cause of obstruction to the building of any canal."[36]

Later that same day, on January 16, 1902, Morgan met with Walker, asking him to attend an emergency meeting of the Senate committee the following day. The admiral turned him down, explaining that, in historian Edmund Morris's words, he was "too busy."[37]

Roosevelt got what he wanted: Every member of the Walker Commission signed a report designating Panama as the preferred canal site. Walker delivered it to Hay, who passed it to the president in the late afternoon. The Friday deadline was important because Roosevelt knew that a press release on Saturday would appear on the front page of the newspapers on either Sunday or Monday morning. And so it did, but with no mention in the article of Roosevelt's position on the matter—"Commission Says Panama Is Best," declared Sunday's *New York Herald*.[38]

The White House sent the report to Congress on January 20, where it encountered strong opposition from Morgan and his supporters in the Senate. The new report was the work of Roosevelt, Morgan charged, not the Walker Commission. "I will strive to defeat it."[39]

The next day, the *New York Times* ran a follow-up story under the headline, "Panama Canal Plan Goes Before Congress." According to the article, the Walker Commission unanimously agreed that Panama was "the most practical and feasible route" for the isthmian canal. Negotiations with Colombia were under way.[40]

The news had a mixed result. Several senators in Washington were excited over the certain bounty coming from a Panama Canal; others were cautious and waited for the recommendation by Morgan's committee. Increasing numbers of lobbyists appeared on behalf of their commercial and financial benefactors, while businessman Edward H. Harriman led others in buying Panama Canal bonds before they skyrocketed in price. Unnoticed in these developments was Panama's reaction: Separatists gained momentum as Colombia seemed poised to seize control of the canal and their future.[41]

III

Two colorful and headstrong figures now emerged as pivotal: William Nelson Cromwell assumed a greater role, joined by Philippe Bunau-Varilla, a French entrepreneur who, in his mid-twenties, had been the chief mining engineer of the de Lesseps operation and was now a major shareholder (along with his brother Maurice) in the new French company. Cromwell and Bunau-Varilla agreed on two points—that the canal should run through Panama, and that success depended on their overcoming the negative feelings they felt for each other when meeting in early 1902. The stakes were so high that they managed to work together throughout that year and into the next, lobbying in Washington for their mutual goal.[42]

Bunau-Varilla and Cromwell implicitly agreed to a truce, but time soon showed that no stage was big enough to hold them both. To Bunau-Varilla, the quest for a Panama Canal was a crusade; to Cromwell, it meant a big check. According to historian David McCullough, Bunau-Varilla regarded Cromwell as a "mercenary" and, even worse, a lawyer. Bunau-Varilla was a self-avowed "Champion of Truth"; Cromwell, a promoter of self. Their common gift lay in lobbying politicians in Washington.[43]

Cromwell took the lead in pushing for Panama against a wall of congressional and American public opinion in favor of Nicaragua. He headed the prestigious New York law firm of Sullivan and Cromwell (which later hired future secretary of state John Foster Dulles) and was now the chief American legal body representing both the French firm and the Panama Railroad Company. Cromwell's first victory came in 1900, when he blocked a plank in the Republican Party's platform calling for a Nicaraguan canal by donating $60,000 to the campaign through Senator Hanna, a close friend of President McKinley and chair of the election effort. Cromwell included the expenditure among his expenses forwarded to the New Panama Canal Company and ultimately received close to a million dollars for his services. According to historian Walter LaFeber, a substantial amount of money changed hands in the long canal process, all amounts impossible to determine because Cromwell burned numerous documents and Dulles and other law partners later disposed of the rest.[44]

Cromwell stands out in the Panama story as an accused conspirator who persuaded the president, his secretary of state, and key figures in Panama to support a revolution on the Isthmus. The *New York World* in 1908 described him as

> about 5 feet 8 inches high, and medium in build. . . . His eyes are a brilliant light blue, as clear as a baby's, and as innocent looking as a girl's. . . . He can smile as sweetly as a society belle and at the same time deal a blow at a business foe that ties him in a hopeless tangle of financial knots. . . . He is a wizard with figures and a shorthand writer of wonderful skill. . . . He talks fast, and when he wishes to, never to the point.

His intellect "works like a flash of lightning, and it swings about with the agility of an acrobat."

Years afterward, in 1912, the chair of a congressional committee investigating the canal controversy, Democrat Henry T. Rainey of Illinois, called Cromwell "the most dangerous man the country has produced since the days of Aaron Burr—a professional revolutionist."[45] Staff member Henry Hall of the *New York World* told the Rainey committee that Cromwell had "conceived and, with the assistance of Mr. Roosevelt, carried out the rape of the

Isthmus and the establishment there of this little Republic." With premature snow-white hair and mustache, all adorned by an elegant suit and silk hat, Cromwell cast the image of respectability, wisdom, and wealth—a mover of mountains.[46]

The second central character in this drama—Philippe Bunau-Varilla—had come to the United States upon learning of the reduced price of the Panama holdings, hoping to convince the government in Washington to settle on Panama by lobbying the most influential people involved in the canal controversy—Roosevelt, Hay, Hanna, and leaders in Panama. Bunau-Varilla was one of the most imaginative and venturesome personalities of his time. According to one contemporary writer, Bunau-Varilla viewed "the earth . . . like a school globe which he, the teacher, made to revolve at his pleasure." Diminutive in stature with a dark red spiked mustache that looked bigger because of his physical size, and just one year younger than Roosevelt, Bunau-Varilla signed on in 1884 as chief engineer of de Lesseps's Panama operation. But like so many of de Lesseps's crew, he was stricken with yellow fever and forced to return to Paris. Still in his twenties, he was nevertheless fortunate to have been among the few to recover from the sickness. Back in Paris, Bunau-Varilla soon resumed his frenetic work pace by building railroads in Spain and the Belgian Congo, masterminding flood control in Romania, editing and co-owning (with his brother Maurice) Paris's morning newspaper *Le Matin*, and, in 1893, helping to establish the New Panama Canal Company as a principal shareholder.[47]

Visionary, crusader, and writer, Bunau-Varilla was also "Napoleonic" in bearing (said a *New York Sun* newsman) and, according to many of his peers, a brilliant engineer who considered himself chosen by destiny to bring to fruition the "Great Idea of Panama," which he defined as a series of locks rather than a sea-level canal. In his account published in 1914, *Panama: The Creation, Destruction, and Resurrection*, Bunau-Varilla wrote, "At every turn of my steps it seemed as if I were accompanied by a protecting divinity."[48]

Bunau-Varilla knew the company was running out of time on the Panama project. The Colombian concessions were less than two years from expiration in late 1904, driving him to sell the rights to another country before they went back to Colombia. The Russians were not interested, dismissing his warning that the Anglo-Saxons would control global commerce if they owned and administered a canal in Panama along with that in Suez. The British likewise refused to buy the rights because of their problems elsewhere, despite Bunau-Varilla's assurances that the rising North American colossus would use the canal to gain worldwide commercial supremacy. Finally, he found widespread interest in a canal upon his arrival in the United States in January 1902, just after the House of Representatives overwhelmingly voted for the Hepburn bill designating Nicaragua as the site for the canal and handing Morgan a resounding victory.[49]

Bunau-Varilla, of course, was not aware of Roosevelt's preference for Panama and felt a great sense of urgency on hearing of the Hepburn vote. The president's role in the Walker Commission's deliberations did not become public at the time, which explains Bunau-Varilla's alarm on February 22, when Roosevelt proclaimed the second Hay-Pauncefote Treaty in effect, authorizing the building an isthmian canal through, it was assumed, Nicaragua.[50]

Bunau-Varilla immediately joined Cromwell and Hanna in an uphill fight in the Senate against the Nicaragua proposal. He warned of volcanoes in Nicaragua (Panama had none), but his argument had little impact until May when a volcano erupted on the island of Martinique in the Caribbean, throwing up a gigantic black cloud and spewing thick and hot waves of molten lava that blanketed and destroyed St. Pierre, a town of 30,000 people. Less than two weeks later, Bunau-Varilla's fortunes soared when the chief volcano in Nicaragua, Mount Momotombo, began rumbling. He realized this was the same volcano pictured on the republic's postage stamps and, with forty-five states in the Union, he scoured Washington, D.C., for ninety of these stamps to distribute, each one pasted on individual pieces of paper placed on the desk of every senator. Below each stamp were these words: "Official testimony regarding volcanic activity in Nicaragua."[51]

Bunau-Varilla's tactics appeared decisive, perhaps in both houses of Congress. After Republican senator John Spooner of Wisconsin consulted the president, he introduced an amendment to the Hepburn bill that substituted Panama for Nicaragua. The Senate approved the amendment on June 19 by a 42 to 34 margin. On that same day, the Senate passed the Spooner bill by a vote of 67 to 6. The House approved the bill a week later by 259 to 8, and the president signed it into law on June 28.[52]

The Spooner Act authorized the president to purchase the land and concessions of the New Panama Canal Company for no more than $40 million and to negotiate with Colombia for perpetual use of a six-mile-wide canal zone through Panama. If he failed to strike a deal with Colombia within a "reasonable time," he was free to negotiate with Nicaragua. Only on the surface is it surprising that Morgan supported the act; he felt confident that negotiations with Colombia would not succeed. In the meantime, as shown earlier, the Colombian concessions would terminate in less than two years. The New Panama Canal Company prepared to sell its equipment and concessions to the United States.[53]

Racing against two deadlines, Secretary of State Hay delivered a virtual ultimatum to the Colombian chargé to the United States, Tomás Herrán. If his country's legislators dragged their feet, Hay warned, the president would turn to Nicaragua, depriving Colombian citizens of the financial stimulus of a canal. Too much time had passed already, according to Roosevelt's watch, and in accordance with his directives, Hay apprised Herrán on January 21, 1903:

> I am commanded by the President to inform you that the reasonable time pro-
> vided in the statute for the conclusion of the negotiations with Colombia for the
> excavation of an Isthmian Canal has expired, and he has authorized me to sign
> the treaty of which I had the honor to give you a draft, with the modification
> that the sum of $100,000, fixed therein as the annual payment, be increased to
> $250,000. I am not authorized to consider or discuss any other change.[54]

Under White House pressure, Herrán signed the treaty the next day in Washington. In his defense, his long-standing instructions had been to sign such a treaty; but, unknown to him, his home government in Bogotá had changed its position on the canal issue, only to encounter communication problems in sending him the new directives. Less than a week later, Herrán received a telegram instructing him not to sign the treaty with Hay and to await further guidance. This note came too late.

In March 1903, the Senate approved the pact over the angry protests of Morgan and others favoring Nicaragua; and the Hay-Herrán Treaty, with the president's signature, went to Colombia for ratification. According to its terms, the United States received a 100-year lease to a six-mile-wide canal zone, renewable at its exclusive option, for an outright payment of $10 million to Colombia plus an annual fee of $250,000 to begin in nine years, the expected time needed for completing the canal. Only the United States could renew the treaty, giving it canal rights in perpetuity. To Hay, Roosevelt confessed to "sweating blood" in persuading the Senate to confirm the Hay-Herrán Treaty on March 17. Morgan called it a "grave mistake."[55]

Opposition to the treaty immediately broke out in Colombia. The govern-ment in Bogotá denounced the pact as a violation of both the nation's sover-eignty and the Treaty of 1846, which had made United States the guarantor of Panama's neutrality. Furthermore, the Colombian constitution did not permit the government to relinquish territory in perpetuity. The greatest objection to the Hay-Herrán Treaty, however, was its provision of only $10 million com-pensation to Colombia. Why, its people asked, should the $40 million pay-ment for equipment and access rights go to the French-owned New Panama Canal Company, particularly when its concessions arrangement was less than two years from sunsetting?[56]

In late March 1903, the U.S. minister in Bogotá, Arthur Beaupré, informed Hay that Colombian popular opinion opposed the ratification of the treaty and that the congressional vote might not take place until the outcome of the recent elections became known. Beaupré was a politician from Illinois who had served as consul in Guatemala City and then Bogotá before becoming minister to Colombia in 1903, when he engaged in a bitter domestic struggle over the treaty. Outspoken and at times abrasive in his straightforward manner, his temperament was not conducive to compromise, particularly when Colombians critical of American policies refused to believe his repeated warning that the United States might drop Panama and turn to Nicaragua.[57]

Major leaders of the National Party in Colombia opposed President José Manuel Marroquín's handling of the canal agreement, making it "probable," Beaupré asserted, that the treaty would not succeed without strong support from the government. Marroquin was a politically inexperienced and elderly scholar who had seized control of the government by a coup in July 1900 after deeming the eighty-five-year-old president, Dr. Manuel Antonio Sanclemente, medically unfit for office. As time passed, opposition to Marroquin grew as every action he took on the canal matter came under vicious attacks as a sellout to the United States. Final election returns would perhaps resolve the issue, but they were almost two months away because of the time required to gather the ballots from remote areas—about May 20, 1903.[58]

Over the last month, both the Bogotá press and the people in the city denounced the Hay-Herrán Treaty as a decree imposed by the imperial United States. The minister of finance had called for a public discussion of the agreement, leaving the misleading impression that the Colombian Congress would make a decision based on the people's wishes. By the time the text of the treaty became public, according to Beaupré, popular opinion had shifted from "suspicion" to "decided opposition." The ministry came under pressure from the press, which denounced the pact as a U.S. "scheme" to take advantage of Colombia's economic crisis by offering "a paltry sum" for one of the most valuable pieces of real estate in the world.[59]

In early May, the Colombian press and public claimed that the U.S. threat to turn to Nicaragua was an effort to squeeze a better deal out of Colombia. The rallying cry became to preserve national honor by refusing to surrender sovereignty. According to Beaupré, the Colombians wanted more money, along with continued U.S. protection of their ports from other countries. "It is entirely impossible to convince these people that the Nicaragua route was ever seriously considered by the United States."[60]

Hay agreed with Beaupré and, in a message meant for confidential delivery to Bogotá's leaders, he issued a warning: Their rejection or undue delay in ratifying the treaty would undermine the "friendly understanding" between the nations and could lead the Congress in Washington to take an "action" in the coming winter session that "every friend of Colombia would regret."[61]

IV

In early June of 1903, a revolutionary plan developed in Panama quietly moved forward when Captain James Beers, an American freight agent and port captain on the Pacific side of the Panama Railroad, arrived in New York to meet with his superior and attorney for the railroad, William Cromwell. Approval of the special mission had come from the white-bearded leader of the separatists, José Arango, who was a senator, land agent, lobbyist, and attorney for the Panama Railroad Company. He had commissioned Beers to confer with Cromwell about the importance of making secession seem "spontaneous." In his later account of the revolution, Arango attempted to make it appear internally driven by not mentioning Cromwell's name in his "Data for a History of the Independence," published in *El Heraldo del Istmo* on December 15, 1905, but his allusion to Cromwell was unmistakable when he referred to "the responsible person who, through Captain Beers, had opened the road to our hopes and thus stimulated the sending of a representative of the committee."[62]

Years afterward, evidence before the House Committee on Foreign Affairs revealed a previously unknown Panama story. Among the figures at the "nucleus of the revolutionary conspiracy in Panama" were Arango, physician Manuel Amador Guerrero of the Panama Railroad Company, and Carlos Arosemena, who later became minister to the United States. Two Americans were involved early on—Beers and the highly popular assistant superintendent of the railroad, Herbert Prescott. "For appearance's sake," Hall noted to the committee, Beers and Prescott stayed in the background.[63]

Soon after Beers's meeting with Cromwell in early June 1903, Senator Hanna convinced Roosevelt to meet with the attorney and discuss Panama. During a three-hour meeting with the president on June 13, Cromwell doubtless shared the details of his meeting with Beers and asserted that a revolution was in the making. In statements the president did not declare confidential, he emphasized his determination to build a canal through the Isthmus. If Colombia rejected the Hay-Herrán Treaty and Panama won independence, he would extend recognition to the new republic and "strongly favor" a new canal treaty.[64]

With no restrictions placed on their conversation, Cromwell felt free to share Roosevelt's views with the public. He sent his press agent, Roger Farnham, to the Washington bureau of the *New York World* to suggest that one of its staff members write an article highlighting the president's position on the canal issue. Farnham explained to his contact at the press that a popular uprising would take place in Panama if Colombia did not ratify the Hay-Herrán Treaty. About a half dozen Panamanians would soon arrive in Washington to consult with Hay and other State Department officials. President Roosevelt, according to Farnham, supported Panama's move toward secession.[65]

The next day, an article in the *New York World* written by a highly respected journalist in Washington, Charles S. Albert, accurately forecasted almost every detail regarding a revolution in Panama, probably on November 3—election day in New York City to detract attention from events on the Isthmus. The headlines on June 14 read:

NEW REPUBLIC MAY ARISE TO GRANT CANAL
The State of Panama Ready to Secede
if the Treaty is Rejected by the Colombian Congress
ROOSEVELT IS SAID TO ENCOURAGE THE IDEA[66]

According to Albert's rendition of Farnham's story, President Roosevelt wanted the Panama route and had no intention of negotiating over Nicaragua. The United States had spent millions of dollars in determining the decision; three different ministers from Colombia had guaranteed their government's willingness to grant concession rights; and two treaties had approved America's right of way across the Isthmus. The Roosevelt administration could not allow a foreign government to build a canal through Panama. If the United States chose Nicaragua, another country could construct a passageway through Panama, which would put the canal outside the American zone of influence. If the United States built a canal in Panama, no one would build another one through Nicaragua because of the high costs and the realization that such a canal would lie within the American zone of influence.[67]

Every day, Albert continued, brought news of swelling opposition in Bogotá to the Hay-Herrán Treaty that could lead to revolution in Panama. The Colombian government demanded more money for the canal zone and the concessions; opponents of the treaty charged that the present treaty required Colombia to relinquish its sovereignty over the Isthmus. Growing numbers of citizens in Panama were prepared to secede from Colombia and negotiate a new treaty with the United States. For diplomatic recognition, they would give the United States "the equivalent of absolute sovereignty over the Canal Zone" (except for Panama City).[68]

Rebel leaders had already drawn up a government for the Republic of Panama but intended to delay action until after the Colombian Congress convened on June 20. Failure to ratify the American treaty within a "reasonable time" would set off the revolution.[69]

Despite Roosevelt's denials of involvement in Panama's affairs, he had implicitly encouraged revolutionary sentiment in mid-June 1903 when he met with Cromwell and never disavowed their conversation about Panama published in two newspapers, the *New York World* and the *New York Sun*. Little doubt can exist about the president's complicity in the scheme since the *World*'s story appeared the day after Cromwell's meeting in the White

House. That same June 14, the *Sun* reported that the president "sent for" Cromwell, who agreed to ask "French company agents" to warn the government in Bogotá in a "semi-official way" that if the United States did not build a canal through the Isthmus, no country would do so. Had the president, like Cromwell with the *World*, leaked that story to the *Sun*? Both articles appeared on the day following the meeting.[70]

Less than a week later, the Colombian Congress convened in a special session at 1 p.m. on June 20 amid widespread vocal opposition to the Hay-Herrán Treaty. In his opening remarks, Marroquin warned that even though a canal would benefit Colombia, the treaty would endanger the nation's sovereignty while failing to secure its fair share of the money changing hands. Yet, he again refused to act. "I leave the full responsibility of the decision this matter brings with Congress. I do not pretend to make my opinion weigh." Final approval of the treaty, congressional members insisted, must come from the legislature, a requirement they claimed the United States had acknowledged at the beginning of the talks and throughout the negotiations, and had twice made clear in conventions signed on November 28, 1902, and on January 22, 1903. The initiation of negotiations did not compel approval of the treaty. The minister of foreign affairs, Luis Rico, argued that to ignore this process would violate the Colombian Constitution.[71]

According to Beaupré, the ministry in Bogotá believed that Herrán had signed the agreement in accordance with the Spooner Act, which authorized the president of the United States to seek canal rights through Nicaragua if Colombia refused to approve an agreement in a "reasonable time." Rico failed to appreciate the gravity of the situation, assuming that, if his government rejected the treaty, the only adverse effect on Colombia would be a U.S. decision to select the Nicaraguan route. In accordance with the law of nations, he emphasized, the United States could not justify any retaliation based on the delayed ratification of a so-called treaty that was still only a "project" bearing no rights or obligations.[72]

The Marroquin government held a clear majority of support in both houses but faced a dilemma: Approval of the Hay-Herrán Treaty entailed a loss of national sovereignty, and rejection would cost money to which Colombia believed it had a right. Marroquin asserted that a canal would establish close relations with the United States and assure industrial and commercial benefits for Colombia. He expressed no concern about the impact on Panama. But instead of taking the lead, he left the decision to Congress.[73]

By early July, the Colombian Senate opposed the Hay-Herrán Treaty as presented. Marroquin had met with senators at San Carlos Palace on July 2 and urged the passage of the treaty. But after an emotional discussion, the majority of senators remained opposed to ratification.[74]

Beaupré learned three days later that the secretary of state's June 9 warning letter had been read aloud in a secret Senate session. "Created sensation," he wrote Hay. "Construed by many as a threat of direct retaliation against Colombia" if it did not ratify the treaty. A statement just issued by the Panamanian members of Congress further complicated matters: They warned that Panama "would revolt" if the treaty did not pass.[75]

A ray of hope came from Colombian General Rafael Reyes, a respected and popular political moderate and realist who urged Marroquin to endorse the Hay-Herrán Treaty as an economic boon for Colombia and the Isthmus. In the interest of compromise, Reyes assured Beaupré that the Colombian Congress would approve the treaty if the United States agreed to two amendments: The New Panama Canal Company would pay Colombia $10 million for the right to transfer its concessions to the United States, and the United States would raise its bonus payment to Colombia from $10 million to $15 million.[76]

Hay assured Colombia that the U.S. Senate would reject both amendments and warned that further delay in ratifying the treaty would "greatly imperil its consummation."[77]

Beaupré recommended that Hay intimate to the Colombian minister in Washington that the government in Bogotá should act before the opposition to the treaty became insurmountable. This was a complex problem, the American minister admitted. If Marroquin signed the treaty, responsibility for the outcome would rest with the executive; if the president did not sign the treaty and the Colombian Senate either ratified or rejected it, the executive would escape responsibility. If not signed, Beaupré thought, the Senate would refuse to act and Congress would adjourn. He repeated his earlier argument—that if Marroquin signed the treaty, the Senate would approve.[78]

Roosevelt was losing his patience. "These contemptible little creatures in Bogotá," he told Hay, "ought to understand how much they are jeopardizing things and imperiling their own future."[79]

American threats to turn to Nicaragua did not work. Colombia appeared immune from pressure and refused to compromise on an issue it thought would never lead to conflict. A week later, Beaupré remained unable to convince the Colombians that the United States was serious about negotiating with Nicaragua if they continued to demand revisions in the treaty.[80]

In the first week of August, Beaupré forwarded the conditions the United States must accept before the government in Bogotá would ratify the treaty. More than two-thirds of the senators required for ratification favored the conclusions of a Senate committee report: exclusion of the cities of Panama and Colón and adjacent territory from the canal zone; U.S. rights to rest on tenancy and not ownership—which meant no perpetuity; American use of other waterways to supply and maintain the canal and its channels; and, finally, if the canal remained unfinished by the termination date, all concessions and properties would revert to Colombia.[81]

Roosevelt warned that any proposed changes would kill the treaty. He regarded any amendment as an attempt to undermine the pact. Beaupré warned Rico that any modification constituted "an absolute rejection of the treaty" and a "breach of faith" by Colombia that "may involve the very greatest complications in the friendly relations which have hitherto existed between the countries."[82]

On August 12, the Colombian Senate met for its first and only time to debate the canal issue. The meeting confirmed Beaupré's belief that the Colombian government had not grasped the seriousness of the situation. Several senators made a move to reject the Hay-Herrán Treaty but at the same time wanted assurances sent to Washington that this was not an act of hostility and that Colombia wanted a U.S.-built canal. Then followed a reading of quotes from Hay's confidential warning of June 9. The packed gallery reacted with "loud murmurs of disapproval" at what appeared to be a threat of force if Colombia did not ratify the treaty.[83]

Rico drew applause when he explained that the government was legally bound to send the treaty to Congress and that if it failed to pass, the United States would respond by negotiating with Nicaragua. The foreign minister saw no reason to fear that a rejection of the treaty would disrupt relations between Colombia and the United States.[84]

At 6:30 that evening, "every senator present" voted "against the ratification of the treaty."[85]

Beaupré nonetheless remained hopeful that Colombia would soften its position. Both the debate and the vote, he argued, were "undoubtedly previously arranged." General Reyes privately told him afterward that the congressional action of that day was part of a plan by the government, senators, and influential citizens to mobilize popular support for the treaty in its original form. In about two weeks, Reyes asserted, Marroquín would present the treaty to the Senate again, where it would pass.[86]

Beaupré thought the plan might work and that the "most intensely critical period" for the treaty had passed. The Senate's rejection of the treaty had caused "an almost hysterical condition of alarm and uncertainty in Bogotá" about what the United States might do—including a rumor that American troops had landed on the Isthmus. Large posters appeared throughout the city, assuring the populace that Colombia's leaders wanted good relations with the United States and that Congress would appoint a joint committee to reach an agreement on the canal's construction. Beaupré sensed "a genuine feeling of relief" throughout the city.[87]

This mood changed to anger when Rico told the Senate that Colombia must either abandon the idea of a canal through Panama or turn over the entire project to the United States. No other power had expressed interest in building a canal, and the United States would not construct a canal coming under someone else's control. The Colombian Congress faced the dilemma of either approving the original treaty or losing all hope for a canal. In a remark that drew "disapprobatory murmurs from the gallery," Rico declared that the government had left the ratification decision in the hands of public opinion "when it could have passed the measure through by dictatorial measures."[88]

c❧ↄ

Were Colombia's actions defensible? It had granted canal rights to de Lesseps until 1904 and insisted that the original deal did not permit the transfer of these rights to another party. It claimed ownership of Panama, having sold only concessionary *rights* in Panama and *not* the *right* to Panama. Colombia needed money. A civil war—the "War of a Thousand Days"—had drained the national treasury. The yearly payment of $250,000 was about the same revenue generated by the Panama Railroad (now under American ownership) and was much less than what it should be.[89] The Bogotá government wanted a share of the $40 million that would otherwise go to French shareholders and leave Colombia without a canal and no funds to build one.

Was the American position justifiable? Years afterward, President Roosevelt explained his concern that Colombia was waiting for the concession rights to expire in October 1904 and then claim the $40 million the United States had agreed to pay the French company. The government in Paris might intervene on behalf of the company and gain a foothold in the Western Hemisphere. A week after the Senate vote in Bogotá, he asserted, "I do not think that the Bogotá lot of jack rabbits should be allowed permanently to bar one of the future highways of civilization." Our decisions will have an impact for centuries, "and we must be sure that we are taking the right step before we act."[90]

U.S. pressure on Colombia, Beaupré had earlier insisted, could have secured ratification of the treaty. "A strong, rather than a velvet hand, was imperative."[91]

Chapter 2

Long Live the Republic of Panama!
Long Live President Roosevelt!

I cast aside the proposition made at this time to foment the secession
of Panama.

—President Theodore Roosevelt
October 10, 1903

I did not lift my finger to incite the revolutionists. . . . I simply ceased to
stamp out the different revolutionary fuses that were already burning.

—Theodore Roosevelt
1913

The Colombians had taken their stand on the treaty but remained uneasy
about their relationship with the Americans—and rightly so.

President Roosevelt privately denounced what he termed Colombia's violation of trust over the canal treaty. Its leaders were, he told Secretary of State
Hay, "contemptible little creatures." To Cecil Spring Rice, he vented, "the
politicians and revolutionists at Bogotá are entitled to precisely the amount of
sympathy we extend to other inefficient bandits." As a young assemblyman
in New York, he had learned to temper his rhetoric, if only in public. But the
language he used in personal letters throughout his life, though not profane,
sometimes seemed uncontrolled.[1]

Roosevelt drafted a message to Congress accusing the Colombian government of extortion and recommending that the United States either turn to
Nicaragua or purchase the rights to Panama from the French canal company.
He preferred Panama because the engineers considered it the better route, but
if Congress supported Nicaragua, he would follow that judgment.

The president refused to incite Panamanian independence, although he had approved a telegram to Colombia from his secretary of state, John Hay, warning that a rejection of the Hay-Herrán Treaty would endanger relations between the countries. The message hardened Colombia's resistance to outside interference while stiffening Panama's support for a revolt if the government refused to ratify the treaty. Roosevelt considered buying the canal rights from the French company, ignoring Colombia, and continuing the construction already begun by the de Lesseps operation. Yet, these steps would virtually guarantee conflict with Colombia. Hay concurred with a Virginian familiar with the Isthmus, who warned that Colombia considered Panama "a financial cow to be milked for the benefit of the country at large." But, the writer added, "This difficulty might be overcome by diplomacy and money."[2]

As separatist sentiment grew in Panama, Roosevelt decided against sending this message to Congress and returned to diplomacy. If unsuccessful through regular channels, the White House could privately encourage the revolutionaries in Panama to break ties with Colombia and, as a new republic, deal with the United States.

Perhaps the best U.S. strategy regarding the unrest in Panama was to do nothing. But that approach did not appeal to the president.

I

Crucial to the president's diplomacy was Secretary of State Hay. Roosevelt thought it a major triumph to convince him to continue in that role after McKinley's death. The new president recognized the importance of experience, patience, and good character in a person holding this pivotal position in his administration. He also knew that Hay would be honest with him in discussing the decisions they would make together. Hay never forgot that his responsibility as secretary was to express his views to the president without disagreeing publicly or acting without his approval.

It may appear surprising that Hay accepted the president's invitation to remain in the cabinet as secretary of state. He was not in good health, and he felt a profound sense of foreboding. Hay knew what problems lay ahead in foreign affairs and that the new president needed his help, but he had a deeper concern. Abraham Lincoln, James Garfield, and William McKinley—Hay had served all three presidents, and all three had been assassinated—the last one preceded less than three months earlier by the sudden death of Hay's twenty-five-year-old son. Duty outweighed despair, and Hay agreed to serve.[3]

Hay somehow maintained his sense of humor while pondering the difficulties in negotiating with the Colombians. Five feet and two inches tall;

he was outwardly calm, scholarly, and grandfatherly in demeanor, seldom departing from what some contemporaries regarded as the very image of a poet. Hay was by no means mercurial like his superior. In a conversation with a close acquaintance of the president, Joseph B. Bishop, Hay criticized leaders in Bogotá in a manner less cutting than that of Roosevelt and yet equally pointed. Bishop recalled from a meeting with Hay that, with "much humor," the secretary recounted the "diplomatic antics" of both sides in the negotiations. Then "he paused, and with that inviting twinkle in his eye which always proclaimed the coming of a happy idea, he said: 'Talking with those fellows from down there, Bishop, is like holding a squirrel in your lap and trying to keep up the conversation.'"[4]

Just as Roosevelt needed the calming influence of Hay, so did the secretary need his own humor and wisdom in dealing with a president fast losing his patience with Colombia—not that Roosevelt's strong reaction to Colombia would have shocked the secretary of state. The *New York Herald* on August 15, 1903, carried the story of a luncheon party the day before at Oyster Bay after which Republican senator Shelby Cullom, chair of the Foreign Relations Committee, told the press that the United States should consider taking Panama "on the ground of universal public utility." The White House "might make another treaty, not with Colombia, but with Panama." Would the United States support a revolution in Panama, asked one news correspondent? "No, I suppose not," Cullom replied, but "this country wants to build that canal and build it now."[5]

That same day, the State Department received a cable from its minister in Bogotá, Arthur Beaupré, declaring that the Colombian Senate had voted against the treaty on August 12. Hay suggested that the administration accept "the simple and easy Nicaragua solution," but Roosevelt rejected the notion, asserting that "I fear we may have to give a lesson to those jack rabbits." The confluence of Cullom's interview and the news of the treaty rejection left the appearance that Colombia was putting pressure on the United States to increase the monetary payment in what the president and others denounced as a holdup. Cullom's declaration, according to historian Edmund Morris, had all but assured Senate support for a presidential use of executive power in acquiring Panama.[6]

Further support for Roosevelt's hardline stance came from the mild-mannered and highly respected John Bassett Moore, an expert in international law who had served as a State Department adviser to both McKinley and Roosevelt and was the first Hamilton Fish Professor of Law and Diplomacy at Columbia University. The assistant secretary of state, Francis Loomis, had asked Moore whether the Treaty of 1846 had any bearing on U.S. negotiations with Colombia on a canal. Yes, Moore responded. The treaty justified U.S. efforts to build a canal through Panama. When the president learned of this conversation, he instructed Loomis to ask Moore to write a memo summarizing his views.[7]

The pressure on the president to act seemed irrepressible when Loomis handed him the memo on August 15, the same day Beaupré's cable arrived and Cullom issued his call for action. Moore asserted that the government in Bogotá had no right to block a canal through Panama. The Isthmus was the only suitable area in the Americas for a project that benefited the entire world. To bolster his argument, Moore referred to a statement by Secretary of State Lewis Cass nearly a half century earlier—that no sovereign state in Central America had the right "to close these gates of intercourse on the great highways of the world, and justify the act by the pretension that these avenues of travel belong to them."[8]

The United States, argued Moore, had correctly dispensed with Colombia's claims to sovereignty over Panama by asserting the right to act on the basis of past interventions that the government in Bogotá had never contested. Article 35 of the Treaty of 1846 had granted the United States transit rights *"upon any modes of communication that now exist, or that may be hereafter constructed."* For nearly sixty years, Colombia called it America's "duty" to protect Panama's "perfect neutrality." The treaty had set a precedent for the United States to send soldiers when needed. Six times since 1846, American troops had entered Panama to safeguard the transit route, and not once did the Bogotá regime object. On four occasions, Colombia *requested* U.S. military help.[9]

Moore concluded that U.S. efforts to protect both Colombia and its railway across the Isthmus gave the White House the right to "require" that country to transfer to the United States the property and the "license" necessary to build and operate a canal. "The United States in constructing the canal would own it; and after constructing it, would have the right to operate it. The ownership and control would be in their nature perpetual."[10]

Moore's argument provided a legal justification for the president's position, perhaps more than he could have expected, which led him to share the memo with Hay and recommend that they "do nothing at present." Roosevelt insisted that the United States could not allow the "Bogotá lot of jack rabbits" to block the construction of "one of the future highways of civilization." Furthermore, the "great bulk of the best engineers" had agreed that Panama offered the best route. And yet, the Spooner Act might require the administration to turn to Nicaragua. Our actions "now will be of consequence, not merely decades, but centuries hence, and we must be sure that we are taking the right step before we act."[11]

Hay remained cautious, counseling the president to adhere to the Spooner Act by waiting "a reasonable time" to act; any forceful attempt to take Panama from Colombia could lead to war.[12]

The Colombian government waited anxiously for the American response, but Hay made it clear that the president would probably not make a decision for a couple of weeks. In the summer White House at his home on Sagamore Hill on August 28, the president and his secretary of state discussed three options in the event Colombia refused to reverse its position on the treaty: move ahead in building a canal based on the Treaty of 1846 and prepare for conflict with Colombia; invoke the Spooner Act and turn to Nicaragua; or delay proceedings until "something transpires" that moves Colombia to accept the treaty. Hay's advice prevailed. When Roosevelt decided that a reasonable time had passed without success, he would pursue the Nicaragua alternative provided in the statute.[13]

The day after the meeting, Hay informed Beaupré of the president's decision, and just two days later the so-called "reasonable time" ran out as the Colombian Congress demanded concessions before it ratified a treaty. Beaupré thought Colombia's previous Congress would have approved the original treaty had the United States added $10–$15 million to the compensation, but popular opposition to the treaty had become so intense that this opportunity no longer existed. The public outcry not only undermined the treaty but proved "immensely disastrous" to that government. The newspapers accused the United States of forcing "an unconstitutional and unsatisfactory treaty" onto a weaker nation and declared that Colombia had preserved its honor by opposing the treaty.[14]

As the president's patience wore thin over the next few days, he narrowed his choices: either turn to Nicaragua or, as he confided to Hay, "interfere when it becomes necessary so as to secure the Panama route without further dealing with the foolish and homicidal corruptionists in Bogotá." Roosevelt's position was clear: "I am not inclined to have any further dealings whatever with those Bogota [*sic*] people."[15]

According to Beaupré, Colombian General Rafael Reyes offered hope for a peaceful settlement when he acknowledged that Marroquin had made a "serious mistake" in refusing to approve the treaty in an attempt to win better terms. The Colombian people concurred, the American minister remarked, thinking the United States would never consider any alternative to Panama and would raise the compensation among other concessions. Reyes and numerous critics accused Marroquin of violating both the law and the custom by making a judgment on a treaty without first submitting it to Congress for consideration.[16]

Roosevelt closely watched events on the Isthmus, pondering how the United States could secure the canal for itself and the world. Buoyed by Moore's legal argument, he told Senator Mark Hanna and Albert Shaw, the latter a friend and editor of the *Review of Reviews*, that he felt legally and morally justified in implementing the Hay-Herrán Treaty and building a canal through Panama. Hanna counseled patience, which the president did not believe would work with these "cat-rabbits." To Shaw, who leaned toward a stronger policy, Roosevelt asserted that the United States could have forcefully occupied the territory. "That is literally the only way it could hitherto have been obtained on the terms on which both you and I would like to see it obtained." But, he added, the American people opposed the use of force, and he knew that "bribery or violence" would be wrong. "As yet no one has pointed out one step we have taken in the matter which could have been better taken."[17]

In the meantime, the Colombian Senate set up the "Panama Canal Committee," which asserted that the government's decision to reject the Hay-Herrán Treaty was consistent with the treaty-making process in the United States— that ratification takes place at home and not at the negotiating table. Article 76 of the Colombian Constitution of 1811 authorized Congress "to approve or reject such treaties as the Government may conclude with foreign powers."[18]

The committee asserted that the Hay-Herrán Treaty no longer existed for two reasons: the Senate's rejection of the treaty on August 12 and the failure by the two nations to meet the September 22 deadline for exchanging ratifications. The key issue remaining was the validity of a legislative decree in 1900, which had granted the New Panama Canal Company an extension of six years for the concessions, thereby changing the expiration date to October 31, 1910. If valid, seven years must pass before the new extension expired, making it "premature" to discuss a congressional law authorizing a transfer of rights. If not valid, the original expiration date of October 31, 1904, remained in effect, meaning that Colombia on that day would gain sole control of the disputed area and the right to negotiate a new treaty. The committee members concluded that Congress needed more time to determine the validity of the extension and "indefinitely postponed" all negotiations.[19]

II

While American freight agent Captain Beers was in the United States, Panamanian separatist leader José Arango sounded out the views of influential Panamanians regarding a revolution. On a Sunday in late July, just before Beers returned from New York, about two dozen Americans and Panamanians gathered for a luncheon at the home of Ramón and Pedro Arias in the savannahs near Panama City. In that highly charged setting, they discussed plans for a revolution and listened to numerous speeches—one by Hezekiah A. Gudger, U.S. consul general in Panama—boldly calling for an independent republic on the Isthmus under American protection. Besides Arango, those present included five Americans: J. Gabriel Duque, proprietor of the

Panama Star and Herald; Herbert Prescott from the Panama Railroad Company; and three engineers, two from the U.S. Army and the other a civilian. The chief American engineer was Major William Black, who had supervised the inspection of the canal excavation by the French Canal Company at the behest of the Isthmian Canal Commission in Washington.[20]

Beers returned to Panama on August 4 with a code book provided by William Cromwell, along with his promise to support the revolution. The conspirators hoped the code system would disguise their plans and the identities of key individuals, including "X" for John Hay and "W" for Cromwell, but none signifying President Roosevelt. Most importantly, Beers reported to Arango and others, Cromwell promised to "go the limit" in their revolutionary project by assuring personal assistance and help from other sources.[21]

On the Sunday following Beers's return to Panama, Arango hosted another luncheon at his country home in honor of his emissary. About a half dozen of Arango's most intimate friends were there, as was Prescott from the railroad company. From this day forward, the revolutionaries' propaganda efforts grew alongside planning conferences in Arango's office or in the adjoining office of his close friend and fellow conspirator, Manuel Amador Guerrero, a physician employed by the Panama Railroad Company.[22]

In late summer, Arango dispatched Amador to the United States to confirm Cromwell's promises of assistance and to specify the types of help Panama needed. To avoid suspicion, Amador established an alibi for leaving Panama. He wrote his son Raoul, a surgeon in the U.S. Army assigned to Fort Revere in Massachusetts, asking that he cable the following message to him: "I am sick; come." When on August 26 Amador left Colón for New York on a steamer belonging to the Panama Railroad Company, he carried coded instructions from the conspirators to seek, "if possible, directly from the American Secretary of State or the President," armed assistance and immediate recognition of the republic when successful; protection from U.S. warships and soldiers against Colombian retaliation; and finances and arms to implement the revolution.[23]

Two other passengers on the steamer were American citizens: J. Gabriel Duque, who was at Arango's July luncheon and was the owner of the Panama Lottery along with the *Panama Star and Herald*, head of the fire brigade of 287 workers, and a wealthy Cuban-American with a Colombian wife; and Tracy Robinson, an American and longtime resident of Panama, who was an official with the Panama Railroad and, like Duque, wielded considerable influence on the Isthmus.[24]

The revolutionary committee lacked substantial funds and erroneously assumed that Americans would pay Amador's expenses, forcing him to improvise ways to cover the costs of his trip, including borrowing money from a Panamanian banker based in New York and subsidizing his accounts with ample winnings at poker with Duque and other passengers on the voyage up the American coast.[25]

Neither Duque nor Robinson was part of the revolutionary group, but they appeared to support Panama's independence. No evidence suggests that Amador and Duque discussed their missions with each other. Amador kept his plans to himself; Duque had major investments in Panama and was reportedly on a business trip to New York. If their presence together was a coincidence, the actions taken by both men in the days afterward in New York demonstrated their mutual concern about Panama.[26]

On September 1, the steamer arrived in New York. Amador first searched for a hotel room he could afford. Within the hour, he checked in and went to the offices of the Panama Railroad, where he asked its vice president, E.A. Drake, to accompany him the following day to Cromwell's office on Wall Street. There, Amador presented a letter from Arango to Cromwell, who, according to Amador, made "a thousand offers" to help the revolution that included repeated pledges of financial assistance and a meeting with Secretary of State Hay.[27]

Amador did not know that on the previous day, Cromwell had met with another passenger on the steamship from Panama—Duque. After disembarking from the steamer, Duque encountered Cromwell's assistant, Roger Farnham, who invited him to Cromwell's office. Duque had met Cromwell two or three years earlier, and though not a close acquaintance, agreed to go. After the formalities, Cromwell emphasized that he saw no chance of Colombia approving the treaty and asked Duque for a loan of $100,000 for the revolution that he would return after the establishment of the republic. Cromwell declared that he would secure the loan and back him as the republic's first president.[28]

Surely Cromwell's request for money raised questions in Duque's mind about the potential of a revolution.

But this was not the end of this strange series of events.

As we have seen, Cromwell had in June conferred with the president about Panama and had doubtless apprised him of the arrival of revolutionaries in New York. If so, Roosevelt had decided to act rather than wait, as he had earlier declared to Hay, until "something transpires" to change Colombia's position on the treaty.

At some point in the meeting with Duque, Cromwell declared that Hay wanted to meet with him. Duque agreed to do so, probably suspecting that the president had approved or suggested the idea. While Cromwell arranged the meeting with Hay by phone, Farnham emphasized the necessity of privacy. To hide any record of the trip, he advised Duque not to register in any Washington hotel and instead take the night train from New York that arrived in the capital at 7:00 a.m.[29]

After leaving Cromwell's office, Duque asked an acquaintance, Charles Hart, former U.S. minister to Bogotá, to accompany him to Washington and introduce him to Hay. As Farnham recommended, they traveled by train on the night of September 2, arriving at the State Department at 9:30 on the morning of September 3 and seeing Hay a half hour later. Hart left after making the introduction. Hay and Duque met for two and a half hours.[30]

In the meeting, the secretary of state did not promise direct American help but left open that possibility by declaring that he "would not cross that bridge until he got to it." He also stated that "the United States would build the Panama Canal" without Colombian interference. If the revolutionaries seized Colón and Panama City, the United States would remain neutral. But if Colombia attempted to land troops in Panama, the United States would honor its commitment in the Treaty of 1846 to maintain "free and uninterrupted transit" across the Isthmus.[31]

The Panama story took another twist when Duque left Hay's office and immediately shared this information with a friend in the Colombian legation—none other than Tomás Herrán, the Colombian chargé who had signed the Panama treaty with Hay. Why would Duque appear to betray his fellow Panamanians? Perhaps he hoped to prevent a conflict between the United States and Colombia that could be a disaster for himself and his family and friends in both Colombia and Panama. Years afterward, congressional testimony called Duque's action a "friendly warning" to the Colombian government to drop its opposition to the treaty before losing everything.[32]

The day after meeting with Duque, Herrán cabled Bogotá: "Revolutionary agents of Panama here." One of them, Herrán disclosed, met yesterday with the secretary of state. If the Colombian government did not sign the treaty by its expiration date of September 22, a U.S.-supported revolution was almost certain. That same day, Herrán sent the same warning to the Colombian consul general in New York, Arturo de Brigard, asserting that the agents had headquarters in the New York offices of Andreas and Company and that the Panama Railroad and canal companies were complicit. "The situation is exceedingly critical."[33]

About a week earlier, the Colombian minister of foreign affairs, Luis Rico, had cabled Herrán, asking about the U.S. reaction to Colombia's rejection of the treaty. The act, the chargé replied in the wake of Duque's warning, had led to a "hostile attitude" in the United States of "favoring indirectly a revolution in Panama." The president had made "threatening statements" in private conversations that Herrán had learned about by "indirect means," all aimed at having the canal's construction under way before he left the White House. His "persistence and decision" were well known. Roosevelt, Herrán warned, would carry out his threats.[34]

To undermine a revolution, Herrán immediately hired detectives to follow Amador and sent letters to Cromwell in New York and the Paris office of the New Panama Canal Company, warning that Colombia would cancel all concessions granted to the New Panama Canal Company if Cromwell or anyone else in the French company took part in the secession plot. Cromwell had been open and encouraging in his meeting with Amador, but Herrán's letter of warning had changed everything.[35]

Cromwell had to protect himself and his clients while secretly keeping the revolutionary plan going. He first severed relations with Amador by dodging him and instructing his secretary to say he was away from his office. Amador was shocked and puzzled by his sudden inability to see Cromwell. His conference on September 2 had gone well. What had changed? Amador told the secretary he would sit and wait until Cromwell returned. Soon afterward, Cromwell emerged from his office, thinking Amador had left.

"Your clerk," Amador remarked, "must have made a mistake." Cromwell tried to persuade Amador to leave but finally had to push him into the hallway before slamming the door. Cromwell also cabled the superintendent of the Panama Railroad, Colonel James Shaler, telling him to avoid any act that could arouse suspicion of an uprising. Shaler and Beers thought Cromwell had written this note to protect the company if the revolution failed. Amador concluded that Cromwell was so "cowed by the threats of the Colombian minister" that in mid-October he bolted to Europe.[36]

Questions remain over the next step in this story—in particular, whether Cromwell cabled Bunau-Varilla in Paris, urging him to take the next steamer to the United States. Bunau-Varilla denied receiving a cable or having any contact with Cromwell, claiming his arrival in the United States at this time was for "personal reasons." He and his wife wanted to bring home their son, who had severe hay fever and stayed the summer on the coast of Maine at the country home of a friend, the former American minister to France during the Civil War, John Bigelow. This argument was not convincing to skeptics of coincidences. Years afterward, testimony before Congress rejected Bunau-Varilla's account, alleging that Cromwell's cable was in the sealed vaults holding the archives of the New Panama Canal Company and was now U.S. property.[37]

III

By mid-September, Amador was downcast after Cromwell's rebuff, but he soon learned through Joshua Lindo, a Panamanian banker working in the New York office of Piza, Nephews and Company, that "help from another quarter" would come if he remained in New York. That help came on September

22, when Philippe Bunau-Varilla and his wife arrived in New York from France, two weeks after Amador had sent a cable to the Isthmus expressing disappointment with Cromwell. The couple registered at the Waldorf-Astoria Hotel, and Bunau-Varilla immediately visited Lindo, asking for an update on Panamanian affairs and the rumors of a revolution. At this point, success for the Panamanian people was far from certain.[38]

They had no money, Lindo asserted. "Without money a revolution cannot be brought about any more than a war." To clarify the situation, Lindo offered to set up a meeting with Amador. "What!" exclaimed Bunau-Varilla in disbelief. "Amador is here?" "Yes," replied Lindo in a lowered voice. Amador's mission is a failure, and he is soon returning home. "He will tell you all. He is in despair."[39]

That same night, Lindo met with Amador and suggested a way to resolve his problems.

"Why don't you see if Bunau-Varilla can do something?"

"Where shall I meet him—in Paris?"

"Nothing of the sort. He has just arrived and is at the Waldorf-Astoria."

Amador was as shocked as Bunau-Varilla over the play of events.

Within the hour, Amador entered the hotel lobby at 11:00 p.m. and, finding Bunau-Varilla out, left a card saying he would return the following day. When Bunau-Varilla returned to the hotel, he telephoned Amador that same night and arranged a meeting for the next morning.[40]

On the eleventh floor of the Waldorf-Astoria Hotel in New York City, Bunau-Varilla and Amador met at 10:30 a.m. on September 23, 1903—fittingly, the day after the Hay-Herrán Treaty expired.

Amador opened up to Bunau-Varilla, detailing the conspiracy and calling Colombia's rejection of the treaty a "sentence of death" that Panamanians had to oppose with armed resistance. They had turned to the United States for help and had received promises of assistance from a person he left unnamed, who had set up a meeting with Secretary of State Hay. "But suddenly the attitude of the person who was to take me to Washington entirely changed." Amador felt betrayed.[41]

If Amador sought sympathy, he got none. Bunau-Varilla rebuked him for trusting that person and identified him as William Nelson Cromwell, the only person capable of such a "childish proposition" and who regularly boasted of speaking with leaders of state.[42] Bunau-Varilla then cut to the seminal question: What do you need to make the revolution a success?

Counsel and money, Amador responded. The revolution must have American support, along with $6 million to buy gunboats and pay and arm the rebel troops. If Colombia discovered the conspiracy, it would sentence everyone involved to death. "If my friends are shot," he declared, choking on emotion,

"I prefer to devote my life to avenging them on the man who will have been the cause of their deaths."[43]

Bunau-Varilla assured Amador of financial support and that he would seek an agreement with the United States to have warships nearby if Colombia tried to land troops. He knew that the Treaty of 1846 applied to the right-of-way across the Isthmus and not to the rest of Panama—as Amador seemed to imply when expressing fear of Colombian retribution against property holders and other citizens if the revolution failed. The United States could intervene on the Isthmus, Bunau-Varilla emphasized, because it had received transit rights in exchange for guaranteeing Colombia (then New Granada) the neutrality of the Isthmus along with Colombia's sovereignty over the area between Colón and Panama City. It would take time to study the situation and provide advice, he told his visitor. In the meantime, Bunau-Varilla devised codenames if Amador needed to phone him: Bunau-Varilla as Jones and Amador as Smith.[44]

After three days of talks, Amador later wrote, "everything was arranged to my satisfaction, and I so informed my friends, announcing to them my early return and giving them complete assurance of the triumph of our project."[45]

Bunau-Varilla later called their meeting "a fortuitous incident" that would have "incalculable consequences." He had published an article on September 2 in *Le Matin*—the Paris newspaper he co-owned with his brother Maurice—in which he argued that the Treaty of 1846 justified U.S. claims to build a canal through Panama. He sent a copy of the article "under sealed envelope" to President Roosevelt at Oyster Bay.[46]

Bunau-Varilla's central objective was to determine how far President Roosevelt would go in supporting his preference for Panama. But how?

Among Bunau-Varilla's closest friends was Professor William Burr, the head of the engineering department at Columbia University in New York. Four years earlier in Paris, he had met Burr, who was then a member of the Isthmian Canal Commission set up by President McKinley to choose between Nicaragua and Panama. Bunau-Varilla had cultivated a friendship with both Burr and George S. Morison, the engineer on the commission who had convinced President Roosevelt that a canal through Panama was technologically possible. Bunau-Varilla later sent Burr a copy of his September article in *Le Matin*.[47]

Burr was not encouraging about Panama. The American people preferred Nicaragua, and he doubted the legality of acting on the basis of the Treaty of 1846. But he mentioned a colleague, Professor John Bassett Moore, whose specialty was international law and who shared Bunau-Varilla's views on Panama. At Bunau-Varilla's request, Burr agreed to introduce him at a meeting set for two days later, on September 29.[48]

At the appointed time, they met in Burr's office, where Bunau-Varilla and Moore discussed the Treaty of 1846, agreeing that it justified U.S. construction of a canal through Panama.[49]

Moore remarked that he was "astonished" to see this idea appear in a Paris newspaper. Bunau-Varilla pulled out a folded copy of *Le Matin*, printed on its familiar off-white paper and immediately recognizable by Moore. "Yes," he declared, "it was in that newspaper." Bunau-Varilla asked Moore if he would make his support for Panama publicly known—that such a statement would assure a canal through that province. Moore replied that he was bound to secrecy. "But why?" asked Bunau-Varilla, emphasizing that the issue was "critical" to Panama. Moore explained, "The conditions under which I was led to formulate this idea are such that I can no longer consider it as my own."[50]

Bunau-Varilla did not push the issue, suspecting he had uncovered the president's legal basis for building a canal through Panama. He concluded that Moore's theory had been "formulated by the highest authority on international law of the United States, conditions that imposed secrecy upon him." Only two government figures "could have any interest in having such an opinion formulated, and formulated secretly"—President Roosevelt and Secretary of State Hay.[51]

To confirm his suspicions, Bunau-Varilla left the meeting and rushed to downtown New York and into the office of his friend and attorney, Frank Pavey. "I am burning to know," he asked Pavey, "who is Mr. Bassett Moore, the Professor of Diplomacy at the University of Columbia? It is extremely important that I should know his connection with the Government." "It is very simple," replied Pavey. "Professor Bassett Moore is the intimate friend of President Roosevelt." The two had supported U.S. intervention in the Cuban insurrection of the 1890s while Roosevelt was assistant secretary of the navy and Moore was assistant secretary of state. Moore was recently a guest in Roosevelt's home in Oyster Bay on September 16 when a huge storm hit that area and made the newspapers.[52]

All the pieces came together. Bunau-Varilla assumed it was during Moore's visit that he presented his theory to the president, who probably showed his guest the September 2 issue of *Le Matin*, which Roosevelt should have received from Bunau-Varilla on September 13.[53]

Within a week of his September 29 conversation with Moore, Bunau-Varilla wrote him a letter that was, as he asserted years later, "really meant for the president." Thinking Moore would share the letter with Roosevelt, Bunau-Varilla declared that he would avoid "any direct contact" with the president while emphasizing that Panamanians intended to launch a revolution for independence and then sign a treaty with the United States based on the Hay-Herrán Treaty. He also called for a greater U.S. role in the hemisphere. "There will be room for a 'Roosevelt Doctrine' in international law, perfecting and completing the Monroe doctrine." As the United States should protect South America from "European interference," so should it protect "European and North American interests" from "South American interference." This would be a justified action, Bunau-Varilla asserted. "The right of protecting involves the duty of policing."[54]

Bunau-Varilla's plan failed. He had intended to use Moore as a "spontaneous intermediary" to learn the president's reaction to an "indirect suggestion" to help the Panamanian rebels. As Bunau-Varilla explained years afterward, he had counted on Moore to "inform me of the desire of the American Government to enter into such a compact." Ignoring Moore's earlier pledge to secrecy (which Bunau-Varilla reasoned was to the White House), he interpreted Moore's silence on this "most discrete" question as his response. "Moore did not manifest in any form or way that the Government desired to encourage a revolution."[55]

Bunau-Varilla now turned to a direct strategy: A meeting with President Roosevelt aimed at winning American support for a revolution without leaving the impression that this was the purpose of his visit. The likely reaction, he feared, "would evidently be repugnant to any member of the Government of the Union."[56]

As Bunau-Varilla sought control over actions in Panama, two recent events threatened his plans—one he knew nothing about; the second he likely did.

In late September, Gabriel Duque wrote Hay, recommending that the White House take advantage of the sinking morale of Colombian troops quartered in Panama City to win their allegiance. They had not received sufficient food supplies and direction from Bogotá, making them and their commanding officer, General Esteban Huertas, susceptible to bribes to gain their support in an uprising. Duque enclosed the translation of a cable sent by the general to Bogotá just three days earlier, in which he complained that he was "very much disgusted" and requested his discharge papers. Duque asserted that the Colombian soldiers were "starving" and had not received almost thirteen weeks of back pay. It would be "easy" to buy their loyalty as "necessity knows no law."[57]

Hay's assistant secretary of state, Alvey Adee, found this letter in the secretary's personal mail of September 30 and, knowing his superior was away from the office for three days, read the letter and forwarded it to the president. In his cover letter, Adee commented that he could not vouch for Duque's information but thought his "political forecast sounds plausible."[58]

Bunau-Varilla played no major role in this scenario and would not have been pleased had he known about it; nor did he support a recent action by his rival, William Cromwell.

Given Bunau-Varilla's penchant for keeping up with newspaper coverage of Panama, he must have seen the report by the Washington correspondent of the *New York Herald* that, on October 7, Cromwell met with the president to discuss Panama and afterward told the press: "The Panama Canal will be built, and by the United States Government." Bunau-Varilla considered himself the leading spokesperson for the Panama project and thought Cromwell had exercised an undue influence over both the president and his secretary of state, along with Amador.[59]

To gain control over the situation, Bunau-Varilla had to act quickly.

On October 10, he visited a friend in the State Department, the acting secretary of state, Francis Loomis, where in their discussion he mentioned his involvement in *Le Matin.* Loomis remarked, "Then you ought to go to present to the President the compliments of *Le Matin.* Do you know Mr. Roosevelt personally?" Told no, Loomis declared, "The President should be glad to receive you. I will go and inquire." He came back moments later, informing Bunau-Varilla that he had telephoned the president, who agreed to a meeting at noon. An hour later, he and Loomis walked over to the White House.[60]

Could it have crossed Bunau-Varilla's mind that Loomis appeared anxious to have him meet the president and that on such short notice the president was available for a conference with someone he had never met? Perhaps Roosevelt *had* read the letter addressed to Moore. On later reflection, Bunau-Varilla mused over the seemingly providential unfolding of events. From the beginning of 1901 through early 1904, "fortune smiled" on him. "Every time I was in need of a man he appeared, of an event it took place." And now the pinnacle: a meeting with the president of the United States.[61]

According to Roosevelt's remembrance of a decade afterward, he quickly sized up the Frenchman as a "keen grey-eyed French duelist who would look you straight in the eye." In their conversation, each figure resorted to feints and parries in attempting to discern what was in each other's heart without saying anything specific.[62]

Bunau-Varilla looked for the opportunity to bring up the Panama matter without revealing his central role in the events. When that moment came, he observed that Panama had become a bitter political issue.

"Oh yes, that is true," declared the president, perking up over a subject of genuine interest. "You have devoted much time and effort to Panama, Mr. Bunau-Varilla. Well, what do you think is going to be the outcome of the present situation?"

After a brief silence, Bunau-Varilla responded, "Mr. President, a Revolution."

Roosevelt, Bunau-Varilla recalled years later, showed "profound surprise." The president then turned to Loomis standing nearby and said almost to himself, "A Revolution! . . . Would it be possible? . . . But if it became a reality, what would become of the plan we had thought of?"

"The plan?" Surely these two words set off questions in Bunau-Varilla's mind that he could not ask aloud. Did "we" include his friend Loomis? Hay and the State Department? Who else? A slip of the tongue—which seemed unlikely—or a signal of the president's interest in events on the Isthmus? Roosevelt and Bunau-Varilla had become, at the least, silent enablers of a revolution or, at the most, secretly complicit in the insurgents' attempt to break from a legitimate government and establish a new republic.

Bunau-Varilla wanted to reveal his knowledge of the plan to coerce Colombia on the basis of the Treaty of 1846 and show how he supported that approach in his letter to the professor. The thought raced through Bunau-Varilla's mind—that the president could work around the sovereignty issue because of the international importance of a canal. Bunau-Varilla wanted to say that his letter to Moore was aimed at the president.

But he remained silent until the president asked about the likelihood of a revolution, "What makes you think so?"

"General and special considerations," replied Bunau-Varilla. The spirit of revolution was "endemic" along the Isthmus and would turn to violence at some point. Colombia's resistance to a canal promised "ruin" to all Panamanians. Their only response could be revolution.

Without hesitation, he asked whether the United States would support an armed insurrection.

Roosevelt did not reply.

Bunau-Varilla openly wondered whether the United States would block Colombian troops from putting down a revolution. Looking into the president's eyes, the Frenchman cagily remarked, "I don't suppose you can say."

"I cannot," Roosevelt just as cagily replied.

Bunau-Varilla tried a direct approach. "Will you protect Colombian interests?"

"I cannot say that," the president responded just as directly. "All I can say is that Colombia by her action has forfeited any claim upon the U.S. and I have no use for a government that would do what that government has done."

Bunau-Varilla had the answer he wanted. Standing, he declared, "Good afternoon, Mr. President."[63]

Bunau-Varilla left the meeting satisfied that the president would, in the event of a revolution, "seize the opportunity" to acquire the area needed for a canal.[64]

Furthermore, Bunau-Varilla reasoned, the rebels would not need the $6 million for arms and ships that Amador had sought. Under the guarantees contained in the Treaty of 1846, President Roosevelt would approve the ships necessary to maintain the neutrality of the Isthmus—including blocking

Colombian ships from the area, as President Grover Cleveland had done in 1885. The rebels would have American military support at no expense if they confined the revolution to the U.S.-protected area authorized by the Treaty of 1846—the isthmian strip of Panama between Colón and Panama City.[65]

Immediately after Bunau-Varilla's departure, the president directed Loomis to send American ships to the troubled area that very night.[66]

Despite his controlled demeanor during his meeting with Bunau-Varilla, Roosevelt had come close to conspiring with his visitor to encourage a revolution by implicitly assuring U.S. military support. In words that have remained the subject of speculation to the present day, he confided to his close friend Albert Shaw later that same day that "I cast aside the proposition made at this time to foment the secession of Panama." The United States cannot engage in "such underhand means." Yet, he would not discourage such an outcome. "Privately," he declared, "I should be delighted if Panama were an independent State, or if it made itself so at this moment; but for me to say so publicly would amount to an instigation of a revolt and therefore I cannot say it."[67]

IV

Bunau-Varilla was elated over his meeting with the president, only to become testy and impatient three nights later when meeting with Amador in the Waldorf-Astoria Hotel. Amador was again in despair about the chances for success. And again, Bunau-Varilla had to convince him the plan would work. On paying troops after the revolution, Bunau-Varilla assured him of $100,000, either from a bank loan or from his own resources. U.S. responsibility under the Treaty of 1846 was to protect only the areas "within gunshot" of the railroad. American forces could intervene only if the revolution took place between Colón and Panama City. "No," Amador objected, "we cannot make the movement in that way." The result would be a divided republic. Bunau-Varilla emphasized that after winning independence and signing a treaty, Panama would have $10 million to "wage war and conquer the rest of the province." Amador replied, "No, 'that wouldn't do'."[68]

Bunau-Varilla did not try to hide his exasperation. "To-day [*sic*], October 13, I offer it to you. If you refuse it, well and good. I have nothing more to say." According to Bunau-Varilla, "We separated coldly." The next day, early in the morning, Amador returned after a sleepless night, apologized for his behavior, and pledged loyalty to the cause. Bunau-Varilla told him to come back on October 19 to make final preparations for the mission.[69]

On the following day, October 15, Bunau-Varilla returned to Washington for President Roosevelt's dedication of the new monument for Union general

William T. Sherman, but he was also hoping Loomis could arrange a meeting with Hay that might confirm the State Department's involvement in isthmian events. Fortuitously, Bunau-Varilla must have thought, this meeting worked out. While he was talking with Loomis in his office, the secretary of state appeared from his office next door to ask a question. Loomis introduced Bunau-Varilla to Hay, who took him into his office to talk. But Hay soon had to excuse himself for a ceremonial duty. When Bunau-Varilla prepared to leave, Hay suggested that they resume their meeting in about an hour. Bunau-Varilla returned to his hotel, where a note from Hay had already arrived at the desk, inviting him to the secretary's home at 3:00 p.m.[70]

When the conversation turned to Panama, Bunau-Varilla predicted a revolution and got the response he wanted. "Yes," Hay agreed. "That is unfortunately the most probable hypothesis. But we shall not be caught napping. Orders have been given to naval forces on the Pacific to sail towards the Isthmus."[71]

A few moments later, the secretary stated that he had just finished reading *Captain Macklin*, a novel by his friend Richard Harding Davis that focused on a West Point cadet who left the Academy "to become a soldier of Fortune in Central America." The young man enlisted in a revolutionary force led by a general once in the French army. Both the American and the former French officer, Hay observed, were "charming types of searchers after the Ideal." He handed the book to Bunau-Varilla. "Read this volume, take it with you. It will interest you."[72]

Bunau-Varilla read the novel on the train back to New York, interpreting Hay's recommendation as "a subtle allusion to my own efforts in the cause of justice and progress." Had the secretary of state explained "symbolically" that the coming revolution in Panama "for the victory of the Idea, was taking shape under my direction?" Bunau-Varilla concluded that *Captain Macklin* was a "password" signaling the secretary's approval of the Panama project. The interview "removed my last hesitations." The White House expected a revolution and had made military preparations. Hay would not have sent such a message without the president's approval.[73]

Roosevelt's reliable cabinet secretary (serving him at both War and State), Elihu Root, offered an analysis of Bunau-Varilla, albeit from the perspective of almost three decades afterward. In a letter to his biographer, Philip C. Jessup, Root referred to Bunau-Varilla as "a very clever person" whose "adroit Latin American diplomacy was something Roosevelt never had patience with and never understood." Bunau-Varilla emphasized that in his conversation with the president, all he did was declare what he thought Roosevelt felt about Colombia's actions. Those observations, Root noted, "got from Roosevelt such violent expressions of opinion unfriendly to the Colombians that when he left he told his people in Panama to go ahead, that Roosevelt would never take sides against them with the Colombians." Roosevelt did not disclose what he planned to do, but his "explosive comments" about the Colombians, Bunau-Varilla insisted, told him all he needed to know.[74]

Three days after his meeting with Hay, Bunau-Varilla gave final instructions to Amador, telling him to take the next ship leaving for Panama on October 20 and arrange for the uprising to begin on November 3, New York City's election day. Such a strategy, Bunau-Varilla calculated, would allow the election results to take prominence over news of the revolt and perhaps temper the attacks in the days and weeks ahead. In a transparently self-serving move, he promised $100,000 from his own funds before asking Amador to support him as Panama's first minister to the United States. Amador, who also coveted that position, replied that he must first consult his friends.[75]

Amador did not trust either Cromwell or Bunau-Varilla and, according to his son, went to Washington determined to secure assistance from the White House.[76]

Uncertainty still exists over Amador's alleged meetings with the president and his secretary of state. In hearings on Panama conducted by the *New York World* in 1909, two members of the revolutionary committee, Ricardo Arias and Federico Boyd (the latter, one of three members of the provisional government at the time), told the attorney for the *World* that Amador never visited Roosevelt or Hay.[77]

The attorney countered that Amador went to Washington at least two times before the revolution. He made several calls at the State Department, hoping to determine what the U.S. reaction would be to a revolution. Hay sent a handwritten message to him, declaring in what Amador termed a "diplomatically discreet and guarded" manner that it was not "proper" for him to speak with someone who was "confessedly and notoriously the would-be organizer of a revolt against a power with which the United States was at peace." Hay's note made no promises of assistance but informed him that the administration would follow a policy of "benevolent neutrality" under the Treaty of 1846 that Amador thought "sufficient for the purpose." Amador later told "various persons" that he met with the president from close to midnight of October 16 until dawn, after which he returned to New York on the morning train.[78]

On the same morning Amador claimed to have left the president, Senator John T. Morgan received a report of a White House visit that he was never able to verify.[79]

Earl Harding, a reporter from the *New York World* who was in Panama in 1910, had first heard this story of a midnight meeting from Amador's son Raoul, who explained that his father had met with the president in the White House two days before Amador mailed his October 18 letter to his son. After the meeting came to a close, Roosevelt arranged for a cab to take his visitor to the train station so he could return to New York in the early morning without being seen. As Amador climbed into the cab, Raoul told Harding, the president put his hand on his father's shoulder and declared, "Go ahead, Doctor; we'll see you through."[80]

In checking the veracity of this account, Harding discovered that Amador and his son had discussed these events with at least three other people. To Harding, Raoul claimed that his father later shared the story with New York attorney Robert B. Alling, who was married to a sister of Raoul's American wife. Raoul discussed the White House conference on numerous occasions during an affair with a twice-widowed woman in New York. Raoul also told longtime friend Dr. Philip Embury of New York, who asserted that Raoul came to his office one evening in October 1903, speaking about a revolution coming to Panama in less than three weeks as he "walked up and down this office like a caged bear the whole time that he was talking." All three sources—the attorney, the widow, the doctor—confirmed Raoul's statements to Harding in 1910.[81]

Two years later, in 1912, Democratic congressman Henry T. Rainey of Illinois opened a series of hearings on Panama that at one point led to a discussion of Amador's alleged secrets pertaining to America's role in the revolution. A committee member held up an unpublished letter by Amador to his son in 1908, the year before his death, that made it "possible to forge many of the missing links in this story of conspiracy." The letter was in Amador's own writing, as Raoul confirmed after looking at it during his testimony. Henry Hall of the *New York World* declared that Amador had sought "to suppress certain facts and to distort others" by a series of "misstatements" and "contradictions of truths." This "confidential correspondence during the days of the conspiracy" revealed a "careful editing out of statements damaging to his friend Roosevelt," all done during Amador's long and fatal illness.[82]

"I am a dying man," Amador wrote his son in the letter, "beyond the need of the help or friendship even of the American Government." But he thought it necessary "for the honor of Panama" and his "friends of the north" to suppress parts of the story. If he revealed everything he knew, the United States "would no longer trust us." We, as readers, are left with Amador's intriguing statement to his son: "I am not going to tell all that I know of our history."[83]

Controversy continues over White House complicity in the Panamanian uprising. According to Henry F. Pringle's Pulitzer Prize-winning biography of the president, "Roosevelt did nothing to incite the revolution, perhaps, but he was extremely well informed regarding the plans." One cannot disagree with the last part of Pringle's assertion, but it is difficult to accept his denial of presidential involvement in a revolution when Roosevelt met beforehand with revolutionary figures Cromwell, Bunau-Varilla, and perhaps Amador, and Secretary of State Hay met with Duque and Bunau-Varilla, and penned a message to Amador.[84]

The implications of these contacts are crucial to the Panama story: They tie the Roosevelt administration to the revolution, if not directly aiding the rebels, then implicitly offering encouragement either by silence or by reminding their visitors of the U.S. obligation under the Treaty of 1846 to implement a neutrality policy that, strictly defined, approved sending American warships and troops to keep order on the Isthmus.

Regardless of what may or may not have transpired between the president and the plotters, the revolution advanced on pace. Amador and Bunau-Varilla met for the final time on October 19, 1903—again in room 1162 of the Waldorf-Astoria, which Bunau-Varilla later called "the cradle of the Panama Republic." There, he showed Amador the first version of the "flag of liberation" for the unborn republic. In John Bigelow's West Point, New York home, his daughter had assisted Bunau-Varilla's wife in sewing this red, white, and blue flag, whose blue silk bore two stars representing Panama City and Colón joined by a narrow white ribbon signifying the canal. Amador found the flag "perfect," Bunau-Varilla later attested.[85]

Amador remained nervous and uncertain, telling Bunau-Varilla, "Fifteen days will be necessary after my arrival in order to carry out the movement."

"What!" Bunau-Varilla exclaimed. "Fifteen days! It is much simpler to say you are going to abandon everything right away. You leave tomorrow, the 20th, you arrive on the 27th. Within two days you can act." Colombian troops, he told Amador, were already amassing in Cartagena for their departure to the Isthmus. "I give you up to the 3rd of November as a final limit for action. If you have not accomplished the revolution on that day or before I shall consider myself free of all responsibility for further events."[86]

"Give me at least till the 5th of November."

"No. If you are not capable within seven days of doing what you would declare yourself to be ready to do immediately, you demonstrate yourself incapable of winning your liberty."

Amador left, promising to return the next day at 9:00 a.m., ready for departure.

In the meantime, Bunau-Varilla prepared a cablegram for Amador to send him once the insurgents proclaimed a republic:

> The government has just been formed by popular acclamation. Its authority extends from Colón inclusive to Panama inclusive. I request you to accept the mission of Minister Plenipotentiary in order to obtain the recognition of the Republic and signature of Canal Treaty. You have full powers to appoint a banker for the Republic at New York, and to open credit for immediate urgent expenses.[87]

The following day, October 20, Amador left New York for Panama, feeling that his mission had been a success. Bunau-Varilla had promised

$100,000 from his own funds for the revolution. If Amador told the truth about a communication from the secretary of state and a meeting with the president, he had reason to believe that Hay had presidential support for American neutrality along the Isthmus that would protect the insurgents from Colombian troops.[88]

Amador's co-conspirators had counted on a written agreement with either Hay or the president, but common sense dictated that this would never happen. Given the political climate in Washington, the best Amador could secure was verbal support.

The original plan had called for taking only the canal zone to establish a small republic that included Colón and Panama City, along with the area between them and fifty miles of territory outside each city—later reduced to ten miles. But when Amador reported to the revolutionary group in Colón on October 27, he encountered general disappointment with the lack of "some secret treaty with a sovereign." His only physical evidence of success consisted of a new Panamanian flag tucked around his waist and under his shirt (which none of his associates liked because of its resemblance to the American flag), along with the declaration of independence and other papers in the safe of the steamship's purser, George K. Beers, son of Cromwell's agent on the Isthmus.[89]

The strongest opposition came from the wealthy inhabitants of Panama's interior, many of whom had real estate and cattle interests and demanded protection throughout the state against Colombian retaliation. One of the conspirators, Tomás Arias, wanted out of the plan for fear of losing everything if the revolution failed. Amador feared that one withdrawal could lead to more. When Amador appealed to Arias's patriotism and declared that he and Arango were willing to die for the cause, Arias replied: "You are an old man, Arango is an old man, and you do not care if you are hung. I do not like to be hung."[90]

Amador had no choice but to go along with the change in the plan. The conspirators unanimously approved of extending the revolution to include the entire state of Panama.[91]

Amador could only have dreamed of what took place behind the scenes in Washington, both during his stay in the United States and the days afterward.

Before Amador's arrival in New York in late September, the president was in the process of gathering firsthand information relating to potential U.S. military action in Panama. A few months earlier, he secretly dispatched two young army officers, Captain Chauncey Humphrey and Lieutenant Grayson Murphy of West Point (the first an instructor, the other a graduate of the institution), to survey the most feasible approaches to the Panama Canal Zone. As the president's secret agents, they spent four months disguised as English tourists in northern Venezuela and Colombia, followed by what Roosevelt later publicly called an "unpremeditated" visit to Panama from September 16 through 20 prior to returning home. The two officers submitted their report to Lieutenant General S. B. M. Young, who considered it important enough to recommend that the president talk with them.[92]

In the White House on October 16, the president's "military spies" (as critics years later dubbed them) detailed everything useful to a U.S. military campaign on the Isthmus—including the number of mules needed in the interior and the best artillery positions near Panama City and Colón. Panama, Humphrey and Murphy declared, was on the precipice of a revolution. They had seen piano boxes and merchandise crates filled with small arms and ammunition arriving in Colón, where the local fire brigade fronted a military organization that distributed the weapons. The *New York Herald* and *Washington Post* confirmed a coming crisis, reporting revolutionary forces gathering on the Isthmus and Bogotá's likely deployment of troops in response.[93]

The president's two agents could not have known that they had witnessed only a small part of the weapons buildup. About two months earlier, an American schooner pulled out of Morgan City, Louisiana, about sixty-five miles west of New Orleans, ostensibly carrying lumber but in reality laden with 4,000 Winchester rifles and more than a million rounds of ammunition, all from a range of American sources and headed for the Panamanian rebels. Along Yucatán's northern coast, the schooner delivered its cargo to a steamer from Kingston, Jamaica, which intended to unload the materiel at Rio Indio, about twenty-five miles north of Colón. But the Colombian governor learned of the shipment and called for troops. The steamer raced for Porto Bello and turned over the weapons to the revolutionaries from nearby Colón.[94]

The day following his meeting with the army officers, the president approved the dispatch of military attachés to the U.S. legation in Bogotá. The State Department's cover story asserted that the White House was assigning them to all American legations in South America, whose task was to enforce the Monroe Doctrine against suspicious German activities in the region.[95]

The day before Amador departed for Panama on October 20, President Roosevelt ordered the navy to station warships—with marines on board—on both the Atlantic and Pacific sides of the Isthmus. Their assignment: Keep the Isthmus open.

True American believers might assert that at this crucial point, Providence intervened: On the day after the Colombian Senate adjourned, October 28, trouble broke out in Panama. The Senate returned to its chamber and went into secret session to discuss the first accounts of seventy men from Nicaragua invading the Isthmus. Two days later, the minister of war informed the Senate that the number of invaders was ten times larger than the initially reported size, that more disturbances had occurred at the same time in the frontier province of Veraguas, and that the unrest was spreading in Panama.[96]

A week or so after Amador's return home, he cabled his co-conspirator in New York: "Send yacht." After Bunau-Varilla figured out that "yacht" referred to a warship, he realized that Amador was again stressing that the rebels must have U.S. military support. Within a week, Bunau-Varilla warned Amador, the insurrection would break out. "Yacht has been sent," he declared on October 30.[97]

The source of Bunau-Varilla's information? The *New York Times*.

In the context of recent events in Panama, news of the USS *Nashville*'s morning departure from Kingston, Jamaica, on October 31 aroused widespread public speculation about its mission. The following morning, the *New York Times* carried a brief note under the heading, "*Nashville* Off—for Colombia?" The warship, according to the story, had probably gone to Colombia under "sealed orders" and, in line with Bunau-Varilla's estimates, would arrive at Colón on the Caribbean side of the Isthmus on the morning of November 2.[98]

Bunau-Varilla read the newspapers to follow the voyages of the USS *Dixie* and the *Nashville*. The *Dixie*, according to the *New York Times*, had transported close to 1,000 marines to Guantánamo, Cuba in preparation for expected trouble on the Isthmus. The *Nashville*, carrying twelve marines and about 250 navy personnel (or bluejackets), had relocated to Kingston on the southeastern coast of Jamaica for the same reason. In accordance with the Treaty of 1846, Bunau-Varilla surmised, the United States was ready to send troops to the Isthmus to protect free transit through the area. All it needed was a warning of imminent armed conflict. Bunau-Varilla intended to issue this warning at the proper time.[99]

President Roosevelt later asserted that Bunau-Varilla made "a very accurate guess" about probable events; Bunau-Varilla claimed he relied on his "mathematical calculation" derived from trigonometry and what he learned from the newspapers.[100]

V

As late as November 1, the Marroquin regime appeared out of touch with the growing unrest in Panama when it publicly accused its lawmakers in Bogotá of politicizing the canal issue by attacking the executive instead of acting in Colombia's best interests. The administration had not changed its opposition to the Hay-Herrán Treaty but had decided to resume talks with the United States, hoping to reach a new agreement subject to congressional approval.[101]

But the time for negotiations had passed with the events rapidly unfolding along the Isthmus. The go-ahead came from Bunau-Varilla's notification to Amador that on November 2, the *Nashville* would be in Colón, presumably to prevent Colombian loyalists from putting down the revolution. The signal for action would be "the smoke of an approaching steamer."[102]

The rebels had received word of the impending arrival of Colombian troops in Colón and devised several contingency plans. Understanding that the limitations on overland access from Colombia to Panama City made it critical to hold the railroad, the insurgents moved all rolling stock to Panama City in the hope of confining the government's soldiers to Colón. If Colombian troops seized control of the train, the rebels would arrange to load the enemies' arms in the rear car and then remove its coupling pins en route to leave Colombia's forces arriving in Panama City unarmed against the resistance. If that plan did not work, the rebels would blow up the train at Miraflores, outside Panama City, leaving Colombian troops stranded and defenseless. In the meantime, railroad employees would interrupt all Colombian communications by cutting telephone and telegraph lines.[103]

U.S. Naval Commander John Hubbard of the *Nashville* arrived in Colón at 5:30 p.m. on November 2 with everything quiet on the Isthmus except scattered loose talk among Panamanians about independence. Hubbard received word from Washington that orders would soon arrive, telling him to maintain open transit on the Isthmus. In the event of hostilities, he was to occupy the railroad line and prevent any armed group from landing, whether government or rebel.[104]

The navy had also ordered five more cruiser commanders to join the *Nashville* and the *Dixie* in Panama. Their task was to occupy the railroad and stop any government or insurgent forces with "hostile intent" from landing within fifty miles of Panama. Reports had arrived of Colombian ships carrying military forces approaching Panama. "Prevent their landing," the cruiser commanders were directed, "if, in your judgment, the landing would precipitate a conflict." If necessary, the navy told its commanders, take a position on Ancon Hill overlooking Panama City and fortify it "with artillery."[105]

At daybreak the following morning of November 3, the Colombian warship *Cartagena* arrived in Colón with 500 troops. Hubbard sent his twelve marines to board the vessel, where they learned that many of the troops were *tiradores*, elite sharpshooters from the army sent to fortify the garrison at Panama City. Having no orders yet in hand, he lacked authority in Colombian territory and could not stop their coming ashore at 8:30 a.m. "With their wives," reported the *New York Times*, the Colombian soldiers "squatted on the street corners."[106]

That Hubbard had still not received his orders was suspicious. It became evident that Colombian authorities had held up delivery of the orders for hours, allowing time for the troops from the *Cartagena* to disembark. The U.S. consul in Colón, Oscar Malmros, noted that both dispatches containing the orders were in cipher and that even if Colombian authorities were unable to read the instructions, they delayed their arrival, correctly guessing that they posed a threat to Colombia's control of the railroad.[107]

The Colombian force was under the command of General Ramón Amaya, chief of staff of the Atlantic Army, and second in command under General Juan Tovar, commander of the *Cartagena*. Both officers wanted to quarter their troops in Panama City. Hubbard discussed the matter with the superintendent of the Panama Railroad Company, Colonel James Shaler, an American who, at seventy-seven years of age, must have impressed the naval commander with his military bearing and quiet confidence. He proposed separating the generals from their troops by declaring that there were not enough cars on hand to transport everyone at once. The governor, Shaler explained to Hubbard, was José Obaldia, who secretly supported the revolution and had authorized a special car for the two officers and their aides; the troops could join them as soon as additional cars arrived. In a decision crucial to Shaler's plan, the generals reluctantly gave in after placing their forces in Colón under the command of Colonel Eliseo Torres.[108]

To complete this part of the revolutionary plan, Shaler arranged for a locomotive and a single car to take Amaya and Tovar (with fifteen aides) to Panama City. The troops, he again assured the two generals now aboard, would arrive on another train shortly thereafter. Troubled by this arrangement, Amaya changed his mind and wanted to get off; Tovar warned that it would look better if they arrived together. While they argued, Shaler slipped to the back of the car, pulled the signal cord for departure, and jumped off, smiling as the train steamed away.[109]

From the U.S. Consulate at Colón, Malmros informed the White House around noon on November 3 that a revolution was "imminent." The vice consul general in Panama City, Felix Ehrman, reported that rebel forces had imprisoned a half-dozen Colombian army and naval officials and that violence would probably break out in Panama City that night. He was correct. Late in the evening of November 3, the White House issued a press release announcing the revolt within minutes of the State Department's receipt at 9:50 p.m. of the following cable from Ehrman: "Uprising occurred tonight, 6; no bloodshed," he wrote. "Supposed same movement will be effected in Colón."[110]

Generals Tovar and Amaya, by now in Panama City, found out about the revolt just before it began and hurried to their soldiers' barracks to take charge. But they arrived too late. A "large and enthusiastic crowd" of several thousand Panamanians, many of them given arms by Duque's fire brigade, gathered around Colombian general Esteban Huertas, who (as Duque had alerted Hay) had switched sides and brought his regulars with him. The former head of the "Colombia Battalion" ordered the arrests of Amaya and Tovar along with three other officers. The boisterous crowd joined Huertas and his soldiers in marching the Colombian officers to police headquarters, all the while cheering their new leader and Amador as they fired their guns in the air despite the danger to women and children in the balconies alongside the streets.[111]

When Amador heard what had happened, he sought to protect his friend, Governor Obaldia, from Colombian forces, arranging his arrest in an effort to conceal his separatist loyalties.[112]

Shortly afterward, a small group of soldiers from the Colombian gunboat *Bogotá* (its commander, among the officers seized by Huertas) came ashore at Panama City to warn that unless the officers were released in two hours, the city would be bombarded. Despite the State Department's warning against such an act, the paymaster of the *Bogotá,* Colonel Martinez, seized control and ordered an assault beginning at 10 p.m. About a half-dozen shells hit different sections of the city over the next half hour, killing a Chinese merchant in his bed and, according to testimony before the Rainey committee years afterward, "mortally wounding an ass in the slaughterhouse." The *Bogotá,* under fire from a shore battery on the seawall, steamed away and stationed itself behind some islands fronting the city.[113]

The next morning of November 4, Washington learned of the previous night's bombardment of Panama City. According to the *New York Times,* the atmosphere in the U.S. state and navy departments was "tense and exciting," much like that of "the morning the news came that the *Maine* was destroyed."[114]

Despite the concern raised by its impulsive action, the *Bogotá* did not return to Panama and had reportedly docked at Buenaventura in northern Mexico. Less than a week later, it departed, presumably to home waters.[115]

Hubbard had meanwhile received multiple copies of orders from Washington to prohibit the landing of Colombian troops in Colón and to keep the Isthmus open. To emphasize the importance of Hubbard's role, Loomis sent him a message a little before midnight on November 3: "Secure special train, if necessary. Act promptly."[116]

"Government troops now at Colón," Hubbard informed the secretary of the navy. To keep the peace, "I have prohibited the movement of troops in either direction."[117]

Early in that morning of November 4, the situation in Colón began to deteriorate when Colonel Torres asked Shaler to provide transportation for his troops to Panama City. Shaler claimed he was powerless to do so. Up to this point, Torres had seen no sign of anything awry. No trouble had arisen over the troop presence and, lacking contact with his superiors in Panama City, he was not aware of any problems. In the meantime, Chief of Police Porfirio Meléndez discussed the matter with Shaler before inviting Torres to the saloon for a drink. There, Meléndez explained that the generals in Panama

City were under arrest and warned that more Americans would soon arrive. If he and his soldiers would board the *Cartagena* and return home, he would receive a generous cash payment. Torres became enraged over this bribe, shouting that if the generals were not freed in two hours, he would set fire to Colón and kill every American in the city.[118]

In an unexpected twist, the fate of the revolution suddenly lay in the young colonel's hands as he commanded hundreds of Colombian soldiers in Colón and encountered no insurgent opposition, while 3,000 rebel forces were fifty miles away in Panama City. Both sides were checkmated by Hubbard's order to "prevent landing of any armed force with hostile intent, either government or insurgent."

Hubbard prepared for trouble in Colón and immediately sought refuge for American citizens in a stone building belonging to the Panama Railroad Company, soon protected by fifty bluejackets sent ashore. Other women and children had found safety on a German steamer and a Panama Railroad steamer, both vessels ready to leave the dock if necessary.[119]

The Colombian troops meanwhile surrounded the building, and for almost two hours, tensions remained high. Hubbard's forces remained calm, and no shots were fired. At 3:15 p.m., Torres arrived and, surprisingly, expressed friendship for the Americans and asserted that the confrontation had resulted from a misunderstanding. Trick or truth? A little more than two hours later, he proposed to withdraw his troops from the town in exchange for the departure of the *Nashville*'s forces, leaving Colón in possession of the police. Hubbard agreed to the arrangement.[120]

Hubbard remained infuriated over the encounter. He wrote his superiors the following day that Torres's actions had "amounted to practically the making of war against the United States," and that only the patience of his men had averted a confrontation with Colombian troops.[121]

On that same morning of November 5, Hubbard discovered that Torres had not withdrawn his troops from Colón as agreed and had occupied buildings on its outer edge. Torres offered what Hubbard termed "some trivial excuse" for violating the agreement but then announced that he intended to reoccupy the city unless his government ordered him to withdraw.[122]

Hubbard re-stationed his bluejackets in and around the railroad office, where they barricaded themselves from attack by mounting a pair of 1-pounders on freight cars behind cotton bales. Numerous citizens armed with rifles and revolvers joined the U.S. contingent as Torres and Panamanian government officials decided to meet in an attempt to negotiate a settlement.[123]

Hubbard soon joined the meeting, where he complained to Torres that his failure to keep his agreement had led to the return of American forces. Torres repeated his intention to occupy Colón unless he received directives from home not to do so.[124]

At about 11:00 a.m., Colombian troops marched into the city but without the "threatening demeanor" of the day before. A Trojan Horse? Hubbard ordered the *Nashville* close to shore to protect the waterfront and offered refuge aboard to American women and children as well as British nationals.[125]

During that afternoon, Hubbard's show of force doubtless encouraged Torres to accept the newly formed provisional government's call for a withdrawal. Hubbard assured the navy department that he did not take part in the negotiations and that his only purpose in sending an armed force was to protect American citizens.[126]

The crisis had abated by the evening of November 5. Shortly after 7:00 p.m., the *Dixie* arrived in Colón and its commanding officer landed part of his marine battalion, allowing the *Nashville*'s forces to pull back. Soon hovering around both Colón and Panama City were five other American warships that, combined with the *Dixie* and the *Nashville*, carried more than 3,000 men. Torres decided to return home.[127]

Torres's troubles persisted. His ship, the *Cartagena,* was no longer at the dock. It had raced out of Panama rather than face the *Nashville.* After more persuasion from Shaler and Menéndez, Torres agreed to depart that evening with his troops on a Royal Mail steamship then in port, the *Orinoco*. The cost was $8,000—guaranteed by a voucher signed by Shaler and Hubbard. Shaler also gave Torres two cases of champagne.[128]

Shortly afterward, Shaler, with Hubbard's approval, authorized a train to transport Generals Tovar and Amaya, and their aides to Colón, where they booked passage on the next ship leaving for Cartagena.[129]

Panama's near-bloodless revolution was briefer and more successful than anyone could have imagined, but problems remained after the celebration of independence.

Bunau-Varilla had chosen New York City's election day of November 3 for the uprising, thinking the press would focus on local election results, but several newspapers also ran the Panama story. The *New York Herald* published a brief dispatch from its correspondent in Panama, Samuel Boyd, the brother of rebel leader Federico, at the bottom of page 1 of its November 4 issue, squeezed between eight-column headlines announcing voting returns, including George B. McClellan's election as mayor of New York. On the same day, the *New York Sun*'s front-page headline read "PANAMA IN REVOLT," and the *Washington Post* announced a "REVOLUTION" aimed at bringing independence to Panama.[130]

The front-page headlines of the *New York Times* encapsulated the story:

PANAMA SECEDES FROM COLOMBIA
Independence of the Isthmus Proclaimed
A Republic Is Declared
Annexation to the United States May Be Object.[131]

American involvement seemed certain to many observers, both inside and outside the United States. The following day, the *New York Times* asserted that the world would find the United States "guilty of an act of sordid conquest" that pursued a "canal policy" rife with "scandal, disgrace, and dishonor." Yet on that same morning of November 5, the *New York Times* published an editorial by the *Times* of London praising U.S. policy in Panama. Colombia was guilty of "wanton procrastination" on the canal treaty by "frankly obstructing" its passage and "trying to blackmail" both the United States and the French Canal Company. The president's reaction was "studiously correct." The revolution made the Panama Canal possible.[132]

Shortly after 8:00 a.m. on November 4 in Panama City, Amador delivered a spirited speech at the Colombian army garrison that made it difficult for the Roosevelt administration to deny complicity in the revolution. "The world is astounded at our heroism! Yesterday we were but the slaves of Colombia; today we are free. . . . President Roosevelt has made good," he proclaimed. "Free sons of Panama, I salute you! Long live the Republic of Panama! Long live President Roosevelt! Long live the American Government!"[133]

Later that afternoon, former Colombian military figures worked with the rebels in setting up a provisional government. General Ruben Varón had also traded his loyalty for the promise of $35,000 in silver and assurances of protection from his government. As commander of the Colombian gunboat *Padilla*, Varón had anchored near the fort off Panama City, where he replaced the Colombian flag with the flag of Panama. At 3:00 p.m., a massive crowd pushed into the Cathedral Plaza for a reading of the proclamation of independence. The Committee of the provisional government—Arango, Tomás Arias, and Frederico Boyd—approved a list of government officials that included Amador as minister of finance and General Huertas as chief of the Army of the Republic. U.S. Consul Malmros assured Washington that the junta was in control.[134]

Before a group of patriots and former Colombian soldiers, General Huertas shouted, "We are free and powerful! Colombia is dead! Long live independent Panama! Long live Dr. Amador! Long live the American Government!" Exuberant Panamanians had earlier hoisted Huertas onto their shoulders and carried him through the city in a chair before dousing him with bottles of champagne. The new government presented Huertas (soon known as the "General of the Revolution") with $30,000 for his services and a retirement grant of $50,000 in gold. It also awarded the $35,000 earlier guaranteed to General Varón, $10,000 to most of his officers, and $50 in silver to every soldier.[135]

Rebel leaders had already made the financial arrangements. Amador had met a number of expenses, including bribing Colombian officers and soldiers, with money advanced from the Panama Railroad and bankers in Panama, including the Bank of Ehrman, whose senior partner was the U.S. consul general, Felix Ehrman. Amador claimed in the ceremony that to pay the soldiers, the U.S. government "sent the money by draft on the Bank of Ehrman in gold," where it was changed into Colombian silver and brought to the barracks in eight boxes on a public coach. Huertas justified the distribution as back pay for unpaid services in the Colombian army in 1901.[136]

At 8:45 that evening of November 4, rebel leaders cabled the State Department in Washington that "a popular and spontaneous movement of the people" had declared the independence of the Isthmus and that the Republic of Panama had established a provisional government. At 10:30 that night, Demetrio Brid, president of the municipal council in Panama City and editor of the *Panama Star and Herald*, informed President Roosevelt that Panamanians hoped for U.S. recognition of their new republic.[137]

This news did not surprise the White House. The "boiling caldron" in Panama, Roosevelt wrote his son Kermit that same night, had begun to "bubble over." The previous morning, the president had been in Oyster Bay to vote in the city election before returning to Washington around 8:00 p.m. to follow the Panama story by cable. For nearly fifty years, the United States had policed the Isthmus "in the interest of the little wildcat republic of Colombia." Yet that republic, he emphasized, had "behaved infamously about the treaty for the building of the Panama Canal." From this moment on, he declared, "Any interference I undertake now will be in the interest of the United States and of the people of the Panama on the Isthmus themselves." This policy will result in "some lively times," but he would "put it through all right."[138]

⟨◈⟩

On November 6, the State Department informed the American consul general in Panama City and the government in Bogotá that the president had approved opening relations with the de facto government of Panama. The Panamanian people, "by an apparently unanimous movement [,] dissolved their political connection with the Republic of Colombia and resumed their independence" after establishing a republican government. The former police chief and now governor of Colón, Porfirio Meléndez, had proclaimed the province part of the Republic of Panama that morning in front of the magistrate's office and before the British and French consuls and a large crowd of civilians, business leaders, and U.S. Army and Navy officers. After a reading of the declaration of independence, Meléndez invited Major William Black of the U.S. Army's Engineer Corps to come forward and raise the flag.[139]

Just before noon, Ehrman pronounced the revolution a success. Colón and the interior provinces had joined the independence movement, and no Colombian soldiers appeared to be on the Isthmus. The Republic of Panama soon appointed Bunau-Varilla as envoy extraordinary and minister plenipotentiary to the United States, authorized to negotiate diplomatic and financial matters in Washington. The chief objective of the two republics was to negotiate a treaty that the principals wanted: a canal through Panama.[140]

Chapter 3

Union of the Oceans

[W]hen the history of this period is written down I believe my administration will be known at least as an administration of ideals.

—President Theodore Roosevelt
January 30, 1909

Mr. Roosevelt avoided, during the first revolutionary attempts anything which could resemble collusion . . . for the very simple but very powerful reason, that such collusion had never existed either directly or indirectly.

—Philippe Bunau-Varilla
1914

As the Republic of Panama celebrated its revolution in early November 1903, Bunau-Varilla waited to hear from the new government about its plans for him as a treaty maker. He had entrusted Amador with a cablegram for the provisional government—that Bunau-Varilla would "accept the mission of Minister Plenipotentiary in order to obtain the recognition of the Republic and signature of Canal Treaty." He became suspicious when the only notes he received from Amador were repeated requests for the $100,000 promised by Bunau-Varilla—with nothing said about his diplomatic status. In an action that did not please him, the provisional government in Panama City appointed him "confidential agent" on November 5. Bunau-Varilla refused to stand aside as others playing lesser roles in this great historical event threatened to destroy his dream of accepting formal U.S. recognition of the new republic he had done so much to create, and of negotiating and signing a canal treaty with the United States.[1]

I

To stabilize the post-revolutionary Isthmus, the White House urged the governments of Colombia and Panama to resolve remaining issues between them. Roosevelt felt obligated, not only by treaty but for the good of civilization, to protect commercial traffic across the Isthmus of Panama from "a constant succession of unnecessary and wasteful civil wars." With that objective in mind, he put Rear Admiral John G. Walker in charge of the military, naval, and civil officers on the Isthmus.[2]

The president spent the first few days after the revolution trying to defend his policy in Panama. He asked Secretary of State Hay on November 6 to assess the argument made by New York attorney Oscar Straus ("a *very* good friend of ours") regarding Panama's status. At a White House luncheon that day with several dignitaries, Roosevelt asked Straus to explain the impact on Panama's sovereignty of the U.S. promise to keep the transit route open in accordance with the Treaty of 1846. Straus emphasized that the American claim rested on the legal principle of "a covenant running with the land" and not on changes in sovereignty. The treaty "goes with territory" and remained in effect with Panama independent. Roosevelt thought the idea "splendid."[3]

Not everyone in the administration endorsed the president's claim that his actions had been "imperative" to building a canal through Panama. In a cabinet meeting, Roosevelt had completed a moral defense of his policies when his secretary of war, Elihu Root, remarked, "The thing I most admire about you, Theodore, is your discovery of the Ten Commandments." On another occasion, the president defended his promotion of "civilization" on moral and legal grounds when he turned to his attorney general, Philander Knox, and declared that "it will be just as well for you to give us a formal legal opinion sustaining my action in the whole matter."

"No, Mr. President," Knox responded. "If I were you I would not have any taint of legality about it."

After further discussion, Roosevelt looked around the table and stopped at Root, who had reservations about the president's Panama policies but did not oppose them. "Have I answered the charges? Have I defended myself?"

"You certainly have, Mr. President. You have shown that you were accused of seduction and you have conclusively proved that you were guilty of rape."[4]

Dark humor perhaps, but not amusing to the president. The suggestion of questionable U.S. conduct in isthmian affairs put him on the defensive, as seen in a private note to his friend Albert Shaw. "I did not foment the revolution on the Isthmus," Roosevelt asserted. The Panamanian people united in favor of a canal and separation from Colombia, whose leaders "signed their death warrant" by refusing to endorse the Hay-Herrán Treaty. "Colombia's grip on Panama is gone forever."[5]

The rapid success of the Panama revolution shocked the Marroquin government into sending General Reyes on a special mission to Panama and Washington. He would first try to convince Panamanians to renounce their revolution and swear loyalty to Colombia. Barring a reconciliation, he was to offer a deal to the Roosevelt administration: If the United States adhered to the Treaty of 1846 by sending troops to defend Colombia's sovereignty and the neutrality of the Isthmus, the government in Bogotá would ratify the Hay-Herrán Treaty. Reyes made clear that his government intended to dispatch 2,000 troops to Panama, half of them from the Pacific and the others from the Atlantic, where they would declare martial law, regain control of the transit route, and squeeze Panama into submission.[6]

But it was too late: President Roosevelt had already decided that the rebels were in control and would receive de facto recognition of their provisional government. Hay notified Herrán in Washington on November 6 that the United States had instructed its vice-consul in Panama City, Felix Ehrman, to initiate diplomatic relations with the new republic.[7]

News of Roosevelt's decision to recognize Panama raised a ruckus in the Colombian Congress on November 9, just two days after General Reyes departed for Panama, accompanied by two other generals, Pedro Nel Ospina and Lucas Cabellero. "Down with Marroquin!" shouted huge crowds demonstrating in the streets the night before a suspected cave-in to the United States. In a mass meeting in front of the palace, the main speaker, a prominent general, called on Marroquin to resign. Troops broke up the gathering, wounding several participants in the fray. The government declared martial law and placed the U.S. legation under guard. A group of protesters moved on to the home of Lorenzo Marroquin, a Senate member and the president's son, and pelted it with stones.[8]

Colombians were bitter toward both their government and the Roosevelt administration. Many of them accused the United States of encouraging the secession movement and forcing Colombian troops in Colón to surrender. The story spread that the current Colombian government was raising an army of 15,000 under Reyes's command to take action against Panama. Some Senate members in Bogotá urged the government to call a convention aimed at amending the constitution to allow immediate approval of the original treaty.[9]

The White House feared that the presence of Colombian troops on the Isthmus might spark a civil war and put the United States in a precarious position. Having already opened relations with the provisional government in Panama, Hay sent instructions to Ehrman in Panama City to use his good offices to facilitate a courteous treatment of General Reyes.[10]

In a note to his friend in England, Cecil Spring Rice, President Roosevelt blamed everything on the Colombians, denouncing them as "not merely corrupt" but "governmentally utterly incompetent." The United States had conceded more than necessary with the treaty and intended to establish a level of stability in Colombia that no other Spanish-American Republic possessed. Despite "the plainest warnings," the Colombians "persisted in slitting their own throats from ear to ear."[11]

In the meantime, the White House learned that neither the French nor the Germans showed any inclination to interfere with events on the Isthmus. The U.S. ambassador in Berlin, Charlemagne Tower, Jr., reported that Germany denied interest in the Panama issue and assured the United States it would not intervene. From the U.S. Embassy in Paris, Ambassador Horace Porter sent a similar assessment, declaring that he expected France and other European powers to follow America's lead in recognizing the Republic of Panama.[12]

Trouble now came from an unexpected source: Bunau-Varilla suspected backdoor maneuvering in Panama City over a canal treaty, probably led by Amador. Their relationship had been uneasy from the start and had worsened as they competed for the credit for success.

On November 7, Bunau-Varilla received two telegrams from Panama City, both dated three days earlier but arriving late because of communication problems. The first telegram declared that the provisional government had appointed him "Confidential Agent" (a "ridiculous title," Bunau-Varilla later remarked) to negotiate formal U.S. recognition of the Republic of Panama (de facto recognition had taken place the previous day) and secure a loan. The other telegram came from Amador, who infuriated Bunau-Varilla by explaining that his new title was the "only diplomatic office which it is possible to give you."[13]

Finally, Bunau-Varilla must have thought, the new government on November 8 gave in to what he later termed a "precise injunction" on his part. It appointed him "envoy extraordinary and minister plenipotentiary" with "full powers to conduct diplomatic and financial negotiations." He immediately released the news to the press.[14]

His elation was short-lived. At a private lunch in the secretary of state's home the following day, Hay congratulated Bunau-Varilla on the appointment and then asked about a story in the morning papers declaring that a special commission from Panama would leave the next day for Washington to negotiate a canal treaty. Bunau-Varilla regularly read the newspapers and was doubtless aware of the story. Hay, of course, had to know who was in charge before negotiations began.

Bunau-Varilla initially dismissed the story as a mistake. But with Hay's question, Bunau-Varilla suspected that the commission was another part of the "intrigue" to outmaneuver him, the first step being reducing his title to "Confidential Agent," and now to replace him in the negotiations. Keeping these thoughts to himself, he explained to Hay that some Panamanians sought to discredit him. There was no reason for concern. "So long as I am here, Mr. Secretary, you will have to deal exclusively with me."[15]

For more than a decade, Bunau-Varilla did not fully explain his reasons for haste in signing a treaty. But in his book on Panama that appeared in 1914, he accused Amador of pushing for the special commission as part of "a plot" to fulfill his "childish desire to sign the Treaty." The three-member commission—Amador, Federico Boyd, and Carlos Arosemena—would "substitute itself for me," at least delaying negotiations for days or longer. There had to be a treaty as soon as possible, Bunau-Varilla asserted. In early November of 1903, the newly established republic consisted of only the Isthmus from Panama City to Colón, which came under U.S. protection by the Treaty of 1846. But the independence movement threatened to expand throughout the entire province without American protection. A new treaty with the United States must encompass all of Panama, justified perhaps by calling this claim "one of the compensations for the Canal concessions."[16]

Immediately after lunch at Hay's home, Bunau-Varilla attempted to counter this perceived attempt to undercut him. He avoided a confrontation with government leaders in Panama City by cabling them about what he called a rumor that a special commission had departed for Washington to negotiate and sign the treaty. He had "explicitly denied" the story to the secretary of state as a contradiction of his instructions that endangered the coming negotiations by leaving a "very bad impression" in Washington of confusion in Panama City. Nothing would block the treaty, he had assured the White House. It was "eminently necessary" to correct this situation before "the formation of an obstructionist group supported by Nicaraguan and Colombian intrigues."[17]

Bunau-Varilla's "formal demand for satisfaction," as he called it, led to a swift reply from Panama City: Amador, Boyd, and Arosemena had "no mission" to the U.S. government except "to avoid loss of time." Not by coincidence did news of this change in directives arrive in Panama City at the same time Bunau-Varilla received word of the revision. Ehrman on November 10 had cabled the State Department that the three commissioners were going to Washington to negotiate the "Canal Treaty." The following day, Ehrman received word of the altered directives for the special commission and cabled the State Department that he had been "officially informed" that Bunau-Varilla was the "authorized party to make treaties" and that the three commissioners would "assist their Minister."[18]

That same day, November 11, Bunau-Varilla cabled the Panamanian secretary of foreign affairs, Francisco V. de la Espriella, praising him for clearing up the "bad impression" left on Hay. He also informed Hay that the Republic of Panama had officially appointed him "envoy extraordinary and minister plenipotentiary with full powers to negotiate." Knowing the commission would arrive in about a week, Bunau-Varilla asked the secretary when he should present his credentials. In two days, Hay's office promptly replied.[19]

On November 13, President Roosevelt met with Bunau-Varilla at 9:30 in the morning to accept his credentials and grant formal recognition to the new Republic of Panama. No need for introductory remarks; they had met a month earlier in the White House and discussed the possibility of a revolution in Panama. After the formalities, Roosevelt could not resist the opportunity to quip about the allegations circulating in the press and elsewhere.

"What do you think, Mr. Minister, of those people who print that we have made the Revolution of Panama together?"

"I think, Mr. President, that calumny never loses its opportunity even in the New World. It is necessary patiently to wait," he continued in his penchant for florid prose, "until the spring of the imagination of the wicked is dried up, and until truth dissipates the mist of mendacity."

Bunau-Varilla praised the president for agreeing to build the Panama Canal as an essential part of the "highway from Europe to Asia." Roosevelt commended Panama for winning independence and establishing a republican government that deserved American recognition. Together, they intended to construct a commercial passageway that would benefit the world.[20]

II

Bunau-Varilla was still racing the clock. Knowing the three Panamanian emissaries were four days closer to Washington, he feared a fight in the U.S. Senate that might result in a switch to Nicaragua. Bunau-Varilla sought to hurry the treaty process—and not only for the good of civilization. If he lost Panama, he would also lose a large part of the $40 million going to the New Panama Canal Company, in which he and his brother Maurice owned 11,000 shares of stock.[21]

Hay had the advantage of knowing that both Bunau-Varilla and Panama desperately wanted a treaty, making it imperative to close the deal before the special commissioners arrived. Their involvement might interfere with Bunau-Varilla's effort to keep the new Republic of Panama reliant on the United States for protection against Colombia. Just two days later, on Sunday, November 15, Hay sent a note to Bunau-Varilla, enclosing "a project of a Treaty" and a request for his recommended changes.[22]

Hay had tried to assure Senate support by revising the Hay-Herrán Treaty in favor of the United States. Only ten of its twenty-eight articles remained in their original form, with three eliminated and fifteen slightly changed. Hay had borrowed from John Tyler Morgan's earlier suggested amendments to the treaty, a move welcomed by the Alabama senator, who considered the changes so pro-American that Colombia would never approve and thereby leave Nicaragua as the only choice. Bunau-Varilla maintained that the draft was "the Hay-Herrán Treaty with insignificant modifications." He noted two changes: The $10 million indemnity for Colombia stipulated in the Hay-Herrán Treaty was not in the new draft, and the line for a monetary award to Panama was blank.[23]

Like Hay, Bunau-Varilla was wary of the Senate and that same day took the secretary's draft treaty and solicited aid from his friend and attorney from New York, Frank Pavey, in making revisions more palatable to the U.S. Senate. For two days and into the night, Bunau-Varilla and Pavey wrestled with the draft submitted by Hay, accepting all but four of his twenty-seven articles and restoring parts of the Hay-Herrán Treaty to give the United States more than the secretary of state had asked.[24]

Bunau-Varilla delivered his revised treaty to Hay in the early morning of November 17, hoping for a quick response in view of the news in that day's press. The three special commissioners had arrived in New York, greeted by Cromwell's press agent, Roger Farnham. Cromwell wanted to meet with them after his arrival from Paris that afternoon, Farnham declared. Bunau-Varilla felt certain that only the looming success of a treaty with Panama could have drawn Cromwell back into the fray. He also knew that Cromwell's decision to drop out of the Panama fight had so angered Amador that he threatened to kill Cromwell for betraying the cause. But with so much at stake, what would the commissioners lose by welcoming Cromwell's support if that was the reason he wanted to talk?[25]

Bunau-Varilla could not have known that Cromwell had never wavered in his commitment to a Panama Canal. Despite the stories that he fled the United States for fear of Herrán's warnings or Amador's threats, congressional testimony in February 1912 shows that Cromwell arrived in Paris in mid-October of 1903 and spent three weeks conferring with the directors of the New Panama Canal Company about how to secure the rights to build a canal through Panama.[26]

Colombia's opposition to the Hay-Herrán Treaty, Cromwell had warned company leaders, would result in the loss of their concessions. Colombia accused the railroad and canal companies in Panama, along with the major powers and commercial interests, of encouraging a revolution. Congressional members in Bogotá opposed the extension of concessions and had done nothing to encourage new negotiations. According to the original expiration date of 1904, the concessions would revert to their original owner—Colombia.[27]

Cromwell proposed to delay any decision by the U.S. Congress for Nicaragua by persuading President Roosevelt to take no action on a canal pending new negotiations with Colombia. Such an arrangement, Cromwell knew, had the added enticement of permitting construction to continue in the interim. On October 31, he cabled Roosevelt that the board had unanimously approved the proposal and praised the president's "masterful policy."[28]

Then came the November revolution three days later and a new negotiator—the Republic of Panama.

Cromwell sailed home about a week later on November 11, intending to honor a "previously arranged" conference with Panama's special commissioners on their arrival in New York on November 17. Amador had balked at meeting Cromwell, but the other two members of the commission, Boyd and Arosemena, thought it might prove beneficial to talk with him. Arosemena later explained to Bunau-Varilla why Amador changed his mind. "I told him that nobody ought to be condemned without a hearing. I added that he should not make an enemy of Cromwell in the delicate situation in which we were placed." He could "greatly harm us."[29]

Bunau-Varilla was not privy to what transpired in that all-day meeting, but he assumed the worst because of the presence of Amador and Cromwell. Amador sought fame as the architect of the new republic; Cromwell wanted to use his influence among government leaders to amass a fortune in fees from the New Panama Canal Company's sale of its holdings to the United States. Bunau-Varilla had worked several months with Cromwell in lobbying Congress to support a Panama Canal and knew that the only way to understand his behavior was to follow the money. As the New York attorney for both the New Panama Canal Company in Paris and the Panama Railroad Company in Panama City, Cromwell would never abandon such a lucrative arrangement. He would tell the commissioners what they wanted to hear—that he had not betrayed the cause and was there to help finish the move to independence.[30]

Bunau-Varilla was furious over the commissioners' meeting with Cromwell. From their vantage point, they were acting within the bounds of the instructions given to them before they embarked from Panama; from Bunau-Varilla's perspective, they no longer had authority over a treaty and had violated—albeit unknowingly—their revised instructions. Bunau-Varilla appeared to project his own motives onto his chief rival for center stage. "My efforts brought about the creation of that new Republic of Panama," Bunau-Varilla later boasted. Amador had a "childish ambition" to negotiate and sign a treaty that "would hand his name down to history." Bunau-Varilla maintained that he had "saved him and his friends," "wrested his country from tyranny," secured "the protection of the United States," and put the new republic onto the path of "fabulous prosperity." For "personal satisfaction," Amador "would jeopardize all the delicate fabric of my work."[31]

By the evening of November 17, Bunau-Varilla had become concerned about hearing nothing from Hay. At 10:00 p.m. he could wait no longer and wrote a note to the secretary of state, expressing his hope of signing the treaty the following day. He feared growing "intrigues" involving the special commissioners and intended to contact them about staying in New York another day and arriving in Washington on the evening of November 18.[32]

Hay responded within minutes. "Please come to-night [*sic*] if you prefer. Or tomorrow at nine here, if you like it better."[33]

Bunau-Varilla left immediately, knowing that circumstances called for quick action. "So long as the delegation has not arrived in Washington, I shall be free to deal with you alone, provided with complete and absolute powers. When they arrive, I shall no longer be alone. In fact, I may perhaps soon no longer be here at all."[34]

At the meeting, Bunau-Varilla expressed opposition to Hay's suggestion that, in the interests of compromise, they equally divide the $10 million indemnity originally allotted to Colombia with Panama. The United States, Bunau-Varilla also asserted, must protect Panama's independence; and Panama must give up its sovereignty in the canal zone—a concession he thought necessary to guarantee Senate approval of the treaty. The United States would not win the *right* of sovereignty over the canal area but the *rights* as "if it were the sovereign of the territory."[35]

Hay wanted to seek the advice of colleagues in the administration.

That night, Bunau-Varilla bought more time by telegramming the Panamanian emissaries then in New York to stay another day.[36]

At lunch on the following day, November 18, Hay met with other cabinet members to discuss his draft of a treaty and the amendments proposed by Bunau-Varilla. Secretary of War Root, Attorney General Knox, and Secretary of the Treasury Leslie Shaw approved all but one of Bunau-Varilla's revisions along with his recommendation to pay Panama the entire $10 million indemnity previously earmarked for Colombia by the Hay-Herrán Treaty. Giving any money to Colombia, Bunau-Varilla had warned in a letter to Hay that morning, would appear to be a blackmail attempt by the United States to hide "a concealed crime"—that of promoting the secession of Panama.[37]

That same day, Hay sent a note to Bunau-Varilla: "Will you kindly call at my house at 6 o'clock to-day [sic]?" He arrived on the minute, encountering two reporters at the door, both asking if he was going to sign the canal treaty. Bunau-Varilla dodged their question by remarking that they had more information than he had. Five minutes ago, one reporter declared, the head of the State Department's Treaties Bureau arrived. "Now you arrive. This shows you are to sign the Treaty."[38]

The reporters were correct: The secretary of state thanked his guest for coming to sign the treaty. Everything in it Hay attributed to Bunau-Varilla's handiwork, which he deemed satisfactory with the lone exception of what he described as an "insignificant question of terminology." In Article II, Hay explained, he preferred changing the words "leases in perpetuity" to "grants to the United States in perpetuity the use, occupation and control" of the canal zone and adjoining territory. "You see," the secretary remarked, "that from a practical standpoint it is absolutely synonymous."[39]

If Bunau-Varilla understood the "insignificant" change to a grant to be what it was—a major extension of American power over the canal zone and surrounding land—he did not show it. Years later, he noted that a lease protected Panama from the charge of abandoning its property. But at the time, the magnitude of signing a treaty had so overwhelmed him that he wanted to do so immediately. In hurrying from his hotel, he had forgotten to bring his seal to place on the document. He and Hay settled on a signet ring bearing Hay's family coat of arms.[40]

At 6:40 p.m., they signed the treaty. As they shook hands afterward, Bunau-Varilla remarked: "It seems to me as if we [have] together made something great."[41]

A half hour later, Bunau-Varilla cabled the news to the government in Panama, two hours before the special commission arrived in Washington.[42]

The Hay-Bunau-Varilla Treaty (or the Isthmian Canal Convention) authorized U.S. construction of a canal linking the Atlantic and Pacific oceans and made the former province of Panama into a protectorate of the United States. Among the treaty's twenty-six articles, the United States guaranteed the independence of the Republic of Panama, which "grants to the United States all the rights, power, and authority within the zone . . . which the United States would possess and exercise if it were the sovereign of the territory." Panama also "grants to the United States in perpetuity the use, occupation and control" of a canal zone ten miles wide, but that did not include Panama City and Colón and their harbors and adjacent territories. Panama would receive $10 million after ratifying this agreement and an annual payment of $250,000, beginning in nine years, the estimated time needed to build the canal.[43]

At about 11 p.m. that evening of November 18, four hours after Hay and Bunau-Varilla had signed the agreement, Amador, Boyd, and Arosemena arrived in Washington, prepared to negotiate a canal treaty—unaware of the instructional changes in their mission after they left Panama City.

Bunau-Varilla met them at Union Station, greeting them with what he later called the "happy news!" Before their feet touched the platform, he declared, "The Republic of Panama is henceforth under the protection of the United States. I have just signed the Canal Treaty." Amador, as Bunau-Varilla recalled, "was positively overcome" and "nearly swooned on the platform of the station." Boyd, according to one story, punched Bunau-Varilla in the face.[44]

The next day, the three commissioners produced the documents defining Bunau-Varilla's mission. Boyd repeatedly insisted that Bunau-Varilla had violated his written instructions to "adjust" the treaty after discussing its clauses with the three commissioners and to "proceed in everything strictly in accord with them." Bunau-Varilla, it appeared, was to be a "mere intermediary" between the secretary of state and the commissioners. If he resigned, they would negotiate without him.[45]

Bunau-Varilla countered their charges by showing them his new instructions, cabled to him after their departure from Panama City. Boyd called for "fresh negotiations" with the State Department. "Cherish no illusion, Mr. Boyd," Bunau-Varilla responded, "the negotiations are closed."[46]

In the late evening of that same day, November 19, Bunau-Varilla received a cable from Panama, asking why he signed the treaty before the commission arrived and what "modifications" he had approved. Suspecting an attempt by its three members to change or reject the treaty, Bunau-Varilla waited for nearly a week to respond. On November 25, he sent a lengthy ultimatum warning that he would resign if Panama refused to ratify the treaty. Two days later, the Panamanian government pledged to approve the treaty on its arrival.[47]

That same day, November 27, General Reyes and his entourage arrived in Washington, having failed to reconcile differences with Panama and now hoping to salvage the second part of his special mission by offering to ratify the Hay-Herrán Treaty. He was too late on both fronts. The United States and Panama had resolved the canal issue nine days earlier by signing the Hay-Bunau-Varilla Treaty; and when Reyes arrived in Panama, the revolutionary government did not allow him to come ashore but sent a delegation to meet with him on a neutral French vessel on November 19. Nothing came of the meeting. Panama had already received recognition by the United States, France, China, and Austria-Hungary.[48]

Reyes nonetheless told the American press that his government wanted to renegotiate the matter. Asked by a reporter, "What can the United States do, now that a Treaty has been signed by Secretary Hay and M. Bunau-Varilla?" the general replied, "That Treaty has not been ratified." Colombians "want the canal." The government in Bogotá had resolved the political issues that blocked the settlement. "I come with instructions from the President of Colombia direct."[49]

Reyes also came with a warning that stirred up talk of war with Colombia. "So tense is the feeling and so national the spirit of determination to bring the Isthmus back into the Republic, that President Marroquin will have no trouble in raising an army twice the size necessary to put down the disturbance." Reyes was aware of Bunau-Varilla's public skepticism about that threat. "It was just as easy," the Frenchman had stated, "to march an army on foot from the Cape of Good Hope to London as from Bogotá to Panama." The 200-mile long terrain was replete with marshes, forests, fevers, and "savage and independent Indians." That did not deter Reyes. Colombian troops, he contended, "can march overland to the Isthmus, despite the contrary opinion of ill-advised persons."[50]

Reyes had a brief conversation with the president, less than a week after Panama ratified the Hay-Bunau-Varilla Treaty on December 2. Roosevelt declined to discuss negotiations and insisted that Reyes take up the matter with Hay. The president asked Hay to "find out whether [Reyes] has any practical proposal."[51]

For almost a month through mid-January 1904, Hay and Reyes met or exchanged lengthy written messages that focused on familiar arguments and reached no agreements. Reyes brought up the most sensitive issue on December 8, when he wrote to Hay, asking how the White House would react to Colombia's landing troops on the Isthmus in accordance with the provisions of the Treaty of 1846, guaranteeing its right to defend its sovereignty. If Colombian troops tried to regain Panama, Hay warned, the White House would regard the move as an invasion certain to cause "bloodshed and disorder" throughout the Isthmus. Roosevelt asserted through Hay that "in the interest of universal commerce and civilization," the time had come "to close that chapter of sanguinary and ruinous civil war in Panama."[52]

Reyes had not achieved anything in either Panama or Washington. He admitted to Hay how difficult it was "to accomplish more than is possible under the circumstances" and expressed fear of an "inevitable period of anarchy and general civil war in Colombia."[53] Reyes conceded that continued attempts to revive negotiations were futile. His only course was to turn the page and focus on stability at home.

Roosevelt and Hay had worked closely together on Panama as their first national security issue. The president had asked him to sit down with Senator John Spooner and go over every line in the Hay-Bunau-Varilla Treaty to avoid a call for amendments by either the United States or Panama that posed the "slightest risk" to ratification. He had monitored Hay's communications with Reyes. The treaty, he later told Spooner, accomplished "practically everything . . . we can possibly desire."[54]

III

President Roosevelt had long faced domestic opposition to his Panama policies. Privately, he characterized critics from New York City and elsewhere in the Northeast as "a small body of shrill eunuchs" who downplayed the global benefits of a canal and opposed any government action not in their own interests. Publicly, he expressed resentment for the charge that he and his supporters wanted an isthmian canal so badly that they ignored moral issues in defending "a business question." The president called it "arrant nonsense" for anyone—especially former Union soldiers—to accuse his administration of "recognizing secession." There was no comparison, he wrote in a lengthy private letter to Chicago attorney Otto Gresham. The South tried to break from the Union to protect slavery. The Panamanians revolted because Colombia, "for corrupt and evil purposes or else from complete governmental incompetency," opposed a canal treaty that meant everything to Panama. "By every law, human and divine, Panama was right in her position."[55]

The Colombians, continued the president in his note to Gresham, were "guilty of deliberate bad faith" and had no right to indemnification. If Congress appropriated the money, he promised to veto the measure. "The United States owes Colombia nothing in law or in morals." This country has been "more than just" and "generous to a fault" in negotiating with the Colombians. "In their silly efforts to damage us they cut their own throats. They tried to hold us up; and too late they have discovered their . . . criminal error." The United States would never betray either the Panamanian people or the "fundamental laws of righteousness."[56]

A few days later, Roosevelt resumed his argument in a private letter to Charles Osborn, a Republican politician from Michigan who later became governor. The problem over Panama, according to the president, was "exactly as if a road agent had tried to hold up a man," except that the victim managed to seize the gun. Why would he return the gun to the agent because it was his? "By every consideration of equity, and of legitimate national and international interest, what we have done was right."[57]

In his Third Annual Message to Congress on December 7, 1903, President Roosevelt attempted to justify U.S. actions by citing the long list of disturbances in Panama that began in May 1850 and continued to the present. According to his count, the Panamanians had rebelled against Colombian rule at least fifty-three times during this period, with some of the uprisings lasting almost three years. Continued unrest across the Isthmus obligated the United States to take corrective action in accordance with the Treaty of 1846. In exchange for guaranteeing New Granada's sovereignty and "perfect neutrality" in the area, the United States received "the right of way or transit across the Isthmus." Six times—in 1856, 1860, 1873, 1885, 1901, and 1902—the United States was "forced" to send military and naval forces to keep the Isthmus open for commerce.[58]

Indeed, he added, the Colombians on four occasions—in 1861, 1862, 1885, and 1900—*invited* the United States to send troops to protect their interests and restore order on the Isthmus. In the latest instance of 1903, "an eminent Colombian" [General Reyes] claimed that if the United States sent troops,

Colombia would declare martial law and then ratify the Hay-Herrán Treaty. This assurance of immediate approval of the treaty, the president stated, demonstrated that the government had control over the treaty and chose not to approve it. Colombia nonetheless expected Americans to protect its "supremacy in the Isthmus."[59]

The United States, President Roosevelt argued, had met its responsibilities under the Treaty of 1846 while Colombia had refused to do so. The government in Bogotá proved unable to quell the repeated revolutions and other domestic disturbances in Panama short of armed action and help from the United States; yet that same government rejected a treaty that would have brought stability to Colombia and peace in Panama. The United States sought a final arrangement that protected "the interest and well-being, not merely of our own people, but of the people of the Isthmus of Panama and the people of the civilized countries of the world."[60]

About a week after the president's message to Congress, Root offered his version of why Colombia opposed the Hay-Bunau-Varilla Treaty. In a note to the American ambassador in Paris, General Horace Porter, Root asserted that the "Bogotá Patriots" had the "very attractive idea of bilking the French people" by declaring null and void the concessions to the New Panama Canal Company and then seizing the canal property as the first step to selling it for the $40 million in American money intended to go to the French company. "They are now in the position of a girl who keeps refusing a fellow, with the idea that she will marry him sometime or other when she gets ready and who wakes up some fine morning to find that he has married another girl."[61]

Roosevelt's Panama policies drew opposition from evangelical groups, according to Lincoln biographer David Decamp Thompson, editor of the weekly *Northwestern Christian Advocate* in Chicago. In a letter to the president, Thompson referred to many readers who opposed U.S. recognition of Panama. Leading Methodists in the Northwest drew a sharp reaction from Roosevelt by suggesting that his action was similar to endorsing Southern secession in 1861.[62]

In a letter to Thompson marked "Personal, not for publication," the president took issue with the conflation of Jefferson Davis's secessionist movement with that of Panama. The secessionists of the 1860s sought to establish "a slave-holding republic," which attempted to "break up the greatest experiment at successful democratic republican government" ever seen in the world. In the present troubles, Roosevelt argued (as he had to Gresham), Colombia for years had "plundered Panama, and misgoverned and misruled her, declined to ratify the treaty for the Canal—which meant giving up Panama's last hope." When the Panamanian people "rose literally as one man," the United States "was bound by every consideration of honor and humanity, and of national and international interest, to take exactly the steps that it took."[63]

On the morning of the same day that Roosevelt penned the above letter, December 22, 1903, a special mission led by the former minister to Argentina, William Buchanan of New York, arrived in Colón as the newly appointed envoy extraordinary and minister plenipotentiary to Panama. Two junta officials provided a private car and arranged for his transportation by rail to Panama City, where the minister for foreign affairs met him at the train station at noon and escorted him to the hotel.[64]

On Christmas Eve, Buchanan handed the minister for foreign affairs a letter from President Roosevelt and a copy of the remarks for the special minister to make at the ceremony set for three o'clock on Christmas Day. On that day, after a carriage ride through two streets lined on both sides with infantry personnel, Buchanan entered the Government House, greeted by a military band playing "The Star-Spangled Banner." The former revolutionary leader, José Agustín Arango, accepted Buchanan's credentials, expressing satisfaction that the "greatest Republic of the American continent" regarded Panama as equal to the other republics of the New World. The new government hoped to succeed in "more closely linking the two nations together in sincere friendship and accord." Among the dignitaries at the reception were the junta, cabinet, supreme court, and high-ranking military officers. All consular officials were present except those from Central America, Chile, and Argentina. As Buchanan left the Government House, the band again played "The Star-Spangled Banner."[65]

In a special to the *New York Times* in late December, J.R. Taylor of Mississippi reported that he had just returned from seven weeks in Panama City, following up on the claim by Panamanians that Hay was more responsible than the president in winning their independence. According to their argument, the secretary of state's "clearness and sagacity" led to the "successful accomplishment of Panama's independence and the speedy signing of the treaty." Roosevelt contributed to the outcome "with his quickness to perceive the wisdom of the policy suggested and outlined by Mr. Hay."[66]

It is unclear whether the president read this article, but even though the populace might have considered Hay chiefly responsible for Panama's independence, the reality is that he did not act without Roosevelt's instructions. And yet the popular perception of Hay as the face of the revolution supported Roosevelt's life-long denials of playing a central role in these events.

In his message to Congress on January 4, 1904, President Roosevelt dismissed Colombia's objections as "an after-thought." The Hay-Herrán Treaty had drawn no criticisms when it first went before the government of Colombia. The treaty guaranteed Colombia's sovereignty over the canal strip, and its government never indicated that U.S. control over that piece of land would impede the construction of a canal. Furthermore, he asserted, the people in the canal area strongly supported the treaty. "I will not for one moment discuss the possibility of the United States committing an act of such baseness as to abandon the new Republic of Panama."[67]

Panama, the president insisted, had the sovereign right of an independent state to protect its vital interests against Colombia's attempt to control the Isthmus and all rights to a canal. Numerous reports had earlier arrived from the Panama region claiming the imminence of a revolution. Daily papers from Costa Rica included travelers' accounts of an insurrection underway. Colombian forces in Panama and Colón sympathized with the revolutionary sentiment, many of them ill-paid by their home offices. Similar stories appeared in the *Washington Post, New York Herald,* and *New York Times,* all warning of strong feelings in Panama that Colombia's government sought to profit itself by negotiating a new canal treaty.[68]

Roosevelt also defended U.S. recognition of the Republic of Panama as an act supporting the "interests of collective civilization." If ever a nation had "a mandate from civilization" to pursue an objective beneficial to mankind, the United States had that opportunity in building an isthmian canal. Colombia had approved the project. Great Britain gave up important rights under the Clayton-Bulwer Treaty with the expectation that the canal would be open to everyone. The second Pan-American Conference in Mexico City on January 22, 1902, had applauded America's efforts to build a canal, with General Reyes as the Colombian delegate signing the resolution and calling the effort a "work of civilization." Now recognition of the new Panama Republic had come from more than fifteen countries, including France, Germany, and Great Britain. All these nations agreed that Panama's separation from Colombia promoted "the interests of the entire civilized world."[69]

In defending his policy, the president referred to a recent article in the December 8 issue of the *New York Evening Post,* in which a native Panamanian spoke for many of his people in calling an American-controlled canal in Panama "a matter of life or death to us." The lack of bloodshed on the Isthmus was "directly due—and only due—to the prompt and firm enforcement by the United States of its traditional policy." Roosevelt praised naval commander John Hubbard and his "little band of men" for acting with "coolness and gallantry" in averting conflict with a force ten times their number.[70]

The United States, Roosevelt emphasized, was not complicit in the revolt and "policed the Isthmus in the interest of its inhabitants and of our own national needs, and for the good of the entire civilized world." No one in the U.S. government had any role in "preparing, inciting, or encouraging the late revolution on the Isthmus of Panama."[71]

Roosevelt urged critics to look at Cuba after the Spanish-American War as a model for America's intentions regarding Panama. The United States stood accused of wanting to seize Cuba as part of its imperial interests, and yet the island was now an independent republic based on self-government. "So will it be with Panama."[72]

Roosevelt placed his concern about Panama's freedom within a global context. An isthmian canal built by the United States, he made clear, was essential to national security and inseparable from protecting civilization in all sectors of the world. Recognition of Panama derived from "the highest considerations of our national interests and safety." In all U.S. foreign relations, there was "nothing of greater or more pressing importance than the construction of an interoceanic canal."[73]

IV

The president prepared for a difficult struggle in the Senate over approval of the Hay-Bunau-Varilla Treaty. Within a week of its signing on November 18, 1903, the leading proponent of a Nicaraguan canal, Democratic senator Morgan of Alabama, accused the president of leading the Panamanian rebels to believe they would receive American help. He did not charge Roosevelt with conspiracy, but with having "armed ships properly posted to protect those engaged in the 'uprising' when it should occur." The Treaty of 1846 authorized him to "check" an independence movement, not "protect" it. The president "authorized war upon Colombia" when he ordered the commander of the *Nashville* to prevent Colombian troops in Colón from advancing to Panama City.[74]

After the treaty went to the Senate for consideration on December 7, 1903, the president invited Republican leaders in that chamber to join him and the secretary of state at the White House to discuss the matter. The senators at first voiced displeasure with the way the administration had handled the situation; but after several hours of intense deliberations, they agreed to support the treaty. As they filed out of the room, a senator from the West, famed for his ability to craft compromises, spoke quietly to Hay: "Do it, but be as gentle as you can with Colombia." Hay later told the president's friend, Joseph Bishop, that this directive "reminded me of the instruction of the Western outlaw chief: 'Kill him, but kill him easy!'"[75]

On January 4, 1904, the president sent his special message on the treaty to both houses of Congress. The Senate immediately began the debate, with Senator Morgan, one of the Democratic leaders, criticizing the treaty and Henry Cabot Lodge, among the Republican strategists, defending it.[76]

In a rapid succession of notes immediately following the opening of the debate, the White House publicly and privately denied any involvement in the Panama revolution. To confirm his position, Roosevelt asked the third person in the room during his conversation with Bunau-Varilla in October

1903, Acting Secretary of State Francis Loomis, to write a memo summarizing what he had heard. "Nothing was said," he wrote the president on January
5, "that could be in any way construed as advising, instigating, suggesting, or
encouraging a revolutionary movement." That same day, Hay wrote General
Reyes that the White House had no contact with "agents of [the] revolution
in Colombia," and renounced "the insinuation that any action of this government prior to the revolution in Panama was the result of complicity with the
plans of the revolutionists."[77]

The administration was on shaky ground. The reader will recall that on
September 3, 1903, Hay met for almost three hours with Gabriel Duque from
Panama, who, technically speaking, was not an "agent" of the revolution
but was on the fringes of the underground movement. The secretary did not
promise American help, but he left room for hope by stating that, if a revolution occurred, the United States would maintain neutrality across the Isthmus
and eventually complete the Panama Canal. Roosevelt likewise implied
support for a revolution without committing to intervention in his October
10 meeting with Bunau-Varilla, who also was not part of the revolutionary
circle but was an advocate of Panama's independence. Less than a week later,
Bunau-Varilla met with Hay in his home and came away confident that if a
revolution broke out, the U.S. Navy would protect the canal project.[78]

The willingness of Roosevelt and Hay to discuss Panama with these two
known associates of the independence movement encouraged the rebels to
anticipate U.S. assistance.

On January 6, 1904, Roosevelt wrote to John Bigelow—Lincoln's wartime
minister to France and a mutual friend of his and the secretary—denying any
part in the uprising, by either himself or Hay. "Of course I have no idea what
Bunau-Varilla advised the revolutionists," he continued,

> but I do know, of course, that he had no assurances in any way, either from Hay
> or myself, or from anyone authorized to speak for us. He is a very able fellow,
> and it was his business to find out what he thought our Government would do.
> I have no doubt that he was able to make a very accurate guess, and to advise
> his people accordingly. In fact he would have been a very dull man had he been
> unable to make such a guess.[79]

That same day, Roosevelt assured Lodge that he was not concerned about
Morgan's charges in the Senate. In fact, "I am much pleased that he should
have done this." His critics, the president declared, had repeatedly warned
that they would release telegrams from Bunau-Varilla proving his knowledge
of White House plans to send ships to the Isthmus and extend U.S. recognition to the rebel government. Roosevelt was "particularly pleased" that Morgan quoted from Bunau-Varilla's article of September 2, 1903. "It really is

a remarkable forecast of what we actually did," in that the article "appeared about a week before I called John Bassett Moore to Oyster Bay and for the first time began definitely to formulate my policy even in my own mind." Morgan and his friends have put themselves into the position of arguing "that Bunau-Varilla knew what we were going to do six weeks before he ever saw any of us and some little time before I had even begun myself to make up my mind what I should do."[80]

Roosevelt followed soon afterward with a note to Moore, declaring that Morgan had stated in the Senate chamber that if Bunau-Varilla's account was correct, he must have gotten the information from either Roosevelt or Hay. Roosevelt denied the allegation, asserting that he did not talk about formulating a policy until about September 9, a week after Bunau-Varilla's article appeared and when Moore stayed the night at Sagamore Hill. Neither he nor Hay saw Bunau-Varilla before October. Bunau-Varilla was "evidently a very clever man."[81]

Moore confirmed that he neither saw nor communicated with Bunau-Varilla, either directly or indirectly, until early October 1903, when he was introduced to him and they briefly discussed the canal issue without mentioning the possibility of a revolt in Panama. On that day or the next, Bunau-Varilla sent him a copy of his September 2 article. Moore had not looked at it since that day but recalled "in a general way its drift." Bunau-Varilla had explained that his position resulted from "the purely logical examination" of a question that he had studied for years. Moore agreed with the president that Bunau-Varilla was "one of the cleverest men I have ever met."[82]

A week later, on January 14, the president and Bunau-Varilla came together for a second time at a State Dinner in honor of the Diplomatic Corps. According to Bunau-Varilla, Roosevelt approached him and declared, "M. Bunau-Varilla, I have never been as astonished as I was when I read the article of September 2, where you described exactly what I was then preparing with Professor Bassett Moore at Oyster Bay."[83]

"But, Mr. President," Bunau-Varilla replied, "it is purely a matter of logic. The same facts are bound to lead logical minds to the same conclusion, however far away from each other they may be."

"Well," remarked the president, "if that is so, you are the greatest logician I have ever known."

At that point, the butler announced that dinner was ready, and the president complimented his guest before leaving for his seat: "They say that I have inspired you. It would be much more true to say that you inspired me."[84]

President Roosevelt complained about the Senate to his friend Spring Rice in England, remarking how difficult it was to deal with "those solemn creatures of imperfect aspirations after righteousness." They have accused the United States of treating Colombia unjustly, when it was "a good thing, a very good thing, . . . for Panama and for the world" that Panama became independent. Mankind "will all be the better because we dig the Panama Canal and keep order in its neighborhood."[85]

On February 23, 1904, the U.S. Senate ratified the Hay-Bunau-Varilla Treaty by a margin of 66–14, with southern Democrats lending their support, not so much for the president's "mandate from civilization" as for a long-standing vision of the practical benefits for the region. Democrat William Randolph Hearst's *Chicago American* called Roosevelt's action "a rough-riding assault upon another republic over the shattered wreckage of international law and diplomatic usage." The president signed the treaty two days later, and it went into effect on February 26, 1904.[86]

Roosevelt denied imperial aspirations, arguing that building a canal was part of his responsibility for maintaining order and civilization in South America. As for the "weak and chaotic governments and people" of that region, he insisted to a friend that America had a duty, "when it becomes absolutely inevitable, to police these countries in the interest of order and civilization." He would have been "delighted" had Colombia ratified the Hay-Herrán Treaty; but when it refused to do so, the only choice for the United States was to interfere "just as little and just as slowly as is consistent with right and justice."[87]

Hard feelings toward the United States persisted in Colombia, as shown by the petitions calling for trade boycotts and government discussions about breaking diplomatic relations. But by the end of March 1904, Colombians realized they could not change the treaty and could hope only for monetary compensation. Hay noted that the Panama issue had "profoundly subsided" and that on July 4 General Reyes had been elected president of Colombia.[88]

Throughout this tumultuous period, Hay defended the president, both privately and publicly. He wrote historian James Ford Rhodes that on the day of the Panamanian revolt, "We had to decide on the instant whether we would take possession of the ends of the railroad and keep the traffic clear, or whether we would stand back and let those gentlemen cut each other's throats" while they damaged American and world interests. "I had no hesitation as to the proper course to take, and have had no doubt of the propriety of it since." To Yale historian George W. Fisher, Hay wrote that if the president had not acted quickly on November 3, the result would have been "an indefinite duration of bloodshed and devastation" across the Isthmus. Speaking at the fiftieth anniversary of the Republican Party in Jackson, Michigan, the secretary asserted in July 1904 that Roosevelt "forged as perfect a bit of honest statecraft as this generation has seen."[89]

Almost a decade later, Bunau-Varilla publicly defended Roosevelt against the charge of collusion with the Panamanian insurgents. The revolution "was not born from a conspiracy fomented by the American authorities," he asserted in his newly published book in 1914. "Mr. Roosevelt avoided, during the first revolutionary attempts, anything which could resemble collusion." No one has proved the allegation "for the very simple but very powerful reason, that such collusion had never existed either directly or indirectly."[90] A year earlier, Roosevelt defended his Panama policy in his *Autobiography*. His actions, he asserted, were "straightforward and in absolute accord with the highest standards of international morality." To have done otherwise would have violated U.S. interests, shown "indifference" to the Panamanians, and ignored "our duty to the world" to build a canal. Colombia had "forfeited" its rights as a nation by engaging in "pure bandit morality." When the threat of revolution became clear, "I did not lift my finger to incite the revolutionists. . . . I simply ceased to stamp out the different revolutionary fuses that were already burning."[91]

⁕

On November 8, 1906, the president and the First Lady departed Norfolk, Virginia, on the USS *Louisiana*, accompanied by two other warships, to view the ongoing construction of the Panama Canal. While on board, Roosevelt befriended the captain, ate with the crew, shoveled coal, and wrote his son Kermit about how excited he was to see "how the ditch is getting along." About eight years earlier, he had sailed to Santiago, Cuba, to fight Spain. It seemed strange to see the same area while president, en route to examine progress on the Panama Canal, "which I have made possible."[92] As the three American war vessels made their way to Panama, Roosevelt thought the fourth day out the most memorable in seeing Cuba on the right and later that day Haiti on the left while thinking about the long history of European rivalry over these islands during the Age of Discovery, three centuries ago.[93] The president and his entourage arrived in Colón in the mid-afternoon of November 14. After the festivities that evening, he and Mrs. Roosevelt the next day boarded a slow-moving, four-car train across the Isthmus that allowed them to see the canal up close. At one stop, he mounted a mammoth steam shovel while in his white suit and Panama hat, sitting at its controls beside the engineer for almost a half hour while asking questions and perhaps imagining himself digging the canal. At another point, in a torrential rain and the danger of landslides, Roosevelt put on white overalls and rode a work train down the funnel-like walls deep into the Culebra Cut to see the drilling and digging firsthand. He also listened to workers' complaints before, by then wet and covered with mud, returning to the First Lady and other dignitaries on his train.[94]

Roosevelt delivered several addresses in Panama, all praising everyone working on the canal so highly that in one instance, he expressed a wish that one of his sons was involved in the project. In front of the Cathedral Plaza on November 15, he warned the Panamanian people to preserve order and freedom against revolutions that could destroy their republic. Roosevelt's lingering bouts with malaria, contracted during the war in Cuba, surely made him pleased with the progress of Surgeon Major William C. Gorgas of Alabama, who led the way in improving sanitary conditions in Panama and suppressing the mosquitoes responsible for malaria and yellow fever. He also expressed satisfaction with being the first sitting president to leave U.S. soil.[95]

As the three American battleships prepared to depart three days later, the president delivered a farewell address at Colón. He then paid a brief visit to Puerto Rico before returning home. While at sea, the president wrote Kermit a long letter expressing a deeper appreciation of the area because of his reading of history and the magnitude of this engineering feat and its global importance.[96]

In March 1907, Roosevelt appointed Lieutenant Colonel George Washington Goethals from the Army Corps of Engineers as the seventh and final chief engineer. Goethals guided the project to completion seven years later.[97]

On Manuel Amador Guerrero's death in May 1909, Bunau-Varilla set aside their differences to write a letter of tribute that he sent to José de Obaldia, complicit in the revolution and now president of Panama. Bunau-Varilla praised Amador's "decisive and courageous" role in liberating his homeland and making possible the "Union of the Oceans."[98]

Looking back on his presidency three years later, Roosevelt remarked to his personal aide that "when the history of this period is written down I believe my administration will be known at least as an administration of ideals."[99]

Chapter 4

Adventures in Statecraft—from Alaska to the Caribbean

Diplomacy is utterly useless where there is no force behind it; the
diplomat is the servant, not the master, of the soldier.

—Assistant Secretary of the Navy Theodore Roosevelt
June 2, 1897

Chronic wrongdoing . . . may in America, as elsewhere, ultimately
require intervention by some civilized nation, and in the Western
Hemisphere the adherence of the United States to the Monroe Doctrine
may force the United States . . . in flagrant cases of such wrongdoing or
impotence, to the exercise of an international police power.

—President Theodore Roosevelt
December 6, 1904

From the beginning of the Roosevelt presidency, the rush of events affecting
national security appeared to unfold as if scripted by the new administration.
The Panama Canal enhanced the commercial and strategic prospects of the
United States and raised the question of which nation would maintain the
security of the Western Hemisphere. Except for the distraction of a festering
boundary dispute over Alaska, the administration focused its "American"
attention on Latin America. A war scare with Germany in the Caribbean over
Venezuela, followed by troubles in Cuba and the Dominican Republic, led
to a White House attempt to resolve those issues with the Roosevelt Corollary to the Monroe Doctrine—a presidential pronouncement that the United
States was the chief guardian of the hemisphere against outside powers. The
Panama Canal would safeguard the United States, and the Roosevelt Corollary would guarantee the security of the canal and the rest of the hemisphere

from outside interference. It should come as no surprise that the president linked his regional peace efforts to his growing commitment to spreading republican principles of civilization to aggressor nations and troubled peoples around the globe.

I

Two years before the war with Spain broke out in April 1898, Theodore Roosevelt revealed his thoughts about the importance of the Monroe Doctrine to hemispheric safety when he told his sister Bamie that he wanted to "really interfere" in Cuba and push out the Spanish. To her husband, Lieutenant Commander William Cowles of the U.S. Navy and aide to President McKinley, Roosevelt explained that he felt "more strongly" about America's attitude toward the outside world than any other policy. The United States must have a strong coastal defense and a first-class navy to implement a "properly vigorous foreign policy." Freeing Cuba from Spain constituted the first step toward detaching all European nations from their colonies in the Western Hemisphere.[1]

Roosevelt gained a public platform for these sweeping ideas when he became assistant secretary of the navy in April 1897. Shortly afterward, he warned Captain Bowman McCalla that the American people must "wake up" to the necessity of a large navy. "I entirely agree with you that Germany is the Power with which we may very possibly have ultimately to come into hostile contact." Speaking at the Naval War College in early June, Roosevelt asserted that the United States faced no threat of invasion from either the north or the south; its enemies would come from either Europe or Asia—or both. U.S. security interests encompassed both the Atlantic and the Pacific and included Hawaii and the West Indies, along with both the East and West coasts of America. The United States required the military strength to uphold the Monroe Doctrine. It cannot bluff.[2]

Roosevelt's goal of a "formidable navy" included the capacity to take the offensive against a hostile nation. Gunboats and light cruisers were necessary; battleships were crucial. The U.S. Navy must have the means for fighting the enemy in American waters and at sea. "Diplomacy is utterly useless where there is no force behind it; the diplomat is the servant, not the master, of the soldier."[3]

In mid-August 1897, Roosevelt privately shared his concern that the most immediate threat to the United States and the Western Hemisphere was Germany. To Cecil Spring Rice, he admitted that from Germany's viewpoint, it had the right to pursue colonial objectives in the Western Hemisphere. The United States must maintain a navy large enough to discourage German efforts to acquire territory in the Americas. "If Germany intended to extend her empire here she would have to whip us first."[4]

Roosevelt emphasized that Americans welcomed the German people into the United States, but only as immigrants whose children would eventually become citizens. They did not dislike the Germans, he told Spring Rice, but regarded them with "humorous contempt." Roosevelt took Germany more seriously. A colonial move in this hemisphere did not appear imminent with Russia on Germany's flank and steadily increasing in power. Yet, the growing troubles between the United States and Spain over Cuba might provide the opportunity for Germany to spread its influence into the Caribbean.[5]

Roosevelt refused to take a chance. Not until the turn of the twentieth century did Germany have sufficient naval strength to threaten the Western Hemisphere.[6] Lacking this information, he nevertheless feared that Germany was poised to expand into Latin America and that now was the time to prepare against that danger. Suspicions of Germany he largely confined to private correspondence; publicly he called for a naval buildup to protect the Americas from outside powers.

In late 1897, as tensions with Spain escalated, Roosevelt wrote his close friend and outspoken imperialist senator from Massachusetts, Henry Cabot Lodge, that the United States must have a stronger navy before taking "firm action on behalf of the wretched Cubans." He also confided to John Hay, then ambassador in London, "I am a bit of a jingo" in hoping to remove Spain from Cuba before Congress meets. Military preparedness was vital in the event of a war. Verbal threats would not work. He emphasized his "horror of bluster which does not result in fight; it is both weak and undignified." To Lieutenant Commander William W. Kimball of the navy, Roosevelt declared that the United States must be willing to intervene in these events before other nations got involved. *"Germany is the power with whom I look forward to serious difficulty."*[7]

By late December, Roosevelt privately advocated what he called a "perfectly consistent foreign policy" based on the principle that no European power should be in the Americas, an expanse he defined as North and South America and the surrounding islands in both the Atlantic and the Pacific. The United States, he wrote William Chandler, former navy secretary and now Republican senator from New Hampshire, must either acquire all these areas or put them under its protection. "With this end in view I should take every opportunity to oust each European power in turn from this continent, and to acquire for ourselves every military coin of vantage; and I would treat as cause for war" he continued, "any effort by a European power to get so much as a fresh foothold of any kind on American soil."[8]

On the eve of war with Spain, Roosevelt again privately expressed his opposition to the presence of Britain or any European power in the Western

Hemisphere, but he still considered Germany "by far the most hostile" to the United States. He denied an innate hostility to any particular country outside the hemisphere. "I am simply an American first and last, and therefore hostile to any power which wrongs us. If Germany wronged us I would fight Germany; if England, I would fight England."[9]

To another confidant, Roosevelt explained that he opposed both entangling alliances and "entangling antipathies." Only the Russians had been consistently friendly, although he dismissed their oft-expressed sentiments as insincere and emanating from their need for an ally against enemies in Europe and Asia. U.S. foreign policy must stand on its own. "Nothing is worse for a country than to shape its policy with the desire of either gratifying or irritating another country, the latter quite as much as the former." The United States should side with or against any foreign power based solely on what was good for America. At this time, Germany posed the greatest potential challenge to the Monroe Doctrine.[10]

After the U.S. victory over Spain in mid-August 1898, the two governments negotiated a peace settlement that solidified America's claim to world power status. In February 1899, after a little more than two months of negotiations, Spain signed the Treaty of Paris in which it assumed Cuba's debt and, for $20 million from the United States, relinquished "all claim" to Cuba, along with the Philippines, Guam, Puerto Rico, "and other islands now under Spanish sovereignty in the West Indies" (Culebra and islands near Puerto Rico along with the Isle of Pines below Cuba).[11]

In the late summer of 1898, Roosevelt returned home from Cuba a war hero, soaking up the accolades while remaining wary of Germany's intentions in the postwar era. He won the election that year as governor of New York, where he became a new leader in the Republican Party while privately continuing his warnings against German interests in the hemisphere. His friend for nearly a decade, diplomat Hermann Speck von Sternburg, was soon returning to Germany where, Roosevelt wrote Lodge in late 1899, "I wish to Heavens he would instill a little common sense into the Kaiser!" Knowing the German emperor loved flattery, Roosevelt sent a note to Sternburg praising his country's leader as "a King in deed as well as in name"—a "fit successor to the Ottos, the Henrys, and the Fredericks of the past."[12] Roosevelt expected him to share this note with the kaiser.

By early 1900, Roosevelt intensified his call for a naval buildup as the best counter to the possible German threat. He told the architect of the war plan with Spain, Lieutenant Commander Kimball of naval intelligence, that he had always regarded Germany as America's "most probable serious opponent." The war with Spain constituted "a warning" that if the United States did not build a bigger navy and army along with stronger forts, it would have "a terrible time against Germany." To his brother-in-law, Lieutenant Commander

Cowles, Roosevelt warned that without a larger fleet, the United States could face a "disastrous war" against Germany or some other power in this hemisphere. The "one unpardonable sin is to bluff," Roosevelt told Elihu Root, then secretary of war. To uphold the Monroe Doctrine, Americans must be ready to fight.[13]

By the summer of 1901, Roosevelt had become vice president and held a stronger position to caution Germany against territorial ambitions in this hemisphere. In his home at Oyster Bay, Roosevelt assured his close acquaintance, the German consul general for New York, Karl Bünz, of his determination to remain on good terms with Germany. He added that he was open to Germans making commercial inroads into South America as long as the United States received equal treatment. But commercial ties must not develop into territorial acquisitions. In words he repeated in a letter to Lodge, no European power "should gain a foot of soil in any shape or way in South America, or establish a protectorate under any disguise over any South American country." To Sternburg, a guest at Sagamore Hill a month later, Roosevelt declared: "If any South-American [*sic*] country misbehaves toward any European country, let the European country spank it."[14]

As president following McKinley's assassination in September 1901, Roosevelt intensified his emphasis on the territorial sanctity of the hemisphere. In his First Annual Message to Congress in early December, he declared the Monroe Doctrine the "cardinal feature" of all North and South American nations—"no territorial aggrandizement by any non-American power at the expense of any American power on American soil." As for commercial matters relating to an American republic, "We do not guarantee any State against punishment if it misconducts itself, provided that punishment does not take the form of the acquisition of territory by any non-American power."[15]

Roosevelt's concern was justified: Germany did not recognize a proprietary right of the United States to control the Caribbean and all points south. Berlin's leaders wanted to expand commerce and finance in Latin America, which could also provide choice spots for naval stations that included southern Brazil (home to 300,000 Germans), the Galápagos, the Virgin Islands, and the West Indies. These ambitions might also include raising European funds to build a canal across Panama. The president could not have known that German strategists were developing a war plan aimed at the United States. The German fleet would lie in wait in the Azores off Portugal and, at the first sign of trouble in the Caribbean, head south and take Puerto Rico as the prelude to a series of attacks on America's east coast. Among the areas hit would be Gardiners Bay on Long Island, where enemy troops would pass by Roosevelt's home at Oyster Bay as they advanced on New York City.[16]

Three months into his presidency, Roosevelt faced the first German threat to the Monroe Doctrine. On December 11, 1901, the German Imperial

Embassy in Washington notified the White House that debt problems with Venezuela had forced Berlin's leaders to take remedial action. The civil wars in Venezuela from 1898 through 1900 had hurt German merchants and landowners, yet Caracas refused to meet its debt (and reparations) obligations. If Venezuela continued to reject these claims, Germany would consider "what measures of coercion should be used." But "under no circumstances" would it pursue "the acquisition or the permanent occupation of Venezuelan territory." After issuing an ultimatum, the German navy intended to blockade the chief sources of income in Venezuela—its two major harbors of La Guaira and Puerto Cabello—and seek compensation from customs duties. If this step was not effective, Germany would contemplate the "temporary occupation" of other Venezuelan harbors as well.[17]

Less than a week later, John Hay, as secretary of state, cited historical precedent in responding to the interventionist threat with a statement of the U.S. position similar to that expressed by the president. Four decades earlier, during the American Civil War, Emperor Napoleon III of France in 1861 engaged in a tripartite intervention with England and Spain to use force in collecting debts from Mexico. Secretary of State William H. Seward allowed that European nations could use force to collect debts in the hemisphere but must not endanger republicanism by demanding territorial compensation. Seward knew that ordering the three countries out of the hemisphere would have been a toothless threat: The Union was at war with the Confederacy, and he had no choice but to acquiesce. To save face, and perhaps to lay the basis for a later reckoning, he stipulated that none of the intervening countries should attempt to acquire territory.[18]

President Roosevelt praised Germany's assurance against territorial ambitions—surely realizing that Hay's response, though consistent with past policy, had virtually invited a foreign power to forcefully settle a debt by intervening in the domestic affairs of an American republic. But the president now recognized a greater danger—that Germany might join Britain and other nations in collecting debts from Venezuela. Once the powers put this process in motion, who could stop them from occupying or acquiring territory? Like Seward, Roosevelt knew that a warning against outside intervention in the hemisphere would be a bluff.

Less than a week before Christmas Day of 1901, the German embassy informed Hay that its navy planned to blockade Venezuelan harbors without declaring war. This was an unorthodox approach in that international law considered a blockade an act of war. Germany insisted on calling it a "peace blockade" that followed the examples set in the past by England and France: no confiscation of goods from neutral vessels if they respect the blockade by turning away from the area.[19]

President Roosevelt feared trouble from the presence of German warships and directed Ambassador Andrew Dickson White in Berlin to inquire into the possibility of Sternburg returning to Washington "if agreeable" to the kaiser. Sternburg had come to the United States as a military attaché and later as the first secretary of the German embassy, where he worked with Roosevelt in resolving a number of issues. Perhaps, the president surmised, they could sit down as friends and settle this one too.[20]

The kaiser, replied White, knew of the president's fondness for Sternburg. "Yes, I know that," Wilhelm had declared, "and I am very glad of it." But the kaiser abruptly changed the subject. White saw no reason to bring it up again. He was aware of the kaiser's regard for Ambassador Theodor von Holleben in Washington, and he had also heard talk that Sternburg was "rather too prone to take the American view" on issues between Germany and the United States.[21]

Over the next few months, tensions rose as Germany and Venezuela failed to reach an agreement on the debt issue. In a memorandum to the president, Rear Admiral Henry C. Taylor warned in the fall of 1902 that Germany's navy would shell Venezuela if its president, Cipriano Castro, opposed a blockade. Germany would demand an indemnity to defray the costs of the blockade, but Venezuela had no money and could either offer payment in property or relinquish control of its customs offices and thereby become a political appendage of Germany. According to Taylor, the United States could be faced with the choice of covering the indemnity or going to war.[22]

The president acted quickly. On November 21, 1902, four American battleships of the North Atlantic Fleet arrived off Puerto Rico, where they joined four cruisers and two gunboats of the Caribbean squadron. Other U.S. warships within the hemisphere also converged on the area. A week later, the German navy took the first step toward establishing a blockade of Venezuela. According to the semi-official Wolff Telegraphic Bureau, three small cruisers left for Venezuela to join six German ships already in South American waters.[23]

Roosevelt's earlier concerns about a joint intervention became real when Britain and other nations followed Germany's lead in pursuing debtor claims against Venezuela. The day after Germany enlarged its naval presence off Venezuela, Washington instructed its minister in Caracas, Herbert Bowen, to make the good offices of the United States available to Britain in the event of its withdrawal from legation headquarters. Two days later, on December 1, Bowen received instructions to extend a similar offer to Germany if it broke diplomatic relations with Venezuela. The next day, Bowen asked Washington for authorization to use his good offices to prevent a diplomatic break between Germany and Venezuela and to explore the possibility of an arbitration settlement of British claims.[24]

Roosevelt could not have known that both Britain and Germany had attempted to avoid alienating the United States by giving up any thought at this juncture of seizing the customs houses as a means for extracting payments from Venezuela. Britain's economic interests in Latin America would suffer from angering the Roosevelt administration, and Germany realized a blockade required more forces than were available. Doubtless, both countries also worried that the possible seizure of customs houses might skirt too closely to taking territory. Years afterward, research in the German and British records revealed no scheme, either individual or joint, to acquire territory in the hemisphere.[25]

Not privy to this archival information, of course, Roosevelt perceived a growing danger and instructed his secretary of state to act. Hay telegrammed the president's longtime friend and chargé in London, Henry White, saying that the White House wanted Germany and Britain to settle the Venezuelan debt issue and would assume no responsibility for any liabilities resulting from the transaction.[26]

The implicit U.S. warning did not slow the progression of events toward a blockade.

II

At 3:00 p.m. on December 7, 1902, the *Times* of London reported, the British and German governments presented ultimatums (identical in form though not in demands) to Venezuela, warning that failure to comply with their claims would lead to "joint military action."[27]

Almost two years earlier, on January 24, 1901, the German ultimatum explained, the Caracas government decreed that a Venezuelan commission would make the final decision on all claims. But the decree, argued Berlin's leaders, ignored claims made prior to Castro's taking control of the presidency in 1899. His regime dismissed diplomatic protests over the pre-Castro period and authorized compensation for only those debts amassed during his regime, with the payments based on the bonds of a new revolutionary loan—which were worthless.[28]

Despite similar claims from the United States, Britain, Italy, Spain, and the Netherlands, Venezuela insisted that foreign creditors receive the same treatment accorded its subjects, defining this as a domestic matter that made outside intervention a violation of the nation's sovereignty. Castro told one news source in Caracas, the *Agencia Pumar*, that he was confident no country having friendly relations with Venezuela would set up a blockade when the issue falls "within the jurisdiction of our laws" and "our justice principles."[29]

Germany accused Venezuela of violating the law of nations by asserting that municipal law prohibited diplomatic interventions. Previous experience showed that continued negotiations would not lead to a settlement. Germany and Britain would therefore cooperate in blockading Venezuela's ports at Maracaibo, Puerto Cabello, La Guaira, and other harbors.[30]

Public opposition in Venezuela to the German and British ultimatums became so threatening that on December 8 the ministers from both countries fled to safety aboard their nations' warships. That same day, Castro announced through the press that his government would make no payments to any nation until the end of the Civil War.[31]

Behind the scenes, President Roosevelt prepared for a conflict with Germany and perhaps Britain. When the representatives of both powers withdrew from their respective legations, breaking diplomatic relations with Caracas, he put Admiral George Dewey in command of the gunboat *Mayflower* and ordered him to move the battle fleet to the Caribbean "in case of sudden war." The legendary hero of the Battle of Manila Bay in 1898 had destroyed the Spanish fleet and, if he could have gotten approval, would have done the same to the German fleet lingering nearby. He now headed the largest American naval force ever assembled at sea—fifty-three warships, including battleships, cruisers, and torpedo boats—and all against what eventually became a combined force of twenty-nine German, British, and Italian smaller craft.[32]

The president immediately warned Ambassador Holleben against acquiring any part of Venezuela or the Caribbean. Roosevelt later wrote to Henry White in England—with "extreme emphasis"—that he had told Holleben to inform the kaiser that he "had put Dewey in charge of our fleet to maneuver in West Indian waters; that the world at large should know this merely as a maneuver, and we should strive in every way to appear simply as co-operating with the Germans; but," he continued, "I regretted to say that the popular feeling was such that I should be obliged to interfere, by force if necessary, if the Germans took any action which looked like the acquisition of territory in Venezuela or elsewhere along the Caribbean." Berlin had ten days to respond. If it did not meet the deadline, he would order Dewey south "to observe matters along Venezuela."[33]

The German ambassador failed to grasp the serious nature of the president's warning and assured him that Germany had no intention of seizing territory on a "permanent" basis. Was this an implied warning from Germany that its government deemed a "temporary" seizure as acceptable? If so, the ambassador knew this claim would further provoke Roosevelt. Yet, Holleben did not transmit an account of this meeting to Berlin for fear of looking like a fool—again. The kaiser may have been a friend, but he had earlier ridiculed his ambassador's concern over anti-German sentiment in the United States.

"We will do whatever is necessary for our navy," he told Holleben, "even if it displeases the Yankees. Never fear!"[34]

Holleben had avoided appearing to be an alarmist. But what if the president was not bluffing? The ambassador braved a snowstorm to make an overnight visit to Manhattan to confer with Karl Bünz. The president, Bünz assured Holleben, was "not bluffing." You "could count on his doing as threatened." Furthermore, Bünz continued, discussions with Roosevelt had revealed the president's "intimate knowledge of the strength and condition of the German fleet," which was spread out and in no position to challenge the U.S. Navy.[35]

For the first time, the German ambassador seemed to comprehend the strong suspicions—even resentment—Americans had of Germany's intentions in the New World. But inexplicably he still did not alert his superiors in Berlin of any problems with the United States, leaving them feeling free to resolve the debt problem with Venezuela by any means short of a permanent seizure of territory.[36]

As the popular protests mounted against the ultimatums, Castro expressed interest in an arbitration settlement and asked Bowen (who had earlier made this suggestion to Hay) to represent Venezuela in the proceedings. But that move came the same day coercive measures began. On December 9, naval vessels from both Germany and Britain escorted six Venezuelan ships to Curacao, placed a seventh in dry-dock in Puerto Cabello, and captured two more. Only one ship escaped. In the midst of growing tension, a British naval captain responded to a perceived "insult" at Puerto Cabello by bombarding the coast. A German cruiser joined the assault, which inflicted extensive damage to two forts.[37]

The seizures of Venezuelan warships in the harbor of La Guaira raised a public outcry that endangered the German consul. To protect him, the commander of the German gunboat *Panther,* then escorting two Venezuelan gunboats to Curacao, received orders to sink the vessels and return to La Guaira. Venezuelan authorities retaliated the following day by rounding up British and German nationals and putting them in jail.[38]

That same day, December 10, Hay authorized Bowen to serve as arbiter for Venezuela if that government proposed arbitration and Britain and Germany agreed. The Venezuelan minister of foreign affairs, R. Lopez Baralt, called for arbitration and Bowen agreed to head the process.[39]

As matters continued to deteriorate, the State Department informed the British government that the United States regarded Germany's so-called pacific blockade as a violation of the rights of neutrals and other nations. The Imperial German Embassy had admitted a year earlier that a blockade "would touch likewise the ships of neutral powers." It now offered assurances that its policy would not lead to confiscations, while ignoring the certain negative impact on neutral trade by insisting that neutral vessels "would have to be turned away and prohibited until the blockade should be raised." The United States warned that, in accord with its position on the blockade of Crete in 1897, it opposed "any extension of the doctrine of pacific blockade" that might "adversely affect the right of states not parties to the controversy, or discriminate against the commerce of neutral nations." This stand included any issue affecting U.S. commercial interests.[40]

German leaders in Berlin soon realized they could not trust the reports of the American situation coming from either their ambassador in Washington, Holleben, or their chargé in Washington, Albert von Quadt. Neither diplomat had reported the rage in America caused by Germany's sinking of Venezuelan ships on December 9. Three days later, Holleben cabled Berlin that the president just moments earlier had expressed admiration for the German navy.[41]

Holleben's assessment contradicted what his superiors in Berlin had learned from Sternburg on December 10 after his return from a visit with Roosevelt. Chancellor Bernhard von Bülow and State Secretary Oswald von Richthofen wanted to know how bad the situation was in the United States. What would his friend in the White House do? "Nothing could have pleased me more," Sternburg wrote Roosevelt, "because it gave me a chance to tell them the truth. I've told them every bit of it and I have used rather plain talk. . . . Fear I've knocked them down rather roughly, but should consider myself a cowardly weakling if I had let things stand as they were."[42]

Bülow told the kaiser that Germany's actions in the Caribbean had led to press attacks in both the United States and Britain. German ambassador Paul von Metternich in London warned his superiors in Berlin that the navy's actions in Venezuela had alienated several countries. Holleben did not cable Berlin about the intense American press and public hostility toward Germany until December 13—*five days* after receiving Roosevelt's warning. The German government tried to blame the British, explaining to Washington that it had originally proposed a pacific blockade, but they insisted on a "warlike blockade." Germany assured the United States that neither power intended "to take any hostile step beyond the declaration of a warlike blockade."[43]

Hay must have thought this delusional. Blockades often led to violence and perhaps an invasion. In present conditions, any incident, whether or not accidental, could elevate trouble into crisis. He instructed his ambassador in Germany, Charlemagne Tower, Jr., to "discreetly" inquire into the meaning of a "warlike blockade without war" and its potential impact on neutrals. Propose arbitration, which, he told Tower, Venezuela favored. That same day, the secretary of state directed White in London to find out whether the report from Germany was accurate—that the British insisted on a warlike blockade. Hay likewise told White to recommend arbitration as a solution to the debt problem.[44]

The prognosis in London remained dire. The British foreign secretary, Lord Lansdowne, told the House of Lords on December 16 that "further measures of coercion will no doubt be inevitable" and that the British navy would join the German navy in a blockade. Like Germany, he emphasized, the British ministry had no plans to send a land force or occupy Venezuelan soil. On the day of Lansdowne's remarks, Italian ships arrived off the Venezuelan coast to add their presence to the blockade.[45]

In response to Hay's directive, White learned from Lansdowne that Germany had tried to draw a distinction between a pacific blockade and a warlike blockade because the latter action required legislative approval by the Reichstag. The British rejected this idea, insisting there was no such thing as a pacific blockade. The British had always considered a blockade to be an act of war and "the only form of blockade admissible."[46]

White was a friend of the British prime minister, Arthur Balfour, and convinced him that working with Germany would alienate Americans. In the House of Commons on December 17, Balfour declared that the British government agreed with the United States that "there can be no such thing as a pacific blockade" and that "evidently a blockade does involve a state of war." From the floor came the question, "Has war been declared?" Balfour was incredulous. "Does the honorable and learned gentleman suppose that without a state of war you can take the ships of another power and blockade its ports?" According to White, the British cabinet that same day "gladly" accepted the principle of arbitration and agreed to ask President Roosevelt to be arbiter.[47]

The White House urged the Germans to accept arbitration—now supported by the British and Venezuelans. On December 16, Holleben again cabled Berlin, attesting to American press hostility toward Germany and warning of the impact of a conflict on Atlantic commerce and Latin America. Rumors suggested that the British might turn from Germany and ally with the United States. Holleben concluded that "now the cannons have spoken, and Germany has shown the world it is willing to assert its fair rights, we would make a good impression on all Americans if our government were to accept arbitration in principle."[48]

The next day, the Reichstag secretly and hurriedly accepted arbitration.[49]

These movements toward arbitration were not publicly known and appeared to have come too late. On December 18, the press reported that the secretary of the navy, William H. Moody, had confirmed that Dewey's fleet would spend the Christmas holidays off the coast of Venezuela at Trinidad, raising widespread alarm that the White House was preparing for war. Minutes after reading the story, Quadt rushed to Hay's office for an explanation. The secretary of state assured the German chargé that Roosevelt trusted Germany, but he added that Congress and the American people did not. They called for a congressional resolution demanding that the administration protect the Monroe Doctrine. Hay urged Quadt to persuade his Foreign Office in Berlin to agree to arbitration. Almost as they spoke, the House of Representatives passed the resolution.[50]

The next day, Germany announced acceptance of arbitration, joining the British who had accepted the day before. Both powers hoped that Roosevelt would serve as arbiter.[51]

In the meantime, however, both Britain and Germany proclaimed a blockade to be in effect on December 20 until arrangements were in place for arbitration. According to the *London Gazette,* the British blockade encompassed La Guaira and eastern ports. Germany installed a blockade of Puerto Cabello, soon followed by the closure of Maracaibo on Christmas Eve.[52]

Two days after the blockade began, White followed Roosevelt's instructions to "discreetly and unofficially" inform the British of his preference that the arbitration case go before the International Court of Justice (World Court) at The Hague in the Netherlands.[53]

Roosevelt was tempted to accept the British and German invitation to head an arbitration, but he turned it down. Perhaps part of his reasoning was Hay's insistence that this step would be improper because the United States also had claims against Venezuela; but in declining to serve as arbiter, Roosevelt acted in keeping with his long-held views on arbitration. The major powers, he explained to Hay, had created The Hague to handle issues that did not involve national honor, foreign policy, or cession of territory.[54]

To his friend Albert Shaw, editor of the *Review of Reviews*, Roosevelt explained that he did not support arbitration of matters involving an "acquisition of territory" because those fell within the national interests guaranteed by the Monroe Doctrine. He also emphasized this point to former President Grover Cleveland, who in 1895 had faced boundary problems with the British relating to Venezuela. British and German acceptance of arbitration by The Hague, he assured Cleveland, meant that the issue did not relate to territorial exchanges. Roosevelt explained in a note to Republican senator Coe Isaac Crawford of South Dakota that an arbitration treaty "would be a lie if it made us guarantee to arbitrate questions of vital national interests and honor." And to Arthur Lee, a member of Parliament, Roosevelt asserted that no nation could arbitrate its "honor, independence and vital national interest."[55]

III

Roosevelt's stand on arbitration was consistent with his views toward the ongoing Alaskan boundary dispute, a contentious issue roused by the discovery of gold in the Yukon region of northwest Canada in 1896 that triggered the Klondike Gold Rush. Bringing definition to the historically ill-defined border suddenly became a matter of urgency. The dilemma was simple—if the line that had been established by the Anglo-Russian Treaty of 1825 and assumed by the United States in the Alaska purchase four decades later remained in place, Canada would have no access from the sea to the gold.[56]

In 1898, exploiting cartographic vagaries in the 1825 treaty, Canadian officials advanced the argument that the treaty negotiators *had intended* the boundary along the Alaska panhandle to track a more direct route south rather than one approximately thirty miles inland that traced the contours of the coastline as previously accepted and as reflected in subsequent maps of the region. In June, they acted on this idea to lay claim to the panhandle's Lynn Canal, the head of which held three critical ports—Pyramid, Dyea, and Skagway, gateways to the gold fields. Knowing this departure from the decades-long understanding of the boundary would threaten U.S. commercial interests in the Alaskan interior, Canadians offered to negotiate, but *only* after Washington accepted their claim to Pyramid Harbor. "It's as if," Hay famously chided, "a kidnapper stealing one of your children, should say that his conduct was more than fair, it was even generous, because he left you two." The secretary of state felt the matter should be left to a joint commission representing the interests of all parties, but his proposal gained no traction at the time. Apart from President McKinley's acceptance of a Hay-proffered *modus vivendi* (temporary agreement pending final settlement) in fall 1899 granting Canada temporary access to land on the Lynn Canal, no further action was taken until Roosevelt became president.[57]

As president, Roosevelt's first inclination was to keep the McKinley *modus vivendi* in place and, as he suggested to U.S. ambassador to Britain Joseph Choate in January 1902, to "let sleeping dogs lie." Within three months, however, the president grew concerned that tensions among the rowdies in the disputed territory could easily spark violence, especially if gold was discovered there. The boundary must be pacified if not resolved. To George Smalley at the London *Times,* Roosevelt suggested in early March that he would "send up engineers to run our line as we assert it" and follow with "troops to guard and hold it." When Smalley described this move as "very drastic," the president retorted, "I mean it to be drastic." At the end of the month, Roosevelt instructed Root to send troops to the disputed area, but did so, at Hay's urging (and to his relief), "very quietly." But by May, he left no doubt of his growing agitation on the matter, volunteering to the British chargé in Washington that he was "going to get ugly" over the Alaska issue. Clearly, Roosevelt's shallow pool of patience was beginning to drain.[58]

Then, in June 1902, Canadian prime minister Sir Wilfrid Laurier suggested revisiting Hay's commission proposal to Henry White in London. Laurier wanted the issue settled, White noted, to "save his face," and he volunteered that the United States would likely receive a favorable outcome regardless of the verdict. If the ruling substantiated the U.S. position, "there would be an end to the whole business" and the prime minister would have "done his best." Even if the decision validated the Canadian argument, the American line should remain the same, and Canada would be satisfied to receive "compensation elsewhere, either in land or in money." But when Hay informed Roosevelt that the Canadians were willing to see the question "arbitrated," the president bristled, arguing that "the Canadian contention is an outrage pure and simple . . . . To pay them anything where they are entitled to nothing would in a case like this become dangerously near blackmail." The most he would consider was American participation in a commission predetermined to not "yield any territory whatsoever" and to "insist on our entire claim." My approach to the matter, Hay replied, "is precisely the same as yours." He pledged that his plan would not constitute an arbitral tribunal. The Canadians, he assured the president, "did not have a leg to stand on," a fact that "any impartial court of jurists would so decide." Hay conceded the hazards of "submitting such matter to an ordinary arbitration, the besetting sin of which is to split the difference;" but he was not suggesting arbitration. Instead, the six-man commission's charge would be to seek a majority opinion on "the question of the interpretation of the treaty of 1825." With an equal number of Americans on the commission, it would be impossible to lose, but entirely possible to gain.[59]

Roosevelt accepted Hay's proposal, and in January 1903—at precisely the moment Venezuela moved toward arbitration—the secretary of state joined British ambassador Sir Michael Herbert in producing a treaty calling for a commission of "impartial jurists of repute" to settle the boundary issue.

It seemed the dispute might now have a path to resolution, but inexplicably the term "arbitral tribunal" appeared in the final copy of the Hay-Herbert Treaty. Remembering his pledge to Roosevelt, Hay could not have been entirely surprised when the president pulled the treaty back from the Senate and insisted that the offensive word be taken out. The term arbitral, Roosevelt objected, was "a foolish misuse of words." He had not and would not agree to anything intimating arbitration on the matter. The word "arbitral" was stricken and the documents sent back to the Senate. Then the president, in a shrewd political maneuver, had Lodge discreetly inform wavering senators of his choices for the American commissioners, information that assured ratification. The *New York Times* celebrated the treaty as a "new pledge of the friendship of the two great English-speaking nations."[60]

Roosevelt stacked the tribunal, as he had promised key senators, with less-than "impartial jurists"—the president's friend and confidant, Lodge (whose rigid position was widely known); former senator George Turner of Washington (a state with a vested interest in securing the American claim); and the president's secretary of war, Elihu Root. There was little confidence that any of these "jurists" would, as stipulated in the treaty, "consider judicially the question submitted to them."[61]

Despite legitimate protests from the Canadians and the dismay of his own diplomats, Roosevelt had made his selections and would not be moved. Hay, while regretting the appointment of Lodge and to a lesser extent Turner, nevertheless knew that, given the Senate's inflexible position on the boundary and the anti-British mood engendered by London's Venezuelan adventure with Germany, this had been the only path to assure Senate approval of the treaty. It was true, as the *Brooklyn Eagle* sniped, that with this group, a favorable outcome for the Canadians was as likely as a snowstorm in hell; but it was equally true, as the *New York Times* admitted, that the choice of hardliners on the U.S. position was to be expected as "no American commissioner could possibly continue to reside in this country if he gave up a single title of the American claim."[62]

Opposite the American commissioners were two Canadians and Lord Alverstone, Lord Chief Justice of England, all three more closely reflecting the treaty profile. As would become evident long before they met for deliberations in London in the fall, the Canadian jurists were every bit as committed to their position as were the Americans to theirs. Thus, Lord Alverstone was the outlier and as such de facto arbiter of the boundary issues. If the vote went as Roosevelt hoped, the Canadians would vote their side, the Americans theirs, and Alverstone, appreciating the utility of preserving the Anglo-American rapprochement, would break the tie in favor of the American position.[63]

To assure this outcome, the president drew a red line for his representatives (those in residence in London and the commissioners en route) beyond which he would not go and directed them to clearly articulate this position to their counterparts, including (perhaps especially) Lord Alverstone. White made it clear to the Lord Chief Justice that Roosevelt had *only* consented to this remedy to provide Britain "a loophole to escape from an untenable position." In other words, the president had no intention of compromising the American claim. When, in the summer, the Canadians called for a delay, Lodge carried to London a letter from the president with a message to Alverstone, Colonial Secretary Joseph Chamberlain, and Balfour that approached an ultimatum. If the matter was prolonged, Roosevelt admonished, "I should ask Congress at its next meeting [November] to make an appropriation to enable me to run the line on our own theory." Lodge, likewise, conveyed the president's message through frequent social sidebars—dining with the prime minister and cabinet members, socializing with Alverstone and others in London, and reaching out by letter to Lansdowne and the King while they were away in Ireland. Choate kept communications moving through Whitehall to ensure that expectations for Alverstone were clear; and, when the Tribunal was seated in September, he hosted a dinner for all the commissioners, an opportunity seized by Lodge and Root to express the president's position informally to Alverstone.[64]

The president also worked other sources, using back channels to intimate a possible breach in the friendly relations enjoyed by Washington and London should the outcome not meet American expectations. Among those carrying his unofficial message was Associate Supreme Court Justice Oliver Wendell Holmes, whose presence in Britain Roosevelt exploited to reinforce the serious nature of the commission's charge. Holmes was directed to share a letter with Chamberlain that made clear that only the president's "intense desire to remain on good terms with England had induced him to allow such a matter to be the subject of discussion at all." But, he emphasized, should the deliberations "not result in a satisfactory agreement, he [Roosevelt] would appeal to Congress in such terms that he felt sure they would give him the appropriation for which he asked, and he would then take possession of the line to which the United States was clearly entitled." Roosevelt also solicited the leverage of Scottish-born American industrialist Andrew Carnegie, who wrote to Balfour that the Canadian position was "trumped up" and added that "nothing but disaster can follow an attempt to prefer Canada over the Republic."[65]

It was, perhaps, the forceful language of Hay in a letter to White toward the end of September that carried the most weight. "The president," Hay wrote White, "will make no further effort to settle the controversy" if this "experiment" fails. "He will hold the territory, as we have held it since 1867, and will emphasize the assertion of our sovereignty, in a way which cannot but be disagreeable to Canadian amour propre." This, Hay lamented, would mean "all the labor of the last few years, to bring about a closer friendship between the two governments will have gone for nothing." White, at Root's encouragement, shared Hay's sentiments with Balfour while on a planned visit to his home in early October. Not surprisingly, Alverstone was soon brought into the discussion and encouraged by his government to press for an amiable resolution.[66]

As it happened, the president's machinations may not have been entirely necessary. He was pushing on a door at least partially open. Alverstone had early decided that the Canadian case was flawed. He only required some minor concession to allow the Canadians, and more importantly the British, to withdraw with dignity intact. In his efforts to be evenhanded with his Canadian colleagues, however, he prolonged the suspense entirely too long for Roosevelt's temperament. Lodge reported to the president on October 12 that he had walked home with Alverstone after that day's session and found "him very set on having his selected summits and . . . creating a range which will narrow the strip," a demand to which, Lodge declared, "we cannot admit." The final terms would either be "our way" or impasse. When the commission adjourned abruptly at midday on the fourteenth, Choate hurried to the Foreign Office to remind Lansdowne that Roosevelt would not accept a hung jury. The president, Choate warned, had made it clear that "there would never be another opportunity" and that "in signing this [Hay-Herbert] Treaty" he "had gone as far as he could possibly go." This meeting was, the ambassador reiterated, "the last chance to settle the question." Not surprisingly, when the commission met again, Alverstone pulled Lodge aside "looking very anxious" and told him that "matters were reaching a crisis & something must be done." It *was* done—he yielded almost entirely to the American position.[67]

Roosevelt, in the end, agreed to forfeit to Canada all four islands in the Portland Channel and accept a slightly narrower strip of coastline, perhaps an indication of his willingness to pair his big stick with a modest face-saving carrot for London.[68] In late June he had told Lodge that "those little islands down at the mouth of the channel . . . are of negligible value." But, despite the president's acquiescence to Canada receiving all four islands, when the commission reconvened on October 17, Commissioner Turner recklessly insisted that the line be redrawn to leave two of the four islands to the United States. Alverstone, understanding the necessity of resolving the festering dispute, accepted.[69]

When the tribunal concluded its work in the third week of October 1903, America's ownership of an uninterrupted coastline on the Alaska panhandle was carried by a vote of four to two, as Roosevelt had hoped, with Alverstone voting with the Americans. "The Alaska and Panama settlements coming in one year," the president wrote White with satisfaction the following month, "make a very good showing, do they not? I shall get Cuban reciprocity through, too."[70]

Roosevelt had won a favorable settlement, not by arbitration, but by a joint commission—an outcome that did more than resolve a thorny boundary dispute; it demonstrated Britain's desire to salve ill feelings over the Venezuelan crisis and to strengthen Anglo-American relations.[71] In fact, Ambassador Herbert had earlier remarked in reference to Venezuela that "The time has almost come in American opinion for us to make the choice between the friendship of the United States and that of Germany."[72]

IV

When Herbert raised the question of "the choice" of friends in the first weeks of 1903, the Roosevelt administration's attention was a great distance south of the Alaska panhandle. Venezuelan president Castro in early January had agreed to pursue arbitration. Both Britain and Germany wanted a guarantee of payment; and Bowen declared that if Hay assured compensation from the customs houses, the two powers should end the blockade. The next day, Castro guaranteed compensation payments through the customs houses.[73]

In the midst of these negotiations, the blockade remained and, as Bowen feared, the situation worsened. On January 17, the German warship *Panther,* which had sunk two Venezuelan vessels, attempted to close a narrow passageway at Maracaibo on the northwest coast of Venezuela. Castro ordered his command at Fort San Carlos to fire on the ship to prevent its entrance. The *Panther* backed off but returned four days later with the *Falke* and caused worldwide revulsion by demolishing the fort with more than 100 shots that set the town on fire.[74]

On learning of this incident, Roosevelt stormed at Quadt, "Are people in Berlin crazy? Don't they know that they are inflaming public opinion more and more here? Don't they know they will be left alone without England?"[75]

Roosevelt's warning of a British break with Germany could not have been news to its leaders. In late December of 1902, Herbert had reported to London that Americans were infuriated with Germany. "The outburst in this country against the Germans has been truly remarkable, and suspicion of the German Emperor's designs in the Caribbean Sea is shared by the Administration, the press, and the public alike." The destruction of the fort, Herbert noted, had caused "intense irritation in the United States against Germany." Henry White wrote to Hay from London that Prime Minister Balfour was so upset with Germany that he and others were talking about terminating the arrangement with Germany and settling the matter on their own.[76]

In mid-February, 1903, Germany joined Britain and Italy in agreeing to lift the blockade.[77]

To prevent recurring crises over claims issues, Argentina's foreign minister, Dr. Luis Drago, had proposed prohibitions on the use of force or the occupation of property in collecting debts. Such measures, he warned, could lead to the "ruin of the weakest nations, and the absorption of their governments." In support of his argument, Drago quoted from the Monroe Doctrine, declaring that the "American continents" were no longer subject to European colonization and that any violation of that principle would constitute "the manifestation of an unfriendly disposition toward the United States."[78]

But neither the Argentine Congress nor the White House supported the so-called Drago Doctrine. Legislators in Argentina feared it would hurt commercial relations with Europe. Roosevelt considered the Monroe Doctrine sufficient to handle these issues. Hay assured Drago that the United States preferred an "impartial arbitral tribunal," where all nations were equal in "international law and mutual duty."[79]

Despite the peaceful resolution of the crisis with Germany, the president found it necessary to clarify the U.S. position on outside intervention in the hemisphere. His opportunity came in mid-March 1903, when Sternburg (ambassador to the United States in July after Holleben's removal) presented a proposal to Roosevelt that, to him, demonstrated Germany's continued failure to understand the U.S. position on the Western Hemisphere. Sternburg, likewise, failed to grasp the gravity of the issue. "Speck was in today," Roosevelt wrote Hay, "evidently inspired from Berlin, to propose for our consideration in the future the advisability of having the great Powers collectively stand back of some syndicate which should take possession of the finances of Venezuela." Such a measure, Sternburg argued, would decrease the chances for revolution in Venezuela by bringing order and prosperity and preventing future punitive expeditions by European nations attempting to collect debts. Roosevelt rejected the proposal, arguing that it "would pave the way for reducing Venezuela to a condition like that of Egypt, and that the American people interpreted the Monroe Doctrine as meaning of course that no European power should gain *control* of any American republic."[80]

Roosevelt considered this proposal a poorly disguised German attempt to undermine the Monroe Doctrine. He admitted to Hay that he often thought that "a sort of protectorate" over the "wretched republics" in South and Central America was the only way to keep peace. But Germany's debt collection arrangement could become a "subterfuge" for seizing territory on a permanent basis in Latin America. As early as the 1890s, Roosevelt maintained that the Monroe Doctrine sanctified freedom not only in the United States but throughout Western civilization. "If the Monroe Doctrine did not already exist it would be necessary to create it."[81]

In a series of arrangements reached in Washington in May 1903, Germany, Britain, and Italy lifted the blockade and agreed with the president (along with Venezuela) to take the matter to the Hague Tribunal for arbitration by a mixed commission. The British realized that cooperation with Germany had threatened to undermine their relations with the United States; the Germans recognized the primacy of the British navy and concluded that the Anglo-American friendship had wrongfully left the public impression of U.S. naval dominance in the Caribbean.[82]

Almost a year later, on February 22, 1904, the Hague Tribunal unanimously upheld the three powers' monetary claims and assigned them 30 percent of the customs revenues each month from Venezuela's two major ports of La Guaira and Puerto Cabello. The payments would go to the Bank of England until The Hague Court ruled on the amounts awarded to each claimant.[83]

Problems nonetheless persisted in Venezuela. Washington received numerous reports of "intimidation" and blackmail of British, Italian, U.S., and other foreign property owners by Castro's forces. Despite Bowen's protests, the situation in Venezuela deteriorated so badly that, according to the minister, Castro "will only yield to force." The Venezuelan dictator blocked the claims settlement awarded to his country's creditors, demanded that foreign businesses pay tribute or have their property confiscated, and seized an asphalt lake belonging to the New York and Bermudez Company, as well as the American company's superintendent. Castro's warning was clear: American property and perhaps lives were in danger.[84]

President Roosevelt was irate. In late August 1904, he told Hay that if Castro "misbehaves," the United States should seize the customs houses and ask the Belgians or other representatives of The Hague Court to run the business. Such a move would teach Castro "a sharp lesson" by showing "those Dagos that they will have to behave decently." Months later, the president was still angry. To Hay again he remarked that Castro was "an unspeakably villainous little monkey," who deserved military punishment. But the president realized that an intervention would not be advisable from either the domestic or foreign point of view.[85]

Roosevelt took Venezuela's behavior personally—that the beneficiaries of his policy did not appreciate or understand what he had done for them. If only they knew the behind-the-scenes maneuvering he had followed in preventing a war.

V

For more than a decade afterward, it remained unclear why Germany abruptly reversed course in December 1902 and accepted arbitration. Roosevelt was straightforward in his explanation: his verbal threat to use force.

Historians have long debated whether Roosevelt gave the kaiser an ultimatum. Skeptics have proclaimed that no documentary record remains in the archives of Germany, the United Kingdom, or the United States—the three principal powers involved in the Venezuelan crisis. But Roosevelt's defenders have insisted that the verbal nature of his warning explains this lack of written evidence. More than three-quarters of a century later, it became nearly certain that Roosevelt's account was accurate.[86]

According to historian Frederick W. Marks III, German, British, and American officials in the post–World War I era tried to hide evidence of a warning by destroying massive amounts of documents covering this critical period of 1902–1903. The Germans scrubbed the historical record because they needed foreign aid from Britain and the United States. The British sought to conceal Roosevelt's angry reaction to their involvement in the Venezuelan crisis in an effort to preserve good relations with the United States. And the United States deleted materials because of Roosevelt's efforts to save the reputation of the kaiser and prevent another crisis. The result, concurred Roosevelt biographer Edmund Morris, is that the full story has "to be inferred circumstantially, from an extraordinary void in the archives of three nations—deletion after deletion hinting at some vanished enormity, a painted-out battle of Titans visible in *pentimento* through layers of pale wash."[87]

Roosevelt was adept at clandestine actions, as shown by his Panamanian and Alaska machinations. His primary focus in all instances was to preserve U.S. security by averting war. In 1913, he wrote that he preferred "that kind of diplomacy which consists in not uttering one word that can be avoided." Not surprisingly, he worked well with John Hay, who, according to his close friend and editor of his published writings, Henry Adams, sought to "settle all questions, if possible, by word-of-mouth, and to write few papers." Quiet threats rather than public attacks characterized Roosevelt's diplomatic efforts to leave his antagonist with a face-saving way out of a confrontation that Secretary of the Navy William Moody called one of the most dangerous in his nation's history. The United States, Moody declared in a speech, was never in "greater peril than at the time of the Venezuelan difficulty. We had a battle fleet within reaching distance," but it "brought peace and not the sword."[88]

Another consideration was Roosevelt's propensity to act on his own, sometimes on the advice of unofficial "kitchen ambassadors," as he called them, or even covertly as the nation's chief diplomat. To Spring Rice in November 1905, the president explained that he had "quietly and unofficially, and with equal courtesy and emphasis," stressed to the kaiser "that the violation of the Monroe Doctrine by territorial aggrandizement on his part around the Caribbean meant war, not ultimately, but immediately, and without any delay." The kaiser "has always been as nice as possible to me since." In his letter of mid-1906 to the U.S. ambassador in London and longtime friend, Whitelaw Reid, Roosevelt argued that Germany's fear of American naval action convinced the kaiser to resolve the crisis. But, added the president, "I suppose we shall never make public the fact of the vital step."[89]

Roosevelt respected and liked the kaiser as "a good man" with an intense ego, he wrote Henry White in London; but he did not trust him and knew better than to offend him. While privately putting pressure on Germany to relent on the Venezuelan issue, he emphasized the Anglo-American friendship and attempted to build "a bridge of gold" that left the kaiser a way out of the crisis without marring his "dignity and reputation" in the world. Roosevelt hoped a "display of force" would convince him that the United States would intervene if Germany sought territory in either Venezuela or the Caribbean.[90]

"This was not in any way intended as a threat," Roosevelt claimed he insisted to the German ambassador, but it was "the position" that "the American people would demand." The kaiser must understand America's reasoning "before the two nations drifted into such a position that trouble might come."

Roosevelt urged the ambassador to assure the kaiser that the world would think the American fleet was there on maneuvers and cooperating with the Germans. But the president stated that he would use force if Congress and the American people suspected Germany of trying to acquire territory in the hemisphere.[91]

Three years later, Roosevelt told more of his story in an unusual setting. Soon after leaving the White House in March 1909, the former president booked passage to Africa. During the crossing, he discussed his tactics in resolving the war scare with Germany in a four-hour conversation with fellow passenger E. Alexander Powell, then a consular official in Syria and Egypt. In late 1902, Roosevelt asserted, "the United States was on the verge of war with Germany." Powell immediately wrote a letter to his wife, detailing the story and, years later in 1932, told it again in his book, *Yonder Lies Adventure.*[92]

In August 1916, Roosevelt revealed to historian William R. Thayer, then writing a biography of John Hay, how back-channel diplomacy led to an ultimatum that persuaded Germany to withdraw from Venezuela.

Roosevelt insisted that Germany was the leading party in this debtor grievance and that Britain only reluctantly went along. He felt certain that the British would not support Germany if it got into a conflict with the United States. Germany, he suspected, wanted to take control of a Venezuelan harbor and fortify it as the first step toward establishing its influence over an isthmian canal and South America itself. Roosevelt warned the German ambassador that if his government rejected arbitration, American public opinion would force him to move Admiral Dewey's ships from the West Indies to a spot close to Venezuela as a demonstration of U.S. opposition to Germany's seizing Venezuelan territory. Germany had opposed arbitration and Holleben would only say that any area occupied would be "temporary"—which, Roosevelt remarked, "might mean anything."[93]

As the debt issue continued to escalate, the president took stronger measures. He first secretly ordered Dewey to station the fleet close to Puerto Rico, ready to move into Venezuelan waters within an hour's notice. In a second meeting with Holleben in December 1902, Roosevelt warned that he "intended to bring matters to an early conclusion."[94]

The German navy's presence along the Venezuelan coast posed a threat to that country and the isthmian canal, Roosevelt emphasized to the ambassador, making it impossible to wait any longer for a German response to his request for arbitration. Holleben again stated that his government could not agree to arbitration and had no plans to take "permanent" possession of Venezuelan territory. Roosevelt reminded him that Germany had recently secured a ninety-nine year lease on Kiauchau, located on the southern coast of China. He "did not intend to have another Kiauchau, held by similar tenure, on the approach to the Isthmian Canal." When Holleben repeated his government's rejection of arbitration, the president replied with an ultimatum: If Germany did not agree to arbitration within ten days, he would order Dewey to lead his fleet to the Venezuelan coast, under orders to block the Germans from seizing territory.[95]

Holleben, according to Roosevelt, expressed "very grave concern" over the U.S. failure to recognize "the serious consequences" of such a move— "consequences so serious to both countries that he dreaded to give them a name." Roosevelt asserted that he had considered the costs of such action and showed the ambassador a map indicating that in no other place in the world would Germany have a "greater disadvantage" in a naval battle with the United States than in the Caribbean Sea.[96]

A week later, the ambassador discussed several issues with Roosevelt in his White House office before rising to leave. Roosevelt asked whether the German government had any response to his request for arbitration. Told no, Roosevelt asserted that the kaiser should know that he, as president, was "very definitely" warning of war. Holleben remarked that he did not like the language. With an attitude reminiscent of that applied to the Alaska issue, Roosevelt replied that "it was useless to wait as long as I had intended, and that Dewey would be ordered to sail twenty-four hours in advance of the time I had set." Holleben expressed concern but again said his government would not arbitrate. Neither the president's secretary, William Loeb, nor anyone in the State Department or German embassy made a record of the meeting, leaving Kaiser Wilhelm an opportunity to back down without losing face.[97]

As the clock ticked toward the deadline, Germany abruptly changed course and accepted arbitration. Less than twenty-four hours before the time originally set by Roosevelt for ordering Dewey to move the fleet, the German emperor sent a message to the president asking him to arbitrate the matter. Roosevelt expressed satisfaction with the decision but declined the request to serve as arbiter. As a counter, he secured Germany's agreement to have The Hague Tribunal conduct the arbitration.[98]

Is Roosevelt's story a fabrication—the product of his well-known skills in embellishment and imagination? This is hardly the case.

Strong contemporaneous support for Roosevelt's version of events came more than a decade after the crisis from Adolph W. Callisen, a former neighbor of Roosevelt's. At some point during the "Venezuelan affair," Callisen had learned from his friend, the German consul general in New York, Karl Bünz, of the actions of Holleben and could now confirm that the ambassador's actions were precisely as Roosevelt recalled. Further, Roosevelt had met Bünz through Callisen and found the consul general highly knowledgeable about American issues and world affairs. They had talked several times in Roosevelt's home about a variety of matters, including the comparative strengths of the German and American navies, with the president thinking the U.S. Navy superior.[99]

When Thayer's biography of Hay appeared in 1916, Callisen read the book—particularly the section on Venezuela—and wrote a friend that he knew both Holleben and Bünz and that Roosevelt's version of the crisis was accurate. The German and British governments counted on what they called the typical "jellyfish squashiness" by the United States and thought Roosevelt was bluffing. Holleben assured his government that Roosevelt would take no action but then reconsidered after asking Bünz for advice. Bünz had, in June 1902, asked Roosevelt for his views on America's relations with Germany, and in a reply the president knew would go to the kaiser, he warned: "No European nation, Germany or any other, should gain a foot of soil in any shape or way in South America, or establish a protectorate under any disguise over any South American country." Bünz assured the German ambassador that Roosevelt never bluffed. Holleben, according to Callisen, had "to eat his own words" and frantically telegraphed the news to Berlin, "where his message fell like a bomb shell."[100]

Roosevelt received a copy of Callisen's letter on May 7, 1916, and showed it to him, asking him to verify its contents. "The above is absolutely accurate," Callisen wrote on the letter before signing it. He had not intended that the letter go public, but several people knew about it, and he authorized Roosevelt to use it in any way he wanted.[101]

The German government had received at least two warnings from Roosevelt about what he would do, but it took both of them (and perhaps others) to convince the Germans that he would use force to defend the hemisphere. Berlin agreed to arbitration and called Holleben home, ostensibly for health reasons. To do otherwise would make it appear that Germany had buckled under U.S. pressure. When the ambassador left Hoboken, Bünz, who was joined in moral support by Callisen, was the only member of either the American or German diplomatic corps willing "to brave official disapproval" to see him off.[102]

Roosevelt provided further evidence for his actions when he responded to a letter in the press charging that his account was apocryphal because, according to the writer, Dewey did not mobilize the fleet at the time of the Venezuelan crisis. The writer had just read Thayer's new book on Hay and sent a letter to Henry Wood of the National Security League, who wrote to Dewey asking him about the matter. Dewey confirmed that he was at Culebra, Puerto Rico, when he received orders from Washington to have the fleet ready to move to the Venezuelan coast "at a moment's notice." He never took that step because the administration had resolved the matter. Dewey's letter appeared in the press, and Wood sent Roosevelt copies of all the correspondence.[103]

Less than a week later, Roosevelt told Thayer that "the really vital point" was the threat of deploying Dewey's fleet to Venezuela. Holleben's implied counter threat was a "bluff," Roosevelt maintained, "an interesting and amusing but subordinate incident." The "decisive factors," the president argued, were his "willingness and readiness" to use America's power while "speaking softly" in private discussions rather than "blustering" in public. As he explained to Thayer, "I did not suppose that there could be any corroberation [*sic*]" of his secret meeting with the German ambassador. "I took no notes, as far as I can remember, of what I did, at that moment. I was trying to achieve results, and never thought of the historical record."[104]

One of Roosevelt's maxims was to avoid embarrassing the kaiser. In about twenty-four hours during the Venezuelan crisis, he had to deal with this issue twice.

In late March 1903, Roosevelt warned Rear Admiral Taylor against "boasting, or saying anything that will hurt the feelings of powers with which we are at peace, and which I hope we will continue on terms of friendship." The United States must be "the most formidable of foes in the event of war, and at the same time . . . make it equally evident that no one need fear a war with us unless from his own fault."[105]

Admiral Dewey violated the president's maxim when he was quoted in the *New York Herald* in late March, exposing his show of force in the Caribbean as an "object lesson to the Kaiser." The German ambassador appeared at the White House, seeking an apology. Roosevelt sent for Dewey to upbraid his lack of judgment. But he cooled off when Dewey appeared.[106]

The president reminded the admiral that his reputation meant that whatever he said could go all over the world. He acknowledged that Dewey's words were not militant in tone, but he cautioned him against saying anything "that can be taken hold of by those anxious to foment trouble between ourselves and any foreign power, or who delight in giving the impression that as a nation we are walking about with a chip on our shoulder. We are too big a people to be able to be careless in what we say."[107]

"Admiral, this is embarrassing," said the president. "You will have to deny the interview."

"Deny it, Mr. President! I said it. I didn't know that fellow who came up to me when I was out walking was going to publish it. The last time I met him he was a consul. I told him what I thought—and he sold it to a newspaper. I said it. I cannot deny what I said. I won't lie."

"Then, Admiral, the only way out is for me to give you a public reprimand."

"Yes, sir. When, sir?"

"Tomorrow," the president replied.

At the appointed time, Dewey later told American journalist and war correspondent Frederick Palmer, "I put on full dress, all the dog, all the medals I had, for the ceremony. The President grinned when I appeared before him, tapped me on the wrist, and said: 'Admiral, consider yourself reprimanded.' Then we had a nice little chat."[108]

One of the strongest critics of Roosevelt's Venezuelan diplomacy is historian Nancy Mitchell, who insists that Germany was making no preparations for war with America and attributes the president's concern over German intervention in the hemisphere to "circumstantial evidence" and "a potent mix of German bombast and American paranoia," all fed by the kaiser's "provocative rhetoric." German and British cooperation in the blockade, Mitchell argues, was "the height of the German challenge." Germany agreed to arbitration only when it realized that intervention would cost more than it would gain.[109]

Whether the alleged threat from Germany was real is not the issue; Roosevelt acted on the best sources of information available to him in perceiving the Germans as ready to violate the Monroe Doctrine. German ambassador Holleben did nothing to allay Roosevelt's fear that Germany would expand any temporary involvement in South America to a much longer stay, as it had earlier done in China.[110]

Throughout the German crisis, Roosevelt made it clear that he would resort to force if necessary. Germany's leaders may have at first doubted his willingness to defend the hemisphere against outside involvement, but they soon realized he was not a novice in warfare and did not bluff. He would use force if Germany's actions threatened the security of an American state, which, by extension, endangered the United States and other nations in the hemisphere.

Roosevelt had tempered the bluster and jingoism of his earlier years by an artful diplomacy that equated the effectiveness of an implicit threat with that of a direct threat, and then allowed Germany to retreat from a confrontation without losing face.

VI

As the Venezuelan crisis wound down in May 1903, Roosevelt's suspicions of Germany melded with American concerns over Cuba and the Dominican Republic in the Caribbean, providing him with the opportunity to issue a public policy statement justifying U.S. efforts to protect the Western Hemisphere from the Old World.

Nearly half of the Paris negotiations following the Spanish-American War had focused on Cuba, which posed a major security issue for the United States. If Cuba were free and independent, it would be vulnerable to European exploitation. The United States could not annex the island without violating the prewar Teller Amendment enacted by Congress on April 20, 1898, which sought to assuage the anti-imperialists by promising against annexation as a result of the war.[111] In actuality, many proponents of the bill had other motives in mind. American sugar interests did not want the island's sugar competing against Louisiana sugar in the domestic market and preferred keeping the Cuban product outside the U.S. tariff wall. Others had racial objections to annexation, fiercely denouncing the prospect of Cuban senators in Washington. To demonstrate humanitarianism, some Americans wanted to assure Cuba's independence once it had a constitutional government. Even then, independence would come with a heavy price.

The McKinley administration tried to follow a middle position by approving a rider to the Army Appropriations Bill of 1901—the Platt Amendment of March 2, which provided quasi-independence to the island and made it a U.S. protectorate. The government in Havana was restricted from borrowing money beyond its capacity to repay and from negotiating a treaty or agreement with a foreign nation without U.S. approval. The United States reserved the right to intervene in domestic disturbances that endangered Cuba's independence by attracting outside powers; to maintain a government safeguarding the liberty of its people; and to assure that it met the obligations for the United States set by the Treaty of Paris and accepted by Cuba. To protect the island's independence—along with the security of the projected isthmian canal and the United States—Cuba's government would sell or lease to the United States in perpetuity the land required for coaling or naval stations. The Platt Amendment laid out a pattern of U.S. behavior aimed at keeping order on the island and in other republics in the hemisphere.[112]

The Platt Amendment proved highly controversial. Critics blasted America's policy toward Cuba as raw imperialism; defenders argued for corrective action when continued unrest so close to the United States endangered American economic and security interests as well as its citizens on the island. The issue became so heated that the president and Congress shied away from citing the Monroe Doctrine as justification for U.S. intervention in Cuba.[113]

The United States attempted to solidify its hold on Cuba by incorporating the Platt Amendment into a treaty and requiring the Cubans to insert its provisions into a new constitution to make them permanent. Despite popular opposition in Cuba, the Cuban Constitutional Convention in June 1901 added an appendix to its new constitution, which contained the Platt Amendment.[114]

That matter settled, and with Roosevelt president in September, the United States in February 1903 implemented one of the Platt Amendment's provisions by leasing two sites in Cuba for coaling and naval stations: Guantánamo Bay, which lay close to Santiago on the southeastern side of Cuba, and Bahia Honda, located near Havana in the north. According to the agreement, the United States recognized the "continuance of the ultimate sovereignty of the Republic of Cuba" over both areas, but it claimed "complete jurisdiction and control" over them during the occupation. The United States also had the right to acquire, under mutually determined conditions, "any land or other property therein by purchase or by exercise of eminent domain with full compensation to the owners thereof." Thus, U.S. military control over these areas would be perpetual. In the following December, the United States opened a naval base at Guantánamo Bay, its purpose, to safeguard Cuba's independence and American security from outside threats.[115]

Before the Cuban Congress, President Tomás Estrada Palma praised the warm relationship between their country and the United States and thanked its "illustrious president" for his assurance of a treaty of commercial reciprocity. On May 22, 1903, despite resistance in Havana, the United States and Cuba signed the Permanent Treaty, which included the Platt Amendment. In July, the two governments signed the lease agreement for the two naval sites. Cuba maintained sovereignty over the Island of Pines and the territory gained by the United States from "sale or lease" that, according to Palma, inflicted the "least wound" on "Cuban sentiment"; Cuba leased land to the United States for only two coaling or naval stations rather than the four sought by Washington; and the conditions regulating the lease were mostly favorable to Cuba. The following month, President Roosevelt kept his promise to Cuba by convening Congress to discuss a U.S.-Cuban reciprocity treaty.[116]

Violence had meanwhile erupted in another part of the Caribbean—an insurgency in Santo Domingo, the capital city of the Dominican Republic—that encouraged U.S. intervention to prevent the involvement of Germany and other foreign powers. The uprising also led to a major declaration of U.S. policy affecting the Western Hemisphere.

At 1:00 p.m. on March 23, 1903, trouble broke out in Santo Domingo, when, during siesta time, rebel forces freed and armed about seventy political prisoners in the city's fort. Within minutes, the escapees disarmed the small number of guards on duty and took control of the fortress. Rebel supporters then banded together and attacked the provisional government and its military authorities along with the police force; and after two hours of fighting resulting in numerous casualties, they seized control of the city. Various officials fled to the foreign legations for asylum, and the insurgents proclaimed General A. W. Gil provisional president.[117]

Peace lasted throughout the city for little more than a week when, on April 2, fighting broke out again. The insurgents seized two Dominican naval vessels; and the United States responded by sending the *Atlanta*, a warship under the command of Captain W. H. Turner, which arrived that same day. Captain Turner immediately dispatched a contingent of sailors to protect the U.S. Consulate and the "La Fé" estate, the latter located about four miles from the city and housing the office of the American mining and railroad companies—and where several officials (one with his wife) and engineers had fled.[118]

As the situation continued to unravel, Roosevelt's worst fears materialized. A German warship arrived the next day in Santo Domingo and sent 150 crew members ashore to protect the German Consulate as well as British interests.

Soon afterward, two more naval vessels, one Italian and the other Dutch, entered the harbor.[119]

Almost three weeks of fighting followed before Dominican forces put down the uprising. Fidelio Despradele from the Department of Foreign Relations in Santo Domingo announced the establishment of a stable provisional government and promised elections within two months. A month later, the United States extended de facto recognition to the provisional government.[120]

The appearance of peace, however, proved an illusion. Almost a year later, on February 1, 1904, the insurgents in Santo Domingo opened fire on the U.S. warship *Yankee,* killing an American sailor and drawing retaliatory fire from other American warships on insurgent positions along the waterfront. Roosevelt ordered Rear Admiral William Wise at Guantánamo on February 7 to take "immediate steps for [the] protection of United States citizens and property."[121]

President Roosevelt confided to his son that Santo Domingo was "drifting into chaos" after a century of freedom. He had "most reluctantly" intervened and hoped he would not have to take stronger action. Yet, he considered it "inevitable" that the United States establish a protectorate over "all these little states in the neighborhood of the Caribbean."[122]

Roosevelt had hoped the situation in the Dominican Republic would improve without U.S. involvement. In a letter marked "personal" to a journalist friend, he declared, "I want to do nothing but what a policeman has to do in Santo Domingo. As for annexing the island, I have about the same desire to annex it as a gorged boa constrictor might have to swallow a porcupine wrong-end-to." The insurgents have carried on a "half chaotic war towards us. If I possibly can I want to do nothing to them. If it is absolutely necessary to do something, then I want to do as little as possible."[123]

Roosevelt rejected the Dominican government's recommendation—that the United States annex the island and take control of its finances. A new protectorate could interfere with his ongoing negotiations over Panama, rouse the anti-imperialists, and provide the Democrats with another issue for the presidential campaign. At that moment, the Dominican foreign minister, Juan Franco Sanchez, was meeting with Hay, pleading for U.S. annexation of the Dominican Republic. And yet, Sanchez also was aware of information (not shared with Hay) from Santo Domingo showing that political forces outside the party in office were trying to make a secret arrangement with the German consul aimed at the United States. Roosevelt did not learn of this possibility until a day or so later, when a dispatch from Santo Domingo informed Washington of this development. It seemed strange that creditors from several countries demanded action, but that Germany was not among them. Later scholarship considers it likely that Berlin's leaders had no interest in the Dominican Republic because of its debilitating debt. If Roosevelt made this calculation, he was correct.[124]

Roosevelt nonetheless remained wary of European intervention and continued to call for naval preparation as the chief means for holding onto America's gains in the Caribbean and Asia. In a letter to Republican Congressman Theodore Burton of Ohio, the president declared that "The one unforgivable crime is to put oneself in a position in which strength and courage are needed, and then to show lack of strength and courage." Americans must not oppose building a navy large enough to protect the areas they had acquired. To give up these new possessions would "inflict a great wrong on the generations who come after us."[125]

In a letter dated May 20, 1904, Roosevelt defended his position to Elihu Root. The United States, according to the president, had freed Cuba from tyranny and then remained on the island long enough to establish civil order and lay the basis for self-government before granting its independence. This act exemplified America's policy toward all Latin American peoples. "It is not true that the United States has any land hunger or entertains any projects as regards other nations, save such as are for their welfare." America sought stability, order, and prosperity in the hemisphere. "Any country whose people conduct themselves well can count upon our hearty friendliness." The United States would not intervene as long as that country met its obligations. "All that we ask is that they shall govern themselves well, and be prosperous and orderly."[126]

Root read the president's letter aloud at an anniversary dinner for the Cuban republic in New York on the evening of May 20, marking this moment as the first public declaration of the "Roosevelt Corollary" to the Monroe Doctrine. It drew a mixed but largely critical review after its full publication in the *New York Tribune* the following day. The *New York World*, no friend of the president, called the letter "a flagrant exhibition of jingoism." Anti-imperialists accused him of "bossing the world," thereby violating "the ideas of the fathers of the Republic, the civilized statesmanship of modern times or the best interests of our people." The *Wall Street Journal* disagreed, declaring intervention in the Western Hemisphere a "national duty."[127]

Roosevelt privately admitted that he had to compromise in certain instances, but he maintained that he had pursued a policy as close as possible to his ideals. He was "amused at the yell" over his letter, he told Root. It was "the simplest common sense," the president asserted,

and only the fool or the coward can treat it as aught else. If we are willing to let Germany or England act as the policemen of the Caribbean, then we can afford not to interfere when gross wrongdoing occurs. But if we intend to say "Hands off" to the powers of Europe, sooner or later we must keep order ourselves.[128]

Roosevelt may have been more bemused than amused, as he put it, but he was also disturbed by what he considered to be the shortsightedness of fellow Americans. To a journalist and friend, he wrote that his "motto has been simply to do justice as between man and man under all circumstances, and to give each man a square deal, no more and no less." Roosevelt assured another friend, President Jacob Schurman of Cornell University, that the charges against him of being a dictator were "so preposterous that they must be made in bad faith." In his letter read at the Cuban anniversary dinner, he declared, "I took the position which is substantially as you [Root] suggested." The only time the United States would use the Monroe Doctrine to justify interference with another nation's affairs was to defend American "interests and honor."[129]

In Roosevelt's Fourth Annual Message to Congress on December 6, 1904, he formally announced what became known as the Roosevelt Corollary to the Monroe Doctrine. It was America's duty, the president argued, "to remember that a nation has no more right to do injustice to another nation, strong or weak, than an individual has to do injustice to another individual; that the same moral law applies in one case as in the other." Americans must also realize that "it is as much the duty of the Nation to guard its own rights and its own interests as it is the duty of the individual so to do. . . . Any country whose people conduct themselves well can count upon our hearty friendship," Roosevelt affirmed. "If a nation shows that it knows how to act with reasonable efficiency and decency in social and political matters, if it keeps order and pays its obligations, it need fear no interference from the United States." When this is not the case, he declared in the corollary to the Monroe Doctrine, the United States bears the responsibility for taking corrective action.[130]

In words similar to those in his May 20 letter to Root, the president explained the responsibilities of a "humane and civilized" nation:

Chronic wrongdoing, or an impotence which results in a general loosening of the ties of civilized society, may in America, as elsewhere, ultimately require intervention by some civilized nation, and in the Western Hemisphere the adherence of the United States to the Monroe Doctrine may force the United States, however reluctantly, in flagrant cases of such wrongdoing or impotence, to the exercise of an international police power.[131]

Roosevelt argued that U.S. intervention should be "the last resort"—when the affected nation's "inability or unwillingness to do justice at home and abroad had violated the rights of the United States or had invited foreign aggression to the detriment of the entire body of American nations." All nations must realize that their independence "cannot be separated from the responsibility of making good use of it."[132]

Roosevelt preferred setting an example of freedom rather than becoming the hemisphere's policeman. "We have plenty of sins of our own to war against," he declared. But sometimes wrongdoing in a nation can occur on such a wide scale that it becomes America's duty as a defender of freedom to intervene, even by force.[133]

The first test of the Roosevelt Corollary came when the president urged the Senate to approve a treaty requested by the Dominican Republic that aimed to resolve its debt problems with several countries, including Germany, France, Italy, and Belgium. Like Venezuela, the Dominican Republic had borrowed money from abroad and now, beset by domestic violence, feared that these foreign powers would use force to collect their money. Encouragement for such action came from The Hague Court's decision in late February 1904, which supported favored treatment for European lenders to Venezuela.[134]

The proposed treaty with the Dominicans would meet their fiscal responsibilities by allotting a percentage of their customs revenues to paying off their debts. The alternative to the treaty would be foreign nations using force to collect their debts and perhaps seizing land as compensation. Under these circumstances, Roosevelt felt it necessary to restore domestic order in the Dominican Republic and to help set up a system enabling the government to satisfy its debtors.[135]

Dominican president Carlos Morales approved the treaty in early February 1905. The primary source of revenue in the republic was the customs house, and Roosevelt recommended accepting the Dominican government's invitation for the United States to set up a receivership to resolve its debt problems. The agreement authorized American officials to collect customs and set aside 45 percent of the funds to meet Dominican internal needs and to deposit the balance with a New York corporation for distribution to claimant nations after ratification of the proposal.[136]

A fierce congressional debate ensued in Washington, angering Roosevelt as conditions in the Latin American republic continued to deteriorate and the European creditor nations warned of intervention. When Roosevelt, on February 15, sent the Senate his proposal for a U.S. receivership, charges echoed throughout the chamber as longtime enemy Senator John Tyler Morgan of Alabama joined Republican anti-imperialists and others in accusing the White House of making the Dominican Republic into a U.S. protectorate. The Senate refused to approve the plan and adjourned.[137]

But the president would not be denied. "Creatures" like Morgan and others in the Senate, he wrote a friend, received support from the "average yahoo among the Democratic Senators" and are "wholly indifferent to national honor or national welfare. . . . The Senate adjourns. I am then left to shoulder all the responsibility due to their failure." Both the French and the Belgians demanded a settlement of their claims; and on March 14, an Italian cruiser arrived in Santo Domingo for the same purpose. The threatened crisis alarmed many congressional members, including Morgan, who infuriated the president by proposing that the United States act in concert with the three creditor governments. This arrangement was exactly what he did *not* want, Roosevelt stormed. It would invite European influence into the hemisphere.[138]

Roosevelt took advantage of Italy's naval presence to emphasize the urgency of the moment and reach an executive agreement with Morales. At the end of March, responding to a recommendation from U.S. minister to the Dominican Republic, Thomas C. Dawson, the president ordered the negotiation of a *modus vivendi* with the Dominican government and proclaimed that he would maintain the status quo on the island until the Senate took action on the treaty. "That this is essentially right, I am dead sure," he asserted to the assistant secretary of state, Alvey Adee. The president ignored the opposition Democrats, who attacked his unorthodox approach as unconstitutional and despotic. Refusing to yield to political pressure, Roosevelt implemented the plan, knowing it did not bind successor administrations but believing it critical to protect the hemisphere at this moment. In the meantime, the receivership program satisfied the Dominican government's creditors and provided funds for new roads and schools. The program's success left the Senate with no choice but to approve Roosevelt's executive agreement as a treaty in 1907.[139]

To Cecil Spring Rice, Roosevelt insisted that the Monroe Doctrine was not "a pretense for self-aggrandizement at the expense of the Latin American republics." Nor was it "a warrant for letting any of these republics remain as small bandit nests of a wicked and inefficient type." The United States must help countries such as the Dominican Republic, but, when necessary, "chastise" them for wrongful behavior.[140]

Roosevelt told Congress that the Monroe Doctrine was essential to keeping peace in the Western Hemisphere. "All that this country desires is that the other republics on this continent shall be happy and prosperous; and they cannot be happy and prosperous unless they maintain order within their boundaries and behave with a just regard for their obligations toward outsiders."
The Monroe Doctrine cannot protect republics in this hemisphere that fail to meet their legitimate responsibilities to foreign powers. The United States would not interfere in the efforts of foreign powers to retrieve money loaned to these republics. But these same foreign powers cannot collect debts by taking possession of the customs houses in these republics when there is every reason to suspect that a "temporary occupation might turn into a permanent occupation."[141]

In response to criticisms by Charles Francis Adams and other anti-imperialists, Roosevelt declared that the United States intervened in the Dominican Republic only after its people made the request. The intervention drew approval from foreign businesses—particularly those in Britain—that had loaned money to that country and wanted to recover their debts. Under America's administration, customs fees were higher than those formerly under Dominican control, which meant that the government in Santo Domingo had more funds than before to improve economic conditions on the island and diminish the chances for revolution, thereby easing U.S. concerns about continued problems in the Caribbean.[142]

At the Second Hague Conference in 1907, the Roosevelt administration took a major step toward the promotion of arbitration in resolving debt disputes and other differences between nations—as long as the matter did not involve America's national interest. No issue of national interest was at stake in the Dominican controversy; thus, arbitration was an acceptable remedy. The United States incorporated the main principle of the Drago Doctrine into its proposal to prohibit the use of force in collecting contracted debts until arbitration had taken place or the debtor nation either rejected arbitration or refused to accept the arbitral decision. The Hague incorporated this principle into international law.[143]

In the meantime, the president faced another test of the Roosevelt Corollary, this time in Cuba, where a revolution entered its fourth year in September 1906. He told his friend and British historian, George Trevelyan, that he did not want to intervene. Yet, the president was upset by the widespread disorder on the island and confided to Henry White, then ambassador to Italy: "Just at the moment I am so angry with that infernal little Cuban republic that I would like to wipe its people off the face of the earth. All that we wanted from them was that they would behave themselves and be prosperous and happy so that we would not have to interfere."[144]

Roosevelt sent 6,000 American military forces to Cuba later that month. From Oyster Bay, he telegrammed his secretary of war, William Howard Taft, that this move was in response to President Palma's request and the threat to life and property resulting from an unstable government. The new provisional government would last until the Cubans formed a permanent one of their own. Lodge approved of the administration's Cuban policy, which he thought was popular with the public. "The conduct of the Cubans is disheartening," he told the president. "After all we did for them and the way in which we started them without debt and the Island all in perfect order, to find them fighting and brawling at the end of four years furnishes a miserable picture of folly and incompetency." It was "almost equally objectionable" to seize the island, as called for by Indiana Republican senator Albert Beveridge. "We do not want to annex Cuba if it can possibly be avoided," Lodge continued, "but we cannot permit the Island to fall into a state of anarchy."[145]

In January 1907, Roosevelt emphasized to Taft that a Cuban protectorate was out of the question. America's objectives were to bring peace, stabilize the government, and pull out its troops. Our "explicit promise," the president continued, was "to prevent a war of devastation last fall," which has been accomplished. The formation of a protectorate would be a violation of the agreement made with Cuba and would tarnish the "good faith of the United States," which "is a mighty valuable asset and must not be impaired." Almost a year later, he told a British writer that Cuba was "prosperous and thriving" and ready to "achieve self-government." The American troops withdrew in 1909 after stability had returned to the island.[146]

Roosevelt wrote to Andrew Carnegie in early 1909 that the successes in Latin America were "entirely Root's." The president claimed that his own contribution lay in "backing him up." As secretary of state, Root had built relations between North and South America and was instrumental in persuading the U.S. Senate to approve the Santo Domingo treaty. Root publicly maintained that the Monroe Doctrine was important because "it rests upon the right of self-protection and that right is recognized by international law." It was not "a warrant for interference in the internal affairs of all weaker nations in the New World."[147]

cᗞᗝᓎ

To a Chicago audience in early April 1903, President Roosevelt declared, "I believe in the Monroe Doctrine with all my heart and soul." But, he warned, "I would infinitely prefer to see us abandon it than to see us put it forward and bluster about it, and yet fail to build up the efficient fighting strength which in the last resort can alone make it respected by any strong foreign power whose interest it may ever happen to be to violate it."[148]

Roosevelt later explained to William Hale of the *New York Times* that in those countries in the Caribbean and South America in which he directly intervened—Cuba, Panama, and the Dominican Republic—he acted with public support, which helped to make his policies effective. In perhaps Haiti as well, the United States should implement "some kind of supervision" that shows the American people that their leaders had acted "in the name of humanity, morality, and civilization" as part of "our general scheme" of dealing with the republics of Latin America.[149]

Roosevelt asserted that he would have intervened in Venezuela and "at least one Central American State" had he been able to convince the American people that it was "in the interest of civilization" to implement "a reasonable and intelligent foreign policy which would put a stop to the crying disorders at our very doors." In each intervention, he insisted,

> I have had to exercise the greatest care in order to keep public opinion here with me so as to make my interference effective, and I have been able to lead it along as it ought to be led only by minimizing my interference and showing the

clearest necessity for it. . . . Our prime necessity is that public opinion should be properly educated.[150]

Roosevelt proclaimed that "the foreign policy in which I believe" is that of "speaking softly and carrying a big stick." All nations, he wrote to Whitelaw Reid, must be confident that he never intended "to wrong them nor to hurt their self-respect." Yet, he declared himself "entirely ready and entirely able to see that our rights are maintained in their turn."[151] Roosevelt's ideal of extending fairness and respect to *all* nations, however, consistently deferred to his commitment to pressing U.S. priorities, with the latter applied more readily to weaker nations and the former offered more generously to the Great Powers. Of the major issues he confronted during 1902–1903, perhaps none validate this assessment more than his approach to the boundary dispute over Alaska. He consistently expressed concern with preserving British honor and "self-respect" (though little was extended to Canada) through the process but was steadfast in guarding America's interests above all else.[152]

Chapter 5

Road to Port Arthur and the Russo-Japanese War

It is always possible that Russia and Japan will agree to make up their differences and assume an attitude of common hostility toward America or toward England, or toward both.

—President Theodore Roosevelt
December 26, 1904

We shall keep the respect of each of them just so long as we are thoroughly able to hold our own, and no longer.

—President Theodore Roosevelt
November 23, 1904

With the Panama Canal under construction and the Roosevelt Corollary a publicly declared policy, the president turned to troubling events outside the hemisphere. By 1905, Roosevelt had taken control of foreign policy with the advent of growing international problems and the declining health and July passing of his secretary of state, John Hay.[1] Americans, Roosevelt knew, remained isolationist, relying on 3,000 miles of Atlantic Ocean as insulation against the militarist and imperialist ways of the Old World. But not only Europe concerned him. He realized that the United States could no longer live in a vacuum—that what happened in East Asia also had repercussions in the Western Hemisphere. The United States, he asserted privately at first, must take a leading role in global matters. His first important step in this direction came in East Asia, where the competition between Japan and Russia for control of this vast region precipitated a war that threatened global stability.

I

As president, Roosevelt embraced a balance of power as the key to world peace. Not that he had turned his back on his belief that the United States must stand on its own: American prestige, he still insisted, rested on military strength primarily dependent on a first-class navy. Yet, he realized that order and stability on a global scale required collaboration with other nations. In his Inaugural Address of March 1905, Roosevelt proclaimed that U.S. policy toward all countries "must be one of cordial and sincere friendship," made clear "not only in our words, but in our deeds."[2]

The potential for trouble remained, leading Roosevelt to reserve military force as a final resort. Conflict between civilized peoples and barbarians was acceptable, he argued, if the objective was to spread civilization. War among civilized countries was not acceptable, although he recognized the reality of imperialist rivalries and possible conflicts regardless of the adversaries' levels of civilization. Knowing he lacked public support for a major U.S. involvement in international affairs, Roosevelt confined his thoughts to private communications until he found it necessary to make secret arrangements and executive agreements in an effort to circumvent the Senate's power to advise and consent on treaties. His paternalistic outlook on the world remained embedded in his diplomacy.

Roosevelt's concerns over Japan were inseparable from his long-held suspicions of Russia and Germany. In 1896, he had written to Cecil Spring Rice in England that Russia's recent expansion into northern China and designs on India would make it the leading power in Asia and positioned to "crush Germany." A year later, Roosevelt warned Spring Rice that the Russians posed "a very much more serious problem than the Germans, if not to our generation, at least to the generations which will succeed us." Russia and the United States have friendly relations, but the Russian and American people "have nothing whatever in common." Roosevelt did not regard the Russians in the way he suspected the British did—"as huge, powerful barbarians, cynically confident that they will in the end inherit the fruits of our civilization" and spread their influence throughout the world. The Russians, he declared, "both despise and fear" America's "political institutions."[3]

While governor of New York after the Spanish-American War, Roosevelt privately continued his support for a balance of power in Asia that required British involvement. He admitted to Spring Rice that Russia's expansion into "barbarous Asia" constituted "a real and great advance for civilization." But it would be a "great calamity" if Russia's actions weakened Britain's position in the region. "If Germany were wise," he wrote, "it would seek allies against the Slavs by creating independent states in Finland, the Baltic provinces, and perhaps in old Poland." Germany, however, showed no interest in this approach, leaving the challenge of Russia's rapid growth to Britain, whose influence was primarily administrative and political. If the Russians drove the British from Asia, Roosevelt felt confident that the West would unite and, along with Australia, tip the world's balance of power in their favor.[4]

As president, Roosevelt confronted what he regarded as a growing international crisis. "Before I came to the Pacific slope I was an expansionist," he told a large crowd in San Francisco in May 1903, "and after having been here I fail to understand how any man . . . can be anything but an expansionist."[5] Roosevelt considered it vital to awaken Americans to the danger of a clash of empires in Asia that would threaten U.S. holdings in the Pacific. In San Francisco, he publicly expressed what he had been saying privately for years: The United States must accept leadership responsibilities in the world. America's advance into the Pacific was part of the "inevitable march of events [that] gave us the control of the Philippine Islands at a time so opportune that it may without irreverence be called providential." This nation wants peace, and "the surest way of obtaining it is to show that we are not afraid of war."[6]

Roosevelt tempered his realist approach with idealistic principles reminiscent of the Puritans' attempt to build a city upon a hill for the world to emulate. In a final statement that day in San Francisco, he drew cheers and applause when he focused on the principles of "exceptionalism" found in Alexis de Tocqueville's *Democracy in America*, which appeared in 1835 and 1840. In his classic two-volume work, the French author wrote that in this new land, the transplanted English people could "enlarge in all directions the empire of mind" because they had the time and energy to do so. "The position of the Americans is therefore quite exceptional, and it may be believed that no democratic people will ever be placed in a similar one."[7]

Roosevelt went on to proclaim that America must be "the example for all the nations of the earth, to make of it a nation in which we shall see the spirit of peace and of justice incarnate, but in which also we shall see incarnate," he continued, "the spirit of courage, of hardihood, the spirit which while refusing to wrong the weak is incapable of flinching from any fear of the strong."[8]

Mahan's call for a strong navy lay firmly rooted in Roosevelt's mind, as did those expansionist doctrines he had discussed for hours in the late 1890s with an inner circle of friends gathered for tea in the new house on Lafayette Square owned by Henry Adams, whom he had met at Harvard. There in Washington DC, with Henry's brother Brooks, Henry Cabot Lodge, and other intellectuals, Roosevelt had explored the importance of greater U.S. involvement in international affairs.[9]

President Roosevelt realized that the growing Russo-Japanese rivalry in East Asia was part of a global struggle for power that affected U.S. interests. In the long run, he was concerned about Japan's expansion in the Pacific, but in the near term, he knew that only Japan stood between Russia and the

Philippines. The Russians had been closing Manchurian ports and siphoning off the profits from mining and shipping. The Trans-Siberian railway neared completion, and, when operational, the Russians would have direct access to their only warm water port at Vladivostok on the west side of the same Sea of Japan that touched the shores of their archrival in that region of the world. In July 1903, Roosevelt publicly denounced Russia's actions in Manchuria and its mass killings of Jews in Kishinev, Bessarabia, rumored to have been sanctioned by Tsar Nicholas II.[10]

Roosevelt's speech in San Francisco marked his emergence from private discussions on foreign policy to public statements urging Americans to accept a responsible role in maintaining world peace.

II

Among his global considerations, President Roosevelt held to his proprietary views toward China, largely because of its alleged inferiority and seemingly unlimited economic potential, but also because that vast country had become the object of Japanese and Russian expansion. In 1894–1895, China had suffered a devastating loss in the Sino-Japanese War that cost it Korea and encouraged Japan to covet Manchuria as a source of raw materials, markets, and employment. However, instead of Japan, Russia and other powers expanded into the area, defending their actions as developing "spheres of influence." The year after the war, China granted concessions to Russia, allowing it to extend the Trans-Siberian Railroad through Manchuria and establish a connection with Vladivostok. In the meantime, Russia joined Germany and France in forcing Japan to give up the Liaotung Peninsula in southern Manchuria (won from China in the war of 1894–1895); and in 1898, Russia took the area for itself by securing a lease to Port Arthur from the Chinese government. Although Russia completed the railroad in 1904, it was unable to send enough ground forces to secure it.

China had long drawn the interest of other nations, including the United States. In late 1899, a secret society of young Chinese nationalists known as the "Boxers" ("Righteous and Harmonious Fists") rebelled against the foreign intruders and seized control of their embassies in Peking. An international force that included American soldiers put down the Boxer Rebellion in 1901; but the uprising encouraged the powers to deepen their intervention, either to redeem the costs of the expedition or to exploit China's vulnerability—or both.

The McKinley administration attempted to stop rapacious nations from carving up China for themselves. Secretary of State John Hay worked with the British in proclaiming an "open door" policy for China, which called on all nations to respect its independence and territorial integrity. Roosevelt continued this policy after becoming president in the fall of 1901, warning Germany to respect the Open Door by informing his friend and diplomat, Speck von Sternburg, that he would oppose any nation seeking territory in China.[11]

In reality, the United States was no different from other nations in wanting to keep China open for American business and religious groups. One by one, Japan, Russia, Germany, France, Britain, and the United States ignored the Open Door principles and staked out economic and territorial claims, creating a chaotic atmosphere of international rivalries in East Asia that could lead to war.

One consequence of confronting the China issue was that the president's attitude toward Russia became more conflicted. Roosevelt had initially regarded Russia's late nineteenth-century expansion into Turkestan and Siberia as a captivating story but one that nonetheless left him apprehensive over the possibility of Russia seizing northern China and building an army out of its people. Yet, as late as the summer of 1901, when still vice president, he hoped that, as a civilized nation, Russia's expansion into the Chinese province of Manchuria would bring stability and progress to this region that was paralyzed by squabbling warlords.

As president in September 1901, Roosevelt's position on Manchuria turned to heightened unease. By December, Russia entered into an agreement with China to evacuate the area but under conditions that drew resistance from Britain and Japan and skepticism from the United States. According to the agreement, the Russo-Chinese Bank, established in 1896 in part to underwrite the Chinese-Eastern Railway, would be "permanently maintained, and protection of railway and Russian subjects . . . undertaken" by China. In addition, restrictions would be placed on the "number of Chinese troops," their positions, and their fighting capabilities. Further, no troops could be deployed by other nations "to protect railways," and the additional construction of railways or bridges in southern Manchuria would be prohibited. If China agreed to these terms and there was "no repetition of disorder," the tsar would schedule a staggered withdrawal to be completed "during 1903." Both the British and Japanese ministers warned China not to sign the agreement; Roosevelt opposed it as a violation of the Open Door.[12]

The president's concerns seemed warranted in early February 1902, when the White House learned that Russia and China had signed the agreement. Secretary of State Hay sent a memorandum to both governments and nine other nations, expressing alarm about China's concessions to Russia in Manchuria. According to the Roosevelt administration, a corporation's sole industrial rights over mines and railways would establish a monopoly that violated China's sovereignty as well as its commercial treaties with other powers, including those with the United States. The Open Door policy in China was at risk.[13]

Russia insisted that it supported the Open Door in Manchuria, arguing that it had no more privileges in Manchuria than did the Germans in Shantung. The White House pointed out that the United States did not recognize German rights there and could not justify Russia's claims. A few days later, on February 9, the Russians provided written assurance that they would withdraw their troops from Manchuria, but not until it was safe to do so.[14] Almost eight months later, in late September of 1902, the Russians began leaving Manchuria and, in accordance with their agreement, expected to evacuate the "territory up to the Liao River" by the second week of October. In other words, it appeared to Edwin H. Conger, U.S. minister to China, that the Russians were moving forward with the scheduled withdrawal.[15]

Roosevelt did not trust the Russians, an opinion reinforced when, in late April 1903, St. Petersburg paused evacuation and levied seven additional demands on China, including a ban on any "new treaty ports or foreign consuls." The Manchurian issue, the president privately asserted to a journalist friend, had become divisive because of the Russian's "well-nigh incredible mendacity." The United States did not want to interfere in Manchuria's politics and, in return, expected the Russians not to impede America's trade. Yet, the Russians were guilty of "persistent lying" and consistently failed to keep Manchurian ports open. The Russians seemed "to be ingeniously endeavoring to force us, not to take sides with Japan and England, but to acquiesce in their taking sides with us." As Roosevelt conceded, the United States had always recognized Russia's special position in Manchuria and would do nothing to prevent its progress in legitimate matters such as equal commercial opportunity.[16]

In a "private and confidential" letter to the editor of *Outlook*, Lyman Abbott, Roosevelt emphasized that the United States wanted only Open Door commercial rights in China. His administration sought no political influence in Manchuria and did not wish to block Russian aspirations. Russia, however, had warned China not to grant such rights. Especially "irritating," declared the president, was Russia's assurance against interference in commerce while prohibiting the Chinese government from doing what it wanted to do. American protests led to ambiguous responses from Russia followed by repeated assurances.[17]

Roosevelt considered Russia's actions in China "appalling," but he admitted that he could do nothing on behalf of Manchuria. As a show of force, he considered sending an American battleship to join the older cruisers of the European squadron moving to the German port of Kiel, but he dropped the idea. "I hate being in the position of seeming to bluster without backing it up," he told Hay.[18]

In the interests of balance-of-power politics, Roosevelt's increasingly negative attitude toward Russia led him to support its chief nemesis in East Asia—Japan. The Japanese people possessed many characteristics that Roosevelt respected, the chief one being their efficiency in military and industrial matters. But he also admired their honesty and willingness to make sacrifices and alterations in lifestyle over the years following their introduction to the West.

Roosevelt's major concerns centered on Japan's attitude toward Russia and the protection of U.S. interests in East Asia. He must court the Japanese. They had heretofore lodged no complaints about America's hold on Hawaii and the Philippines, but that situation could change if they continued to expand in East Asia. To slow expansion by both nations, Roosevelt pursued a delicate policy that favored a Japan strong enough to balance off Russia without encouraging Tokyo's leaders to challenge U.S. holdings in the Pacific.

According to a mid-July 1903 cable from U.S. minister Lloyd Griscom in Tokyo, the Japanese government wanted to negotiate with Russia over Manchuria and had convinced China to reject Russian demands pertaining to its province. The Japanese hoped for a settlement in Peking and intended to pursue the matter with the Russian government in St. Petersburg. They wanted to discuss all aspects of the Manchurian question with Russia in what the Japanese called a "friendly spirit."[19]

Trouble seemed likely, given what Griscom reported as Japan's probable proposals to Russia: recognition of China's integrity and sovereignty in Manchuria; no Russian troops in Manchuria except those needed to guard the railroads; Japan's recognition of all Russian rights in Manchuria based only on published treaties; and acknowledgment of Japan's political, commercial, and industrial interests in Korea, as declared in Japan's alliance with Great Britain in 1902.[20]

In mid-September 1903, the Russian government countered with demands on China. Russian troops would evacuate Manchuria in one year if China accepted the following terms: no cession of any part of Manchuria's three provinces to a foreign power; Russian access via the Chinese Eastern Railways in securing Manchurian goods; Russian troops to protect merchant vessels operating on the river along with the telegraph lines strung on both banks; and Russia's right to establish stations along the roads through the provinces.[21]

The immediate concern for the United States was the impact this might have on a pending trade treaty with China slated for signing on October 8. The April announcement of restrictions on new treaty ports had thrown Hay and Conger into a series of Russian and Chinese counterclaims with assurances from both over the following weeks that U.S. opportunities would not be undermined. Hay and Conger erroneously translated these assurances into a belief that a treaty opening new ports for the United States remained on schedule. But this latest move by Russia in September promised to derail the treaty. China faced two unpleasant outcomes—an irate America on one side and the continued presence of Russians in Manchuria on the other. Hay was asked by the Chinese if the United States would intercede with Russia on their behalf. The secretary sent word through Conger that this question might best be considered *after* the treaty was signed. The two nations signed, as agreed, on October 8. The Russians, as suspected, made no further moves to evacuate Manchuria.[22]

Griscom had reported from Tokyo in late September that Japanese-Russian negotiations over Manchuria were not going well. He had asked the Japanese minister for foreign affairs, Baron Jutaro Komura, whether the negotiators had made any breakthroughs.

"They are making no progress at all," he replied. "The only desire of the Russian Government seems to be to delay matters."

"Has the situation become critical?"

"Yes; it is very serious," Komura declared. "The Japanese people are getting into a very excited condition."

"But the Government is able to control them?"

"Yes; we can control them," Komura assured the U.S. minister, "but the fact remains that something must be done—some action must be taken."

Griscom observed that Komura wanted to leave the impression that his government had taken "a firm line of action, and that its patience is nearly exhausted."[23]

On Christmas Eve, Griscom informed Washington that Komura found the Russian reply to Japan's proposals "entirely unsatisfactory" and that the Japanese press almost unanimously called for war.[24]

A week later, Griscom reported that war was "almost inevitable."[25]

By the new year, relations between Russia and Japan had further deteriorated over Manchuria and Korea. A triple barrier comprised of Japanese islands, Korea, and the upward bulge of Manchuria had virtually isolated Russia's port in Vladivostok, making it imperative to secure access due east via the Chinese Eastern Railway across Siberia and through the heart of Manchuria. However, the acquisition of railway rights strengthened an expanding Russian presence built on special zones, mining and timber concessions, and the soldiers required to guard the long passageway. Russian control over Manchuria posed a threat to Korea, which, according to traditional fears, was a dagger aimed at the heart of Japan.

The security agreements won by the Japanese in their war with China had unraveled within a decade. Both Japan and Russia mouthed assurances of Korean independence, but in the aftermath of the Sino-Japanese War, Tsar Nicholas moved to tighten Russia's grasp on the peninsular country while solidifying his hold on Manchuria. On January 16, 1904, the Japanese issued a "note verbale" outlining what they believed to be reasonable compromises on the Russian position, and they wished to convey this message in "a spirit of perfect conciliation." But the St. Petersburg government showed no interest in Japan's call for hegemony in Korea in exchange for Russian control of Manchuria. East Asia was just the beginning for the Russians. According to one scholar, they sought all Asia.[26]

Back and forth went the demands until the Tokyo government in late January informed the Russian minister that a response was "now about due" to its note of January 16. Still hearing nothing, Japan feared that Russia was preparing for war and recalled its minister from St. Petersburg. The following day, February 6, Japan broke diplomatic relations.[27]

Less than twenty-four hours later, the Russian minister made arrangements to leave Tokyo, breaking diplomatic relations with Japan and making war all but certain.[28]

On the night of February 8–9, 1904, Japanese naval forces under the command of Admiral Togo Heihachiro launched a surprise attack on the Russian Oriental fleet based at Port Arthur in southern Manchuria, igniting the Russo-Japanese War. The attacks shocked Nicholas, who had felt certain that Japan would not go to war without first issuing a formal declaration and whose advisers had assured him that Japan would not fight. On February 10, the *New York Times* headlines reported "Japan's Crushing Blow to Russia," belying both Russian presumptions. According to a Russian account, a squadron of fifteen battleships and cruisers bombarded Port Arthur for about an hour, disabling three battleships and four cruisers, and landing troops in various other ports. In less than an hour, according to the *Times*, Japan became the leading naval power in the Yellow Sea.[29]

Japan declared war on Russia the following night, and the next morning published its objectives in *The Japan Times* of Tokyo: Japan intended to defend its vital interests in both Korea and Manchuria.[30]

According to Griscom, Japanese leaders envisioned seizing Korea and the Liaotung Peninsula, which would cut off Port Arthur from the rest of Manchuria before their forces laid siege to the port city. From there, they planned to push northward, driving the Russians back to Mukden and into a final stand in China's northernmost Manchurian province.[31]

Russia declared war on Japan a week later.

III

To keep a close watch on the crisis in East Asia, President Roosevelt ordered a naval squadron to Chinese waters and, at the kaiser's suggestion, sent notes to the belligerents and the European nations asking them to join the United States in reaffirming their pledges to neutrality in China. Japan agreed to do so, provided Russia did the same. Komura furnished Griscom with written confirmation of Japan's respect for Chinese neutrality and asserted that instructions had gone out nearly three weeks earlier to Japan's ambassador in Washington, Baron Kogoro Takahira, to inform the United States of Japan's position.[32]

Roosevelt initially noted with satisfaction that the war began "most disastrously" for Russia. The Russians had "behaved very badly" toward the United States, as well as Japan and other nations in East Asia. The president worried that if Russia defeated Japan, it might pursue an "intolerable" policy toward Americans in Asia. He informed Secretary of State Elihu Root that the German kaiser's note calling for the neutrality of China was unsatisfactory because he recommended guaranteeing the integrity of China only south of the Great Wall, "which would have left Russia free to gobble up what she really wanted." The kaiser immediately retracted the restrictive provision, demonstrating that Germany "behaved better" than other powers in the area. Roosevelt told his son that, for the moment, he was "thoroughly well pleased" with the Japanese for "playing our game."[33]

Roosevelt nonetheless became concerned about Japan's rapid successes and sought greater naval preparations to safeguard U.S. interests in East Asia and the Caribbean. Those Americans who supported the acquisition of the Philippines, the incorporation of Puerto Rico, the annexation of Hawaii, the building of naval stations in Cuba, the construction of the Panama Canal, and the tenets of the Monroe Doctrine must now support a navy large enough to secure these interests. Not everyone in Washington, however, shared his commitment. Foremost in his mind were those who opposed fortifying the naval station at Subic Bay as a threat to Philippine independence. The president saw this as recklessly shortsighted. Clearly, Roosevelt believed Japan's attack on Port Arthur posed a new danger to the United States.[34]

The president, meanwhile, invested in learning all he could about Japan. He built a close relationship with Minister Kogoro Takahira in Washington, who provided information to both his home government and the White House—always following protocol by communicating with the president through the State Department or, when Roosevelt was home at Oyster Bay, to his secretary. Roosevelt also relied on information from Japan's special envoy, Baron Kentaro Kaneko, the president's friend from Harvard College days. When Roosevelt made clear that he wanted to read books on Japan, Takahira and Kaneko compiled a reading list that included items written by Kaneko as well as books that schooled the president in Bushido, which emphasized the self-discipline needed to become a samurai or professional warrior trained in the martial arts—particularly the hand-to-hand combat of jujitsu.[35] White House personnel and visitors must have been both shocked and amused when learning that the president was tussling with two Japanese wrestlers three times a week, especially when they heard the loud slams coming from upstairs as his sparring partners repeatedly picked him up over their heads and threw him onto a mattress.[36]

Returning to the global mat, Roosevelt intended to remain neutral unless one of the belligerents made "a preposterous demand," he wrote his close friend and editor of the *Boston Pilot*, James Roche. To Spring Rice, Roosevelt expressed surprise at the "hysterical side" of the Russians, brought on by their perception of American hostility and Japan's success at Port Arthur. "I believe in the future of the Slavs, if they can only take the right turn. But I do not believe in the future of any race *while it is under a crushing despotism*." Americans tended to sympathize with Russia, but if Japan won the war, the Slavic peoples and everyone else "will have to reckon with a great new force in eastern Asia." Japan would emerge as "a formidable power in the Orient," determined to "reorganize China" and shift the balance of power in East Asia against the white nations.[37]

Privately, the president informed Spring Rice that Russia had never frightened him. He was astonished by the Russians' lack of preparation for war and could see no permanent good coming from them unless they followed "the path of orderly freedom, of civil liberty, and of a measure of self-government."[38]

Roosevelt surprised the Japanese by telling Kaneko that "Japan's entrance into the circle of the great civilized powers was of good omen for all the world."[39]

But his compliment came with a word of caution.

At lunch in June 1904 with Kaneko and Takahira, Roosevelt warned against getting the "big head" if victorious in the war. He further cautioned against pursuing a policy of aggression that "would undoubtedly be temporarily very unpleasant to the rest of the world, but" would be even "more unpleasant for Japan." He hoped Japan would take its place among the civilized nations after having satisfied its "paramount interest" in the area around the Yellow Sea, just as the United States had done in the Caribbean—with no "conquest of the weak."[40]

Both guests rejected the possibility of Japan's "becoming intoxicated" with a victory, insisting that they were not "barbarians" and desired to be part of the broader world community. To ease the president's concern about the Philippines, they renounced any interest in the islands as "nonsense." When Roosevelt expressed hope that China would remain intact and asserted that all parts of the world must be "prosperous and well policed," they "grinned" as they considered the likely problems in applying this standard to Korea. To get the Russians out of Manchuria, Japan must have Port Arthur as the first step toward establishing primary influence in that huge area before turning it over to the Chinese. Yet Takahira was not confident that China was strong enough to stand on its own, nor did he believe that the Russians would keep their promises about evacuating Manchuria. An international agreement was vital to guarantee China's autonomy in Manchuria.[41]

Roosevelt insisted that he was not laying the basis for American intervention in Asian affairs, but he privately admitted to Spring Rice that it could happen because of reasons beyond U.S. control. If Japan won the war, he foresaw a U.S.-Japanese struggle for hegemony in the Pacific; if Russia won, he worried that it would block U.S. commercial interests in northern China.[42]

Race had nothing to do with this issue, he assured his friend. The reality is that "a good man is a good man and a bad man a bad man wherever they are found." Roosevelt declared that he liked the Russian people but considered their despotic government "incompatible with the growth of intelligence and individuality in a civilized people." As for Russia's enemy in the war, "I see nothing ruinous to civilization in the advent of the Japanese to power among the great nations."[43]

Roosevelt came to believe that the best interests of both America and the rest of the world lay in a Japanese victory. He knew that war between the United States and Japan was possible unless the two nations respected each other's interests in East Asia. But this would be difficult if Russia won the war. Before the Russo-Japanese War was six months old, he shared these sentiments with Spring Rice: If Russia "wins she will organize northern China against us and rule us absolutely out of all the ground she can control. Therefore, on the score of mere national self-interest," he conceded, "we would not be justified in balancing the certainty of immediate damage [from Russia] against the possibility of future damage [from Japan].[44]

A little more than a month later, Roosevelt felt more confident that the Japanese would win the war. If they held onto Port Arthur, Russia could not dislodge them by sending its Baltic Squadron to the war zone. The Japanese, he told Hay in the summer of 1904, "have played our game because they have played the game of civilized mankind." If they win, the United States must oppose any effort to deny them the fruits of victory.[45]

Roosevelt and the leaders of the European powers involved in Asia expressed concern about building a balance of power in that region if Japan won the war. The president had told Sternburg that he supported the Open Door in the Yangtze area—stretching 4,000 miles across China—as much as he did in Manchuria and preferred that Germany (rather than Britain) appoint a Chinese viceroy to control Manchuria. The kaiser suspected the British of wanting to establish influence in Manchuria and on the Yangtze River but regarded Roosevelt's suggestion as premature, warning that "one must not divide the hide of the bear before he has been shot."[46]

The White House, meanwhile, took steps aimed at maintaining U.S. neutrality. In late August, the president emphasized to the navy department that without direct orders, no Americans were to interfere with fighting between Russian and Japanese vessels in China's neutral ports. Hay soon afterward instructed Conger to encourage the Chinese to maintain neutrality. Roosevelt expressed concern about China's resiliency to Hay. "What nonsense it is to speak of the Chinese and Japanese as of the same race!" He praised Hay's memorandum to the Russians, which clarified their erroneous position on contraband and led him to remark that they "think only with half a mind." If the Russians won the war, "they would be so intolerable as to force us to take action."[47]

Less than two months after accepting his party's nomination for the presidency in late July 1904, Roosevelt wrote a long letter to the Republican speaker of the House of Representatives, Joseph Cannon, in which he warned that if the United States gave up the Philippines and did nothing on behalf of China, it would lose influence in East Asia. Since America's victory over Spain in 1898, Cannon had resisted naval expansion almost as much as when, as a conservative representative from Illinois, he had opposed Roosevelt's conservation efforts and other progressive ideas.[48]

America's governmental system, Roosevelt declared to Cannon, rested on the basic idea that "each man, no matter what his occupation, his race, or his religious belief, is entitled to be treated on his worth as a man, and neither favored nor discriminated against because of any accident in his position." Roosevelt admitted that the U.S. promise to grant independence to the Philippines would take place only when they were capable of standing on their own. To take such action now would result in anarchy and violence throughout the islands, but to abandon them would hurt American trade in East Asia as well as threaten the people under U.S. protection. They have made advances in education, health, roads, self-government, individual rights, and civil liberties, he acknowledged, but this "wholly new experiment in Asia" needed more time to develop.[49]

By the fall of 1904, Roosevelt expressed surprise that so many Americans thought Russia would defeat Japan. "I do not," he told Hay. True, the Japanese had found Port Arthur a bigger challenge than expected, but he saw no sign that Russia could prevail.[50]

However, in mid-October, Roosevelt altered his initial pro-Japanese stance to support a postwar balance of power based on no victory by either side. He shared these views with his friend Jules Jusserand, the French ambassador to the United States, who passed them to the French foreign minister, Théophile Delcassé, whose government was an ally of Russia. Rather than support

Japan, Roosevelt explained to Jusserand, "I would like to see the war ending with Russia and Japan locked in a clinch, counterweighing one another, and both kept weak by the effort." Only this standoff would protect U.S. interests in Hawaii and the Philippines.[51]

Roosevelt remained wary of Britain and other foreign powers seeking to take advantage of the war in East Asia to satisfy their own interests. In comments that suggested both the magnitude and the loneliness of his job, he told political commentator and humorist Finley Peter Dunne, "We shall keep the respect of each of them just so long as we are thoroughly able to hold our own, and no longer. If we got into trouble, there is not one of them upon whose friendship we could count to get us out; what we shall need to count upon is the efficiency of our own fighting men and particularly of our navy." Thus, our friendship can go only as far as "our self-respect" will allow.[52]

On the day after Christmas, 1904, Roosevelt asked his longtime friend and then ambassador to Italy, George Meyer, to transfer to that same position in St. Petersburg, Russia, which the president called "the most important post in the diplomatic service" at this moment. Roosevelt and Lodge had known Meyer since their college days at Harvard, all three going on to become active in Republican politics. Both the president and Lodge thought the political adeptness he had displayed as speaker of the Massachusetts House of Representatives would continue to serve him well as a proven diplomat. "I want a man who will be able to keep us closely informed . . . of everything we ought to know," the president determined; and one "who will be, as an Ambassador ought to be, our chief source of information . . . and you are the man to do it." Lodge wrote Meyer that the president wanted "private letters" from him. Roosevelt emphasized to his new emissary that he had been disenchanted with the lack of professionalism in the diplomatic corps. Too many of the appointees, he complained, regarded the position as "a kind of glorified pink tea party" in which they were more interested in social niceties than in doing the actual work of an ambassador.[53]

Roosevelt alerted his ambassador-select of potential dangers involving Japan. "It is always possible that Russia and Japan will agree to make up their differences and assume an attitude of common hostility toward America or toward England, or toward both." The United States, he warned Meyer, "cannot count upon any ally to do its work. We must stand up on our feet." The Japanese considered Russia "their most dangerous permanent enemy," but Roosevelt thought they harbored similar sentiments about other nations, including the United States. They "dislike" and "resent" white people and consider the "yellow civilization" to be superior.

Russia, Roosevelt continued, had consistently opposed U.S. policies in East Asia and demonstrated a "literally fathomless mendacity" and "profound contempt" for the United States, Britain, and Japan. Germany and France had their own reasons to restrain Russia and did not care about American interests. Britain appeared friendly to the United States and probably would support Japan against Russia, but the English were "pretty flabby" and lacked "tenacity of purpose."[54]

Roosevelt did not trust either Russia or Japan. Russia, he told Spring Rice, had treated the United States as poorly as it had treated Britain and Japan. Russian diplomats had "lied to us with brazen and contemptuous effrontery" while showing "with cynical indifference their intention to organize China against our interests." Russia lacked the capacity to attack either the United States or the Philippines, but its leaders had displayed "a brutality and ignorance, and arrogance and shortsightedness, which are not often combined." The Japanese, however, had treated the United States well and appeared to seek the same outcome desired by every civilized power in East Asia. Yet Roosevelt suspected that they considered all white nations as "white devils inferior to themselves" and treated the United States "politely only so long as would enable the Japanese to take advantage of our various national jealousies, and beat us in turn." American military attachés with the Japanese army reported its officers' insolence over their initial success at Port Arthur and seemed to hold America responsible for blocking Japan's expansion into the Philippines and Hawaii.[55]

The hard truth in international relations, Roosevelt emphasized to Spring Rice, is that every nation's security depended "upon its own forethought and industrial efficiency and fighting edge." Whatever the outcome of the Russo-Japanese War, the victor would respect the United States or Britain more for its power than its friendship. Russia and Japan were longtime rivals because of their common interests in Korea, Manchuria, and China. Nevertheless, to achieve their ends, the two powers might ally against the United States, the Dutch, and perhaps the British in the Pacific; but the Japanese surely recognized that the maritime powers could inflict more damage on them than on Russia.[56]

In this frenetic atmosphere, Roosevelt expressed alarm to Speaker Cannon over a proposed cut in funding for the navy. No one can predict the outcome of present events in East Asia, the president declared. "No one can tell how long the war will last, or whether other powers will be drawn into it, or whether when peace comes a great effort may not be made to save the honor of both combatants at the expense of outsiders, or by the aid of some outsiders at the expense of the remaining outsiders." We must demonstrate to other nations "that our policy is definite and permanent, and that we shall not abandon it." The United States must have a strong navy and could not rely on bluster to secure its interests in that embattled region.[57]

The president did not receive enough congressional support for the navy he wanted. In his Fourth Annual Message of early December 1904, he argued again for a naval upgrade in view of the realities on display in the Russo-Japanese War. Torpedo destroyers he considered "indispensable" and "fast lightly armed and armored cruisers very useful," but the "main reliance" must be on "great battleships." Roosevelt called for three battleships, five cruisers, six destroyers, six torpedo boats, and two coal-carrying colliers for the fiscal year ending June 1906. Not until late February 1906 did Roosevelt get a response: Congress reduced his requests to two battleships and three cruisers, while approving the two colliers.[58]

IV

On January 2, 1905, after a five-month siege of Port Arthur, the Russians surrendered. Three days later, Kaiser Wilhelm cabled Roosevelt, conceding that "a grant of a certain portion of territory to both belligerents eventually in the North of China is inevitable." Roosevelt realized that Germany could play a major role in a realignment of powers and told Sternburg—now German ambassador to the United States—that he hoped Wilhelm would continue to support "the open door and the integrity of China." That same day, the kaiser cabled the president about a French-led coalition aimed at partitioning China and suggested that the White House urge European powers to renew their pledge of support for China's territorial integrity. Roosevelt wrote to Sternburg saying he interpreted this recommendation as a demonstration of the kaiser's "disinterestedness" in the region. Two days later, the president wrote to him again, attempting to allay his fears about France and Britain's territorial intentions after the war.[59]

In early February 1905, Roosevelt informed Ambassador Meyer in St. Petersburg that American military attachés with the Russian army thought its leaders wanted an alliance with Japan against the United States and European powers and called them "colossal in their mendacity and trickery." Roosevelt, as was his habit, distinguished between the Russian people whom he admired and the government that he dismissed as "most insincere and unscrupulous, and most reactionary."[60]

To hold Russia in check, Roosevelt anticipated a postwar Japan balancing off its territorial ambitions. The Japanese should take control of Port Arthur, support Manchuria's restoration to China, and establish a "protectorate" over Korea because of its "utter inability to stand by itself." The United States, he told Hay, could not intervene on behalf of the Koreans against Japan, and the Koreans "couldn't strike one blow in their own defense."[61]

After the fall of Port Arthur, the battle scene shifted northward to Mukden in Manchuria. In late February and early March, military observers from numerous countries gathered to watch the largest armies ever amassed on a single field—more than 600,000 troops, 330,000 of them Russians and 270,000 Japanese. The battle raged for almost three weeks, its more than forty miles of trenches offering a stark preview of the warfare along the Western Front in the Great War. The resulting stalemate at Mukden came with heavy casualties on both sides: 89,000 Russians and 71,000 Japanese. Russian forces evacuated northward, leaving Japan in control of a major part of Manchuria. Although not realized at the time, the Battle of Mukden marked the first major step toward the establishment of a balance of power in East Asia.[62]

During the last week of the battle, Roosevelt informed King Edward VII of England that he had warned Russia weeks earlier to make peace before the Japanese took Mukden and moved north of Harbin. He also wrote to British historian George Trevelyan that he had unofficially warned the Russian government to sign an early peace—unless it was certain its fleet could defeat the Japanese and the government could follow that victory with the deployment of 600,000 troops to stabilize Manchuria.

The Russians' conduct in that province had alienated Americans by making it appear that "they intended to organize China as a step toward the domination of the rest of the world." By contrast, Roosevelt added, the Japanese continued to treat Americans fairly; but he nonetheless remained cautious. "What they will do hereafter, when intoxicated by their victory over Russia, is another question which only the future can decide." In the meantime, Russia's despotic regime had shown that in both diplomatic and military matters, it "has during the last year or two done as badly as any republic could possibly do; and much worse than either of our governments has ever yet done."[63]

Anticipating an end to the war, Roosevelt wrote to John Hull, the chair of the House Committee on Foreign Affairs, expressing his thoughts on what policies should guide the United States in the postwar period. Americans must be courteous to all foreign governments, striving "neither to wrong them nor talk about them in ways which will make them think we are hostile or intend to wrong them, and yet to keep steadily prepared to hold our own." He hoped the Japanese had no intention of taking the Philippines, but the United States must be militarily prepared to hold them against any power. "If we do this, and act justly towards and speak courteously of, our foreign neighbors, we shall have taken the only effective steps to make our position good."[64]

Roosevelt realized a settlement would be difficult, given the different objectives of those nations affected by the Russo-Japanese War. The Chinese wanted the fighting to continue until both sides were exhausted. The kaiser suspected France of wanting to establish a congress of all nations except Germany. Roosevelt thought the British did not want the Japanese to take Vladivostok. Neither the Japanese nor the British, he wrote Sternburg, wanted a congress of the nations.[65]

Roosevelt perhaps sensed the danger of another war of broader proportions when he declared to Hay that the kaiser had become a "Mono maniac" about contacting him every time he sensed a conspiracy against him and his country. However, Roosevelt thought Wilhelm was "playing our game—or, as I should more politely put it, his interests and ours, together with those of humanity in general, are identical." The kaiser was convinced that the British intended to destroy his fleet and ally with France in a war against Germany. Ironically, as Roosevelt noted, the British had no such objectives but were in "panic terror" that the kaiser would ally against them with France or Russia in an effort to destroy the British Empire. "It is as funny a case as I have ever seen of mutual distrust and fear bringing two peoples to the verge of war."[66]

In early April, Roosevelt worried that the Russians intended to continue the war, even though their ambassador in Washington, Arturo Cassini, insisted that his government would agree to peace on "honorable terms" as long as they did not include the payment of an indemnity. Roosevelt feared that if the war dragged on and the Japanese took more Russian territory—Harbin and Vladivostok—they would demand harsher terms.[67]

Cassini's views were often suspect in Washington. Hay did not trust him. Cassini was a liar and a dilettante, according to historian Edmund Morris. "For all his Italian nomenclature," Morris wrote about Cassini, he "was as Russian as *borscht*, and lied with fabled virtuosity. The Ambassador, who mysteriously depended on his teenage daughter, Marguerite, for social purposes, introduced her around town as 'Princess Cassini,' when she was neither a princess nor, according to rumor, a Cassini. His numberless jeweled decorations," Morris observes, "may not all have been earned in the Tsar's service, but they were the glittering envy of Embassy Row. When he stood under a chandelier at receptions, he looked like a section of the Milky Way."[68]

Despite his well-earned derision in Washington circles, on this occasion, Cassini's fears and those of the president were equally justified. Sensing victory, Takahira insisted on an indemnity in addition to all the demands his government had made publicly when going to war. Roosevelt confided to Hay, "Did you ever know anything more pitiable than the condition of the Russian despotism in this year of grace?" The tsar was "a preposterous little creature" who "has been unable to make war, and he is now unable to make peace."[69] Nicholas lived in terror not only of the wrath of the tsarina who wanted the war to continue, but from the anger of war advocates at home who, even after the fall of Port Arthur, refused to consider the possibility of defeat and appeared ready to decapitate the throne and its court if peace came without victory.[70]

Roosevelt told his longtime friend and now secretary of war, William Howard Taft, that if the tsar had "an ounce of sense," he would have made peace in January. At that time, according to the president, Japan would have settled for Korea, Port Arthur, Dalny, control of the Harbin-Port Arthur Railway, and the return of Manchuria to China. Roosevelt approved of these terms, along with China's promise of an Open Door in trade. But Nicholas refused to commit to either an indemnity or the cession of territory.[71]

The seemingly certain Japanese victory in the war with Russia raised the specter of the so-called "yellow peril"—largely a figment of Kaiser Wilhelm's imagination in the 1890s but real to many contemporaries around the world.

In late 1895, the kaiser had witnessed the widespread shock across the continent caused by Japan's victory in the Sino-Japanese War and warned white people of a new threat to civilization coming from this rising new power on the Pacific horizon. "Under the glitter of the Christmas-tree candles," as "Willy" wrote cousin "Nicky" (Nicholas II) in St. Petersburg, he had sketched a picture that soon became the basis for a painting that garnered wide publicity. On a dragon rode Buddha through a dark and thunderous sky, destroying civilization along his drive toward Europe. In the west, seven blonde and long-haired female warriors waited, clad in armor and helmets and representing the seven European nations prepared for battle. Germania stood at the lead, sword unsheathed, and her long golden hair tucked inside a headband bearing the emblem of an eagle. Hovering over the protectors of the continent was the Archangel Michael, urging them to be strong. "Peoples of Europe, guard your most precious possessions."[72]

Engraved copies of this drawing went to every embassy in Berlin and to the ruling families of Europe. "William the Sudden," as contemporaries dubbed the kaiser, had used fear tactics that reverberated throughout Europe and in the United States. Japan's acquisition of vast areas in East Asia raised anxieties among Americans not only about their interests in that region but also about the growing number of Japanese in the United States.[73]

The president's domestic and foreign policies meshed into a major problem for his administration when, in early March 1905, the California legislature asked for federal legislation barring entry into the United States of the "immoral, intemperate, quarrelsome men bound to labor for a pittance." Two months later, the San Francisco Board of Education approved a resolution segregating Chinese and Japanese schoolchildren, a program to begin in 1906. Roosevelt repeatedly denounced that legislation as damaging to relations with Japan, but to no avail.[74]

The president exploded over the discriminatory legislation passed by lawmakers he privately belittled as the "idiots of the California Legislature." In a letter to George Kennan, a Russo-Japanese War correspondent for *Outlook* news magazine in New York City, he admitted that Californians had the right to protest against the admission of Japanese laborers as competitors to America's working class—a problem already serious in Hawaii. But he saw no need to foment anger, particularly during the ongoing war. The Japanese, he knew, did not allow foreigners to own land in Japan and therefore had no right to object to the same restrictions on Japanese in the United States. He would not have opposed a "courteous and proper" resolution, but he felt "humiliated" by "the foolish offensiveness" of California's resolution.[75]

Roosevelt largely agreed with Kennan's assessment of the Japanese. "I admire them and respect them," he wrote Kennan. "I regard them as a highly civilized people" and am "keenly mortified that any American should insult such a people." But he rejected Kennan's recommendation to join with Japan to bring about a Japanese-Anglo-American alliance. "Have you followed some of my experiences in endeavoring to get treaties through the Senate?" he chided. "Mind you, I personally entirely agree with you." But, he added, "I might just as well strive for the moon."[76]

"I am powerless," Roosevelt continued, "to do anything more than I have done; that is, in every possible way, personally and officially, to show the utmost courtesy and consideration to the Japanese." It was "deeply exasperating" to see Americans "doing just exactly the reverse of what I have made the cardinal doctrine of my foreign policy"—to "talk offensively of foreign powers and yet decline ever to make ready for war." The United States must treat Japan with "scrupulous courtesy and friendliness so that she shall have no excuse for bearing malice toward us." Americans must understand the importance of "common decency" as well as the necessity of having a navy strong enough to leverage a deal with Japan.[77]

The president's attempt to maintain neutrality in the Russo-Japanese War became more problematic when the California legislature prepared to exclude the Japanese from the United States as Congress had done to the Chinese in 1882. Roosevelt privately declared to Lodge that he was "utterly disgusted" with the California state legislators for actions that were in the "worst possible taste and in the most offensive manner to Japan." They were cut from the same cloth as the senators and congressmen who had opposed a naval buildup the previous year and now were willing to antagonize the Japanese. "How people can act in this way with the Russo-Japanese war going on before their eyes I cannot understand."[78]

By mid-May, Roosevelt was frustrated over his inability to persuade Russia and Japan to end the war. He reminded a confidant that he had no issue with the Russian people, but he found their leaders, according to Ambassador Meyer in St. Petersburg, to be in "a comatose state," waiting for more bad news from the battlefront. The Japanese would promote civilization, but they did not trust the white race. As he had feared, they felt "rather puffed up over their strength." Even if they won the war, it would have been better to make peace after Mukden without seeking a monetary indemnity from Russia. Prolonging the war, the president emphasized, would cost the Japanese whatever they might get from an indemnity. But they rejected his argument, and the Russians never gave a "straightforward" reply, which meant there was "nothing to do but let them work out their own fates."[79]

V

In the meantime, Roosevelt anxiously awaited the outcome of the imminent clash between the Russian and Japanese fleets. "Just at the moment," he wrote Spring Rice, "Russia is riding a high horse and will not talk peace." With the Russian fleet in Asian waters since early May, Roosevelt told Lodge, it seemed that Japan would want peace. Takahira and the Japanese Foreign Office, he thought, agreed with him, but the army, navy, and other hardliners in Japan demanded an indemnity and territorial concessions and were willing to risk everything to secure them.[80]

Roosevelt concluded that the forces for continuing the war were stronger than those calling for peace. Russia had been too cocky over its fleet to follow his advice and make peace after the surrender of Port Arthur, and Japan had become overly confident after winning the Battle of Mukden. Roosevelt informed Lodge that he had advised the Japanese "to build a bridge of gold for the beaten enemy." But they refused. The president realized that the Russian fleet was superior in matériel and feared that a Japanese defeat at sea could leave them "crushed to earth."[81]

The president remained insistent on acting independently of Germany but came under heavy criticism from the British for allegedly following the lead of the kaiser. Roosevelt assured Lodge this was not the case. Wilhelm recently gave a speech attacking both belligerents. Not even a congressman "could be guilty of quite such folly," declared the president. "It always amuses me to find that the English think that I am under the influence of the Kaiser. The heavy witted creatures," he asserted, "do not understand that nothing would persuade me to follow the lead of or enter into close alliance with a man who is so jumpy, so little capable of continuity of action, and therefore, so little capable of being loyal to his friends or steadfastly hostile to an enemy." The Germans sought to take advantage of Russia's weakened position by expanding their holdings in Europe. Perhaps to temper Wilhelm's ambitions, Roosevelt committed to remain on friendly terms. "I shall be friendly to the Kaiser as I am friendly to everyone. But as for his having any special influence with me, the thought is absurd."[82]

Lodge agreed with Roosevelt's assessment. The kaiser was "unstable, crazy for notoriety—not to be trusted. Not a man to rely on at all—with a saving sense of the danger of war and a strong inclination to bully up to the verge of war."[83]

Roosevelt also expressed concern to William W. Rockhill, soon to become U.S. minister to China, that Americans might alienate the Chinese inside the United States and damage commercial relations between the countries. The president noted China's growing disapproval of the way U.S. immigration officials treated its merchants and students. This bad feeling provoked anti-American riots, a boycott on U.S. goods, and the cancellation of the Hankow-Canton Railroad concession.[84]

Despite these forces pulling at him, the president remained determined to defend U.S. security without violating either neutrality or his sense of integrity. Both Japan and Russia must perceive him as honest and above the fray. According to the Greek philosopher Socrates, Roosevelt asserted, there was a "difference between a private man, who only has to do what is right, and a public man, who ought so to conduct himself that no one can have an excuse for *saying* that he has not done what is right." As president, Roosevelt was a public man.[85]

Also, as a staunch proponent of the balance-of-power principle, Roosevelt regarded the outcome of the Russo-Japanese War as integral to American interests and to the entire civilized world. Stability in East Asia remained uppermost in his mind as he attempted to use Japan's preoccupation with the war to solidify American ties with the Tokyo government. Japan's victories in the ongoing war, he continued to remind himself, posed a potential threat to U.S. control over the Philippines and perhaps Hawaii.

Isolationist sentiment in the United States led the president to keep his intentions secret and unofficial. In early 1905, he instructed his special emissaries in Britain and Japan, Senator Lodge and Secretary of War Taft, to privately assure their host governments of U.S. support for the Anglo-Japanese Alliance. In an unauthorized action that Roosevelt later approved, Taft signed an "agreed memorandum" with the Japanese prime minister, Count Taro Katsura, by which Japan disavowed any aggressive designs on the Philippines in exchange for the U.S. promise not to disturb Japan's interests in Korea.[86]

The plight of Korea became a major concern to the White House, for both humanitarian and economic reasons. Stories soon arrived of Japan's brutal treatment of the Korean people. The president also feared that the Japanese would obstruct U.S. economic interests in that small country. But he could do nothing in view of isolationist feelings at home. Moreover, in keeping with his pragmatic core, he insisted that moral sentiment must not determine

American foreign policy. Growing protests against the actions of Japanese occupation forces in Korea would alienate the Tokyo government and endanger his efforts to establish a balance of power in East Asia. The president had to stand by as critics claimed he had "sold out" the Koreans.[87]

In reality, Korea was under Japan's control and had never been susceptible to American influence. As Root declared more than two decades afterward:

> Many people are still angry because we did not keep Japan from taking Korea. There was nothing we could do except fight Japan; Congress wouldn't have declared war and the people would have turned out the Congress that had. All we might have done was to make threats which we could not carry out.[88]

Roosevelt was not inactive, however. Following Hay's announcement of the Open Door in China, the United States secretly and unofficially joined the Anglo-Japanese Alliance of 1902. By early 1905, all three nations—the United States, Britain, and Japan—stood on the same side of the Open Door in China. An Anglo-American-Japanese entente had quietly developed that could not have been more incongruous. Such is the world of diplomacy.

The president's backstage arrangements remained secret for two decades. A rumor had circulated just months after the clandestine negotiations, alleging that the United States had become a silent partner in the Anglo-Japanese Alliance. The Roosevelt administration quickly issued a denial. Not until 1925 did historian Tyler Dennett discover this unofficial tripartite pact in the Roosevelt Papers at the Library of Congress.[89] The president had taken unilateral and private actions that he considered vital to American security and in keeping with his moral code.

Roosevelt's support for Japan soon became evident, however, as he joined fellow Americans in sympathizing with the Japanese underdog fighting to uphold the Open Door in China against the Russian behemoth. But Roosevelt's favor ran deeper than protecting a nearly helpless China. Japanese efficiency demonstrated their increasingly "civilized" status based on Western economic, technological, and military advances. They, indeed, would be a postwar power.

In Roosevelt's push for a mediation by the concerned neutrals, he argued that a peace agreement must reflect the reality of Japan's decisive victory at Mukden and its succeeding spread northward into Manchuria. But no one—Japan, Russia, China, France, Germany, or Britain—showed interest in his year-long appeal for a mediated peace. Both belligerents felt confident of victory: China feared that it would become the sacrificial lamb for peace, and France and Germany did not trust each other. Neither the French nor the Germans wanted to alienate the Russians with the war's outcome uncertain. France hoped to maintain its alliance with Russia, and Germany sought to cultivate the tsar's friendship. Britain felt bound to France by the Entente Cordiale of 1904, which seemingly pushed the British into Russia's camp because of its Dual Alliance with France. Yet, Britain was tied to Russia's wartime enemy by the Anglo-Japanese Alliance of 1902. The secrets of the European alliance system had now revealed themselves at their worst.

Out of this diplomatic mire came a glimmer of hope when Roosevelt leaked information to the Japanese government on March 10, 1905, that he was willing to help bring about negotiations to end the war. Japan responded favorably and expressed interest in the president acting as mediator.[90]

The Tokyo government had realized it lacked the financial means and manpower to continue the war. The irony of its historic victory at Mukden in early 1905 had become clear: Japan's successful campaign had depleted its villages of young males, draining the national pool of soldiers and leaving females to work the fields and raise their families. Moreover, the time seemed propitious for ending the war because of the Japanese army's advances on the Asian mainland.

Problems remained. Japan insisted on a treaty that reflected its victory, and one of its most important demands was a Russian indemnity that would cover the costs of the conflict. Equally problematic was Russia's belief that it could win the war in spite of its glaring setbacks.[91]

Tsar Nicholas rejected all peace overtures and prepared for a naval Armageddon that would dwarf the legendary battle between the English fleet and the Spanish Armada in 1588. Despite the signs arguing against continuing the war—a nearly bankrupt Russian treasury; one battle defeat after another; all sea communications severed; the outbreak of a popular revolution at home in January 1905 that the St. Petersburg government could not put down because most of its troops were in Manchuria; and French warnings about the war exhausting their ally while they were on the verge of their own war with Germany—the tsar ignored these realities and cast his nation's future into one climactic battle with Japan. His Baltic fleet headed for East Asia, first to relieve Russian forces holding Port Arthur, and then to destroy the Japanese navy in its own waters.

Along the way, the Russian naval officers learned of the fall of Port Arthur on January 2, 1905, and in early May, as they approached the Sea of Japan, decided that the only course of action was to seek safe harbor in the Russian port of Vladivostok by taking the shortest and most dangerous of three northeastern routes—through Tsushima Strait between Japan and Korea.

Japan's officers had expected the Russians to choose this narrow path and ordered the imperial fleet to lie in wait off the south Korean coast.

The thirty-six warships comprising Russia's Baltic fleet had steamed 18,000 miles from the other side of the world—out of the Baltic Sea and around three continents to what became a showdown at Tsushima Strait on May 27–28, 1905. Admiral Togo Heihachiro's Japanese navy, already victorious at Port Arthur and in the Yellow Sea, bombarded the Russian fleet with a blizzard of shells that reached 2,000 blasts a minute and sent twenty-two of Admiral Zinovi Rozhdestvenski's vessels to the bottom. The Japanese navy captured or detained in port all the other Russian ships except three that escaped to Vladivostok. At the cost of three torpedo boats and just over 100 lives, Japanese forces killed 4,000 Russians and, in a final humiliation, took their admiral as prisoner.[92]

Roosevelt wrote Kaneko, "No wonder you are happy! Neither Trafalgar nor the defeat of the Spanish Armada was as complete—as overwhelming."[93]

⌒∞⌒

The tsar had been correct about the impending magnitude of the naval encounter: The near-total annihilation of the Russian fleet far surpassed the level of defeat experienced by the Spanish Armada.

One of the most iconic images of Roosevelt, this photograph carries the simple title "Theodore Roosevelt Laughing." *Source*: Library of Congress.

Sagamore Hill, Roosevelt's "Summer White House" at Oyster Bay. *Source*: Library of Congress.

President Roosevelt and his Cabinet. From left to right around the table in this photograph are Lyman J. Gage, Philander C. Knox, John D. Long, John Hay, James Wilson, Elihu Root, Ethan A. Hitchcock, and Charles E. Smith. *Source*: Library of Congress.

The First Spadesful. Roosevelt towers over ships in the harbor and pitches dirt toward Bogotá, Colombia, as a flag bears the words "new treaty"—a reference to Hay-Herrán and the Panamanian canal initiative. *Source*: Library of Congress.

President Roosevelt's Peace Messenger. Roosevelt dispatches a carrier pigeon from "The Hague" with an arbitration message as "War!" clouds hover over "Venezuela." *Source:* Library of Congress.

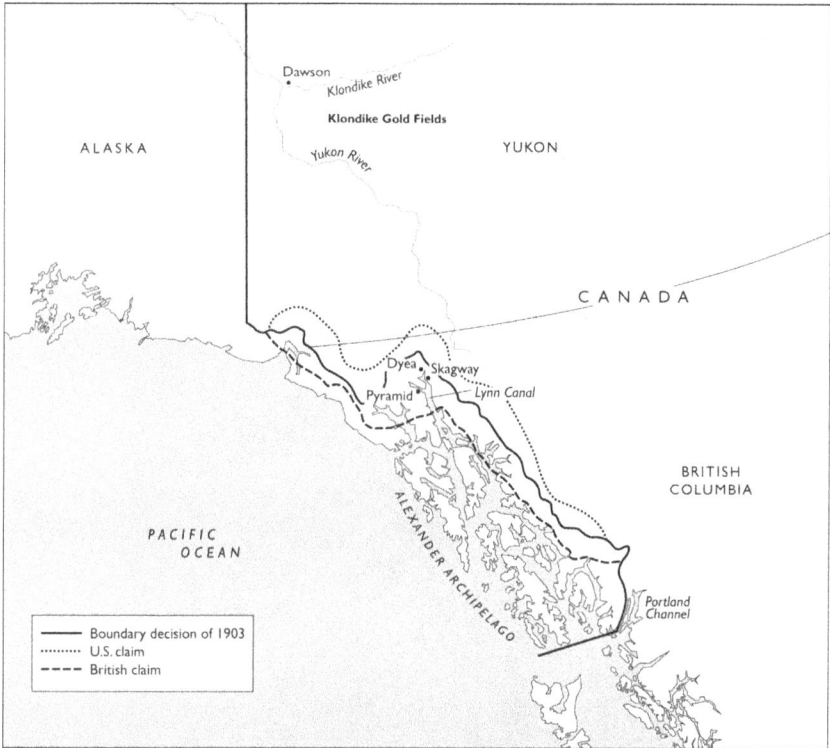

The Alaska Boundary Dispute. The map shows the extreme British (Canadian) claim and the extreme U.S. claim. The commissioners' boundary of 1903 shows a slightly narrower coastline, but contains everything Roosevelt required. *Source*: From Howard Jones, *Crucible of Power* (2008).

Portraits of Envoys at the Portsmouth Peace Conference. Appearing on this postcard proclaiming "We are fighters for peace" are, clockwise from top left, Baron Komura, Sergei Witte, Baron Rosen, and Kogoro Takahira, with Roosevelt in the center. *Source:* Library of Congress.

Theodore Roosevelt with Kaiser Wilhelm II. This photo was taken in Döberitz, Germany, in 1910 with German troops flanking the two mounted leaders. *Source*: Library of Congress.

Welcome home! Roosevelt greets the Great White Fleet on its return to Hampton Roads, Virginia. Behind him are sketches portraying George Washington and Uncle Sam as they join in the celebration of this major Roosevelt accomplishment. *Source*: Library of Congress.

THE BUSY SHOWMAN.—III.

The Busy Showman – III. In this third installment of *Harper's Weekly*'s "The Busy Showman" series on Roosevelt, the president's "Big Stick" rests on his shoulder while sailors manning turrets atop elephants follow to "Morocco via [the] Algeciras [Conference]." The message is clear: with strength comes respect and a critical role in maintaining peace. The original caption has the president dismissing a need for "precedent" as he addresses the people's perennial concern over international engagement with: "You need anticipate no so-called 'entanglements'." *Source:* Alamy.

Chapter 6

Peace at Portsmouth

I thought it my plain duty to make the effort. I have done my best to succeed and shall continue to do it to the end.

—President Theodore Roosevelt
August 5, 1905

The man who had been represented to us as impetuous to the point of rudeness, displayed a gentleness, a kindness, and a tactfulness mixed with self-control that only a truly great man can command.

—Professor Frederic Frommhold De Martens
January 1920

On May 31, 1905, three days after the Japanese navy destroyed most of the Russian fleet at Tsushima Strait, Tokyo's leaders secretly asked Roosevelt to mediate a peace. Negotiations should be between the belligerents, they asserted, although the United States as a neutral power could seek help in bringing the two antagonists together. Concerned about appearing weak, the Japanese did not want to publicly reveal their interest in peace and hoped that Roosevelt would present the idea to the Russians as "entirely of his own motion and initiative." If he agreed to do so, the Japanese would approve his choices on procedures to follow and whether to turn to another country for consultation. Japan would not make an overture to Russia.[1]

The president saw no value in offering to mediate an end to the war. "I do not want to do anything futile," he told a confidant. He and the French government had quietly tried to secure peace over the past four months, but Russian "folly" had led to the belief that the Japanese could not take Mukden and that the Russian fleet could defeat the Japanese navy. "Now Russia has nothing to offer and no threat to make." Japan would demand a heavy cost for peace; Russia would be unable to meet such a demand and be forced to continue the war. The conflict would move "from disaster to disaster."[2]

Senator Lodge agreed with the president, remarking that the Russians "did not so far as I can judge show as much pluck or fight as the Spaniards against us." The Japanese were "very formidable" both on land and at sea. Roosevelt and Lodge knew the odds were in Japan's favor, but they and most others had initially thought the Russians could win at Tsushima Strait. "No one," Roosevelt declared, "anticipated that it would be a rout and a slaughter rather than a fight; that the Russian fleet would be absolutely destroyed while the Japanese fleet was left practically uninjured."[3]

Roosevelt emphasized that he wanted the "best for Russia." To put pressure on its government to negotiate directly with Japan, he sent a memo of his thoughts to Ambassador George Meyer in St. Petersburg. He also had copies of the memo sent to German ambassador Sternburg, French ambassador Jean Jules Jusserand, and British chargé Hugh O'Beirne, hoping their governments would instruct their representatives in St. Petersburg to make the same argument. Roosevelt agreed with "all outsiders"—including Russia's friends—that continuing the war would cost all its holdings in East Asia.[4]

Perhaps Russia would meet if the invitation came from Washington.

I

Under the guise of his own initiative, President Roosevelt met on the same day Japan made its secret proposal—June 5—with the Russian ambassador in Washington, Arturo Cassini, asking him to inform the tsar that the United States would make a proposal for peace if both nations approved. The war appeared "absolutely hopeless for Russia," the president emphasized to Meyer, making it advisable that the two antagonists come together and draw up peace terms.[5]

Roosevelt privately asserted that the Russians had shown themselves inferior to the Japanese. The Russians, he wrote Lodge, "are hopeless creatures with whom to deal. They are utterly insincere and treacherous; they have no conception of truth, no willingness to look at facts in the face, no regard for others of any sort or kind, no knowledge of their own strength or weakness."[6] Despite having earlier listed Russians among the peoples advancing civilization, he now joined fellow Americans in criticizing their imperialism in Asia, along with the government's arbitrary sentencing of domestic dissenters to the frozen prisons in Siberia, its brutal attempts to absorb Finland, and its cruel treatment of Jewish people.

Roosevelt's offer drew no interest—not that this surprised him. Neither he nor Meyer trusted the Russian ambassador in Washington. To Lodge, the president remarked that Cassini had responded to the call for peace with his "usual rigmarole," insisting that Russia was fighting the "battles of the white race" and was "too great" to concede defeat.[7]

The situation abruptly changed that same day when Washington learned that Kaiser Wilhelm wanted the president to take the lead in making peace. The kaiser feared that the turmoil of what became known as the Russian Revolution of 1905 had made conditions inside Russia so volatile that news of the recent defeat at Tsushima Strait could escalate domestic insurrection and put the tsar's life in danger. He had written to his cousin Nicholas, pleading with him to seek an immediate peace. The United States, he assured the tsar, was the only nation the Japanese respected, making the president "the right person to appeal to" in persuading the Japanese to accept "reasonable proposals." To Ambassador Charlemagne Tower in Berlin, the kaiser made a request: "Please inform the President privately, from me personally, of the steps that I have taken, which I hope will be for the benefit of the world."[8]

Roosevelt interpreted this message from Wilhelm as an implicit invitation by Nicholas II to set up a meeting with his adversary. Like Japan, Russia did not want to publicly propose negotiations and appear to capitulate.

Roosevelt immediately instructed Meyer to inform the tsar that "by personal direction of the President," he was inviting Russia to join Japan in a conference to discuss peace. In a private letter soon afterward, Roosevelt explained that he did not want to be in the position of attempting "to squeeze out of Japan favorable terms to Russia." To avoid playing the role of mediator, he recommended that the two sides meet with no intermediary present. Afterward, they could seek suggestions from anyone on the outside. If Russia agreed to the offer, Roosevelt would act "simply on his own initiative" in trying to win Japan's approval, not revealing to either antagonist that the other one was interested in peace. To save face for both belligerents, he would not go public with his proposal until both parties agreed to meet. At that point, the president would openly ask each government to agree to a meeting between the belligerents.[9]

Roosevelt knew the Japanese wanted to end the war but that the Russians were undecided. Both the Japanese minister, Kogoro Takahira, and Cassini had come to him separately after the battle at Tsushima Strait. The Japanese "evidently want peace," the president told Lodge, but "pretty nearly on their own terms"; the Russians "seem helplessly and soddenly unable to decide what they want or how they are to get anything if they do want it."[10]

On that same stressful day of June 5, the president received a report from Meyer, who was equally confused about the Russian position. Despite widespread calls for peace, Nicholas appeared to prefer war over agreeing to pay a "large money indemnity." Meyer warned that a Japanese demand for an "excessive" indemnity would drive all Russian groups into their emperor's camp. "Everyone is really in the dark as to the Emperor's future policy," Meyer concluded. "Procrastination, lack of decision, no determined plan of action appear to be the order of the day."[11]

Roosevelt admitted to Lodge that there was little chance for peace, largely because the tsar "will refuse to do anything." If he rejected the proposal, "his blood must be on his own head."[12]

The president privately considered Japan a "formidable new power—a power jealous, sensitive and warlike, and which if irritated could at once take both the Philippines and Hawaii from us if she obtained the upper hand on the seas." Less than a week earlier, he had directed Secretary of War Taft to convince Congress of the need to fortify Subic Bay in the Philippines if the United States intended to keep them and Hawaii. Japan's "soldiers and sailors have shown themselves to be terrible foes . . . none more dangerous in all the world."[13]

Roosevelt cautioned that America should show "a spirit of generous justice and genuine courtesy toward Japan," while maintaining a strong U.S. navy. "That Japan will have her head turned to some extent I do not in the least doubt, and I see clear symptoms of it in many ways. We should certainly as a nation," he confessed, "have ours turned if we had performed such feats as the Japanese have in the past sixteen months."[14]

The Japanese, Roosevelt remarked, could not behave any worse than Californians in their legislature. They "wish grossly to insult the Japanese" by barring their immigrants from the United States as "an immoral, degraded and worthless race"—just as they had belittled the Chinese with the Exclusion Acts.[15]

In the meantime, on June 7, Meyer met alone with the tsar for the first time. His initial interview in early April had been with both the emperor and the empress, the latter, Meyer wrote the president, wanting the war to continue until Russia won. In his diary entry of April 12, Meyer wrote that she had drawn in close and watched her husband "like a cat," embarrassing him while implicitly warning against crossing her. This time, without her presence, Meyer could see that Russia was in an "absolutely hopeless" position and that continuing the contest would cost all its possessions in East Asia. The time had come for the two adversaries to meet and, "without intermediaries," discuss peace terms.[16]

After several exchanges—including Meyer's summarizing Roosevelt's instructions, later followed by his reading them verbatim to the tsar for added emphasis—Nicholas agreed with the president's assessment, calling this moment pivotal in that the Japanese had not yet invaded Russia. He had confidence in the president and hoped a restoration of the "old friendship" between Russia and the United States would facilitate a settlement. But, he added, "I realize that at almost any moment they [the Japanese] can make an attack on Sakhalin. Therefore it is important that the meeting should take place before that occurs."[17]

The news of Nicholas's decision had not yet reached Washington, leading to further confusion in Russian circles that the president recounted in a long note to Lodge nearly two weeks afterward. On June 6 (the same day Meyer secured the tsar's decision to meet the following day), Cassini informed Roosevelt that the Russian government had rejected his proposal for peace but asked him to attempt to moderate Japan's demands when they became known. The next day, however, the president received Meyer's note, saying that the tsar had approved the president's acting "on his own initiative" in proposing a meeting of the "plenipotentiaries" of both sides (with no "intermediary") to determine whether it was "possible for them to agree to terms of peace." As if a hidden hand had scripted a formula for peace that each belligerent had independently proposed, the tsar had made the same stipulation earlier made by Japan: His decision must be "absolutely secret" until his enemy also agreed—as Meyer reported.[18]

Cassini had received no word from St. Petersburg of this change in policy and suggested that Meyer "might have misinterpreted or forgotten what the Emperor had said." The president had Cassini's claim cabled to Meyer, who secured the permission of the Russian minister of foreign affairs, Count Vladimir Lamsdorff, to affirm that the account was accurate—which he did. To Lodge, Roosevelt quipped, "Is not this characteristically Russian?"[19]

Cassini, meanwhile, tried to justify the tsar's shift in position by raising suspicions about the president's recent behavior. Roosevelt was meeting too many times with the Japanese minister and representatives of the neutral powers. He was trying to make Russia act before it was ready. Finally, the president had interned Russian ships at Manila, an act that Cassini indignantly denounced as out of order. "This," he objected, "is not the time to establish new principles of international law."[20]

Roosevelt considered the first protest "impertinent," the second unfounded, and the third worthy of only a brief explanation. He had refused to allow the Russian ships to enter that port for repairs resulting from the battle and then had interned them. In response to Cassini's protest, Roosevelt stated that it was exactly the time to establish a new principle in international law and that it was now in effect.[21]

Nicholas had finally agreed to Roosevelt's proposal for peace, primarily because of the dire prognosis for Russia in the war. The president's task had not been easy, given the tsar's inability to grasp the enormity of Russia's defeats at Mukden and Tsushima Strait. Nicholas relented out of fear of a Japanese attack on Sakhalin and the strong pressure for peace coming from several sources, particularly from his cousin, the kaiser. Roosevelt understood that he needed to maintain the delicate balance of playing up to the tsar's adolescent fantasies while upholding a resolute but openly fair respect for the emerging Japanese power. From the beginning of this peace enterprise, Roosevelt remained outwardly calm while inwardly seething with anger.[22]

Only later did the president privately remark that he was "amused" at both sides for wanting him to appear to take the initiative on peace proceedings.[23]

Roosevelt prepared to inform the Russian government that Japan had agreed to the proposal, and that he intended to publicize the news. He hoped the two antagonists could resolve the issue by themselves, but he would help arrange the time and place of their meeting.[24]

II

Roosevelt moved quickly. On June 8, the acting secretary of state, Francis Loomis, informed Russia and Japan that the president had made his good offices available for urging the two belligerents to meet without an intermediary to negotiate peace terms. Cassini verbally agreed to the proposal, and two days later Japan gave its approval.[25]

Trouble came in less than a week when the Russian foreign office equivocated about determining peace terms by instead agreeing to a meeting "to see if it is not possible for the two powers to agree to terms of peace." Roosevelt volunteered to Lodge that this less than "definite committal" had "most naturally irritated Japan."[26]

Roosevelt assured Russia that no risk would come from joining Japan in talks aimed at reaching a final settlement when its terms were subject to ratification by both home governments. He emphasized to Cassini that it was "nonsense" to argue over details that would prolong the war and result in his country's losing its possessions in East Asia, while leaving Russia with "well-nigh irreparable" problems at home. "I should be very sorry, because of my real regard for the Russian people and because of my regard for the interests of the world generally, to see her driven out of territory which had been hers for a couple of centuries." Russia's "military position was now hopeless" and the war "assuredly a failure."[27]

Roosevelt now turned to the Japanese, warning against excessive demands that might cause Russia to fight another year when they had already won Port Arthur and Korea, along with a dominant position in Manchuria. Japan nonetheless refused to meet without a "categorical answer" from Russia about whether to appoint representatives who had authorization to make peace. As he had done with Russia, the president warned Japan that quibbling over details would leave "a most unfortunate impression" in the United States and in Europe. The general feeling was that Japan wanted peace on fair terms, and that the Russians had held back for no good reason. Prolonging the war would come at a debilitating cost in Japanese manpower and finances, all for the *possibility* of gaining control of Eastern Siberia, an area of no importance to Japan. In a statement that Roosevelt had to explain to Takahira afterward, he asserted that "I should have been only too glad to give Russia the shell as long as I kept the kernel."[28]

To Lodge, Roosevelt emphasized his overriding concern—that a decision by Russia to continue the fight would leave no nation strong enough to stem Japan's postwar expansion in the region. Even though a Russian victory would be "a blow to civilization, her destruction as an eastern Asiatic power would also in my opinion be unfortunate." The best outcome would be Russia standing "face to face with Japan so that each may have a moderating action on the other."[29]

By mid-June 1905, Roosevelt was losing patience with both Russia and Japan as well as with the kaiser. "In short, the more I see of the Tsar, the Kaiser, and the Mikado the better I am content with democracy, even if we have to include the American newspaper as one of its assets—liability would be a better term." Russia, he told Lodge, was "so corrupt, so treacherous and shifty, and so incompetent, that I am utterly unable to say whether or not it will make peace, or break off the negotiations at any moment." Japan was "entirely selfish, though with a veneer of courtesy, and with infinitely more knowledge of what it wants and capacity to get it." Russia "does not believe in the genuineness of my motives and words, and I sometimes doubt whether Japan does."[30]

To press the issue, and, as he noted, "ease the Japanese mind," Roosevelt sent a memorandum to Cassini on June 15, informing him that the Japanese government had authorized its two plenipotentiaries to negotiate a peace, subject to ratification by the home government.[31]

The big break in the standoff unexpectedly came later that day, when Roosevelt learned that his use of the word plenipotentiary in his memorandum to Cassini had inadvertently won over Russia. Japan's reference to plenipotentiary, Cassini explained, removed his government's greatest objection to the talks, because the term left the door open for Russia to reject unfavorable terms. Although its delegates would have full authority to negotiate a treaty, its final approval must come from home—the point Roosevelt had repeatedly emphasized to both antagonists from the beginning of the process.[32]

The president must have been puzzled by Cassini's claim that the word plenipotentiary provided an honorable way out of the stalemate. Over a week before, on June 6, Meyer had met with Nicholas and followed Roosevelt's instruction to propose that the "plenipotentiaries" of both Russia and Japan meet without "intermediaries." The tsar had agreed. Two days later, Roosevelt notified Meyer that Japan had agreed to the proposal and that the news would become public when both sides were aware of the agreement. Apparently, Roosevelt remarked, no one had told Cassini.[33]

That issue settled, Japan and Russia suggested locations for the peace talks, neither of which satisfied the other one. Roosevelt recommended The Hague, but both parties strongly opposed that move and preferred Washington. Roosevelt agreed to the proposal and assured them he would select "some cool, comfortable and retired place for the meeting of the plenipotentiaries, where the conditions will be agreeable, and there will be as much freedom from interruption as possible."[34]

The impending end to the Russo-Japanese War set off a flurry of activity not only in East Asia but in other parts of a world that had become entangled in alliances and competing national interests. It was no coincidence that Lodge had warned Roosevelt in early June that Germany was taking advantage of the imminent peace in East Asia to expand its interests in the Western Hemisphere. He noted in the morning's dispatches that, under the guise of the Danish Asiatic Company, the Hamburg-American Company intended to build a coaling station at St. Thomas in the Caribbean. "It is the thin edge of the wedge and I do not like the move at all." The kaiser was "restless and tricky," only pretending to be on friendly terms. As a precautionary measure, Lodge recommended that the United States try to buy the Danish West Indies and Denmark's colony of Greenland. Roosevelt seemed amenable to the ideas once the administration had resolved the ongoing domestic problems in Santo Domingo.[35]

The president recognized the dangers posed by the kaiser, even when he seemed to be on America's side by encouraging Russia to end the war and warning the White House that, like Asia, Europe and Africa were not immune from the growing danger of world war. The fear of a global conflagration was, in fact, rising over a dispute between France and Germany over Morocco. The European powers were taking sides and weighing alliance obligations. From Berlin, Sternburg sent a memo informing Roosevelt of the kaiser's belief that Britain would support France in a war, "not on account of Morocco," but over Germany's expansionist policy in East Asia. The kaiser thought the Anglo-French navies "would undoubtedly smash the German Navy," opening East Asia to Britain, France, Japan, and Russia; and Nicholas, he suspected, "might try to cede a portion of China to Japan as a war indemnity, instead of parting with the island of Sakhalin." To ease the growing international tension, the kaiser urged Roosevelt to convince the British of the need for a conference on Morocco that might, in turn, facilitate peace in East Asia as well as Europe and Africa.[36]

By mid-June 1905, Roosevelt feared an outbreak of war in Europe and tried to hurry the peace process between Russia and Japan. Not only would a European war threaten France, he told his friend and ambassador to Britain, Whitelaw Reid, it could lead to a global conflict that affected all nations.[37]

Roosevelt still had little faith in the Russians making peace and being truthful. "What I cannot understand about the Russian is the way he will lie when he knows perfectly well that you know he is lying." Neither the tsar nor the Russian government and its people would face the facts. It was in Russia's interest, along with that of the world, to make peace. "I should be sorry to see Russia driven completely off the Pacific coast and driven practically east to Lake Baikal, and yet something like this will surely happen if she refuses to make peace."[38]

Roosevelt also remained wary of the Japanese: Even though their government claimed the war was more about self-defense than territorial gains, it admitted to wanting Sakhalin, along with what Takahira called a "moderate and reasonable" indemnity. Roosevelt understood the airy feeling of certain victory, yet remained suspicious of Japan's raising its demands. "No power could fail to," press its advantage, "after such astounding victories," he told Lodge. He must remain in good standing with the Japanese. Once more he explained that he had intervened at their request and had taken each step with their knowledge ahead of time—not only with their approval but with their "expressed desire." Roosevelt remarked that this provided "a rather comic turn" to the British criticism that he had acted primarily in the interest of Russia and that Japan was moving "rather magnanimously" in agreeing to the talks. "My move is really more in the interest of Russia than of Japan, but it is greatly to the interest of Japan also."[39]

The Japanese were, he wrote Spring Rice, a "wonderful people" and well advanced in industry and warfare. Japan was already expanding trade throughout the Pacific and into China and would soon be a formidable rival to the United States and other countries in that region. The United States must treat the Japanese in a just and courteous manner to discourage trouble with them or any other people.

> But if we bluster; if we behave rather badly to other nations; if we show that we regard the Japanese as an inferior and alien race, and try to treat them as we have treated the Chinese; and if at the same time we fail to keep our navy at the highest point of efficiency and size—then we shall invite disaster.[40]

Roosevelt warned that in a decade or so Japan would be an even more formidable military power and the leading industrial nation in the Pacific.

He had thought (despite his earlier faith in the Baltic Fleet) that the Japanese could win the battle at Tsushima Strait, but as he told Spring Rice, he never expected "a slaughter." Japan, he wrote Lodge, would turn to the Philippines after resolving its problems with China.[41]

At one point, Roosevelt asserted to Spring Rice, "I should not be surprised if the peace negotiations broke off at any moment." Both powers appeared to distrust him. His difficulties as a peace negotiator had been "rather worse than getting a treaty through the United States Senate!" Both sides were "so suspicious," "so unreasonable," and "so foolish." If the war continued another year, the Japanese would, indeed, push Russia out of East Asia but with no compensating indemnity and a huge expenditure in manpower and money for the acquisition of territory of little value. An immediate peace would require Russia to give up Sakhalin and pay an indemnity, while recognizing Japan's control over areas it had already taken. Still, Russia would emerge with its territories in East Asia largely intact and with some semblance of self-respect. He hoped France and Germany would encourage Russia to agree to these terms, and that the British would convince Japan to accept.[42]

On June 18, Roosevelt's patience won out. Russia agreed to meet with Japan in Washington to explore the possibility of drawing up peace terms, all subject to approval at home.[43]

III

With the two antagonists now having settled on the meeting, Lodge voiced his concern that the greatest obstacle to peace would be the Russians, not the "excessive demands" by the Japanese. The continuing war, Lodge asserted, was attributable to the "hopeless, sodden stupidity of the Russians who either will not or cannot look facts in the face but think that they can win by lying without limit to themselves as well as to others." Russia's leaders were "desperate adventurers who care nothing for the country but only for their own place and power." They were "autocrats without intelligence, the sole thing which can excuse the existence of autocracy for a moment."[44]

Roosevelt concurred, acknowledging the Japanese as civilized and equal to other civilized people. His policy, he assured a missionary to Japan, was to "treat Japan the Nation just exactly as I would like to have Japan treat the United States; and to treat each individual Japanese strictly on his merits, just as I would like each American treated." He added, "I should hang my head with shame if I were capable of discriminating against a Japanese general or admiral, statesman, philanthropist or artist, because he and I have different shades of skin."[45]

The president thought the Japanese had soundly defeated the Russians both on land and at sea. If Russia continued the war, he told Meyer, it might avoid paying an indemnity but at the risk of losing Eastern Siberia and eastern Asia, areas it had held for more than two centuries. It should agree to Japan's call for Sakhalin and a reasonable indemnity. It was in the interests of Russia and the world to end the war now.[46]

The Japanese assured the president that they would appoint high-ranking plenipotentiaries and expected Russia to do the same. Fellow Harvard graduate Kentaro Kaneko reminded his friend in the White House that Japan had felt insulted in earlier negotiations with European powers who sent mere representatives. Their victories at Mukden and Tsushima Strait entitled them to equal status and respect at the peace table. Roosevelt agreed. The Russian government must appoint emissaries of equal rank whose aim was to work with the Japanese in negotiating a peace treaty that would go to each home government for approval. The Japanese remained dubious about whether the Russian representatives would have the authority to reach an agreement. To relieve this suspicion, the president stipulated that before an armistice took place, both sides must have their plenipotentiaries named and bearing public instructions to work toward a treaty of peace, subject to approval at home.[47]

The kaiser, Roosevelt wrote Ambassador Tower in Berlin, must convince the tsar to accept peace while I "endeavor to make them [Japanese] moderate" their demands. But under current circumstances, the president suggested, Russia should be relieved to pay a "substantial indemnity" and forfeit Sakhalin. "If she is wise she will thus welcome it."[48]

The president welcomed German assistance in ending the Russo-Japanese War, not because he was under the influence of Wilhelm but because he needed German cooperation to defuse the tense relations among the major powers that could endanger world peace. He had followed the kaiser's advice in talking with France about the necessity of averting war in Europe; and in late June, he informed Sternburg that the French had agreed to attend a conference on Morocco. The president had been hesitant to intervene and risk charges of "officious interference," but he chose to do so after the kaiser's appeal. The French concession, Roosevelt declared to Sternburg in words the president knew would make their way to the kaiser, marked "a diplomatic triumph of the first magnitude." In a purposeful use of hyperbole, Roosevelt called him "the leader among the sovereigns of today who have their faces set toward the future."[49]

President Roosevelt notified the Japanese government that Russia had agreed to meet in the first ten days of August. The Japanese were considering as their two chief envoys Baron Jutaro Komura, the secretary for foreign affairs, and Baron Kogoro Takahira, the Japanese minister in Washington and friend of the president. Russia approved both selections. On July 7, eight

Japanese advisers, headed by Komura, boarded the steamer *Minnesota* for Washington, DC, where they would join Takahira.[50]

In the meantime, Roosevelt agreed to Russia's request to ask Japan for an armistice, even though he was not optimistic. Russia, he wrote Meyer, must make major concessions before Japan agreed to peace. The Japanese were confident they could win the war and did not trust the Russians in the negotiations. "The Japanese triumph is absolute and Russia's position critical in the extreme." If the tsar did not make peace and focus on domestic difficulties, "the disaster to Russia will be so great that she will cease to count among the great powers for a generation to come." On the other side, he explained to Lodge, Japan feared that "magnanimity on her part would be misinterpreted and turned to bad account against her." Only after the Russians had arrived in the United States did Roosevelt think they might reach an armistice.[51]

One of Roosevelt's greatest challenges was to preserve the Open Door in China in the face of competing national interests while not becoming directly involved in the negotiations. Before the delegates from Japan and Russia departed for the United States, U.S. minister William Rockhill in Peking informed Washington that China welcomed President Roosevelt as mediator in ending the Russo-Japanese War but emphasized that he must protect Chinese territorial rights in the process. The White House quickly assured China that the United States would do everything possible on China's behalf but would have nothing to do with the talks. China warned that it must have the right to approve any territorial arrangements made by Russia and Japan in the negotiations.[52]

China was by no means the only hindrance to the talks: Roosevelt was still exasperated over Russia's continued refusal to face reality. "Oh Lord! I have been growing nearly mad in the effort to get Russia and Japan together," he privately told Ambassador Reid in London. The Japanese had earned the right to make demands that Roosevelt did not consider excessive. Russia, however, was "so suddenly stupid and the Government is such an amorphous affair that they really do not know *what* they want." To Lodge, the president asserted that Russia had the choice of either accepting "severe defeat" or suffering the "far greater penalty of irretrievable disaster."[53]

Roosevelt emphasized to Meyer that he must convince the tsar that the Japanese had gained the upper hand in East Asia and that extremists in Japan would call for pushing the Russians into the Pacific if they did not agree to peace. Moderates would probably accept a high indemnity, the island of Sakhalin (which they had just invaded and would have a firm grip on by the end of July), and continued control over Manchuria and Korea. Russian insistence on pursuing the war would be a disastrous mistake.[54]

Complications also arose from non-participants in the war. The British dawdled over mediation, choosing not to press their Japanese ally and, in fact, appeared agnostic about ending the war altogether. In mid-June, Roosevelt instructed Loomis to cable Ambassador Reid in London that "The President desires you to find out whether the English Government really does wish peace." It was in the British interest, Roosevelt told Reid three weeks later, "to have peace come with Russia face to face with Japan in east [*sic*] Siberia." Such an outcome would guarantee against any Russian move toward India or Persia; if the war continued, however, and the Japanese took East Siberia, they would inflict significant damage on Russia but would themselves sustain crippling losses in manpower and matériel.

In late July, Roosevelt sought and received assurances from Spring Rice that the British were not contemplating acquiescence to a "hostile combination against Japan." Any development of this nature he strongly opposed as injurious to the construction of a balance of power in East Asia. The president informed Spring Rice that shortly after war broke out, he had privately warned France and Germany that if they allied against Japan as Russia, Germany, and France had done in 1894, he would "side with Japan" in protecting its interests. Roosevelt did concede to his old friend that, at the moment, "most of this talk as to what England ought to do is academic, because I think the Japanese have probably made up their minds just about what they will accept and what they won't."[55]

Roosevelt further confided to Spring Rice that he had made no attempt to bring about peace talks until the Japanese had asked him to do so. They assured him of no interest in East Siberia or any other territory aside from Sakhalin. Roosevelt expected them to take over Russian rights and possessions in Manchuria and to spread their influence over Korea.[56]

In a "Confidential" note to Reid, the president explained that Japan had two battlefield choices for ending the war, both of which he had repeatedly emphasized to Komura and Takahira would cost more than $1 million a day while disabling Russia so badly that it would not be able to pay any indemnity. Either push the Russians out of East Siberia and into the Pacific or drive them out of Manchuria and Korea, seize Sakhalin, and leave East Siberia vulnerable to Japanese armies in Manchuria who could hold the region as a perpetual "hostage for Russia's good behavior." Although the Japanese have "informed me," that they "do not want east [*sic*] Siberia and do not want the war to continue," they have, nevertheless, adopted the second choice.[57]

Roosevelt lamented that neither party would listen to reason. In either case, the Russians would suffer a "serious defeat" or "further and perhaps overwhelming disaster." If they "persistently refuse to see any light, all we can do is to shrug our shoulders and let them go on to their fate." As for the Japanese, "I am not at all sure" that anyone can influence them.[58]

The Russians had, meanwhile, put together a peace delegation by mid-July that prepared for immediate departure to Washington. Heading its twelve members were the ambassador to the United States, Baron Roman Rosen (already in Washington), and Secretary of State Sergei Witte, who was also president of the committee of ministers and first plenipotentiary of Russia. On July 26, 1905, the Russian delegates left Cherbourg, France, and arrived in New York on August 1.[59]

In the meantime, the president had to deal with a private understanding that did not become public until the 1920s but had immediate ramifications in East Asia. On July 27, 1905, Japanese Prime Minister Taro Katsura and Secretary of War Taft shared a conversation in Tokyo about Japan's objectives in the Philippine Islands and Korea. Taft believed that the Japanese wanted the Philippines under the direction of a "strong and friendly" United States, rather than under Filipinos incapable of self-government or an "unfriendly European power." Katsura stated in the "strongest terms" that his country had no "aggressive designs" in the Philippines and that the so-called "yellow peril" was no more than "malicious and clumsy slanders" intended to denigrate Japan.

As for Korea, Katsura considered that small country an issue of "absolute importance" to Japan and the central cause of the war with Russia. If Korea remained independent after the war, it would "certainly drift back" into unfavorable treaties with other powers and revive the international issues that helped bring on the war. Taft thought it necessary for a general peace that Japanese troops establish a "suzerainty" over Korea that prohibited it from entering any treaty without Japan's approval.

Katsura emphasized that the Japanese wanted peace in East Asia that rested on the Open Door principle supported by Japan, the United States, and Great Britain. A "good understanding" would assure a peace that benefited everyone, without the unnecessary commitments entailed in the creation of a multilateral alliance.

Taft warned that it would be nearly impossible for the president to enter into any agreement without Senate approval, but he added that the American people wanted peace in East Asia and would work with the Japanese and British as closely as if the government in Washington had signed a treaty. In the "agreed memorandum of conversation" of July 31, 1905, Japan consented to U.S. supervisory control over the Philippine Islands in exchange for U.S. recognition of Japan's hegemony over Korea. Taft assured Katsura that he would recommend presidential approval; Katsura promised to do the same with the prime minister.[60]

Would the president approve? This informal agreement marked a major reversal in policy from three months earlier, when Roosevelt told George Kennan that there was little chance for Senate approval of an American alliance with Japan and Britain.

That same day, the president telegrammed Taft: "Your conversation with Count Katsura absolutely correct in every respect."[61]

IV

The president had meanwhile kept his promise to find a cooler place than Washington for the peace talks in late summer: the big hall of the Naval Building at the Portsmouth Naval Shipyard in Kittery, Maine, located near the small town of Portsmouth, New Hampshire. To prevent interruptions from reporters and onlookers, the president had chosen an isolated site that required the delegates to leave their hotel in nearby New Castle and be ferried by navy cutters across the Piscataqua River to the navy yard.[62]

Before the two sides convened on August 6, Roosevelt had to deal with several sensitive matters of protocol. He had already met privately in his home with each delegation's leaders—on July 28 with Japan's foreign minister, Komura, and its minister in Washington, Takahira, and on August 4 with their Russian counterparts, Secretary of State Witte and Ambassador Rosen.

These personal meetings were as different as day and night. Komura and Takahira were cordial and candid in their expectations, but amenable to the president's recommendation against using the word indemnity in the talks. The Russians were stiff and unfriendly—the tone of their meeting set by Witte, who towered over everyone at six-foot four inches tall and seemed humorless. Even though he wanted peace, he did not think Russia had lost the war and refused to approve paying an indemnity to Japan. "If the Japanese do not come around to our point of view," he warned the president, "then we will conduct a defensive war to the last extreme and we will see who will last the longest."[63]

There was little reason for optimism. The president's expression of concern about reaching a peace agreement led Witte to telegraph Foreign Secretary Lamsdorff that the chances for an agreement were small. Witte read his host correctly. "I do not think the Russians mean peace," Roosevelt wrote Lodge. To Spring Rice, he remarked that "Witte impressed me much while he was here, but by no means altogether pleasantly."[64]

These two meetings proved a less than auspicious beginning for the proceedings. How would the two delegations act when they came face to face over specific issues? The first test came during the president's formal welcome at a reception on board the USS *Mayflower*, Admiral George Dewey's flagship during the Venezuelan crisis and now a presidential yacht temporarily moored at Oyster Bay. At noon on August 5, in the midst of bands playing and guns firing salutes, the delegations came aboard as the flag of each party joined that of the United States waving above, the Japanese first and then the Russians, with the order of their boarding based on their order of arrival in the United States.[65]

The pivotal occasion was the first meeting of the antagonists—a luncheon where the questions of precedence and order took top priority. How to import a European and imperial style into the proceedings that both antagonists would welcome as familiar? Which language would the conferees use? Who would be the first to enter the dining area? Who would sit on the president's right-hand side? Which nation would he toast first?

Petty issues? Perhaps—when raised within a reasonably sedate context. But this was no gathering of friends. The two peoples were still at war, with the Japanese insisting they had won and the Russians maintaining they had not lost. Failure at this initial point could end the proceedings before the negotiations began. The minuscule thus became the monumental, compelling Roosevelt to navigate his way through this delicate tangle of longtime ethnic and racial animosities, visceral anger and personal resentment, and intense national pride on both sides. How to bring peace to a historical relationship built on war and rumors of war?

Roosevelt handled the touchy affair with a masterful blend of personal and diplomatic charm, and he later boasted of being "dee-lighted" with the outcome. As the delegates of each nation boarded the ship, the Japanese were escorted into the salon below to meet the president; the Russians followed a few moments later. After introducing both party's delegates to each other, the president briefly conversed with them, the Russians in French and the Japanese in English. He then broke an awkward silence by easing them to the doorway of an adjoining room for lunch. "Mr. Witte," the president asked, "will you come to lunch with Baron Komura?" With one on either side of him, Roosevelt led them into the dining room.

The luncheon, to the guests' surprise, was not a formal sit-down affair but a stand-up event at which servers from behind a round buffet table filled the delegates' plates. Chairs dispersed unevenly around the room provided seating if desired. Roosevelt had meanwhile taken a seat in the corner and invited the heads of each delegation to join him.

Once everyone had settled with their food, their champagne glasses filled and the luncheon underway, President Roosevelt stood and announced with glass in hand: "Gentlemen, I propose a toast to which there will be no answer and which I ask you to drink in silence, standing." With everyone now out of their chairs, he declared,

> I drink to the welfare and prosperity of the sovereigns and to the peoples of the two great nations whose representatives have met one another on this ship. It is my most earnest hope and prayer, in the interest of not only these two great powers, but of all civilized mankind, that a just and a lasting peace may speedily be concluded between them.

A photograph session followed on the deck, after which the president departed for home to a twenty-one-gun salute.[66]

Roosevelt's grace and elegance had brought a better result than anyone could have imagined. Each side had watched for any slight to its honor, but neither delegation could find anything worthy of complaint. The frozen atmosphere gradually thawed into an almost warm surrounding in which civil conversations took place that astounded the participants as well as the observers. When the luncheon came to an end, Takahira and Rosen shook hands.

That night, in his home at Oyster Bay, Roosevelt admitted to his guest, Joseph Bishop, that he had "looked forward to the meeting with anxiety, realizing that a single slip of any kind on his part that could be construed as favoring one set of envoys more than the other would be fatal. No such slip had occurred and . . . the first and very important step toward a successful outcome had been taken." The "whole world" was watching him, he declared, and if he failed as peacemaker, he would be the object of "universal condemnation." Despite his resistance to personally mediating peace, he knew that his role was both visible and critical. In the end, it would prove decisive.[67]

In a scripted text with a storybook ending, the ensuing negotiations would have gone easily, but they did not. The president never attended the negotiations but maintained daily back-channel discussions by cable with representatives of both Japan and Russia, listening to their advice and offering some of his own while attempting to moderate each side's demands. Japan initially demanded the entire northern Siberian island of Sakhalin and more than $600 million in war indemnities. The tsar rejected both demands, doubtless suspecting that the Japanese government faced a desperate domestic situation that necessitated peace. He also sensed a shift in American popular sympathy away from Japan, largely the result of Witte's suave demeanor and appearance of reason—but also perhaps attributable to U.S. fears of Japan's continued conquests threatening the China market and stirring up American racial animosities toward both the Japanese and the Chinese. Would the tsar continue the war?[68]

Roosevelt understood that intervening in other countries' affairs was dangerous, especially during an ongoing war. If the issue is a "simple misunderstanding," he explained to Ambassador Reid in London, he would consider accepting an invitation to step in and offer suggestions on how to prevent the matter from reaching the "danger point." But if those parties were to have a "genuine conflict of interest" that has led to war or could do so, "there is no use of my interfering." Hence his great care to avoid direct participation in the Russo-Japanese negotiations. "I do not try and never shall try in such case unless I am myself willing in the last resort to back up my action by force."[69]

Roosevelt put it on a personal level: Intervention to stop a war was equivalent to trying to stop a fight and then becoming involved in that fight. "I have a horror of the individual who bluffs and, when his bluff is called, does not fight, and have always acted upon the cardinal principle of the Western man in the good old days when I first struck the cattle country—'Never draw unless you mean to shoot.'"[70]

Roosevelt continued talking with both sides while hoping that someone could help him convince the two antagonists to sign a peace treaty. Even if the British wanted peace based on only their interests, he told Reid, they could put pressure on the Japanese to end the war. Germany or France, he suggested to Sternburg, might persuade Russia to accept peace terms. He agreed with Russia's opposition to Japanese demands to hold onto its interned ships and he concurred with Japan's desire to place limitations on the Russian navy in the Pacific. The Japanese had surprised him by offering to return the northern half of Sakhalin to Russia in exchange for a "substantial sum" of money that would also facilitate the return of the Russian prisoners. This would be a "just and honorable" peace, the president wrote Sternburg. Such a settlement would be in both antagonists' interests, but more so for Russia.[71]

Continuing the war, Roosevelt had long realized, would hurt Japan financially while Russia would lose the East Siberian provinces it had held for centuries. The proposed settlement would protect ancient boundaries, requiring Russia to give up only the southern part of an island that had belonged to Japan just three decades ago. The Russians could not hope to retake Sakhalin with their navy, but they knew that holding onto the northern half of the island would help secure Vladivostok along with Eastern Siberia. For the interests of both warring nations, along with "military expediency" and "broad humanity," this would be a wise settlement. Roosevelt hoped the kaiser would persuade the tsar to accept its terms.[72]

Roosevelt maintained communications with Japan's negotiating team through his friend Kentaro Kaneko, who was in New York and kept the president at Oyster Bay in contact with Japanese foreign minister Komura at the Portsmouth proceedings. Roosevelt warned Kaneko of the widespread opposition among Japan's friends to continuing the war over the insistence of an indemnity of up to $600 million. To make an exorbitant demand would harden Russia's opposition to an indemnity and thereby encourage Japan to take East Siberia, though at the cost of considerable manpower and perhaps $500 million or more. And worse, it would leave the Russians unable to pay any amount to ease that financial burden. "Every interest of civilization and humanity forbids the continuance of this war merely for a large indemnity."[73]

Roosevelt strongly advised Witte to approve the terms under consideration as "an absolutely just and honorable peace." Even though Sakhalin was militarily important to the safety of Eastern Siberia and Vladivostok, Russia's leaders must recognize that the Japanese were in possession of nearly the entire island and that their victory at Tsushima Strait had left the Russian navy so weakened that it could not dislodge them. The best approach would be a compromise: Russia should offer to purchase the northern half of Sakhalin and leave the southern sector to Japan.[74]

The president added a personal touch to his pleas to Nicholas by offering assurances that this advice was his own, extended from an "earnest well-wisher" of Russian welfare. The Japanese had dropped several demands and now, in exchange for a "substantial sum" of money, were willing to release Russian prisoners and return the northern half of Sakhalin to Russia. As he had reminded Witte, the destruction of the Russian navy had cost it any chance of retaking the rest of the island in the future, but the guarantee of the northern half assured the safety of Vladivostok and East Siberia. These terms, the president contended, would be "just and honorable" and avert a "dreadful calamity."[75]

Roosevelt knew that the tsar opposed buying half of Sakhalin from Japan; the payment, the emperor feared, would leave the appearance of an indemnity paid by a "vanquished nation." Roosevelt insisted that the exchange of money could not be open to interpretation as a war indemnity and argued to the Russian representatives that the southern half of Sakhalin had once belonged to Japan and its disposition was not at issue. Roosevelt instructed Meyer to make clear to the tsar that he intended to persuade the Japanese to set a fair price for northern Sakhalin. The alternative would be a "terrible disaster" for Russia.[76]

V

Meyer met a second time with the tsar in the late afternoon of August 23 and cautioned him that, with Japan currently occupying all of Sakhalin, the wisest course for Russia was to divide the island. Japan at one time had owned it, and Russia should settle for the northern half. Nicholas insisted on an honorable peace, which meant no indemnity and no territorial changes. Meyer pointed to a map and emphasized how important northern Sakhalin was to Russia and that to refuse a compromise could lead to the Japanese keeping the entire island and leaving Vladivostok and East Siberia virtually unprotected. Even then, the tsar insisted, his people would continue the war rather than pay an indemnity. "If necessary, I will go to the front myself and join my army."[77]

Meyer had to counter a number of arguments in trying to convince Nicholas that the destruction of the Russian navy made the division of Sakhalin the best outcome. When the tsar insisted that his troops could cross the strait when frozen, Meyer asserted that they would then "be surrounded by the Japanese fleet after the ice breaks." There would be continuous trouble on the island, Nicholas asserted. The two nations could cohabit Sakhalin, Meyer argued. Referring to the map again, he turned his host's attention to the success of a compromise in North America. The boundary between Maine and Canada was not the St. Lawrence River, Meyer asserted, and yet the United States and Britain had had no problems after drawing the line by treaty in 1842. Nicholas had no arguments left and agreed to a division of Sakhalin. The meeting lasted two hours, but by 6 p.m. Meyer had convinced the tsar to accept the compromise.[78]

An ocean away, Roosevelt appealed to Kaneko in two notes of August 22 and 23 that it was in the interest of both Japan and the world to withdraw the indemnity demand and accept the peace proposal. "Remember, I do not speak of continuing the war rather than give up Sakhalin, which I think would be right; but of continuing the war in order to get a great sum of money from Russia, which I think would be wrong." It would cost Japan too much to extend the war another year; and if it still did not get the money, it could never make up for the humiliation and the great losses in blood and treasure. Manchuria and its railroad, Korea, Port Arthur, Dalny, and Sakhalin—Japan controlled them all while in effect doubling the size of its fleet by "destroying that of Russia." Better to end the war in triumph than to prolong it by expending more than it could ever get from an exhausted and depleted Russia. Japan's "duty" to the civilized world was to end the war in the name of all that was "lofty and noble."[79]

Still unable to forge a peace, the president vented his exasperation on the U.S. ambassador to Italy, Henry White. "I am in the last throes of trying to get the Russians and Japanese to make peace." Russia was worse because it refused to consider itself defeated. But the Japanese should not continue the war merely for money. The British government had been "foolishly reluctant" to urge the Japanese to be reasonable and had not performed as well as the German and French governments had in advising Russia to accept the terms under consideration. "I have not much hope of a favorable result, but I will do what I can."[80]

As fate would have it, on that same day, August 23, representatives of the two delegations at Portsmouth inched closer to a peace treaty. Meyer had convinced the tsar that the southern half of Sakhalin, like Port Arthur, had only belonged to Russia temporarily and that its best course would be to retain northern Sakhalin by buying it back. The tsar accepted the idea but insisted that the amount of the payment not appear to be an indemnity.[81]

Roosevelt believed that only two substantial issues remained—the money question and Sakhalin. The proposed settlement included the return of the northern half of Sakhalin to Russia after the payment of "redemption money" for buying back the restored territory and the return of Russian prisoners. If Russia and Japan failed to agree on the amount, they could seek the advice of a high French or German official appointed by or with the approval of Russia and some high English official appointed by or with the approval of Japan. The amount set would not be binding on either nation. If Russia agreed to the amount, Roosevelt would try to persuade Japan to do the same. If Russia refused to approve, Roosevelt would warn that Japan might take Harbin, Vladivostok, and East Siberia.[82]

On August 25, Roosevelt declared to his son Kermit, "I am having my hair turn gray by dealing with the Russian and Japanese peace negotiators. The Japanese ask too much, but the Russians are ten times worse than the Japs [*sic*] because they are so stupid and won't tell the truth."[83]

Two days later, the conference descended to its nadir. That afternoon, Komura met with the Russian plenipotentiaries, where Witte declared he had "absolutely no hope" of convincing his government to accept any Japanese compromise. The military party in Russia complained that its emissaries had already gone too far in granting concessions on the Manchurian issue, which left no reason to consider the issues of an indemnity and cession of Sakhalin. Komura telegrammed Kaneko in New York that "the last hope for peace is gone." Kaneko forwarded the telegram to the president with these words, "I fear that the last day has come." Did he have any advice?[84]

Perhaps, Roosevelt determined, another attempt through Wilhelm might prove effective. He asked the kaiser to persuade the tsar to accept the following peace terms: Russia would pay no indemnity to Japan but receive northern Sakhalin for an amount set by a mixed commission. The Japanese, he noted to Wilhelm, had "reluctantly" accepted this proposition "only under strong pressure from me." Each party would appoint an equal number of commission members who would then agree on another member. The Japanese claimed that Witte had agreed that Russia would pay for their half of Sakhalin if the figure was fair—which Roosevelt, borrowing Meyer's thought, declared was "something on the scale of that for which Alaska was sold to the United States." Roosevelt thought these terms moderate and hoped Wilhelm would convince cousin Nicholas to accept them. If successful, the president emphasized, the civilized world would thank him.[85]

The next day, August 28, Komura telegrammed Kaneko that Nicholas II had rejected Roosevelt's advice to offer concessions. The tsar had scribbled on the president's letter "no further consideration" and put it away. Komura expressed appreciation for Roosevelt's "earnest and sincere effort" to promote peace. "I grieve extremely to put the President into so much trouble" by trying to fashion a compromise. He wanted to thank him personally before returning home. Kaneko was distraught over Russia's rejection of Roosevelt's "sincere and disinterested advices for peace and humanity." He added, "I fear before this letter reaches you that we might hear an awful result of the conference."[86]

Roosevelt shared his frustrations over the proceedings in a confidential note to Ambassador Jusserand of France. He fumed over having to be

> polite and sympathetic and patient in explaining for the hundredth time something perfectly obvious, when what I really want to do is to give utterance to whoops of rage and jump up and knock their heads together—well, all I can hope is that self-repression will be ultimately helpful for my character.[87]

Then, on August 29, the logjam suddenly broke when Japan dropped its indemnity demand in exchange for the southern half of Sakhalin. Kaneko exclaimed to the president, "The peace is concluded at last!" Emperor Mutsuhito had followed Roosevelt's "line of policy" set out in his two letters to Kaneko of August 22 and 23. Kaneko again praised the president: "Your name shall be remembered with the peace and prosperity of Asia."[88]

The State Department also telegrammed the news to the president, who wanted a note sent to Komura that would "heartily congratulate" Japan. When the treaty became official, the "civilized world" would thank Japan for its "magnanimity in its hour of triumph."[89]

Meyer from St. Petersburg had likewise informed the president of the developments at Portsmouth. At 10 p.m. on August 29, Meyer received a telegram from the Associated Press representative at New Castle, declaring "Peace Concluded." He immediately wired the president, congratulating him on his "great achievement" in saving perhaps 250,000 lives and putting "humanity under a lasting debt of gratitude to you." It was especially gratifying that your success came after the entire European press had "prophesied that you had undertaken the impossible." Both antagonists had wanted peace, Meyer believed, but each party thought it had an advantage—the Japanese calculating that Russia's domestic turmoil would force it to sign a peace treaty and pay a war indemnity, and the Russians convinced that Japan was at the brink of financial collapse and must end the war. The two belligerents had settled their differences by the combined efforts of Roosevelt's persuading Japan to drop indemnity demands and Meyer's convincing Russia to surrender the southern half of Sakhalin.[90]

Also on August 29, Witte reported to the tsar that "Japan has accepted our demands . . . in exact conformity with Your Majesty's plans." Witte rejoiced that "Russia in the Far East will remain a Great Power." He had recognized the necessity for peace, that "we were threatened by a complete debacle, involving the revolution of the dynasty." He also knew that opponents in Russia would hold him responsible for the treaty. Peace at Portsmouth heightened Witte's popularity at home and led Nicholas to bestow on him the rank of count.[91]

On September 5, 1905, the two warring powers agreed to the Treaty of Portsmouth, which underlined Japan's victory by confirming the return of holdings lost to Russia in the decade following the Sino-Japanese War of 1894–1895. Port Arthur and the Liaotung Peninsula, including the port at Dairen; a dominant economic position in Manchuria (still nominally under Chinese control) that included the South Manchurian Railway and associated privileges; and recognition of its "predominant political, military, and economic interests" in Korea, which remained quasi-independent until its annexation by Japan in 1910—all these areas, plus the acquisition of southern Sakhalin, provided the basis for a Japanese empire in East Asia. Russia held on to northern Sakhalin and Eastern Siberia while paying no indemnity, but Japan's victory in the war awarded it legendary status as the first time in modern history that a non-white people had defeated an allegedly superior white nation.[92]

Roosevelt kept his post-conference assessment private. To historian and friend George Trevelyan, the president expressed dislike for Witte. "I thought his bragging and bluster not only foolish but shockingly vulgar when compared with the gentlemanly and self-respecting self-restraint of the Japanese." Whereas the Japanese, Roosevelt submitted, were truthful and likely to join civilization, the Russians were liars, anchored in "widespread corruption and selfishness." Roosevelt confessed to "feeling much contempt" for the Russian secretary of state. At Portsmouth, he appeared to be "a very selfish man, totally without high ideals."[93]

If much of diplomacy is political theater, Roosevelt had played his part well. He hid his negative feelings so masterfully that at least three members of the Russian delegation were impressed by his part in the settlement. Witte was one of them. On September 8, four days before the president wrote Trevelyan, Witte expressed his thoughts about Roosevelt in a private letter to a friend. That same day, however, extracts of the letter were published in a cable from Berlin, praising Roosevelt's "moral point of view" and assessing him as a "statesman of high caliber." His "personal qualities" shine through "in actions requiring decision, tact and clear vision." Roosevelt has "an ideal and strives for higher aims than a commonplace existence presents." He is one of the "soldiers who cannot be relieved from the danger line."[94]

Baron Rosen, head of the delegation, could not yet have known of Witte's surprisingly positive evaluation of the president when recording his own feelings about the Portsmouth experience. In his *Reminiscences*, he declared it unfortunate that Witte had not read *Roosevelt's Letters to His Children*, where he would have found it "impossible not to love the man who wrote these letters." The Portsmouth Treaty was the "crowning achievement" of Roosevelt's "brilliant career as a statesman and Chief Magistrate of this great Nation."[95]

A third Russian admirer of Roosevelt was Professor Frederic Frommhold de Martens, a world-recognized Russian expert on international law who served as an adviser to the delegation. In an essay published in *Outlook* in January 1920, Martens asserted that he had found the president "exactly informed" on all issues and numerous times "intervened in the most discreet manner by conveying a hint of a message" to the delegates on both sides that "cleared the skies and brought things back to their true level." The Portsmouth Conference was the first attempt by the United States "to stand as an equal" with "the great nations of other continents." The treaty was "essentially Roosevelt's work," done without either "showing openly his hand" or interfering in issues "not supposed to concern him." He was "one of the most powerful personalities" in the world. "The man who had been represented to us as impetuous to the point of rudeness, displayed a gentleness, a kindness, and a tactfulness mixed with self-control that only a truly great man can command."[96]

It is, perhaps, surprising then that both Japan and Russia expressed dissatisfaction with the agreement. That neither party returned home happy is, strange to say, a tribute to the fairness of the settlement and further highlights Roosevelt's success in securing a balanced peace in East Asia without his physical presence in the negotiations. But as is the nature of a compromise, its chief architect became a scapegoat for the inflated expectations of each antagonist at the outset of the negotiations as they attempted to put the best color on their efforts to pacify their people at home. Consequently, the treaty strained American relations with both Japan and Russia.

Many issues remained after the war. The Japanese masses, struggling with a famine, complained about the lack of an indemnity—a crisis brought on in part, according to President Roosevelt's private assessment, by the government's mistake of bluffing when demanding an unreasonable indemnity. The Japanese people were already under a heavy tax burden and, in response to the treaty, rioted against their government and damaged a number of American church buildings. The Russians, Roosevelt privately noted, "all pulled against one another, rarely knew their own minds, lied so to others that they finally got into the dangerous position of lying to themselves, and showed a most unhealthy and widespread corruption and selfishness." The Russian people likewise were suffering from famine and threatening to riot while fantasizing that they could have won the war had it not been for the so-called Portsmouth betrayal.[97]

⟨✺⟩

Roosevelt nonetheless won international acclaim for the Portsmouth Treaty. It was a great personal victory in that he had earned the reputation as a world peacemaker. Praise came from all quarters—including the kaiser, the king of England, and, most notably, Emperor Mutsuhito of Japan and Tsar Nicholas II of Russia. The culmination came in 1906, when Roosevelt received the Nobel Peace Prize.[98]

Roosevelt expressed no regrets about his new image as peacemaker, even as Americans at home reacted in a mixed way to the events that had further thrust the United States onto the international stage. He explained to his daughter Alice that hosting the Russo-Japanese peace negotiations in the United States had ultimately forced him into the position of having to intervene when the two sides deadlocked.[99]

American critics worried about becoming involved in the outside world's tangled web of secret alliances and looked back nostalgically to the simpler times of an isolationism that safeguarded the country by relying on thousands of miles of Atlantic and Pacific waters. Writer and anti-imperialist Mark Twain joined others in objecting to a peace that prolonged the autocratic Romanov regime in Russia and left untold numbers of people in chains. Others predicted trouble with the Japanese, pointing to their allegations that the United States had tried to block their rise to imperial greatness.

Roosevelt, however, extolled the peace that had ended the war and hoped to construct a balance of power that stabilized East Asia while bestowing international prestige on the United States. "I thought it my plain duty to make the effort," he explained to his friend Joseph Bishop at Sagamore Hill in the evening after the luncheon on the *Mayflower*. "I have done my best to succeed and shall continue to do it to the end."[100]

Chapter 7

Navigating Turbulent Japanese Waters

I certainly do not intend to go into peacemaking as a regular business.

—President Theodore Roosevelt
November 1, 1905

It was evidently high time that we should get our whole battle fleet on a practice voyage to the Pacific.

—President Theodore Roosevelt
July 23, 1907

By the end of 1905, Roosevelt's views toward war had changed. In his younger days, he championed war as a demonstration of masculinity or a major means for advancing civilization; at some point earlier in his presidency, he had developed a better understanding of the costs of war and would accept it only as a last resort in resolving international problems. In his annual message to Congress in early December, he emphasized the peacemaking role of The Hague, a statement doubtless driven by the recently concluded war between Russia and Japan and his difficulties in bringing about the peace treaty. War was a "lamentable and evil thing," he asserted. Wars of aggression, pursued in a "conscienceless spirit," constituted a "peculiarly atrocious crime against all humanity."[1]

Roosevelt nonetheless considered certain kinds of wars justifiable. "Our aim is righteousness," he assured Congress. "Peace is normally the handmaiden of righteousness; but when peace and righteousness conflict then a great and upright people can never for a moment hesitate to follow the path which leads toward righteousness, even though that path also leads to war." In these times, "only that nation is equipped for peace that knows how to fight, and that will not shrink from fighting if ever the conditions become such that war is demanded in the name of the highest morality." The Golden Rule should be the guide to keeping peace, but it should never prohibit the use of police power.[2]

I

In the aftermath of the Russo-Japanese War, Roosevelt expressed concern about relations with Germany and Britain as well as Japan. He feared an outbreak of war in Europe, in part attributable to what he regarded as the kaiser's provocative actions toward France in Morocco, but also because of the "wild talk" coming from both the British and the Germans. The president wrote Cecil Spring Rice in England that even though he would do anything to keep peace in Europe, he did not want to become known as a "Meddlesome Mattie" who was ready to intervene in every trouble spot. "I certainly do not intend to go into peacemaking as a regular business."[3]

Roosevelt assured Spring Rice of his support for the Anglo-Japanese treaty of 1905 renewing the 1902 alliance, despite Count Witte's claim to French ambassador Jusserand that the United States agreed with Russia in opposing the alliance. In a communication shared with Japanese minister Takahira in Washington, Roosevelt asked Jusserand to inform his government that the White House considered the Anglo-Japanese treaty a step toward keeping the peace in Asia and in the world.[4]

The Russo-Japanese War and the Portsmouth Treaty left a host of problems in East Asia that meshed with European issues to raise the specter of a global conflict. Japan posed a challenge to U.S. interests in East Asia and the Pacific, ironically making Roosevelt, as the architect of the peace treaty, partly responsible for the possibility of a Pacific war. But the Japanese threat did not affect only the United States. "In a dozen years," Roosevelt wrote Spring Rice, "the English, Americans and Germans . . . will have each to dread the Japanese more than they do any other nation." Japan would soon become a major power, forcing the United States to treat it "in a spirit of all possible courtesy, and with generosity and justice." To do otherwise would, indeed, "invite disaster."[5]

After Japan and Russia resumed diplomatic relations in early February 1906, the Tokyo government reassured the United States that it would respect the Open Door in Manchuria. Japan first wanted to open Mukden and the rest of Manchuria to foreign trade. Marquis Kimmochi Saionji, the new Japanese prime minister and minister of foreign affairs, explained that the safe withdrawal of his country's troops from the Asian mainland had necessitated temporary restrictions on the movement of foreigners into these war-torn regions.

But this process was nearly complete, and Japan would soon adhere to the Open Door policy in Manchuria. By May 1, a few of the ports welcomed diplomatic representatives, and within a month Mukden would be ready to accept diplomats. Foreign travelers could enter at their own risk in areas where they did not hinder the military withdrawal, and the port at Darien would be open to world trade as soon as possible.[6]

The president was cautiously satisfied with the Japanese explanation for not yet restoring the Open Door in Manchuria. At the moment, he wrote Ambassador Whitelaw Reid in London, he treated the Germans "much more cavalierly" than he did the Japanese. As for the kaiser, however, "I am very polite with him, but I am ready at an instant's notice to hold my own." Similarly, with Japan, he was careful "to be scrupulously polite, to show a genuine good will toward her," but to maintain a strong navy that would make it risky for Japan to turn on the United States.[7]

According to Roosevelt, the civilized countries bore the responsibility for maintaining world peace. They must encourage China to become more westernized like Japan, cooperate in abolishing the Turkish Empire, and put the uncivilized parts of Africa and Asia under the control of advanced countries such as Britain, France, Germany, or (despite his low opinion) Russia. This arrangement, he privately wrote a friend and career diplomat, could lead to an international agreement that reduced the need for armies and navies except for domestic and foreign police work.[8]

Japan's attempts to firm up its economic interests in Manchuria nonetheless challenged America's Open Door policy in China. Months before the end of the war, Roosevelt had quietly strengthened the U.S. hold on the Philippines while repeatedly assuring Takahira that he did not oppose Japan's hegemony in Korea. Such control, the president knew, enhanced hope for a postwar balance of power. Yet Japan's show of military and naval strength in the Russian war raised concerns that its further expansion into China and the Pacific might encroach on U.S. interests.[9]

While these sweeping and long-standing international issues dominated the president's attention, he suddenly faced a more pressing problem at home that threatened relations with Japan. The rapidly growing influx of Japanese immigrants to the West Coast alarmed many Americans. U.S. annexation of Hawaii near the close of the nineteenth century had laid the basis for this migration. The Hawaiian islands had provided a safe haven for about 60,000 Japanese émigrés from their homeland's population surplus, but now, with Hawaii a U.S. possession, passports were no longer necessary for any of these workers wanting to relocate to the United States as part of the wave of "New Immigration" hitting both the Atlantic and Pacific shores in the 1890s. Fewer than 200 Japanese lived in the United States in 1880; in 1900 alone, more than 12,000 Japanese made their way to Hawaii and the U.S. mainland.[10]

Popular protests against the Japanese erupted in California in August of 1900, leading the Tokyo government to deny passports to laborers wanting to go to the continental United States. The restriction had little impact on the inflow, however, because laborers could still get a passport to Hawaii and then enter the mainland either directly or through Canada and Mexico. The year before the Russo-Japanese War broke out, about 8,000 more Japanese settled in the United States. As Japan courted victory in the war, widespread fear developed along the Pacific Coast that the number of Japanese émigrés would multiply in the postwar period. When they came, most settled in California, including former soldiers who refused to return home to a life of exorbitant taxes and backbreaking work in the rice fields.[11]

But California's promise of the good life did not extend to those outside the mold of white, Anglo-Saxon Protestants. The Japanese reception suffered from Californians' recent experience with the Chinese who had flocked into the state after working as cheap labor on the transcontinental railroad completed in 1869. Chinese émigrés were primarily male who, instead of plowing back their wages into the economy in the form of purchases, saved their money to take home, where they could enjoy a far higher standard of life than when they first left for the United States. These "sojourners," Californians charged, had forsaken the American dream of sharing the bounty and deserved the poor treatment they received from loyal Americans.[12]

Now the Japanese—also "Orientals" and therefore, according to many Americans, no different from the Chinese—had come to California, threatening white workers' welfare by accepting lower wages and, according to the sensationalist press of William Randolph Hearst and others, personifying the "yellow peril" conjured up in Kaiser Wilhelm II's dark imagination.

The growing anti-Japanese sentiment centered in San Francisco, where the Board of Education sought to separate Asian students from their white classmates in school. In the *Plessy v. Ferguson* case of 1896, the U.S. Supreme Court had approved black and white racial segregation with the stipulation that local officials provide "separate but equal" public facilities. The school board in San Francisco advanced the argument that the color line applied not only to Black people but to other nonwhites as well. According to its reasoning, the overflow of Japanese children in the city's schools had crowded the classrooms, pushing out whites and replacing them not just with school-age youths but also with Asian men twenty-one years of age and older.

On October 11, 1906, a year after initial approval, the San Francisco School Board assigned all Chinese, Korean, and Japanese children to the Oriental Public School. Public reaction in Japan was explosive and, combined with ongoing efforts to exclude the Japanese from entry into the United States, endangered relations between the countries. Later in October, the Japanese ambassador, Viscount Shuzo Aoki, met with Secretary of State

Elihu Root to alert him of his government's concerns over this discriminatory action. "The exclusion of children from ordinary public schools,
because of their Japanese origin," Aoki protested, "is based on racial distinction and is as such resented by the Japanese people as derogatory to their
dignity."[13]

President Roosevelt warned the chair of the Senate Committee on Naval
Affairs, Eugene Hale of Maine, that the growing unrest in California could
lead to conflict with Japan—a prospect that, he emphasized, necessitated
building up the U.S. military, especially the navy. It should come as no surprise that the president seized this opportunity to advance his plans to enlarge
the fleet.

The trade unions had further inflamed the populace in San Francisco and
other cities in the state by boycotting Japanese restaurant owners, supporting
segregation in public schools, and threatening mob action—all violations of
Japanese rights in this country guaranteed by treaties between the nations.[14]
Roosevelt soon took steps to resolve the problem. He asked the Department of Justice to explore the potential for legal action, and he sent Secretary
of Commerce and Labor Victor Metcalf to California to warn authorities
and labor union leaders that their conduct jeopardized relations with Japan.
Perhaps Metcalf, a Californian, might lead the school board to reason. It was
clear that Roosevelt felt circumstances might call for more severe action. As
Metcalf prepared for his trip, the president informed Hale that he might send
the army to the area because of the boycotts and the potential for violence.[15]
Roosevelt had been watching events in California and knew that all the ingre-
dients were present for a major crisis.

The president asserted that the "proud, sensitive, warlike" Japanese people
were "flushed with the glory of their recent triumph," and determined to be
the central power in the Pacific. Roosevelt reminded Hale of U.S. efforts to
prevent Japan from forcing Russia out of East Asia. But Russia's military
strength had declined after the war, raising doubt about its ability to balance
Japanese expansion in that region, leaving the United States as a counter-
weight to Japanese dominance of Manchuria. If Americans continued to
humiliate the Japanese, the two nations could soon be on the path to war.[16]

U.S. policy toward Japan, Roosevelt emphasized to Hale, must rest on
"absolute good faith, courtesy and justice," along with a navy strong enough
to discourage Japan from considering war. The U.S. Navy needed battleships
armed with eight twelve-inch guns. And considering the Hague Conference's
hesitation in restricting the size of battleships, he felt "that we ought to go
ahead with the steady progress of building this year the ship authorized last
year and the ship to be authorized this—that is, two ships the equal of any
laid down by any nation."[17]

Roosevelt told his son Kermit at the end of October that war could come because of the "infernal fools" in California, who "insult the Japanese recklessly" and make all Americans "pay the consequences." The president proclaimed his readiness to fight any nation if need be, but he would hate going to war when the United States was in the wrong.[18]

His fears seemed validated. Reports from the Office of Naval Intelligence suggested that Japan was preparing for war. Roosevelt remained doubtful of this warning, but he could not take a chance and therefore approved Admiral George Dewey's recommendation to send the battle fleet to East Asian waters as quickly as possible. The three-month preparation time needed to fortify the area, Dewey warned, would allow Japan to "capture the Philippines, Honolulu, and be master of the sea." Despite Dewey's warning, the president opted for grandeur over expediency and laid plans for what would become the voyage of the Great White Fleet.[19]

In the meantime, Metcalf's investigation in the autumn of 1906 eased Japan's concern about the White House reaction to the school crisis, but it also led him to conclude that the Board of Education remained obstinate that the issue was a local matter and would not rescind the segregation order. The *San Francisco Chronicle* highlighted Metcalf's failure, chiding that "the presence of a Cabinet officer vicariously waving the big stick" had not worked.[20]

There might yet be a legal opening for the president to probe in America's treaty obligations. In Aoki's instructions from Viscount Tadasa Hayashi in late October, the Japanese foreign minister had raised the issue of a treaty violation. An 1894 commercial treaty between the two countries contained, it was believed, a most-favored-nation clause. If this was the case, did it extend to the education provided for children of the signatory nations? Were the Japanese students entitled to attend the same schools as students of other nations, especially Europeans? Finally, did the treaty obligation of the federal government supersede the California law? The Board of Education agreed to accept a ruling on this by the California Supreme Court. Metcalf conferred with justices of the California court before moving the case forward and found them amenable to taking it up when the case made it to their docket, but in the meantime, he and the U.S. District Attorney in San Francisco studied the treaty and both agreed that its terms did not support their argument. In Washington, Root disagreed and, although Roosevelt concurred with Metcalf, the president authorized the secretary of state to proceed with the suit. Root believed that the "whole purpose and end of the treaty of 1894 was to do away with and prevent just such exclusions as are now provided by the San Francisco School Board."[21]

Roosevelt understood that the courts were not likely to provide relief and that the most practical solution to the school crisis lay in direct intervention to prevent unskilled Japanese laborers from entering the United States. Federal intervention in local school policies, he explained to Metcalf, would cause problems with California over the states' rights doctrine. The prohibition must therefore come from Japan. He had emphasized to Ambassador Aoki in Washington that his government must stop unskilled workers from entering either the United States or its Hawaiian territory. Aoki agreed, declaring that he had always opposed their migration. The essential action, the president knew, would require calming the Japanese government and people over the San Francisco school action. In his annual message to Congress, he hoped to placate the Japanese while their government restricted emigration.[22] The president had to guarantee fair treatment of the Japanese without violating states' rights principles and angering Americans in California.

II

In his annual congressional message in early December 1906, Roosevelt called on Congress to grant him the judicial and military power "to enforce the rights of aliens under treaties." The school segregation policy was a "wicked absurdity" and the failure to treat everyone fairly was "a confession of inferiority in our civilization." To put pressure on California legislators to rescind the separation order, he warned that failure to do so could cause war with Japan. To prevent conflict, he would use "all of the forces, military and civil, of the United States which I may lawfully employ." The president "fired a bomb" at the state, according to a leading Californian. His hardline tactics, as anticipated, infuriated west coast Americans, but they relieved the concerns of Japanese, both in the United States and in Japan.[23]

To a friend, Roosevelt explained his objectives in the school controversy. California must know he would not let political considerations prevent him from "using the armed forces of the country to protect the Japanese if they were molested in their persons and property." He must calm the Japanese in order to arrange a mutual agreement with them that would prohibit workers of either country from migrating to the other. He also must assure the California delegation in Congress that if he resorted to federal troops, his purpose would be to keep order, not to integrate the schools.[24]

Roosevelt realized that Britain's alliance with Japan put him in a delicate position. If Japanese workers continued to enter the United States, he told British foreign secretary Sir Edward Grey, Congress would have to pass a prohibitive law, which could cause international problems. He did not want to alienate Japan, whose role was vital to counterbalancing Russian expansion in East Asia. But in mid-December, he warned that Russia might seize the opportunity to again challenge Japan for supremacy in East Asia, which would force Japan to protect its holdings in Manchuria and perhaps broaden its interests in the Western Pacific and East Asia. Roosevelt felt confident that Canadian and Australian workers would likewise object to a major influx of Japanese laborers. He also assumed that the Japanese would feel the same about the entry of foreign workers. The only solution was for Japan and the United States to police themselves by unilaterally stopping the flow of workers from either country to the other.[25]

Roosevelt emphasized to the president of the University of California, Benjamin Wheeler, that San Francisco's school action had threatened his administration's attempt to persuade the Tokyo government to prohibit Japanese workers from entering the United States. Roosevelt told his friend and editor of the *London Spectator*, John Strachey, that he wanted a mutual U.S.-Japanese agreement to stop the laborers of either country from migrating to the other. The existing treaty with Japan included a prohibition against the entry of Japanese workers, but to enforce it now would worsen relations— "unless I can have it done on Japan's initiative."[26]

Perhaps the president was thinking about what one of his major advisers on Asia, William Sturgis Bigelow, had told him about the Japanese: "They don't care—broadly speaking—what is done to them as long as it does not seem to be done to them as *Japanese.*" Roosevelt knew that the Japanese already in the United States must receive the same treatment given to European migrants. He hoped to avoid charges of racial discrimination by arguing that the problem in assimilating the Japanese was attributable to racial differences and not to racial inferiority.[27]

Roosevelt's sixth annual message drew praise from the Japanese, both at home and in the United States. His friend, Baron Kaneko, held an advisory position to the government in Tokyo, and, in an interview, called the president's message "the greatest utterance by an American President since Washington's farewell address." The Japanese consul in Seattle told the *San Francisco Chronicle* that Roosevelt was the "best friend Japan ever had." In late January 1907, the Japanese minister for foreign affairs, Viscount Hayashi, told legislators in Tokyo that the president's message "showed that the American government was sincerely endeavoring to arrive at an amicable settlement of the question."[28]

Roosevelt assured the publisher of the *Los Angeles Times*, Harrison Gray Otis, that the opposition to Japanese children was "simply nonsense." Metcalf's report showed that the overcrowding charges had no merit: Only ninety-three Japanese (including twenty-eight females) were in the twenty-three schools in the city system. Roosevelt agreed with the opposition to having "grown-up Japanese" in the schools, but even this fear was exaggerated. Of the total number of Japanese in the schools, about thirty were fifteen years old, and only two were twenty. Furthermore, teachers attested to the good behavior of the Japanese children.[29]

Presidential pressure did not work in California, causing Roosevelt to try personal diplomacy. At the end of January 1907, he invited the California congressional delegation in Washington to visit the White House to discuss the matter. There, he worked with Root and Metcalf in convincing the legislators to send two telegrams to their state: the first one to the governor, James Norris Gillett (a Republican the president had supported in the campaign of 1906), asking him to put a hold on legislation relating to the school crisis; the second telegram to the San Francisco School Board's leaders, asking them to accept an invitation from the president to meet with him in the White House.[30]

Shortly afterward, the city school superintendent and the president of the Board of Education of San Francisco responded to the president's invitation with conditions. A quick meeting of the city school board led to a telegram to the president insisting that no action on school policies could take place without the presence of all eight members. Roosevelt agreed. Another request came the following day: extend the invitation to the city's mayor, Eugene Schmitz, who had appointed each member of the board. Roosevelt had met Schmitz in the White House about five years earlier and agreed to this request as well. Adding to the novelty of this occasion, every member of the group boarding the train in San Francisco in early February 1907 was a target of an ongoing investigation into corruption in the city government. Mayor Schmitz had been indicted for extortion and was out of jail after posting $25,000 in bail.[31]

At the board's request, the mayor headed the delegation that met for six days with the president and two cabinet members—Secretary of War Taft and Secretary of State Root—to resolve a local matter that affected national security. Schmitz unenthusiastically agreed to a repeal of the school segregation order and the admission of Japanese children who could speak some English and were the proper age for each grade.[32]

Roosevelt now had to convince the California state legislature to prohibit the school systems from blocking the admission of Japanese children. He explained to Governor Gillett that the "central difficulty" was the "violent extremists" in San Francisco who used the school issue as a means for preventing the entry of Japanese workers. With the passage of a new immigration bill (outlined below), Congress made it possible for the president to bar all Japanese laborers from the United States, except for those who had passports allowing them direct entry into the country. The only way this law would work was for the Tokyo government to deny passports to its laborers entering the country indirectly. But that government refused to take such action until American schools ended discrimination against Japanese children.[33]

Roosevelt assured the governor of White House support for the new law as soon as the San Francisco School Board admitted Japanese children on an equal basis with those of other nations. His support also hinged on state legislators passing no more laws establishing school discrimination, the deployment of "'Jim Crow' [train] cars for Japanese," or any other action denying fair treatment.[34]

The California legislature ignored the president's warnings of conflict with Japan and unanimously passed a bill establishing separate schools for the Japanese, the Mongolians, and other "Orientals." This was a "foolish and wanton insult to Japan," he wrote the governor. If the state's legislators were trying to undermine the February agreement between the government in Washington and the San Francisco School Board and mayor, the effort was "exceedingly mischievous." This "absolutely useless" California law insulted the Japanese and threatened to undermine the international negotiations aimed at blocking Japanese workers from entering the United States.[35]

To the governor, Roosevelt explained that he had hoped to convince the California officials visiting the White House of their duty as Americans to accept a compromise. Roosevelt wanted an international settlement by which Japanese youths of the appropriate age who demonstrated *some* ability to communicate in English could attend any school without restrictions in exchange for the Tokyo government's halting the migration of workers to the United States. The February agreement crafted in the White House permitted Japanese (and all alien) children meeting the above criteria (proper age for grade level, and acceptable proficiency in English) admission into regular public schools.[36]

The Japanese government, Roosevelt announced, had agreed to deny passports to workers wanting to migrate directly to the United States if its Japanese citizens in the United States received equal treatment. Congress passed and the president signed in the third week of February the Immigration Act of 1907, making it possible to bar certain Japanese workers. This so-called "San Francisco Compromise" provided that

> whenever the President shall be satisfied that passports issued by any foreign government to its citizens to go to any country other than the United States or to the Canal Zone are being used for the purpose of enabling the holders to come to the continental territory of the United States to the detriment of labor conditions therein, the President may refuse to permit such citizens' entry into the United States.

This includes, the act noted, anyone attempting to pass through other countries or through "insular possessions" or "the Canal Zone" to the continental United States. While not explicitly naming the transition venues, the meaning was clear: no skirting the process by entering through Mexico, Canada, or Hawaii, the common routes for such movement.

The only obstacle left was the "unwise and sinister agitators," who sought to undermine the mutual exclusion attempt and bar *all* Japanese laborers. Since workers made up the vast majority of those wishing to enter the United States, this rigid position would, in essence, catch almost all Japanese in the exclusion net. This simply could not stand. The president knew that fair and equal treatment of the Japanese was the only way to secure the same treatment for Americans in Japan and to assure an "honorable agreement" between the nations.[37]

The tension eased when Roosevelt notified Mayor Schmitz that, after he rescinded the segregation order, the White House would order dismissed the suit Root's office had filed against the San Francisco Board.[38] This, perhaps worth noting, was not a difficult concession for the president to offer. As the case had percolated through the California courts, Root became increasingly skeptical about the language of the 1894 treaty meeting the threshold of most favored nation. By February 1907, both he and Hayashi determined that the treaty supported the spirit but not the letter, and an argument on those grounds would be unpersuasive to the California Supreme Court.

When the segregation order was finally rescinded as agreed, Schmitz could not resist issuing a meaningless disclaimer that the decision should not be taken as an admission that the Board had violated terms of the Japanese treaty. Besides, he proclaimed, local law would render null any contrary treaty obligations.[39]

In late 1907 and early 1908, Roosevelt settled the international dimension of the school crisis by negotiating the "Gentlemen's Agreement" with Japan. He had three objectives: withdrawal of the segregation order; Japan's denial of passports to unskilled workers wanting to immigrate to the United States; and federal legislation closing immigration routes through Hawaii, Canada, and Mexico. Japan refused to stop emigration to Hawaii, but the United States prohibited Japanese laborers in Hawaii from migrating to the mainland.[40]

Resorting to an executive agreement (as the president had done with the Dominican Republic in 1905), he exchanged diplomatic notes with the Tokyo government, thereby circumventing the Senate's role in the process and avoiding heated public battles over the issue. In an arrangement designed to save face on both sides, Japan took the lead in prohibiting unskilled laborers from moving directly to the United States in exchange for the school board's revocation of the segregation directive.

The issue nonetheless lingered. Japan continued to fear for its children's safety in San Francisco and considered exclusion from the United States a near certainty. And yet, it also realized that marking passports for "Hawaii only" did not close the door on further migration of its people to the American mainland. What could stop them from entering the United States from either Canada or Mexico? Furthermore, the Gentlemen's Agreement did not apply to Japanese migrants outside the category of unskilled labor, and it had no impact on the passports granted to females who went through the paper process of marrying Japanese males already in the United States and then joining them as "picture brides."

"Nothing during my Presidency," Roosevelt wrote Kaneko in the wake of anti-immigrant violence in San Francisco, "has given me more concern than these troubles."[41] The images of "nativists" in San Francisco descending on Japanese restaurants and bathhouses as an angry mob in the riot of May 1907 prompted Roosevelt's comment to Kaneko. The scene would be repeated later in the year as white residents of Bellingham, Washington attacked the Asian community there with cries of "drive out the Hindus." The president's concern was well founded.[42]

III

Roosevelt worried that the immigration compromise might signal American fear of the Japanese, leading him to look for a way to publicly display the nation's naval strength as a means of warding off conflict. His "prime purpose," he remarked years afterward, "was to impress the American people" and increase their support for enlarging the navy. The U.S. Navy ranked second to the British but was three places higher than the Japanese, and he wished to drive home this reality to their most ardent nationalists. "I am exceedingly anxious," he wrote a friend, "to impress upon the Japanese that I have nothing but the friendliest possible intentions toward them, but," he stressed, "I am none the less anxious that they should realize that I am not afraid of them and that the United States will no more submit to bullying than it will bully."[43]

In the United States, Roosevelt explained to a friend in London, he encountered many Americans who opposed a large navy and thereby interfered with his efforts to resolve problems with Japan. These people "invite trouble and refuse to prepare the means which would avert disaster if trouble came." Some Americans, he privately declared, denounced armaments while demanding a strong policy that could lead to a "humiliating backdown" or a "disastrous war unless we are already armed."[44]

The president remained wary of Japanese expansionist intentions in East Asia, and in July 1907 he explained his central objective to Lodge: send the U.S. battleship fleet on a "practice cruise" aimed at exposing and correcting any performance problems before hostilities broke out. Roosevelt had learned from the Russo-Japanese War not only the importance of battleships but also of training their officers and men through lengthy experience at sea. His correspondence throughout the ensuing controversy affirmed that Japan's navy weighed heavily on his mind.[45]

On July 12, Roosevelt met with Japanese ambassador Shuzo Aoki and Admiral Gombei Yamamoto (former cabinet minister) for lunch in the president's home at Oyster Bay, where he sought to alleviate any worry they might have about relations between the countries. He had told Lodge that the task would not be easy in light of the "prize jingo fools" in both countries, along with the "worse than criminal stupidity of the San Francisco mob" and the inflammatory stories in the city's newspapers and the *New York Herald*, among others.[46]

Despite the immigration agreement, Yamamoto remained apprehensive, repeatedly insisting that the United States must not distinguish between the Japanese and the Europeans in deciding whom to keep out of the country. Roosevelt countered that the Japanese government had already done this by prohibiting the entry of American workers on the grounds that they would deflate the wages of Japanese laborers. For economic reasons, he later told Root, the United States must stop the entry of Japanese workers who would compete with Americans for jobs. The Japanese government must refuse passports to these workers; otherwise, Congress might enact a Japanese exclusion law like the one applying to the Chinese.[47]

Roosevelt later explained to old friend and German ambassador to the U.S., Speck von Sternburg, that he saw "literally not one reason" why the United States and Japan would go to war. As president, he would seek to eliminate every wrong Americans had inflicted on the Japanese while treating them with "every courtesy and consideration." Americans should ask nothing from the Japanese that they would not grant in return. "I am not in the slightest degree influenced by fear of them," the president asserted in mid-July, and "I will no more permit my country to be wronged than I will sanction its committing wrong in return." Yet he wanted to keep the fleet ready for action by sending it "around the world" as a "mighty good practice."[48]

Later in July, Roosevelt's worst fears appeared to materialize when a war scare with Japan spread across the United States. In addition to the alarm expressed by what he called the jingo press in both nations, a number of reports arrived at the White House, including one from Secretary of War Taft, offering a firsthand account of the widespread belief in Hawaii that perhaps 10,000 of the 70,000 Japanese in the islands were well-organized former soldiers. A *New York Times* front-page article titled "Admiral Predicts War" reported that retired Rear Admiral W. J. Thompson had just returned from East Asia and predicted war with Japan as "inevitable" within five years. The

Washington correspondent of the *New York Times* found the danger more immediate if not imminent. Surely, according to the writer, "no grown man in Washington will believe that if the whole navy goes at once to the Pacific Coast it can be for any other reason than because trouble is expected with Japan."[49]

Warnings of war between the United States and Japan also came from Europe. Two private letters from Sternburg asserted that France and Germany expected war to break out in the next few years between the Americans and the Japanese—a war the European powers did not believe the United States could win. Sternburg warned of claims that the Japanese were reorganizing their army and had dispatched 4,000 troops to Mexico—many of them disguised in civilian clothing. Charles Denby, the U.S. consul general in Shanghai, visited Germany and sent the same cautionary message to Root that Ambassador Tower in Berlin confirmed. Both France and Germany, Denby reported, believed that Japan had decided for war.[50]

Roosevelt remained dubious of the reports of Japanese military activities in Mexico and Hawaii, but he could not be certain. He also knew of similar trepidation in Britain and repeated his belief to Root on July 23 that the only way to prevent war was to build a U.S. navy large enough to convince Japan it could not win. "It was evidently high time that we should get our whole battle fleet on a practice voyage to the Pacific."[51]

The president assured Assistant Secretary of the Navy Truman Newberry that the U.S. fleet would not go into the Pacific as a war measure but as an incentive for peace. The only way to avoid the charge of military aggression was to conduct this operation in peacetime. The cruise "will show other nations what we can do and it will let us ourselves tell what we can do and what the shortcomings that must be remedied are."[52]

Roosevelt regretted that recent American actions and press reports had angered the Japanese people, but he assured Root that this was no "pretext" for going to war. If British, German, and French authorities were correct, the Japanese wanted the Philippines, Hawaii, and perhaps Alaska. "I do not think they will attack us." Yet, there was "enough uncertainty" to put us "very much on our guard" and "ready for anything that comes."[53]

For several reasons, both the press and politicians in the eastern United States opposed the voyage of what became known as the Great White Fleet after the application of the ships' new coats of white paint to lower inside temperatures driven upward in the tropics. The fleet's long absence, critics warned, would leave the Atlantic Coast vulnerable to attack. Rough weather and turbulent seas over the long voyage would damage the ships, resulting in expensive and unnecessary repairs. The act could provoke war with Japan. To stop the trip, one press editor from the South called for impeaching the president. Many opponents convinced Congress to investigate how much the spectacle would cost—which turned out to be more than $1.6 million. The chair of the Senate Committee on Naval Affairs, Eugene Hale, had earlier told the president there was no reason to fear war with Japan and rejected his call for large capital ships as being too costly and unnecessary. Hale now led the congressional opposition to the cruise by announcing that "the fleet should not and could not go because Congress would refuse to appropriate the money."[54]

Roosevelt accepted the challenge. In a response best recounted in his *Autobiography*, he declared that "I had enough money to take the fleet around to the Pacific anyhow, that the fleet would certainly go, and that if Congress did not choose to appropriate enough money to get the fleet back, why, it would stay in the Pacific. There was no further difficulty about the money."[55]

In a letter to a congressional member in September, Roosevelt ended the debate: "I am Commander in Chief, and my decision is absolute in the matter."[56]

Roosevelt explained to his close friend and editor of *Outlook*, Lyman Abbott, that the Great White Fleet would consist of sixteen battleships joined by two other ships on the Pacific Coast, along with eight armored cruisers in San Francisco and six torpedo-boat destroyers from the Atlantic Coast. The battleships would carry 12,000 officers and men; the armored cruisers would transport another 6,000 officers and men. In the meantime, protection of the Atlantic ports and coastline would come from fortifications and mines, along with torpedo boats, cruisers, and other vessels left behind.[57]

Impressive as they were, the American naval vessels remained a distant second to Britain's Royal Navy—which had recently solidified its position at the top. A year earlier, after a long period of secret construction, the British had launched HMS *Dreadnought*, a revolutionary "all big-gun" ship that was larger, faster, and at least two times more powerful than anything on the water. Roosevelt realized that Congress would not support a dreadnought at this time but hoped the Great White Fleet would stir up national interest in a larger and more technologically advanced U.S. Navy while implicitly warning Japan of America's growing strength.[58]

On December 16, 1907, the Great White Fleet hoisted its anchors from the murky harbor waters of Hampton Roads, Virginia, and steamed into the Atlantic. The massive flotilla was bound for "a feast, a frolic, or a fight," according to the commander of the armada and speaker at a farewell banquet in New York the night before—the same commander who sank the Spanish flagship at the Battle of Santiago in the Spanish-American War, Rear Admiral Robley D. "Fighting Bob" Evans.[59]

For the president, this was a dream come true. "Did you ever see such a fleet and such a day?" he bellowed from the presidential yacht *Mayflower* after reviewing the procession amid a twenty-one-gun salute from each battleship as the last one filed past him. So excited was the president that he ordered the captain of the *Mayflower* to follow the ships beyond the Virginia Capes before the caravan disappeared at sea and he returned to port.[60]

It soon became evident to the fleet's officers and crew that they would see more than the Pacific Coast on their voyage. Roosevelt had confided to Evans just before departure that the fleet would go around the world and return home through the Suez Canal. Once at sea, the admiral used the ship's new wireless system to inform the other commanders of their real destination, but he did not encode the message and it was picked up on shore. Roosevelt denied the highly publicized claim and insisted that he had only stated his belief that this was the navy's intention.[61]

The armada moved south and around South America, then turned northward to California, stopping for several visits in Latin American ports before reaching San Francisco in the spring of 1908. In a move that would not have surprised recipients of the president's private letters, Root leaked a story to the press that confirmed Admiral Evans's wireless message and the president's attempt to disavow it by asserting that the White House had expanded the Pacific voyage into a cruise around the world. The official acknowledgment came from the U.S. Navy on March 13, when Victor Metcalf, now secretary of the navy, declared that the fleet would return to the East Coast after visiting Australia and the Philippines, and then pass through the Suez Canal and into the Mediterranean Sea en route to the Atlantic. The ships soon departed from California and into the Pacific, now under the command of Admiral Charles S. Sperry after Evans withdrew for health reasons.[62]

Roosevelt's global itinerary included stops at numerous places, but most notably at Yokohama in October. He had instructed Sperry to be careful with the Japanese. If he permitted enlisted men to take leave while in Japan, he should choose only those who would not raise any "suspicion of insolence or rudeness." Above all, he must exercise the "utmost consideration and courtesy to the Japanese."[63]

Sperry, however, had faith in his men's conduct and virtually ignored the president's instructions by permitting nearly all officers and men to go ashore before leaving Japan. This was a risky move and not only because the president had instructed him to prevent behavior insulting to the Japanese. In previous stops at Rio de Janeiro in Brazil, Auckland in New Zealand, and Melbourne in Australia, riots had broken out between Americans and locals. Sperry had worked out a tight schedule of entertainment before his men arrived in Japan. For the signal event, he selected 150 "special first-class men" for a gala pageant in the Imperial Palace Gardens attended by the emperor, the empress, and princes. The admiral's orders emphasized that good behavior was a "military duty." No incident occurred there or anywhere else, even though 3000 men were on land at one point during the visit.[64]

In late July 1908, almost seven months into the cruise, the president appeared before the U.S. Naval College to praise the voyage for winning international respect for the Monroe Doctrine. If the United States went to war, he declared, it must "hammer its opponent until that opponent quits fighting." The fleet was not for coastal defense; fortifications protect ports. The United States must have a first-class navy that was "footloose to search out and destroy the enemy's fleet." It must safeguard not only the homeland but also Hawaii, the Philippines, Panama, Puerto Rico, Alaska, and Cuba. The United States cannot be a "great nation" unless other nations respect its navy. The chances for war will become "infinitesimal" after the fleet goes around the globe. The voyage will be "the most instructive object lesson that has been afforded as to the reality of the Monroe Doctrine."[65]

Reports of the enthusiastic reception accorded the American fleet in Japan had eased Roosevelt's apprehension as he learned that throngs of native youth sang the "Star-Spangled Banner" in English while American sailors marched by. The fleet then headed home after circumnavigating the globe and arrived back in the United States on February 22, 1909—George Washington's birthday, Roosevelt later noted. The fourteen-month, 43,000-mile journey provided a fitting finale to his augmentation of the navy while affirming his nation's prestige in the international arena.[66]

Staring into binoculars as the steady rain and gray mist blanketed the harbor at Hampton Roads, Virginia, Roosevelt shouted with glee upon seeing the first ship of the seven-mile-long flotilla and hearing the swelling sound of the bands on all twenty-six ships playing in unison "The Star-Spangled Banner" while accompanied by the cadenced booms of cannon. The last echo had barely ended when came a twenty-one-gun simultaneous salute by all the ships as they approached the president, followed by a second twenty-one-gun salute from each ship as it passed by him. From the bridge of the *Mayflower*, the president triumphantly declared as he gazed at thousands of onlookers, "I could not ask a finer concluding scene for my administrations."[67]

Years afterward, Roosevelt declared in his *Autobiography* that "the most important service that I rendered to peace was the voyage of the battle fleet round the world."[68]

This "important service" was, perhaps, to be short lived. The United States and Japan had been trying for more than a year to avoid a collision course in China and the Pacific. Barely a month after the fleet's visit to Yokohama, Ambassador Takahira proposed that the two nations recognize the status quo in the Pacific by pledging mutual respect for each other's holdings. The result was another executive agreement—the president's third—that helped squelch the kaiser's dream of an American-German-Chinese alliance, but it also contained contradictory terms that ensured trouble in East Asia. In the exchange of notes that made up the Root-Takahira Agreement of November 30, 1908, Japan guaranteed U.S. interests in the Philippines, Hawaii, and Formosa in exchange for U.S. support of Japan's dominion in Manchuria, followed by a mutual acceptance of the Open Door principles upholding the "independence and integrity" of China.[09]

Roosevelt defended the agreement despite criticism from China. The Chinese criticized America's apparent approval of Japan's hegemony in Manchuria and the White House's decision not to reveal the terms until after the American fleet had completed its visit to China and steamed out of the port of Amoy. China's government and people, according to the *New York Times*, also felt "humiliated" by the U.S. decision to dispatch only half of the American fleet to China after sending the full complement to Japan. The British praised the agreement for undercutting the kaiser's efforts to build an understanding with the United States and China. The Japanese expected recognition of their territorial advances in East Asia after defeating Russia. Roosevelt realized he could do nothing to reverse these gains; the Japanese navy was stronger than he had thought. As he later emphasized to his successor in the White House, William Howard Taft, Tokyo's leaders regarded Manchuria and Korea as a "vital interest." To accept Japan's primacy on the Asian continent was realistic; to defend the Open Door in China was unrealistic and could lead to war with Japan.[70]

Japanese hardliners were not impressed by the Great White Fleet. Less than a month after the last ship left Tokyo Bay, the emperor presided over a huge pageant in Kobe that highlighted a twenty-mile-long parade of 123 warships. "Don't anger us!" warned one organ of the ultra-nationalist press, Tokyo's *Hochi Shimbun*. "Japanese patience is fast being exhausted."[71]

The global cruise of the Great White Fleet may have raised the profile of the United States as a naval power, but it did not mobilize sufficient congressional support for Roosevelt's call to construct four new battleships. He had not expected to win funding for all four ships, but he got approval for two ships along with the assurance of two more each year—"a great gain," he wrote a confidant. Alarmists feared a naval race in the Pacific, but no evidence indicates a sudden rise in competition either in the United States or anywhere else.[72]

By securing congressional appropriations for six battleships between 1907 and 1909, the president maintained his policy of keeping the United States Navy ahead of Japan and Germany and second only to Britain. Furthermore, Congress in 1908 authorized the building of a base at Pearl Harbor that widened the gap in naval strength between the United States and Japan. In 1902, the United States had two battleships; by 1909, that number had jumped to sixteen. Congress opposed greater naval expansion in 1912 and 1913, putting the United States behind both Britain and Germany when the Great War broke out in 1914. The ships built during the Roosevelt administration would make up almost half of the American fleet used in the war after U.S. entry in April 1917.[73]

Roosevelt doubted that war would occur in East Asia during his presidency, but, as he explained to Root, "there is a sufficient likelihood to make it inexcusable for us not to take such measures as will surely prevent it." The success of the cruise may have encouraged the president to believe that the navy would become a vital arm of diplomacy, but he also knew the training and experience gained by the sailors in peacetime was not the same as in combat conditions. Nor did he fail to recognize the need for more coaling stations. Militants in Japan were confident that in war they would establish "naval supremacy of the Pacific." If the United States bolstered its coastal defenses and built a formidable navy, the president argued, "war cannot take place." Two days later, he wrote his son Kermit that the U.S. Navy must be strong enough to "forbid Japan's hoping for success." Extremists in Japan believed "they could land a large expeditionary force in California and conquer all of the United States west of the Rockies."[74]

Perhaps with that thought in mind, that same day Roosevelt wrote his secretary of the treasury, George B. Cortelyou, "I do not at all like having so much gold in San Francisco. Have you yet shipped much of it to Denver? If not please take steps to get at least the bulk of it there during the next six months. San Francisco is on every account an undesirable place in which to leave it, a fatal place should there ever be war."[75]

⁂

On March 3, 1909, just one day before relinquishing the presidency to Taft, Roosevelt still had Japan uppermost in mind when he cautioned his close friend not to divide America's battleships between the Atlantic and the Pacific oceans before the completion of the Panama Canal. The Russians had made a fatal decision to divide their fleet into three unequal parts before its destruction at Tsushima by Japanese warships fighting as a single unit. Station the entire American battle fleet in one ocean or the other, urged Roosevelt, and have the armed cruisers ready to provide supportive action.[76] President Taft followed that advice.[77]

Four years later, in May 1913, Roosevelt told his cousin, Franklin Delano Roosevelt (then assistant secretary of the navy), that he anticipated no trouble with Japan, "but it may come, and if it does it will come suddenly." The former president offered the same advice he gave Taft based on the outcome at Tsushima: "Russia's fate ought to be a warning for all time as to the criminal folly of dividing the fleet if there is even the remotest chance of war."[78]

Nearly three decades later, the U.S. Navy stationed its Pacific Fleet at Pearl Harbor to discourage an attack in the Pacific.

Chapter 8

Algeciras—A Seat at the Table

Germany had no idea of making an attack, but was sure that England did intend to attack; and on the other hand, England had no idea of making an attack, and was sure that Germany intended to attack her.

—President Theodore Roosevelt
February 22, 1907

I feel . . . that the events which led to the Conference at Algeciras forbid me to omit any effort within my power to promote a settlement of the differences.

—President Theodore Roosevelt
March 7, 1906

Events in Europe after the Franco-Prussian War of 1870–1871 dragged much of the world into the cataclysmic Great War of 1914–1918. An intricate and often clandestine system of alliances failed to keep the peace, proving to be a symptom of, rather than a cure for, international distrust. Ironically, many of the ruling houses stretching from England in the west to Russia in the east were related by blood, making the suspicions and hatreds often caused by familial ties take on deep intensity. For years, the British had maintained a navy at least equal to that of their two closest rivals combined. But after the Prussian victory over France in 1871, Germany strengthened its army and navy. These actions combined to fuel bitter rivalries around the globe.

I

For nearly a century, the Congress of Vienna of 1815 helped to avert another war similar in scope to the Napoleonic Wars. The balance of power underpinning this peace settlement was working, or so it seemed. Beneath the surface stirred rumblings of discontent, spurred by competing nationalisms, mutual suspicions, rival commercial aspirations, and seemingly insatiable appetites for more territories. Never in peacetime had the continental states maintained such massive military forces as at the turn of the twentieth century. The powers boasted expanded navies and large standing armies, along with huge numbers of reserves ready to don uniforms at a moment's notice. Only the most fanatic and irrational people wanted war, and yet many assumed it would come despite the best efforts of peacemakers.

Germany joined other nations in the late nineteenth-century Industrial Revolution that swept the continent and the world, demanding what Chancellor Bernhard von Bülow's speech in 1897 called its "place in the sun" alongside the British and the French.[1] By the turn of the century, Germany produced more steel than its two competitors combined and appeared ready to lead Europe into the modern age. Such a development meant dethroning Britain and France, who had held firmly to their positions at the top of the power pyramid since the 1600s.

The Germans, claiming racial superiority and advocating the widely popular principles of Social Darwinism, pushed forward into economic and territorial domains once monopolized by the British and French. By the Treaty of Frankfurt ending the Franco-Prussian War in 1871, Germany annexed the longtime hotly contested French provinces of Alsace and Lorraine, located along its common border with France. In succeeding years, German businessmen penetrated greater numbers of world markets while their military and diplomatic leaders in Berlin entered the imperial race by winning the loyalties of European states and seeking colonies in Africa and Asia.

For nearly two decades following the Franco-Prussian War, German chancellor Otto von Bismarck masterminded a peace policy in Europe intended to give the new German Empire a chance to mature. This, he determined, could be advanced by isolating France from Britain, keeping the two states enmeshed in colonial rivalries outside the continent. In 1879, Bismarck negotiated a military pact with Austria-Hungary and three years later invited Italy to join. The result was the Triple Alliance of 1882, which linked the security of the three signatory nations and committed mutual support for Germany and Italy in an unprovoked conflict with France as well as the promise of military assistance to any member of the pact that went to war with two or more other powers. In another move five years later, he signed a "re-insurance" treaty with Russia that remained secret because of that country's long-standing animosity toward Austria—still allied with Germany. The Triple Alliance of Germany, Austria-Hungary, and Italy lasted into the Great War; the German-Russian treaty did not.

This uneasy alliance arrangement began to crumble in 1890 when Germany's new ruler, Wilhelm II, forced Bismarck into retirement. Instead of maintaining the delicate balance engineered by Bismarck, the mercurial leader—determined to put his own stamp on foreign affairs—virtually ignored its demise. He did nothing to preserve his country's pact with Russia, driving that huge state into a partnership with France in 1894. The Dual Alliance of France and Russia had two direct results, both threatening continental peace: It focused the signatory nations' attention on the European power structure and, by creating an opposing armed camp, helped to lay the basis for the Great War.

The aftermath of the Sino-Japanese War of 1894–1895 provided a brief interlude of accommodation before the storm clouds gathered over the cooperative effort by Germany, France, and Russia to slow Japanese expansion in East Asia.

One more power must be accounted for in this unstable mix—Great Britain. By the close of the nineteenth century, the British had no allies in Europe. Seizing the opportunity, the kaiser spoke of building a European union that would oppose the British Empire. No longer could Britain follow a policy of "splendid isolation." Germany's decision to build a world-class navy set off a naval race with Britain that led leaders of both nations to tailor new alliances. The two countries had been at an uneasy military standoff at sea, with the British unable to threaten Berlin and the German army, in turn, unable to cross the channel and threaten London. This equation would change dramatically, however, if the Germans built a competitive navy.[2]

Admiral Alfred T. Mahan's theories on sea power had provided the basis for Britain's maritime supremacy, but they rendered an even greater impact on Germany and Japan. A navy would safeguard German colonies and maritime lanes, ensuring the new empire's rise to greatness. The same factors that drove Germany's naval buildup elevated Britain's insecurity. The nascent German Empire forced London to mend relations with France and to embrace rapprochement with the United States. The British also turned to the Japanese, who welcomed an alliance that would protect their interests against a vengeful Russia in East Asia.

By 1904, the British had built an alliance system that posed a challenge to Germany's rise to global prominence. After signing a military pact with Japan in 1902, London reached an informal understanding with France two years later that guaranteed each other's spheres of influence. The Entente Cordiale pledged British support for French interests in Morocco in exchange for French recognition of the British occupation of Egypt. The dangerous pattern continued as the French remained allied with the Russians and the British with the Japanese. Further, the outbreak of the Russo-Japanese War in February 1904 severely tested Anglo-French relations by exposing their competing interests in Asia and North Africa.

The eruption of a crisis in Morocco in March 1905 underlined the perilous nature of the European alliances. Russia's war with Japan afforded Germany the opportunity to test the strength of the Anglo-French entente. Would the British protect French interests in Morocco? At stake was more than that small country in northwest Africa. The British feared that if Germany established a sphere of interest in Morocco, it would threaten their hold on Gibraltar and the entrance to the Mediterranean; the Germans feared that a French protectorate in Morocco would encourage their expansion into the Mediterranean and North Africa. Either outcome could lead to war.[3]

On March 6, Ambassador Sternburg delivered a message from the kaiser to the White House, asking President Roosevelt to join him in urging the sultan of Morocco, Moulay Abd al-Aziz bin Hassan, to reform his government in exchange for U.S. and German assurances of an open door[4] commercial policy. The kaiser further suggested that Roosevelt inform the sultan that the United States would stand with Germany in opposition to any French attempt to threaten Moroccan sovereignty. The implication was unmistakable—an alignment of German, American, and Moroccan military force to resist French designs on controlling Morocco. The next day, Sternburg informed Roosevelt of the kaiser's suspicion that France and Spain intended to divide Morocco between themselves and seize control of its commerce. If France occupied the country and Spain controlled the city of Tangier, they would dominate all passageways "to the Near and Far East." Roosevelt declined the invitation, explaining to a confidant that American interests did not justify his intervention and that he felt certain the kaiser did not want war. When the president looped Hay in on Sternburg's missive, the secretary of state was incredulous, confiding to his diary his shock at the level of "indiscretion and of such implicit reliance upon our discretion. By giving England and France the least hint of what he has said to us in the last few weeks," Hay continued, "we could make serious trouble."[5]

The situation sharply escalated a few weeks later when, on March 31, the kaiser altered the route of his Mediterranean cruise on the imperial yacht to enter Morocco's principal port of Tangier and deliver a spirited address at the German legation (with French officials in attendance) calling for Morocco's independence. He had been dubious about provoking the French but followed the potentially dangerous direction of Chancellor von Bülow and the political secretary to the Foreign Office, Friedrich von Holstein.[6]

The kaiser's words had worldwide repercussions, for he had orchestrated his hardline presentation to test the will of the Anglo-French Entente Cordiale by publicly calling for an open door in Morocco. The sultan, proclaimed the kaiser, was the sovereign head of this free state, requiring all nations, including Germany, to deal with him. French imperial designs, Wilhelm charged, were invalid. His provocative speech at Tangier ignited a crisis in Morocco that threatened the balance of power in Europe and East Asia.[7]

Less than a week later, Sternburg sent word to Roosevelt that Britain and France were allied on the Moroccan issue and that Germany wanted a conference of the powers to save the open door. The kaiser, his ambassador insisted, expected nothing in return except equal commercial opportunities for Germany and other nations. In a series of notes, Sternburg emphasized that Wilhelm's sole objective was to protect Germany's "national dignity," making it necessary that his government work with the French in settling this issue. The kaiser felt certain that British aid to France would come only from "diplomatic support" and that France would remain on its own. Britain's position depended on the American attitude toward an international conference. Kaiser Wilhelm thought the conferees would approve an open door policy in Morocco.[8]

A few days later, on April 13, the kaiser sought Roosevelt's help in persuading the British to participate in such a conference. Italy, according to Sternburg, had assured Wilhelm of support on the Moroccan issue, and France would "only continue her aggressive policy in Morocco, aimed at all non-French interests, if she feels sure that Britain will stand by her and eventually shows herself ready to back her up by force of arms."[9]

The kaiser's request put the White House in a bind. A refusal to stand with the French in Morocco could alienate their British ally (which had interests in Egypt protected by the Entente Cordiale with France) and fracture the Anglo-American rapprochement. Roosevelt knew that the principles of the Open Door in China had become a public part of the U.S. pledge to peace on a global basis. How could he turn down the kaiser's offer to defend an open door in Morocco? And yet, to side with Germany meant to oppose France, leaving an imbalance of power on the continent that would threaten peace there and across the globe.

Roosevelt had earlier agreed with Secretary of War Taft, who counseled against any involvement in the Moroccan issue. En route to a hunting trip in the West, the president wrote Taft—in charge during his absence—that "I wish to Heaven our excellent friend, the Kaiser, is not so jumpy and did not have so many pipe dreams." The United States could do nothing in Morocco, he declared with seeming finality.[10]

But Germany persisted. Sternburg sent Roosevelt "an urgent appeal" on April 20 to find out whether the British government intended to support France in "gobbling Morocco." The president remained steadfast in his noninvolvement. While still on his bear and wolf hunt in Colorado, he sent word to Taft that "I do not feel that as a Government we should interfere in the Morocco matter." The United States had "no real interest in Morocco" and should not take sides between France and Germany. "Each Nation is working itself to a condition of desperate hatred of each other from sheer fear of each other." The kaiser remained "dead sure" that Britain planned to attack Germany. Likewise, the British government was certain that Germany intended to attack Britain.[11]

The president wrote to Taft that he was "sincerely anxious to bring about a better state of feeling between Britain and Germany." Wilhelm's dispute with France over Morocco was "proof positive" that he did not want a war with Great Britain at the same time. The British government "utterly overestimates as well as misestimates Germany's singleness of purpose." The United States must determine London's position on this matter without raising suspicions that "we are acting as decoy ducks for Germany." He suggested to Taft that he raise the issue with the British ambassador, Sir Mortimer Durand, but only if he was "in any rational mood and you think the nice but somewhat fat-witted British intellect will stand it."[12]

Taft met with Durand the last week of April to sound him out on Britain's position on the Moroccan affair. Durand informed Taft that London no longer considered Morocco important. He was aware that Berlin had floated the idea of European nations, including Britain and Italy, joining in a conference concerning Morocco. But his government, he added, had expressed no interest in such a meeting. Not surprisingly, Durand reported to the foreign secretary, Lord Lansdowne, that "Mr. Taft says that America does not care a cent about Morocco, and has no desire whatever to take sides between Germany and France."[13]

Roosevelt intended to stay out of the Moroccan controversy while keeping informed. He asked Taft to assure the British ambassador that the United States was not taking sides with either France or Germany but would like to forward Germany's inquiry regarding the British stance on Morocco. Roosevelt emphasized that his only purpose was "to make things as comfortable between England and Germany as possible."[14]

The president knew that mutual interests tied the United States to Britain, which had helped forge an informal Franco-American bond out of the Entente Cordiale, but Germany was a different matter. Its administrative and military efficiency had been impressive, even though the kaiser's combative behavior threatened order both inside and outside his country. Most importantly, Roosevelt considered Germany a rival worth watching. He instructed the American minister to Morocco, Samuel R. Gummeré, not to make any commitment to either the French or the Germans in Morocco and to emphasize that the U.S. government would never interfere in matters involving loans made by American financiers. To Sternburg, the president declared that American interests in Morocco were "not sufficiently great to make me feel justified in entangling our Government in the matter."[15]

Despite his disclaimers, Roosevelt surely recognized the international ramifications of the Moroccan controversy and had not shut the door on intervention. He was well aware that the United States and Morocco had a long history of commercial relations and that Morocco was rich in minerals and agricultural potential. He also realized that the collapse of the open door in Morocco would have serious implications for China and other vulnerable places in the world. Worse, the partition of Morocco could lead to Great Power confrontations that extended beyond that state. German involvement in North Africa posed a potential danger to all nations—including the United States—by providing a base for the kaiser's warships at the entrance to the Mediterranean. The outbreak of a Franco-German war would most likely pull in the United States. The Moroccan crisis could become America's crisis.

II

The kaiser did not accept the president's "no" as final and again, on May 13, urged him to persuade the British to cooperate with Germany in an international conference on Morocco. Wilhelm alleged that he had refused a French invitation to settle the matter between the nations because he was more concerned with broader participation and wanted the open door for every nation. If he received no support from others, he would have to consider the possibility of war with France. The kaiser warned the president of another concern—that Britain, France, and Russia, along with possibly Japan, intended to partition China. Reflecting later to U.S. ambassador Whitelaw Reid in London, Roosevelt noted that he had dismissed the kaiser's anxieties as "mere lunacy."[16]

The president tried to allay British concerns about his apparent support for Germany. To Spring Rice, he noted that many English friends in government feared he had come under the influence of the kaiser, "but you ought to know better, old man." Roosevelt admitted to admiring both Wilhelm and the German people, but they "are too completely under his rule for me to be able to disassociate them from him, and he himself is altogether too jumpy, too volatile in his policies, too lacking in the power of continuous and sustained thought and action."[17]

America's security, Roosevelt continued, must never depend on an alliance. All nations must understand that fighting the United States was "too expensive and dangerous a task." Maintaining "a spirit of justice and good will toward others" was essential to building "a general attitude of peacefulness and righteousness in the world at large." He focused this policy primarily on Britain, but also extended its sentiments to France, Germany, and Japan. As for the Russian government, "I loathe it."[18]

Germany, Roosevelt assured Spring Rice, had no plan to attack Britain. The kaiser was "too erratic to think out and carry out any such policy." Any trouble Britain might have with Germany "will come from some unreasoning panic which will inspire each to attack the other for fear of being attacked itself"—a scenario that Bismarck famously described as "suicide for fear of death." Roosevelt admitted to becoming "exasperated" with the kaiser for sudden actions like those in Morocco, or his speech about the "yellow peril"—a "speech worthy of any fool congressman." He could not take seriously a leader whose policy rested on "such violent and often wholly irrational zigzags."[19]

Roosevelt could not understand why the British were afraid of Wilhelm. Last December, he told Spring Rice, they feared imminent war with the Germans. "But it is perfectly obvious that [the kaiser] had no such a thought, or he would never have mortally insulted France by his attitude about Morocco." If trouble developed with the kaiser, it would stem from his "jumpiness and not because of a long-thought-out and deliberate purpose." He will continue to be "exasperating and unpleasant" but not a "dangerous neighbor."[20]

Roosevelt repeatedly asserted that the British were wrong in saying he was acting on behalf of the kaiser in the Moroccan crisis. Using similar language as that penned to Spring Rice just two days earlier, the president declared to Lodge on May 15 that the "heavy-witted creatures do not understand that nothing would persuade me to follow the lead of or enter into close alliance with a man who is so jumpy, so little capable of continuity of action, and therefore, so little capable of being loyal to his friends or steadfastly hostile to an enemy." It was "absurd" to believe he was under Wilhelm's influence.[21]

Roosevelt nonetheless felt that the kaiser's concern about French and Russian "designs" against Germany encouraged him to seek better relations with the British. Given that Wilhelm "dwells on his desire to be friendly with England," Roosevelt asserted to Spring Rice, "I can not [sic] believe that the Kaiser has any deep-laid plot against England." The kaiser's effort to block French interests in Morocco proved that he never intended to rely on them as an ally in a war against Britain. Besides, the president observed, "I don't believe he has the Bismarckian continuity of policy and resolution of purpose."[22]

At the end of the month, the kaiser repeated his warning to Roosevelt. If Germany found "no support from the interested treaty powers in connection with the open door" and, further, if the British failed to convince France to join a conference, the result could be a realignment of European alliances in a conflict that affected East Asia as well as Europe. Again, he stressed the importance of Roosevelt convincing London to support a conference—a move he thought likely if the president participated.[23]

Sternburg followed the message from the kaiser with another visit with the president where he noted that American participation in addressing the Moroccan affair was warranted if not expected. Not all "interested treaty powers" were European. The United States, he reminded Roosevelt as he had Taft in early April, joined other nations in signing the Treaty of Madrid in 1880 regarding Morocco. The implications were clear; the Americans had treaty rights with and obligations to Morocco.[24]

On Roosevelt's return to Washington in May, he noted the growing unease in France, Germany, and Britain over the possibility of war. French ambassador Jusserand understood his country's anger with Germany but thought a conference far better than war. Roosevelt did not believe that Sternburg agreed with his government's policy but had to follow directives. The British government, the president felt, welcomed Germany's humiliation by the French opposition to a conference over Morocco and appeared willing to go to war. If the British and French fleets united, Roosevelt thought, Germany could not have done anything; but on land, its forces would face only France.[25]

As tensions rose in the spring of 1905, the sultan took the lead and invited the interested states to a conference. In early June, it appeared Hassan's initiative might find a more favorable reception when word circulated that the Paris government had dismissed the anti-German foreign minister, Théophile Delcassé, who had precipitated the crisis earlier in the year by announcing expanded French control over the sultanate. But instead of calming matters, the move encouraged the kaiser to intensify pressure on Roosevelt to urge Britain and France to agree to the meeting. The British expressed concern that Delcassé's removal might embolden Germany to take actions conducive to war. Was the kaiser's pressure for a conference part of a plan to break up the entente?[26]

In the second week of June, the kaiser informed Roosevelt that the British offered the French a formal alliance aimed at Germany. Despite a lack of enthusiasm among a number of French statesmen who nurtured hope of an amicable solution with Germany, the Moroccan problem necessitated tighter commitments between London and Paris. The French government, Wilhelm went on to say, had expressed a willingness to award Germany a "sphere of interest" in Morocco while keeping most of the country to itself. Germany, he asserted, rejected this arrangement because of its pledge to support the sultan and the open door. Strange to say, he remarked, "we may be forced into war not because we have been *grabbing* after people's land, but because we *refuse to take it*."[27]

The situation worsened when the kaiser expressed alarm to the president that Britain and France would go to war with Germany, if not over Morocco then because of their competing interests in East Asia. The British and French navies "would undoubtedly smash the German navy and give England, France, Japan, and Russia a more free hand" in the region. The Russians might award part of China to Japan as a war indemnity and thereby maintain control over all Sakhalin. This dark scenario caused the kaiser to reassert his call for Roosevelt to seek British participation in a conference on Morocco.[28]

By mid-June, Roosevelt also feared a war in Europe. Morocco was not vital to U.S. interests, but averting a war involving Britain, France, and Germany over Morocco was. The small country had suddenly become the linchpin for continuing the peace or beginning a war. As for Wilhelm's request for American mediation, Roosevelt privately declared,

> I felt in honor bound to try to prevent the war if I could, in the first place, because I should have felt such a war to be a real calamity to civilization; and in the next place, as I was already trying to bring about peace between Russia and Japan, I felt that a new conflict might result in what would literally be a world conflagration.[29]

Roosevelt emphasized to Jusserand that war could be disastrous for France. British assistance would mean "very, very little," because of French vulnerability to a land invasion. With French support for a conference, the attending powers would likely reject "any unjust attack" by Germany, making it "well-nigh impossible" for Germany to succeed.[30]

Roosevelt considered it essential to massage the kaiser's vanities. To promote his strategy, the president relied on Jusserand. Roosevelt expressed "a real sentiment for France" and promised his friend that he would never advise the French "to do anything humiliating or disgraceful." To avoid a war, the remedy must "save the Emperor's [Wilhelm] self-esteem; that for such purpose it was wise to help him save his face." If the powers agreed to a conference, they could convince the emperor to abandon any thought of an invasion. Roosevelt also assured Jusserand that the United States would not take part in a conference France did not support and that he would treat both sides fairly and oppose any German action that seemed "unjust and unfair." In reassuring his friend, he declared, "Let not people in France take it amiss if I am found particularly flattering toward the Emperor."[31]

The president's tactics proved effective, leading Jusserand to defend Roosevelt in his missives to superiors in Paris. "Examining . . . the means by which he might help us in avoiding war," Jusserand advised, "the very idea of which struck him with horror, the President has concluded that the only chance to do what might be useful, would be perhaps to flatter this excessive vanity of William II, to which he attributes, in large measure, the present difficulties."[32]

The first sign of success came when Sternburg notified the president on June 18 that the kaiser praised his efforts to convince the French to ease their resistance to a conference concerning their policy on Morocco. "Your diplomatic activity with regard to France, the Emperor says, has been the greatest blessing to the peace of the world."[33]

Facing the possibility of war, the French government had, indeed, relaxed its opposition to an international conference. On June 23, a dispatch from Premier Maurice Rouvier (now heading the Ministry of Foreign Affairs) directed Jusserand to inform the president "that however unjust," it appeared Germany was prepared to go to war. "Under present circumstances," Rouvier continued, the application "of conciliation" seemed necessary and, "that among the concessions which we might make [,] a conference would without doubt be the least undesirable." That same day, Jusserand watched as the president transmitted a message to the kaiser through Sternburg informing him of the softened French position.[34]

The letter of the 23rd was the second of three to Sternburg in less than a week, all of which Roosevelt showed to Jusserand before sending to remove any suspicions of American actions. The first, on June 20, was simply to thank Wilhelm for the compliment he had paid him for his efforts on the Morocco issue. A third letter, on June 25, contained an excerpt from a telegram received by Jusserand from Rouvier verifying French acquiescence to a conference. The letter then extended congratulations to the kaiser for his "diplomatic success" in securing the French agreement to "accept a conference" that should keep the peace. "It is a diplomatic triumph of the first magnitude."[35]

Roosevelt further informed Sternburg in the third letter that it would have been "useless" to consult the British on the matter. If war broke out, Britain would "profit immensely," regardless of what happened to France. Germany would lose most of its fleet and probably all its colonies. Nothing he could have said would have swayed the British. He must persuade them to approve the French decision to join a conference. The kaiser trusted him not to pursue any action that threatened Germany's interests or honor. "I am advising," the president maintained, "just the conduct that I would myself take under like circumstances; and I venture to give the advice at all only because, as I took the action I did on the Emperor's request, it seems but right that in reporting the effect of this action I should give my own views thereon."[36]

The president had gained the trust of both France and Germany. Rouvier felt confident that Roosevelt could undercut any move toward war and now welcomed the conference. "Tell him," he wrote Jusserand, "that the exceptional authority which attaches to his counsel, not only because of his office, but also because of his character, his sense of right and justice, and his clear perception of what are the highest interests, qualify him in supreme degree to intervene in favor of the maintenance of peace." The German emperor's appeal to the United States gave President Roosevelt the opportunity "to take the initiative that we expect from his friendship."[37]

To Sternburg, the president explained that he had been hesitant to intervene because the step "might savor of officious interference." He had only one objective when complying with the kaiser's request: to preserve peace. The French agreement to meet marked "a genuine triumph for the Emperor's diplomacy." Wilhelm now "stands as the leader among the sovereigns of today who have their faces set toward the future." His triumph was greater than either Britain or France could have expected. "I myself," Roosevelt continued, "did not believe" it possible. The outcome was a "striking tribute to him personally no less than to his nation."[38]

III

But even with France favorable to a conference, problems arose with Germany over the agenda. It should be noted that Berlin entered the discussion understandably skeptical of French sincerity, having received the incongruous opinion from Paris that the meeting would likely be "dangerous if it were not preceded by an understanding and useless if it were." The French government wanted the other powers to acknowledge its hegemony in Morocco before the meeting convened; Germany countered that all matters must be open for discussion at the meeting.[39]

Roosevelt intervened, warning the kaiser that a dispute over "minor details" would not only tarnish his "high and honorable fame," but it could lead to a war with France in which Britain would profit from Germany's loss of its colonies and perhaps its navy. Roosevelt wrote a memorandum to both Jusserand and Sternburg, recommending that the two governments have no agenda when going to the conference and agree to discuss all questions relating to Morocco, except those matters prohibited by an earlier agreement with another power. Both governments approved his memorandum, after which the president insisted that there must be no public reference to his role in the matter—far better that any agreement be "freely entered into by themselves."[40]

It appeared the president's strategy had worked. On June 28, Sternburg wrote to Roosevelt that "The Emperor has requested me to tell you that in case during the coming conference differences of opinion should arise between France and Germany, he, in every case, will be ready to back up the decision which you should consider to be the most fair and the most practical."[41]

Roosevelt was so relieved over the possibility of reaching a settlement that he decided to inform Jusserand of this "confidential note." The powers were moving toward war, the president feared; he must convince the French that the German note provided a way to keep the peace. The kaiser, explained Roosevelt, wanted to prove that "what I have done has been done in the interest of peace alone and not to aid the selfish purposes of any power."[42]

Unfortunately, Sternburg had misread his instructions.

On the previous day, June 27, Chancellor von Bülow had telegraphed his ambassador that in the event of Franco-German disagreements in the pre-conference proceedings, he would be amenable to taking before the emperor whatever recommendations Roosevelt made that seemed fair. Bülow *did not* pledge to support a presidential directive during the conference, nor did the emperor make any such promise. Yet, Sternburg mistakenly read the instructions to mean that the kaiser would follow Roosevelt's lead, both in the pre-conference talks with France and during the conference itself.[43]

To Lodge more than a week later, Roosevelt expressed skepticism about Sternburg's claim that the emperor had instructed his delegate at the conference "to vote as the United States delegate does on any point where I consider it desirable." In sharing what the president termed his "dead secret" with his closest friend, he recalled that he had considered Sternburg's assurance "extraordinary" and would be "very wary" about raising the matter.[44]

But Roosevelt had not ruled out the possibility.

Three days before the president received the German note, the French ambassador forwarded an excerpt from a telegram sent by Rouvier, saying that he and the other members of the French Council had been persuaded by the president's "reflections and advice" and were "ready to accept a conference."[45]

On June 30, Roosevelt informed Jusserand of the note from the German ambassador. In a brief summation, the president assured his friend that Berlin's leaders had declared that if a conference takes place and "any difference of opinion" arose between Germany and France, "Germany will in every case be ready to back up the decision which I may consider the most fair and practical."[46]

If any doubt remained in Paris, Roosevelt's decision to share Sternburg's note surely removed it.

Jusserand shortly informed the president that France had agreed to accept his recommendations and support a conference and thanked him for his "benevolent influence." The president's longtime cultivation of French friendship had combined with his perceived influence on German policy to assure the Paris government that it would not lose its favored position in Morocco.[47]

In Paris on July 8, 1905, France signed an arrangement with Germany, agreeing to attend an international conference on Morocco. The pre-conference assurances contained in their exchange of notes that day included Germany's approval of French special interests in Morocco, but on two conditions—that the exercise of these rights did not violate that country's independence and that its economic affairs adhered to the open door policy. France's greatest victory in the pre-conference proceedings was Germany's recognition of French control over Morocco's domestic stability; its Algerian neighbor due east also remained under French influence.[48]

Lodge was in Paris that day and reported to Roosevelt that the French people hailed the United States as their "natural ally." France accepted Morocco's invitation to meet with Germany—with the stipulation that all parties leave the open door untouched.[49]

Roosevelt had secretly acted as "intermediary" between Germany and France. To Lodge, the president confided that "I suggested the final terms by which they could come together." Sternburg served as the "mouthpiece of the Emperor; but with Jusserand I was able to go over the whole matter, and we finally worked out a conclusion which I think was entirely satisfactory." Roosevelt wanted to keep his role unknown. "Not a word of it has gotten out into the papers." The president remained mindful of his domestic constituency's aversion to U.S. involvement in European affairs and wanted no publicity attached to him. It should appear that the two governments had reached an agreement on their own.[50]

Roosevelt must have realized that his secret could not remain hidden. Through the U.S. ambassador in Berlin, the German government praised Roosevelt for bringing about "a speedy and peaceful solution of the questions at issue." Jusserand likewise expressed his government's appreciation, noting that "the agreement arrived at is in substance the one we had considered and the acceptation of which you did so very much to secure." Letters from Paris confirmed that "your beneficent influence at this grave juncture is deeply and gratefully felt." Everyone in France knew "there was a point where more yielding would have been impossible." The French people had already "braced up silently in view of the possible greatest events."[51]

Once more, the president cautioned the French not to "boast or be disagreeable and try to humiliate the Kaiser in connection with the conference."[52]

With most of the preliminary issues resolved, France and Germany agreed to ask Spain to host the conference in its small seaport town of Algeciras, located near British Gibraltar and close to the entrance to the Mediterranean. Gummeré reported from Tangier at the end of October that the sultan had approved the program and location and that the conference would be brief, "no more than two weeks," opening before the end of the year or in early January. The next day, the same news reached Secretary of State Root's desk from the German embassy but with a question directed from the chancellor as to whether "the Government of the United States, as one of the powers which signed the convention concluded in Madrid on July 3, 1880, concerning the exercise of the right of protection in Morocco," would participate in the conference.[53]

The chancellor's question, though innocuous, raised the dreaded specter of entanglement for the president. Roosevelt wanted American representation there; but, again, he knew that isolationist sentiment at home had long opposed any involvement other than commerce with Europe. And had not Roosevelt asserted (albeit privately) that the Moroccan matter had no impact on American security? Jusserand recognized the political peril of the interventionist issue in the United States and advised his home government against making a public appeal for U.S. participation. The American people must not suspect the White House of taking sides at the conference and thrusting itself into European political and military affairs.[54]

Roosevelt nonetheless felt free to offer advice and recommendations from his desk in Washington. After receiving copies of the Franco-German arrangement, Root informed their governments that the United States would have representatives at the Algeciras Conference in fulfillment of its obligation under the 1880 Convention of Madrid to guarantee the independence of Morocco. At the president's direction, the secretary appointed a two-member delegation: Minister Samuel Gummeré in Morocco, and Ambassador Henry White in Rome, the latter an experienced diplomat who would head the delegation.[55]

Root emphasized to the two delegates that their primary objective was to promote "equality and stability" in the region based on the open door. Toward that end, the United States preferred an international agreement establishing a Moroccan police force outside the border area that could provide the security necessary for trade with all countries. "Fair play is what the United States asks—for Morocco and for all the interested nations."[56]

A problem arose in Washington that December of 1905, when Senator Augustus Bacon of Georgia led a group of southern Democrats in proposing a congressional resolution against U.S. involvement in a conference on Morocco and demanding that the White House turn over all related documents to Congress. It had been, proclaimed Bacon, "the settled policy of this Government since its foundation to abstain from taking part in such political controversies between European nations." But Lodge worked with the president's supporters in the Senate to kill the resolution in the Foreign Relations Committee.[57]

The president was less tactful in his response. After venting his anger in a personal note to a friend, he publicly accused his Democratic opponents of attempting to "reduce the Executive to impotency." Privately, he attacked them as "wholly incompetent" in foreign policy. He never admired the Senate, calling it "helpless" when asked to do something good. It had earlier that year refused to confirm the treaty with the Dominican Republic, leaving him to take the blame for its failure. "Creatures like Bacon, [John Tyler] Morgan, et cetera, . . . are wholly indifferent to national honor or national welfare" and "too ignorant and too silly to realize the damage they are doing." The Senate's "action on the treaty-making power should be much like that of the President's veto over legislation. In other words, it should be rarely used."[58]

IV

In mid-January 1906, the delegates of thirteen countries, including Britain in support of France, gathered at the opening session of the Algeciras Conference. Throughout nearly three months of meetings, Roosevelt maintained steady communication with Sternburg and Jusserand in Washington, but he had no contact of consequence with Britain's ambassador, Sir Henry Mortimer Durand. He and Roosevelt had been uncomfortable with each other from the time they met in 1903. As the president saw it, Durand was not skilled in diplomacy; nor was he an outdoorsman interested in hiking and rock climbing; and, perhaps most of all, he was not Cecil Spring Rice, Roosevelt's close friend and personal preference for the ambassador's post in Washington. Roosevelt and Root felt certain that Sternburg did not believe Durand's government was acting as it should, whereas France was "more reasonable," and the president more at ease working with Jusserand.[59]

Durand did not intend to play an active role in these negotiations. His government supported the open door and did not believe its commerce threatened by either pirates or French dominance in Morocco. The president, along with Root, Sternburg, and Jusserand, soon abandoned hope of working with the British ambassador. Durand, remarked Roosevelt privately after the conference, had "a brain of about eight-guinea-pig-power." He did not know why the British kept him in Washington. "If they do not care for an Ambassador, then abolish the embassy; but it is useless to have a worthy creature of mutton-suet consistency like the good Sir Mortimer."[60]

Roosevelt needed no convincing when Russia and Italy urged him to help block a German sphere of influence in Morocco. Austria, he later wrote Reid in London, was "a mere cat's paw for Germany" in its effort to partition Morocco. The president had already told Sternburg that the United States opposed Germany's proposal that each power assume responsibility for one port. The kaiser, Roosevelt knew, sought a port, along with another port ostensibly for either the Netherlands or Switzerland, which, not by coincidence, sat next to German territory and in effect would become a second German port. He also knew that the French opposed any form of German partition, making it certain that trouble would break out between these rivals.[61]

In late January, Wilhelm found no support in Washington for his proposal that the president suggest entrusting the sultan of Morocco with the task of organizing the police forces within his country under international control and with monetary assistance from the powers. Root assured Ambassador White that the administration would never support a proposal that "involved responsibility for seeing it carried out, and it is difficult to see how we could make the proposal without assuming some such responsibility." White concurred, adding that France would never accept a proposal in which Germany took part in financing the police program.[62]

A few days later, France made clear to Germany that it would support the open door in commerce and share supervision of the police with Spain. If Germany approved French and Spanish control over the police, White told Root, he would attempt to "save German prestige" by including a provision for the appointment of another power to the police program. White expressed concern that the kaiser did not understand how rigid the French were in their position.[63]

Seeing the conference in danger, Roosevelt decided to intervene directly. He understood Root's hesitation to get involved in a matter that appeared to be inconsequential to the United States, but White's telegram had convinced him that failure to reach an agreement could lead to a conflict affecting everyone.[64]

Based on White's recommendations, Roosevelt on February 19 sent the kaiser several suggestions that left the appearance of U.S. acceptance of the German position but in reality supported the French. Roosevelt urged him not to quibble over "details" that, the president knew, could change the direction of the German proposal of late January into one favoring the French. His suggestions included the following: the police force in every port to be organized, maintained, and "entrusted to the Sultan, the men and officers to be Moors"; the international bank for Morocco to finance the police force through equal allotments of stock to all powers "except for some small preference claimed by France"; "French and Spanish officers and non-commissioned officers" selected by the sultan from a list provided "by their legations" to instruct, "discipline, pay," and "assist in management and control"; the French and Spanish to submit annual reports to Italy; and the open door to guide all commercial and financial matters. Only the sultan's control of the police force and the Franco-Spanish guarantee of the open door were in the German proposal. The first appeared in name only—that is, the French and Spanish officers would actually be "named by their respective legations"; the second had always been on the list of French priorities at the conference.[65]

The kaiser objected to only one recommendation—the one that made the settlement work: French and Spanish control over the police. This proposal, he claimed, would deny equal treatment to other nations.[66]

Roosevelt—and perhaps Sternburg at this moment—did not know that Berlin's leaders were softening their position. The same day that Sternburg rejected the president's plan, Bülow told Baron von Holstein in the Foreign Office that no German political or military leaders wanted a war over Morocco. The only solution, argued the chancellor, was "an acceptable compromise." Holstein later remarked that he hoped the French did not intend "to gobble up the whole of Morocco at once."[67]

Unaware of these changing feelings in Berlin, Roosevelt replied to Wilhelm's objection by declaring that he could not ask France to make more concessions than those contained in his note. At Germany's request, he had persuaded France to agree to the conference by guaranteeing a fair outcome. Fearing an aborted conference, Roosevelt turned to the leverage (albeit errantly) granted him by Sternburg: He reminded the kaiser of his assurance that if differences arose between Germany and France "during the coming conference," he would approve any decision that Roosevelt considered "the most fair and the most practical." At Roosevelt's instruction, Root sent a telegram to the kaiser on March 7, quoting his alleged commitment appearing in Sternburg's letter of June 28, 1905. As the "disinterested spectator" that Roosevelt professed to be, he considered the terms fair and practical. They would achieve the purpose of Germany's intervention in Morocco—to protect the open door—and the kaiser could claim a victory for German diplomacy.[68]

As Roosevelt initially suspected, Sternburg had misinterpreted Bülow's advice to the kaiser. The chancellor had not told him to accept any proposal in the negotiations that Roosevelt considered fair and practical; he had emphasized to Wilhelm that his order applied to only the preliminary proceedings—or so he said. In fairness to Sternburg, the chancellor's wording in the June 27 cable was open to interpretation: "If after the resulting acceptance of the conference by France we shall be negotiating and in the process shall run up on differences of opinion, I (Bülow) shall at all times be ready to urge upon his Majesty the Kaiser those decisions that the President shall recommend as fair and practical."[69]

Bülow later reprimanded Sternburg for giving his word about differences with France "during the *Conference* while I had in mind only the then forthcoming special discussion between us and France."[70]

Meanwhile, in Algeciras, the German delegation expressed interest in a compromise proposal by Austria that offered a major concession to France and yet appeared favorable to nearly everyone in the hall. French officers would supervise the police forces in four ports and the Spanish in three, leaving the eighth port to either a Swiss or Dutch inspector-general, who would also inspect the police at the other seven ports and report his findings to the diplomatic corps at Tangier.[71]

Roosevelt objected to the Austrian proposal, calling it a shift from the German and American position that Morocco must be open to equal commercial opportunity. The Austrian arrangement would lead to a tripartite partition that violated the open door principle by establishing three spheres of influence, with each power having special rights. The president insisted on jointly charging France and Spain with supervisory powers to make it unlikely that an individual government could take over.[72]

Chastened by words attributed to him now exposed in print by Root's March 7 telegram, the kaiser approved Roosevelt's proposal that French and Spanish officers cooperate in each of the ports, and he supported the appointment of an inspector-general that France had already accepted in principle. The following day, March 20, the White House learned that the Austrian ambassador would present a new proposal at the next meeting, revised along the lines suggested by the president in his February 19 note to Germany.[73]

But there was another aspect of the story. Roosevelt had also verbally warned Sternburg that if the conference failed, he would publish all correspondence with the kaiser relating to a promise made and a promise broken that would raise suspicions about Germany's "justice and good faith." If Wilhelm accepted the proposals, however, Roosevelt would publicly credit Germany for reaching that settlement.[74]

That acceptance affirmed, Roosevelt kept his promise.

In a talk before a delegation of German-American war veterans (the transcript of which he first shared with Sternburg and Jusserand), Roosevelt commended the kaiser for repairing relations with France and for bringing Germany and the United States closer together. The Algeciras Conference took place at the kaiser's initiative and achieved his objectives of promoting international peace and improving conditions in Morocco. Both Sternburg and Jusserand thanked Roosevelt for the speech. The French government expressed its "high appreciation" to the president for his assistance in arranging a "just solution" to the differences with Germany over Morocco.[75]

Roosevelt refused to allow the publication of any of the documents, calling them "most strictly confidential."[76]

The conferees reached a final settlement of all issues on March 31, 1906. The U.S. delegates noted "good-fellowship" and "general relief and satisfaction" by all delegates as they adjourned until the final meeting of April 7 to sign the General Act. Throughout the conference, the delegates used "no uncivil or unkind word" toward each other. White and Gummeré noted two major reasons for success: The conference supported "every principle of international interest advocated by Germany," and it recognized the French financial position in Morocco without violating the open door.[77]

The secretary of state instructed the two U.S. delegates to sign the General Act of the International Conference of Algeciras but only after declaring the United States free from any obligation to enforce the provisions. The U.S. government, Root explained, had no political interests at stake and took part in the proceedings only to secure the open door in Morocco. Two days later, on April 7, White and Gummeré made the declaration and signed the act.[78]

V

Roosevelt and Root were satisfied that their efforts in the Moroccan crisis had secured American interests and prevented a possible war. The president assigned praise for the success of the conference to Jusserand, writing him a few weeks after the signing ceremony "the simple and literal truth" that "in my judgement we owe it to you more than to any other one man that the year which has closed has not seen a war between France and Germany" that "would probably have extended to take in a considerable portion of the world." His achievement, the president felt, owed much to his ability to serve his own country without "deviating by so much as a hand's breadth from the code of mutual good faith and scrupulous regard for the rights of others, which should obtain between nations no less than between gentlemen." A few days later, the secretary of state commended the two U.S. delegates, White and Gummeré, for working together to resolve issues that endangered peace in Europe. To White, he acknowledged that the "task was exceedingly delicate and difficult, and it was admirably performed."[79]

In his Sixth Annual Message to Congress in December 1906, Roosevelt expounded on his views on war within the context of the Moroccan crisis. Peace must rest on a righteousness that will "bind the conscience of a nation" as it does that of an individual. "A just war is in the long run far better for a nation's soul than the most prosperous peace obtained by acquiescence in wrong or injustice." America must prepare for war to avoid defeat in war. A defeated nation was "not necessarily a disgraced nation," but it was a disgrace for the nation to avoid the responsibility of defending its vital interests and promoting an honorable peace. The greatest assurance of peace was a strong United States Navy.[80]

Roosevelt attributed the war scare over Morocco in 1905–1906 to mutual fear by each country that the other country was going to attack. To John Strachey, a British friend and editor of the weekly *Spectator*, the president declared that "Germany had no idea of making an attack, but was sure that England did intend to attack; and on the other hand, England had no idea of making an attack, and was sure that Germany intended to attack her." Contention over the French position in Morocco had exposed potentially catastrophic distrust among the Great Powers. Conflict became possible as each side suspected the other of planning a preemptive strike. The chief threat in Britain and the United States was "not of too brutal and warlike a spirit, but of a curious indifference to, and inability to grasp" the dangers of a "foolish peace spirit which is not merely harmless, but fraught with the possibility of mischief." This, despite (or, perhaps, because of) the fear of war that had been on the rise in Britain for years—a fear reflected in popular literature and political rhetoric and one shared by any Americans who cared to take notice.[81]

In reality, the kaiser had suffered a humiliating blow at Algeciras. The German chief of staff, Helmuth von Moltke, remarked that the Germans had to "slink" out of Algeciras "with our tail between our legs" and would no longer rely on international conferences. At least two historians have agreed with this negative assessment: Allan Nevins called it a "diplomatic defeat for the Germans." Raymond Esthus concluded that the Germans suffered a "virtually total diplomatic defeat." Germany failed on several counts: to undermine the Anglo-French entente; to secure a tripartite partition of Morocco; to win a Moroccan port or one under its control; and to become part of an international police force under French and Spanish command.[82]

Roosevelt resolved to convince the kaiser that he had emerged the victor— a disingenuous strategy he had followed from the beginning of the Moroccan affair—consistently praising Wilhelm's leadership in reaching the settlement. Roosevelt sent the kaiser his "sincerest felicitations on this epoch making political success at Algeciras" and lauded his diplomacy as "masterly from beginning to end." In a private note to a friend, the president boasted, "You will notice that while I was most suave and pleasant with the Emperor, yet when it became necessary at the end I stood him on his head with great decision."[83]

Was anyone fooled by the flatteries exchanged between the president and the kaiser? Roosevelt found the experience amusing. To a friend in England, he asked, "How could anyone with even a glimmer of humor swallow such stuff? We might as well have been addressing each other from behind ancient Greek masks." Sternburg assured the president that "the Kaiser was delighted with it all."[84]

President Roosevelt's behind-the-scenes but integral role in the Algeciras settlement contributed to slowing temporarily the momentum of events that would accelerate again to ignite the Great War eight years later. While maintaining relations with Germany, he also helped to preserve America's growing ties with France and Britain and strengthened the Anglo-American rapprochement by supporting the French position on Morocco. In writing

Jusserand, Roosevelt expressed confidence that he "would treat all that was said and done between us two as a gentleman of the highest honor treats what is said and done in the intimate personal relations of life." According to historian Howard K. Beale, Germany, France, and Britain had looked to the United States for counsel out of a crisis that not one of their three leaders wanted. Much of that advice came from Roosevelt.[85]

In the Moroccan crisis, the president had taken the United States into European affairs and, by combining this move with his involvement in the Portsmouth Treaty, expanded his country's interventionist course on a world-wide scale. At Algeciras, historian Allan Nevins declared, the three powers "looked with anxious eyes upon the course which Roosevelt would take at the conference." The U.S. presence, Henry White insisted, "was exceedingly welcome" by all the powers, who listened to his suggestions and "often adopted" them.[86] America's national security, Roosevelt argued, depended on peace in Europe as well as in East Asia, making it a U.S. responsibility to help maintain a global balance of power.

꙳

President Roosevelt was no longer in the White House when the kaiser brought on another Moroccan crisis in 1911 by attempting to secure the French Congo in exchange for recognizing France's privileged position in Morocco. The Germans won some concessions in Africa, but their actions further stiffened the Anglo-French entente while also driving the British and Russians together. Europe divided into two armed camps: the Triple Entente of Britain, France, and Russia (the Allies), and the Triple Alliance of Germany, Austria-Hungary, and Italy (the Central Powers).[87] These two forces confronted each other in the Great War of 1914–1918, with the United States eventually entering on the side of the Allies in April 1917; but only, as Roosevelt had articulated while president, when grievously wronged and having exhausted all options for peace.

Epilogue
It Is Not Having Been in the Dark House, But Having Left It, That Counts

Alike for the nation and the individual, the one indispensable requisite is character—character that does and dares as well as endures, character that is active in the performance of virtue no less than firm in the refusal to do aught that is vicious or degraded.

—Governor Theodore Roosevelt
March 31, 1900

But in addition I am an idealist, as I feel every practical man ought to be, and I endeavor to reduce my ideals to practice.

—Theodore Roosevelt
December 2, 1914

On February 13, 1905, President Theodore Roosevelt addressed an enthusiastic audience of 400 at the annual dinner of the New York Press Club, where he summed up his foreign policy in the words of a West African proverb: "Speak softly and carry a big stick." He had been late in arriving, and he followed two other speakers, one of them Speck von Sternburg. But Roosevelt was the main attraction, as evidenced by the menu cards bearing his portrait and the boisterous applause when he rose to speak.

Roosevelt's remarks were similar to those of another address he gave while vice president. His foreign policy remained consistent with the one he rolled out at the Minnesota State Fair on September 2, 1901, shortly before he became president. Now, in the middle of his presidency, he punctuated with his customary fist pounding and high-pitched voice his belief that an effective foreign policy results from dealing with other nations in the same way an individual treats his neighbor.

"Besides acting squarely, talk politely."

From the crowd: "How about the big stick?"

"Yes, and have that too, but don't brandish it."

Americans must understand the importance of "speaking courteously and considerately of all foreign nations." In private as well as in public life, the person who "speaks loudest" is the one most likely to ignore "the feelings of others upon whom we can most rely in the event of a quarrel." The person most respected is "perfectly able to protect his own rights" and is "scrupulously careful neither to insult nor to wrong anyone else." That is "the ideal I want to see set before us as a Nation, and the ideal to which I hope to see our people live up."

The "most contemptible of all attitudes" is to talk loudly and act indecisively. So it is with nations. Maintain "a state of preparedness" that makes it "evident that we are scrupulous not to wrong others because we believe it right to adopt such an attitude, and not because we are afraid of adopting any other attitude."[1]

Three weeks later, on March 4, 1905, President Roosevelt repeated these themes in his Inaugural Address, which highlighted his understanding of what makes America great in foreign policy. "Our relations with the other powers of the world are important, but still more important are our relations among ourselves." To be great, we must follow the example set by our Founding Fathers, "not merely in great crises, but in the everyday affairs of life, the qualities of practical intelligence, of courage, of hardihood, and endurance, and above all the power of devotion to a lofty ideal."[2]

A few months later, Roosevelt declared in his Fifth Annual Message to Congress, "The Golden Rule should be, and as the world grows in morality it will be, the guiding rule of conduct among nations as among individuals."[3]

I

As the engineers and workers continued their construction of the Panama Canal, so too did accusations of criminal conduct in the story continue to dog the president. In October 1908, the *New York World* resurrected the allegations of fraud, graft, and corruption made four years earlier about the Panama treaty that could tarnish what Roosevelt called his signature achievement. The president filed charges of criminal libel that wound their way to the U.S. Supreme Court, which on January 3, 1911, threw out the case as having no legal merit.[4]

Roosevelt, by then out of office and a contributing editor of the weekly *Outlook* in New York City, was at work when the wires carried the news of the Supreme Court's decision. Surely, at least one reporter surmised, the former president would weigh in on the case.

That same evening, Earl Harding from the *New York World* sought an interview with Roosevelt on his return home from his *Outlook* office. On a cold and bitter night, Harding stood on the big porch at Sagamore Hill, knowing not to expect a warm welcome. At long last, Roosevelt arrived by motorcar shortly before 7:30 p.m. Quentin rushed down the steps to greet his father as Harding followed, repeatedly asking Roosevelt his opinion of the court decision and receiving the same answer: "I have nothing to say."[5]

The area was dark, recalled Harding, lit only by the reflection of the receding motorcar's lights on Roosevelt's "world-famous glistening teeth and eyeglasses." But being the persistent reporter Harding was, he tried one more time as Roosevelt reached the door: "Colonel, won't you at least give the public the satisfaction of knowing" your reaction?[6]

Roosevelt's answer came just before he slammed the huge door. Harding reported the response the next day in an all-caps headline of his front-page story in the *World*: "I HAVE NOTHING TO SAY!"[7]

Harding wanted to raise another issue, but he had pledged not to do so until the source of his information had died or if the president's case against the *World* had gone to trial: "Did Dr. Manuel Amador and his son, Raoul, visit you in the White House, late at night, before Dr. Amador left for Panama to start the 'revolution' and did you promise to see them through?"[8]

The questions remain unanswered.

Roosevelt often boasted that he was responsible for the canal, which, as he told historian James Ford Rhodes in 1904, allowed him to "nearly double the efficiency of the navy." In another private letter four years later, Roosevelt declared that no feat had more "far-reaching importance" in recent affairs than the Panama Canal, "and this I can say absolutely was my own." To Lodge, Roosevelt again denied any wrongful actions when asserting that the "vital work, getting Panama as an independent Republic, on which all else hinged, was done by me without the aid or advice of anyone, save in so far as they carried out my instructions; and without the knowledge of anyone."[9]

In March 1911, years after the American phase of construction had begun on the canal, Roosevelt proclaimed to a large crowd at the University of California, "I took the Canal Zone and let Congress debate, and while the debate goes on, the canal does also."[10]

The following October, Roosevelt published an editorial in *Outlook* that again defended his actions. "The acquisition of the Canal, and the building of the Canal, in all their details, were as free from scandal as the public acts of George Washington and Abraham Lincoln." In a national crisis, Lincoln "gave the people the benefit of the doubt and was not afraid to take responsibility . . . for the good of the people the great powers of a great office." History has "taught the lesson that the President has very great powers if he chooses to exercise those powers." Whatever action was necessary to support the American interest, "I did it unless it was specifically prohibited by law."[11]

Roosevelt publicly insisted in 1913 that "the most important action I took in foreign affairs . . . related to the Panama Canal." Yet, "at different stages of the affair believers in a do-nothing policy denounced me as having 'usurped authority'—which meant, that when nobody else could or would exercise efficient authority, I exercised it."[12]

The charge of collusion still trailed him. In a letter to historian William R. Thayer in July 1915, Roosevelt once more denied involvement in a conspiracy with Bunau-Varilla. He had just read Thayer's article in *Harper's Monthly* and disputed his claim that Bunau-Varilla "laid the train for the explosion" and then "communicated the plan to President Roosevelt." The former president insisted that he never received a "plan of any kind" from Bunau-Varilla. He could not prove that Bunau-Varilla began the revolution but thought he had made ready the powder for the explosion.[13]

Colombia's leaders, Roosevelt continued, had failed to fulfill their duties as heads of a responsible nation. "You could no more make an agreement with them than you could nail currant jelly to a wall." When he realized he could not persuade them to "act straight," he acted without them. The Panamanians wanted the canal and that necessitated independence. "If they had not revolted, I should have recommended Congress to take possession of the Isthmus by force of arms; . . . I had actually written the first draft of my Message to this effect." On news of the revolt, "I promptly used the Navy to prevent the bandits who had tried to hold us up from spending months of futile bloodshed" in trying to hold on to the Isthmus and causing damage to the area and to everyone wanting a canal. "I did not consult Hay, or Root, or anyone else as to what I did, because a council of war does not fight; and I intended to do the job once for all."[14]

Perhaps the last word in the Panama story belongs to Roosevelt in his response to the work of a House committee investigating his conduct. As the reader may recall from Chapter Two in this work, Democratic congressman Henry T. Rainey of Illinois headed an investigation in 1912 that focused on whether President Roosevelt was guilty of wrongdoing in the Panama affair. Like the press, Rainey and his congressional colleagues failed to uncover any nefarious action by the Roosevelt administration, but the publication of their committee hearings in 1913 did not close the discussion. Instead, it revived Colombia's demands for monetary reparations and an apology from the United States for taking Panama.[15]

Roosevelt was infuriated by the idea, and not only because it drew support from his bitter rivals; such a payment would constitute an admission of guilt. "One of the rather contemptible features of a number of our worthy compatriots," he privately wrote Bunau-Varilla in July 1914, "is that they are eager to take advantage of the deeds of the man of action when action is necessary and then eager to discredit him when the action is once over."[16]

Seven years later, in 1921, the United States awarded an indemnity of $25 million to Colombia, an action that had begun earlier in the Democratic administration of Woodrow Wilson and culminated in approval by the Republican presidency of Warren G. Harding. The Thomson-Urrutia Treaty of 1921 completed the transaction after the clearing of three critical impediments—the removal of American "regret" from its text; the disavowal of U.S. interest in the oil reserves of Colombia; and the death of Roosevelt two years earlier. In exchange for Colombia's recognition of Panama's independence, the United States made the payment to Colombia. Skeptics sneered at the award as "canalimony."[17]

II

Roosevelt knew that making America a world power involved more than amassing wealth and military strength; it included a duty to keep the peace. A civilized nation must have leaders with character, integrity, empathy, and a vision of where they want to take the people. To officers at the Naval War College in July 1908, he asserted that he "would not pretend for a moment . . . that merely military proficiency on land or sea would by itself make this or any other nation great." An exemplary nation must respect the rule of law, administer justice, and protect freedom, both abroad and at home. The republican values shaping global responsibilities also define "the duties within the gates of our own household."[18]

In putting his personal stamp on foreign (and domestic) policy, Roosevelt drew attention to another dimension in effective presidential leadership—that of decency grounded in doing what was morally right, both publicly and privately, regardless of conflicting views of enemies, as well as friends and supporters. He reminded Lodge that one cannot dismiss "Socrates's maxim" about "the difference between a private man, who only has to do what is right, and a public man, who ought to so conduct himself that no one can have an excuse for saying that he has not done what is right." Roosevelt despised hypocrisy. In a private letter to historian William E. Dodd a few years later, he declared, "I always object to a man's getting in power by denouncing our doing what he himself does when he gets the power."[19]

On a policy level, the president promised a square deal for everyone in what had become one of the great powers in the world. Before a large group of labor union members, he asserted that he was "President of all the people of the United States, without regard to creed, color, birthplace, occupation, or social condition." Every person bore a responsibility to help those less fortunate. Economic fair play was Roosevelt's priority—people's rights above property rights. All Americans deserved "equal and exact justice."[20]

Roosevelt's views on race and imperialism were, of course, a product of the times in which he lived. Like many Americans of his generation, he developed a stereotypical outlook on race based on his personal experiences: his youthful readings of novelist James Fenimore Cooper and the mythologized American frontiersman struggling against the indigenous savage; his interest in the popular magazine, *Our Young Folks*, that helped to shape the young boy's racial beliefs; and his mother's romantic reminiscences of antebellum life on the Georgia plantation that made him critical of slavery. In college, his exposure to new ideas, including Teutonic (Germanic) theory on eliminating barbarism in the world, Social Darwinism and the survival of the fittest, and Rudyard Kipling's arguments for the white man's burden fed his intellectual curiosity. Finally, there was the inspiration of Henry Cabot Lodge and Captain Alfred T. Mahan, who both advocated imperial expansion as the chief means for fulfilling the duty of the "English-speaking race" (British, Americans, South Africans, Australians) to spread the cultural and technological advances of Western civilization around the globe.[21]

In his private letters, Roosevelt made disparaging remarks about numerous nonwhite peoples, similar to comments openly expressed by bigoted Americans of his time. He nevertheless denied being a racist, insisting that his support for white supremacy did not mean he was prejudiced against Blacks and other nonwhite peoples. The publication during the 1950s of his personal correspondence, however, exposed some of his innermost thoughts and, when viewed through the lens of an America struggling to address systemic racism, raised questions about his character and his presidency.

There was clearly tension in Roosevelt's thinking at the time. He had argued for years, both privately and publicly, that Blacks could rise in society only as individuals. Equality for African Americans, he believed, was not yet conceivable because of their "natural limitations" at this stage of their evolutionary development. In a speech at the Lincoln Day dinner sponsored by the Republican Club of New York on February 13, 1905, he called for "equal justice" for all men—"equality of opportunity, equality of treatment before the law." Yet, more than a year later, he wrote Owen Wister that Blacks were "altogether inferior to the whites." Roosevelt stood out from many, if not most Americans, in thinking that Black equality and opportunity would come—but only, he thought, after a long and bitter struggle to incorporate the features of white civilization.[22]

In a private letter to African American Reconstruction figure Albion W. Tourgée, Roosevelt conceded that he had "felt a moment's qualm" about inviting Booker T. Washington to the White House for dinner because of his color, but that thought made him "ashamed" and solidified his decision to send the invitation in late 1901. If a merit system was not the "right solution," he asserted, "all my thoughts and beliefs are wrong, and my whole way of looking at life is wrong." In public life, he felt "honor bound" to act in accordance with his "beliefs and convictions." He would never "offend the prejudices of anyone else." Nor would he "allow their prejudices to make me false to my principles."[23]

Roosevelt had always tried to work within the bounds of political reality, which often required compromise to achieve something when demanding everything would gain nothing. He did not regard the early twentieth century as the time to press for Black equality. He nonetheless valued Washington's advice on racial and political issues and continued to meet with him in the White House—but never again during dinner hours.[24]

More problematic was the Brownsville affair in South Texas in the fall of 1906. Racial tensions were high in the border town over the recent arrival of the first battalion of African American soldiers at nearby Fort Brown on the Rio Grande. The president received a telegram from the town's residents in August, alleging that about thirty Black soldiers had rioted and opened fire on the populace, killing one citizen and severely wounding a police officer. The mayor had originally found no evidence of Black soldier involvement, but rumors of a rape along with pressure from his white constituents discredited his position.[25]

Roosevelt ordered an investigation by the army, which resulted in thirteen months of Senate hearings before a verdict was rendered in March 1908 that found the soldiers guilty as charged.[26]

President Roosevelt declared the army's findings to be final and refused to reconsider his position. Later research found the army's verdict and, consequently, Roosevelt's support for that verdict to have been wrong. In September 1972, the U.S. Army cleared the African American soldiers accused of the crime. A year later, journalist John Weaver, who had uncovered the truth about the incident, published his findings, vindicating all the soldiers.[27]

After Roosevelt's death in 1919, an NAACP editorial in *The Crisis* recognized him as a flawed human being who had always tried to do what was morally right. "We have lost a friend," the newspaper declared.

> That he was our friend proves the justice of our cause, for Roosevelt never championed a cause which was not in its essence right. He had his faults—of the head, not of the heart. . . . Even in our hot bitterness over the Brownsville affair we knew that he *believed* he was right, and he of all men had to act in accordance with his beliefs.[28]

After the United States entered the Great War in April 1917, Roosevelt wrote numerous editorials for the *Kansas City Star,* including one that stressed the importance of truth in assessing a president's performance in office.

> To announce that there must be no criticism of the President, or that we are to stand by the President, right or wrong, is not only unpatriotic and servile, but is morally treasonable to the American public. Nothing but the truth should be spoken about him or anyone else. But it is even more important to tell the truth, pleasant or unpleasant, about him than about anyone else.[29]

Roosevelt's leadership in public service drew from an image as one of the people and a vision of leading the nation to greatness grounded in civil behavior. He understood the importance of empathy—a trait learned from personal tragedies—and showed his concern for fellow Americans by identifying with them and trying to help them out of their own dark places. They knew him as much as he knew them. As America's first celebrity president, he made the White House into the people's house as Americans followed the news stories about him and his family on their daily ventures, made countless requests for autographs, and waited in long reception lines outside the White House to see him and perhaps shake his hand. These were, indeed, the "plain folks" he first met in the Dakota Badlands and came to know as the heart and soul of America.[30]

Too often overlooked is the importance of Roosevelt's wife as First Lady, best friend, and confidant. Edith occasionally harnessed her husband's exuberance at White House dinners with one word—"Theodore!" Then followed his sheepish response: "Why, Edie, I was only . . ." She carried the family, both inside and outside the White House, always supported her husband as president and devoted father, and regularly kept him mindful of public opinion and urged him to appreciate the value in projecting personal humility.[31]

No greater testament to his partner in life: Edith enabled him to do everything he could for his family, fellow Americans, and the country.

III

When the Great War broke out in 1914, the Panama Canal had just opened in mid-August, providing the United States with the potential for building a two-ocean navy that could safeguard the nation. The engineering skills of George Goethals and others had brought success, all made possible by Dr. William Gorgas, the physician who led the way in conquering the two chief obstacles to Ferdinand de Lesseps's failed efforts in the 1880s—yellow fever and malaria. Roosevelt had put his country in the position to protect its interests in what became a global conflict that ended a century of relative peace, dating back to the Final Act crafted at the Congress of Vienna in 1815. Roosevelt's views about war had not changed by the time the fighting in Europe began in August 1914. He had earlier declared that there was "no nobler cause" than "the peace of righteousness," never straying from his assertion that the chief guardians of peace were moral leadership and military strength. According to Elihu Root, Roosevelt sought peace, "not because he had any objection to fighting himself but because he had a genuine sympathy for the multitudes to whom war inevitably brings suffering and misery." The United States must be fair to all nations, regardless of size or power, and it must demand justice from others, while maintaining "such moral and physical strength as to command respect."[32]

As Roosevelt stated to the public in 1913:

> I abhor unjust war. I abhor injustice and bullying by the strong at the expense of the weak, whether among nations or individuals. I abhor violence and bloodshed. I believe that war should never be resorted to when, or so long as, it is honorably possible to avoid it. . . . I advocate preparation for war in order to avert war; and I should never advocate war unless it were the only alternative to dishonor.[33]

Roosevelt testified to the effectiveness of his diplomacy: "Throughout the seven and half years that I was President," he asserted, "I pursued without faltering one consistent foreign policy, a policy of genuine international good will and of consideration for the rights of others, and at the same time of steady preparedness." Not one American soldier or sailor died in action against a foreign power during his presidency.[34] As commander in chief of the armed forces, Roosevelt considered military action his last resort in trying to keep the peace. He realized that the United States did not have lethal weapons so Washington's leaders could use them; it had lethal weapons so they would *not* have to use them.

Roosevelt considered himself a practical idealist. His prime objective had always been to defend America's rights. "But in addition I am an idealist, as I feel every practical man ought to be, and I endeavor to reduce my ideals to practice." He sought a world order in which civilized nations worked together in opposing "international wrongdoing."[35]

Roosevelt received several honors for his public service. He won the Nobel Peace Prize for his role in the Treaty of Portsmouth ending the Russo-Japanese War. Much later, in 1939, a dedication ceremony took place in the Black Hills of South Dakota, where Roosevelt's bust had been carved in stone on Mount Rushmore alongside the likenesses of George Washington, Thomas Jefferson, and Abraham Lincoln. More than sixty years afterward, in 2001,

Roosevelt was posthumously awarded the Medal of Honor for his bravery at San Juan Hill in the Spanish-American War, presented to his great-grandson Tweed by President Bill Clinton. Roosevelt thus became the first president to receive this award but the second recipient in his family—the first going to his son Theodore Jr., who had been badly injured in the Great War. He returned to action in World War II as brigadier general to lead his forces at Normandy Beach on June 6, 1944. A few days after the historic landing, he died of a heart attack.[36]

If legend is one of the markers of greatness, no story of Roosevelt's inspiration to Americans then and now would be complete without tying the failed assassination attempt of 1912 to his seeming invincibility at San Juan Hill in Cuba. Roosevelt survived not only the war with Spain in 1898 but perhaps a closer brush with death fourteen years later that enhanced his legendary status.

The former president had a falling out with President Taft over policy and personal matters and decided to run for president again in the election of 1912. Lacking support from the Republican Party, Roosevelt ran on a third-party Progressive ticket bearing the insignia of a Bull Moose.

Then, on the eve of a campaign speech in Milwaukee, Wisconsin, he confronted a crazed assassin. Shortly after 8 p.m. on October 14, 1912, Roosevelt left the Gilpatrick Hotel for his speaking engagement, accompanied by six people, including his bodyguard and a Progressive Party security agent. Passing through hundreds of spectators along the dimly lit street, he climbed into the rear seat of the roofless automobile and then stood up to wave at the crowd. As his entourage filled the other six seats, his stenographer caught a glimpse of a gun about seven feet away and lunged at the man wielding the weapon. But John Schrank got off one shot before being thrown to the ground. A copy of Roosevelt's hefty speech and his steel eyeglass case inside his jacket pocket had blunted the bullet's impact, but it entered Roosevelt's chest and broke a rib before lodging near a lung.[37]

Roosevelt pulled himself up, shrugged off his wound as minor, and demanded to see his would-be assassin. Kneeling down and turning Schrank's head upward with both hands, Roosevelt asked, "What did you do it for?" The only response he got was a blank look on the face of a little man in disheveled clothing he had never seen before. Not until later did he learn that Schrank had read in the newspapers that Roosevelt intended to subvert the Constitution and that Schrank had had a dream more than a decade earlier in which McKinley's ghost had appeared and pointed to Roosevelt while saying, "This is my murderer, avenge my death."[38]

"I am all right," Roosevelt insisted, acknowledging that he was bleeding but refusing to go to the hospital. "I am a little sore," he admitted, but he intended to deliver his speech. "Anybody has a right to be sore with a bullet in him. . . . If I was in battle now I would be leading my men just the same. Just the same way I am going to make this speech."[39]

Roosevelt soon appeared before an overflow crowd of 10,000 people jammed into Milwaukee's Auditorium (with many more milling around outside), where a party spokesman took the stage and, with a shaking voice, announced that Roosevelt had just survived an assassination attempt. "Fake! Fake!" yelled skeptics until Roosevelt stepped forward with his coat hanging open to reveal a bloodied shirt and holding his fifty-page speech folded in half from his jacket pocket and displaying two holes showing the bullet's path to his chest. "I have been shot," he declared, "but it takes more than that to kill a Bull Moose!"

Waiting for the chaos and screaming to subside, he spoke for an hour and a half, his voice steadily weakening and his body slowly rocking from one side to the other between two security agents ready to catch him if he fell.

Perhaps Roosevelt's near-death experience led him to reflect on the growing violence in the United States that could culminate in "two recognized creeds fighting one another"—the "Have-nots" and the "Haves." Violence would become "commonplace" when "the poor man as such will be swayed by his sense of injury against the men who try to hold what they have improperly won." On that day, "the most awful passions will be let loose and it will be an ill day for our country."[40]

A little before 10 p.m., he was rushed to the Emergency Hospital.[41]

Roosevelt recovered from the wound but carried the bullet in his upper body for the rest of his life. Earlier that year, he had declared in a speech that "we need leaders of inspired idealism, leaders to whom are granted great visions, who dream greatly and strive to make their dreams come true; who can kindle the people with the fire from their own burning souls." The leader's responsibility is to carry on "the long fight for righteousness. . . . It is of little matter whether any one man fails or succeeds, but the cause shall not fail, for it is the cause of mankind." Roosevelt lost his second bid for the presidency, but these words had already become nationally identified with the assassination attempt.[42]

Along with Roosevelt's many successes came the personal tragedies that repeatedly upended his life but in doing so revealed a resiliency that helped him develop that essential feature of an effective leader noted in the Preface—an empathy that enabled him to look beyond his own problems to understand, sympathize, and care for the weak, the downtrodden, and the aggrieved.[43]

Years earlier, in the spring of 1905, Roosevelt demonstrated his concern for forgotten people when he privately helped a struggling young poet continue his craft by finding employment for him in the New York Custom House. That poet was Edwin Arlington Robinson, who went on to win three

Pulitzer Prizes for Poetry and become a four-time nominee for the Nobel
Prize in Literature.

More than a decade afterward, in February 1916, Robinson sent Roosevelt
a copy of his latest work, *The Man Against the Sky*, accompanied by a letter of
thanks for helping him "escape from the Dark House." In a handwritten reply
from Sagamore Hill, the former president declared that this letter "deeply"
touched him because, as he had told Robinson in an earlier note, he too had
lived in a dark place and understood his despair.

> There is not one among us, in whom a devil does not dwell; at some time, on
> some point, that devil masters each of us; he who has never failed has not been
> tempted; but the man who does in the end conquer, who does painfully retrace
> the steps of his slipping, why he shows that he has been tried in the fire and not
> found wanting. It is not having been in the Dark House, but having left it, that
> counts.[44]

IV

Despite his own counsel, Roosevelt's struggle with grief over the loss of
his youngest son Quentin finally broke his spirit and took him back to the
"Dark House." Quentin had followed three brothers (the "Golden Lads," as
sister Ethel called them) into the Great War, where he became an Army Air
Corps pilot and was shot down in France by two German planes on July
14, 1918. In the skirmish, Quentin was struck in the head by two machine-
gun bullets and was dead before hitting the ground. When the two German
aviators landed to inspect the damage, they discovered that they had killed
the son of the former president and, according to Germany's semiofficial
Wolff Bureau, had Quentin buried with "military honors" at Cambrai, the
place where he fell.[45]

Before this tragedy, according to writer Edward Wagenknecht, Roosevelt
exposed "a strong Tom Sawyer strain" running through him when he ignored
the warnings against going on a treacherous trek through the Amazon in
1913. But his boyish enthusiasm once again belied his age. "I had to go,"
he declared. "It was my last chance to be a boy." He had barely survived
this ordeal in the jungle, only to have Quentin's death extinguish that boyish
spark. Friend and biographer of the family, Hermann Hagedorn, observed
after having had lunch with Roosevelt that "the old side of him is gone, the
old exuberance, the boy in him has died."[46]

Roosevelt's grief intensified from his belief that he had been partly responsible for his son's death. In replying to a letter of condolence, Roosevelt
expressed a personal concern. "To feel that one has inspired a boy to conduct

that has resulted in his death, has a pretty serious side for a father—and at the same time I would not have cared for my boys and they would not have cared for me if our relations had not been just along that line." Perhaps the most heartrending display of his sorrow came at Sagamore Hill, when he walked alone from the house to the stable and was found crying uncontrollably, his face all but hidden in the mane of Quentin's pony as he choked out the words, "Poor Quentyquee!"[47]

About three months later, just days short of Roosevelt's sixtieth birthday, he garnered enough consolation to tell Owen Wister, then a guest at Sagamore Hill: "It doesn't matter what the rest is going to be. I have had fun the whole time."[48]

Roosevelt's body was older than what the calendar showed to be his sixtieth year. He nonetheless welcomed the milestone with humor, signing a letter to his sister Corinne, "Ever yours Methuselah's understudy." He had not complained about losing sight in one eye and hearing in one ear, but he admitted to a friend that "the Brazilian wilderness stole away ten years of his life." His body was stiff and wracked by sciatic rheumatism. High blood pressure, hardening of the arteries, gout, recurring episodes of "Cuban fever" (malaria), and the dire effects of infection and other maladies stemming from the Amazon jungle, all conspired to accelerate old age. As early as 1904, John Hay recorded in his diary that the "President will of course outlive me, but he will not live to be old." Fifteen years later, according to one writer, Roosevelt was "completely worn out." His voracious appetite had won the battle with exercise, leaving him with a weak heart and overweight.[49]

Among Roosevelt's last publications was an article titled "The Great Adventure" for *Metropolitan Magazine* that appeared in the newspapers on September 17, 1918, before becoming part of a book published later that year. The opening passage and the last sentence in the article read, "Only those are fit to live who do not fear to die; and none are fit to die who have shrunk from the joy of life and the duty of life. Both life and death are part of the same Great Adventure." Never was a nation worth living in or dying for "unless its sons and daughters" regarded every person as essential to that nation. "These are the torch-bearers; these are they who have dared the Great Adventure."[50]

When asked by friend and historian Joseph Bishop about the subject of the essay, Roosevelt replied, "Ah, that was Quentin."[51]

Roosevelt seemed to accept the coming end as he turned sixty in late October. On Christmas Eve of 1918, he told Corinne that no matter what happened to him now, he had kept a promise made to himself when he was twenty-one years old.

"What promise, Theodore?"

"I promised myself that I would work *up to the hilt* until I was sixty, and I have done it."[52]

Nearly two weeks later, after remaining in bed all day reading, dictating letters to Edith, and completing some work (including, in his audacious style, making plans for his third presidential run in 1920), he opened a book and began reading while Edith played solitaire at a table beside the bed. Roosevelt's former valet, James Amos, had arrived from his New York job as a detective on January 4, after receiving a phone call earlier in the day from Edith. The following day, Roosevelt felt better and finished editing his article for *Metropolitan Magazine* that advocated for a constitutional amendment establishing equal voting rights for women.

About 10 p.m. on January 5, Roosevelt asked Edith to help him sit up in bed—that he had the "strange feeling" his heart was about to stop. Both the live-in nurse hired by Edith and the family doctor she sent for agreed that Roosevelt's heart and lungs were fine. As the doctor prepared to leave a few minutes before midnight, Edith asked him to approve a shot of morphine to help her husband sleep. After the nurse administered the dose, she and Edith retired to their bedrooms while Amos stayed at the president's side. Around midnight, Roosevelt asked, "James, will you please put out the light?" Those were his final words. He died in his sleep at 4:15 in the morning of January 6, 1919.[53]

In speaking of her father's death, Ethel told her brother Kermit, "Mother and I felt that part of his illness was due to his grief for Quentin—It took the fight from him . . . must have been his heart."[54]

Amos shared that sentiment. He had accompanied Roosevelt on several Liberty Bond campaigns to finance the war, but he never heard the former president talk about the loss of his son. Yet, according to Amos, Roosevelt was "a changed man." He came close to breaking down when he walked past a gathering of crying "gold star mothers" and had to swallow hard before saying to them, "We must not weep. Though I too have lost a dear one, I think only of victory. We must carry on no matter what the cost." But Amos noted that "something had gone out of him." On occasion, he heard Roosevelt say to himself, "Poor Quinikins!" This sorrow, Amos declared, "prepared the way for his death." In a letter to an elderly friend, Roosevelt wrote, "You and I are within reach of the rifle pits—any moment we may go down into the darkness." Amos concluded that the "one disaster that I have always felt was too much even for his brave heart—that was the death of his son Quentin."[55]

Biographer Edmund Morris has offered the most poignant analysis of Roosevelt's death. Modern-day physicians conclude that he died from a "myocardial infarction, secondary to chronic atherosclerosis with possible acute coronary occlusion." If the above family and professional assessments are accurate, Morris writes, Roosevelt "could be said in more ways than one to have died of a broken heart."

"Death had to take him sleeping," remarked Vice President Thomas Marshall, who represented the Wilson administration at the funeral. "If Roosevelt had been awake, there would have been a fight."[56]

V

Few would argue with Marshall's assessment of Roosevelt, a fighter to the end, but as president and chief diplomat, was he more fighter or peacemaker? Was Roosevelt correct in claiming that his administration had safeguarded American security by preserving world peace without wronging any nation and increasing the chances of war?[57]

Critics of his foreign policy have differed with his supporters over the period under scrutiny. Negative assessments rest primarily on Roosevelt's post-presidency, when he no longer held executive power. Opponents generally focus on his legacy without analyzing whether he could have done more to maintain a tenuous peace despite the lack of public support for international involvement. His advocates have mostly approved his presidential statecraft as a model for later diplomatists. More than a few analysts have attributed his successes to a diplomacy based on power, while others praised the moral force of his character.[58]

Still, according to historian Howard K. Beale, Roosevelt "failed . . . to create a stable world in which the great civilized nations would refrain from war upon one another."[59] But this assumes that Roosevelt was capable of producing a self-sustaining system that would have prevented "civilized nations" from going to war five years after he had relinquished any real ability to balance or reset the scales.

In office, his defenders note, he had to act within rigid domestic constraints. He could only buy time during his tenure as president, hoping that collective efforts at peace through diplomacy or international organizations such as The Hague would work. Roosevelt won the respect and trust of the leaders of the Great Powers by personal diplomacy, but he lacked the leverage to challenge their imperial interests.

Beale admits that a foreign policy not backed by voters "was as bad as bluffing about something the executive lacked the intention or the power to carry out."[60] If he is correct—that Roosevelt refused to make empty threats and would not act without gauging popular support—what more could he have done in an international environment teeming with competing nationalisms and mutual suspicions?

Roosevelt had several tools in his diplomatic chest. He preferred personal diplomacy, whether through private correspondence with leaders or conversations with their representatives in Washington. This approach, Frederick Marks III observes, was representative of the "gentlemanly behavior" of the Victorian period and exemplified by Roosevelt and his secretaries of state, Hay and Root. In steering clear of confrontations over vital interests, Roosevelt knew that the best he could hope for were short-term agreements perhaps built on flattery, as with the kaiser. Or he could engage in adroit machinations, as seen with Panama and Colombia over the canal, Germany and the Venezuelan debt issue, Britain and the Alaska dispute, Japan and Russia during the Portsmouth negotiations, and Germany and France at Algeciras. Of course, speaking softly was only half of the dictum. Roosevelt commanded a sizable stick, a modern navy that he proudly dispatched on a world cruise as the Great White Fleet—a cruise clearly meant to deliver an implicit message of intimidation.[61]

Roosevelt exhausted all approaches to diplomacy short of military force. In the aftermath of his presidency, international matters began to spiral downward, leading to problems that appeared irreconcilable except by war. As president, Roosevelt had secured for America a seat at the table. "For the first time," Marks notes, "America was taken into account by world leaders, not only in questions affecting the Western Hemisphere, but in all major diplomatic decisions." But how that role would be played would be left to his successors after he relinquished control in early 1909.[62]

An evaluation of Roosevelt's foreign policy should, then, rest more on his actions while president than on foreign developments after he left office. He frowned on intervention, but he did support unilateralism, an independent course of action that left him free to withdraw from any involvement, all the while laboring to educate Americans about the dangers of isolation. He had early recognized that with the technological advances of the twentieth century—including submarines, airplanes, wireless connections, and huge battleships such as the British *Dreadnought*—the United States could no longer live safely apart from the world.

In a speech published by *The Independent* on December 21, 1889, he laid the basis for a peace that depended on the "expansion of the domain of civilization at the expense of barbarism." Every expansion by "a great civilized power" in the nineteenth century benefited "the whole world" by putting down "barbarous and bloody violence" in "a victory for law, order, and righteousness." A "barbarian conquest," he warned, "would mean endless war." At that time, he admitted, "only the warlike power of a civilized people can give peace to the world." As a last resort, "peace may come only through war."[63]

After McKinley's assassination, the new president resumed his call for civilizing the world by including the use of military force if necessary. In his First Annual Message to Congress in December 1901, Roosevelt noted the recent drop in wars among the "great civilized powers" before emphasizing that wars with "barbarous or semi-barbarous peoples" fall into "an entirely different category." They require "a most regrettable but necessary international police duty" to protect "the welfare of mankind." The "civilized peoples" have apparently recognized the "wicked folly of war" and now understood the importance of a global peace based on "the rights of others."[64]

If Roosevelt was correct in assuming the goodwill of so-called civilized nations, he had not prepared for the racial implications inherent in a plan infused with white supremacy. He did not publicly come to grips with the world's angry reaction to lynching in the United States, a sentiment that could potentially undermine peace efforts abroad. He privately declared to Attorney General Philander Knox that he deplored lynching as "the inhuman aspect of putting to death by torture." Mob action, he asserted, was lawlessness that struck at the soul of a civilized nation.[65]

Admittedly strong words, but private expressions not equaled by consistent public statements denouncing racial violence threatened his efforts to remake the world in America's image—a stark juxtaposition between the ideal and the real world. Peace, he believed, would come only after the civilized nations rid the world of savagery. According to Beale's understanding of the president's plan, "the spread of English-speaking peoples meant attainment of world peace and the spread of civilization, and this belief dominated [Roosevelt's] views on foreign policy." The advanced nations exemplified the standards of civilization that would convince barbarous peoples around the globe to forgo nationalist feelings and racial differences to incorporate the political and economic reforms needed to transform their cultures.[66]

President Roosevelt failed to explain how he would persuade a complex mixture of cultures and nationalities around the globe to adopt republican principles. Would democratic concepts appeal to all peoples designated as backward? Ironically, the more he exalted America's freedoms, the more those peoples under scrutiny might see hypocrisy in America's racial violence and oppose his program. How could a nation posture as a righteous leader invested in uplifting the downtrodden while headlines exposed such graphic contradictions? His laudable ideals of fairness and just treatment of his fellow man clashed with his learned and deeply held racial biases that created tension between his goal to export civilization and his belief that only certain peoples were capable of embracing it.[67]

At the heart of Roosevelt's problem was the fundamental premise of exceptionalism—that backward nations would welcome Anglo-Saxon and Teutonic traditions and culture. But his peace plan contained a major barrier to success. Beale feels that the president never expected widespread opposition from colonial subjects to the "English-speaking, white man's dominance of the world that [he] spent a lifetime trying to create." Roosevelt, Beale adds, could not conceive of unfortunate peoples rejecting benevolence as the pathway to liberty. As the *Nation* remarked at the time, the president showed no awareness of their preference for the liberty of "doing things their own way." He "is almost painfully conscious of his own benevolence, but he does not see that benevolence at the tip of a bayonet may be hateful."[68]

In Marks's estimation, Roosevelt felt "imperialism to be a temporary phase in the march of civilization." But, while its relevance may have waned for some, such as Ireland and South Africa, for others it remained essential to global order. In the meantime, Beale notes, Roosevelt was convinced that backward peoples who flirted with "nationalist movements" would collapse into chaos without proper guidance by "civilized" powers.[69]

While in the White House, Roosevelt argued that the protection of America's security necessitated honest and frank diplomatic exchanges with adversaries as well as friends. Such actions, he knew, would raise popular concern about foreign entanglements and set off a nationwide outcry against imperialism. He, nevertheless, pressed it forward and exited the White House having firmly established the United States as a major world power with a respected navy capable of projecting force to maintain peace—a legacy of pressing "peace through strength" with far-reaching influence on U.S. foreign policy.

Roosevelt's impact on how the United States did and should conduct itself in international affairs continued throughout the remainder of the twentieth century, with successive presidents of both parties looking to his approach for guidance. Except for the period between the two world wars when America recoiled from the carnage of modern warfare and naively attempted a retreat into isolation, the United States would never again adopt a posture of disengagement. Instead, its role would continue to evolve into that of a critical and essential agent in global affairs. This role, as with Roosevelt, would focus not on territorial expansion but on the projection of power and influence as, it was hoped, a positive force in both war and peace. In fact, during Roosevelt's presidency, the cession of a small bit of territory in the Alaska settlement left fewer square miles under the American flag when he left office than when he was sworn in. "While he admired enlightened imperial rule . . . for the benefits of peace and progress that it might confer," Marks argues, "he did not, as a rule, recommend it to Americans."[70]

Roosevelt left office in 1909, honoring the tradition of two terms, but he did so with an impressive resume in foreign affairs. While not adding territory to the United States, he had, in fact, added something more—prestige, power, and influence with the ability to project it globally. His accomplishments include: building the Panama Canal and, with the Roosevelt Corollary to the Monroe Doctrine, safeguarding both the nation and the Western Hemisphere from predator powers; resolving the potentially explosive Alaskan boundary dispute with Britain; intervening in the Russo-Japanese War and orchestrating the Portsmouth Treaty that earned him a Nobel Peace Prize; keeping the nation at peace while holding Germany and Japan at bay during two war scares; settling an immigration controversy with Japan that eased Americans' suspicions of its expansionist aims in the Pacific; playing a critical role in resolving the Moroccan crisis through the Algeciras Conference that arguably slowed the rush of European events toward the Great War; and supporting an Anglo-American rapprochement that helped to establish his credibility as a world leader and proved vital to the outcome of two world wars.

⊂✕⊃

Among the gems in the Theodore Roosevelt Center's impressive collection at Dickinson State University is a photo negative of a short article written by William Williamson, who, as congressman from South Dakota, had been instrumental in the creation of Mount Rushmore. The article, published three years after Williamson's death in 1972, begins with brief observations on the monument before focusing on Theodore Roosevelt, the youngest of the four presidents whose granite likenesses tower over the Black Hills National Forest.

The congressman believed that of "all the great leaders of the country," Theodore Roosevelt "was the most typically American." After suffering tragic personal loss, he recalibrated his life in the Dakotas and emerged from his dark house with renewed purpose, "cool courage and resourcefulness," and a determination to drive "hard and steadily toward his goal"—"to strike when a bold stroke was required." While it is no surprise that Williamson highlighted the Panama Canal as one of Roosevelt's "outstanding achievements," his emphasis on the president's "injection of morals into our politics" might have pleased Roosevelt just as much. The president maintained a commitment to fair play whether dealing man-to-man or nation-to-nation, making him, in Williamson's words, "one of the greatest moral forces that has taken possession of the hearts and minds of men in any age." "Every word that he spoke and every manifestation of his personality," Williamson continued, "left a profound impression" and his "fight for the betterment of his fellow men will ever be like a beacon going before to inspire men and women everywhere."[71]

As a reflection on Roosevelt published decades after the monument's dedication and half a century after the president's death, the congressman's words provide an example of what Michael Patrick Cullinane describes as *Theodore Roosevelt's Ghost*. In his 2017 study, Cullinane examines how the memory and legacy of the 26th president have continued to penetrate the American consciousness, making him "as germane today as a century ago." Writing just two years before the centennial of Roosevelt's death and over thirty years after Williamson's article, Cullinane concludes that in the ebb and flow of Roosevelt's reputation, "the only apparent constant is" his "popularity." America's perception of Roosevelt may change, and his image, "like the Cheshire cat," may "fade" . . . "but until the time when his memory is entirely insignificant—a scenario that seems utterly unlikely—Roosevelt's ghost will continue to inspire debate and interest."[72]

Williamson is one among countless Americans for whom the various images of Roosevelt have shown no signs of fading or failing to inspire debate and interest. In the piece referenced above, the congressman had clearly tailored his words to commemorate Mount Rushmore, so his remarks must be weighed accordingly. But as we conclude this study, it may be useful to ask the reader to consider whether the congressman's comments as well as Cullinane's broader conclusions might apply to Roosevelt's direction of U.S. foreign policy and, if so, to what degree. This book has attempted to provide insight into this assessment by offering a glimpse into Roosevelt's character, what contributed to the development of that character, and how it guided his behavior after an assassin's bullet placed him front and center on the international stage.

Throughout these pages, Roosevelt, as promised, has been allowed to speak directly to his vision for America's role in the world and how and why he pursued it as he did. When viewed in the context of his time, Roosevelt's direction of foreign policy, much like his approach to life, sought balance between the ideal and the attainable—with eyes on the stars and feet on the ground.

Notes

PREFACE

1. Theodore Roosevelt, "Citizenship in a Republic" (commonly known as "The Man in the Arena") Speech at the Sorbonne in Paris, April 23, 1910, Theodore Roosevelt Center, Dickinson State University in North Dakota, online at https://www.the odoreRooseveltcenter.org/Research/Coections.aspx (hereafter cited as TRC).

2. For an insightful discussion of Roosevelt's "American exceptionalism" and the various factors contributing to his views on America's national identity, see Gary Gerstle's 2023 essay "Theodore Roosevelt and the Divided Character of American Nationalism," *History Cooperative*, https://historycooperative.org/journal/theodore -roosevelt-and-american-nationalism/#more-5834.

3. Doris Kearns Goodwin, *Leadership in Turbulent Times* (New York: Simon and Schuster, 2018), xii, 38, 129–37; TR quoted in ibid., 25.

4. George C. Herring, *From Colony to Superpower: U.S. Foreign Relations Since 1776* (New York: Oxford University Press, 2008), 341.

5. Ibid., 339–41.

6. Lewis L. Gould, *Theodore Roosevelt* (New York: Oxford University Press, 2012), 50; TR quoted in Edward Wagenknecht, *The Seven Worlds of Theodore Roosevelt* (New York: Longman's, Green and Co., 1958), 104.

7. Adams quoted in Edmund Morris, *Theodore Rex* (New York: Random House, 2001), 82; other quotes in Wagenknecht, *Seven Worlds of TR*, 105, 107–08, 110. The observer was Richard Washburn Child, an attorney, writer, and diplomat.

8. Joseph Bucklin Bishop, *Theodore Roosevelt and His Time*, 2 vols. (New York: Charles Scribner's Sons, 1920), 1: 240. In 1901, Roosevelt officially renamed the "Executive Mansion" the White House to distinguish the president's home from the Executive Mansions housing the governors in nearly every state.

9. Kermit and Alice quoted in Kathleen Dalton, *Theodore Roosevelt: A Strenuous Life* (New York: Random House, Inc., 2002), 211; James quoted in Edmund Morris, *The Rise of Theodore Roosevelt* (New York: Coward, McCann and Geoghegan,

1979), 481; Henry Adams, *The Education of Henry Adams* (Boston: Houghton Mifflin, 1918), 256–57.

10. Hermann Hagedorn, *The Roosevelt Family of Sagamore Hill* (New York: Macmillan, 1954), 226–29; TR's defense of his going down in the submarine in a letter to his German friend, Hermann Speck von Sternburg, cited ibid., 229; TR to Kermit Roosevelt, Aug. 25, 1905, Elting E. Morison, John M. Blum, and Alfred Chandler, eds., *The Letters of Theodore Roosevelt*, 8 vols. (Cambridge, MA: Harvard University Press, 1951–54), 4: 1316; Morris, *Theodore Rex*, 413; TR quoted in Wagenknecht, *Seven Worlds of TR*, 16.

11. "Our Submerged President," *New York Times*, Aug. 27, 1905, 6.

12. Ibid.

13. Hagedorn, *Roosevelt Family of Sagamore Hill*, 294–95; Wagenknecht, *Seven Worlds of TR*, 16. Less than three months later, Hoxsey went down with his plane. For a video of Roosevelt's flight, see https://www.smithsonianmag.com/videos/teddy -roosevelt-goes-flying/.

14. Wagenknecht, *Seven Worlds of TR*, 11–12; Mikel B. Classen, *Teddy Roosevelt and the Marquette Libel Trial* (Charleston: History Press, 2015), 12–13, 15, 17, 20, 97–98; Edmund Morris, *Colonel Roosevelt* (New York: Random House, 2010), 277–82, Newett quoted on 243.

15. For Roosevelt's contribution to the evolving Anglo-American rapprochement, see William N. Tilchin, "Setting the Foundation: Theodore Roosevelt and the Construction of an Anglo-American Special Relationship," in William N. Tilchin and Charles E. Neu, eds., *Artists of Power: Theodore Roosevelt, Woodrow Wilson and Their Enduring Impact on U.S. Foreign Policy* (Westport: Praeger Security International, 2005), 45–65; Theodore Roosevelt, *An Autobiography* (New York: Macmillan, 1913; unabridged paperback ed., New York: DaCapo Press, 1985; introduction by Elting E. Morison), 54.

16. Wagenknecht, *Seven Worlds of TR*, 14; Theodore Roosevelt, *Ranch Life and the Hunting Trail* (New York: The Century Co., 1899), 59. Roosevelt would face a number of tragedies that understandably invited darkness and depression, but he committed to working past (staying ahead of) the depression and melancholy.

17. Hermann Hagedorn, *Roosevelt Family of Sagamore Hill*, 176–77; Wagenknecht, *Seven Worlds of TR*, 14–15; TR, *Autobiography*, 355. The guest was Colonel Cecil Andrew Lyon of Texas. TR quoted ibid., 15.

18. See David McCullough, *The Path Between the Seas* (New York: Simon and Schuster, 1977), 347.

19. Hagedorn, *Roosevelt Family of Sagamore Hill*, 146, 167–68.

20. Ibid., 148–49, 186. Years afterward, Wister's account of this episode involving Alice slightly differed from that of Hagedorn. On the third time she entered the room, according to Wister, the president warned that "the next time you come, I'll throw you out the window." Sometime later, "a friend" asked Roosevelt, "Why don't you look after Alice more?" To which he replied, "Listen, I can be President of the United States—or—I can attend to Alice." Owen Wister, *Roosevelt: The Story of a Friendship, 1880–1919* (New York: Macmillan Company, 1930), 87. Roosevelt's successor, William Howard Taft, was the first president to occupy the Oval Office sometime in October 1909.

21. TR quoted in Dalton, *TR*, 301, 303.

22. Wister, *Roosevelt*, 331–32; Theodore Roosevelt, *Realizable Ideals* [The Earl Lecture Series at Pacific Theological Seminary in Berkeley, California in 1911] (San Francisco: Whitaker and Ray-Wiggin Co., 1912), 2, 29; Frederick W. Marks III, *Velvet on Iron: The Diplomacy of Theodore Roosevelt* (Lincoln: University of Nebraska Press, 1979), 116.

23. TR, *Realizable Ideals*, 7, 10–11, 13–14, 22. In an article, Roosevelt earlier attributed this quote to Lincoln. See Theodore Roosevelt, "The Coal Miner at Home," *The Outlook*, 96 (Dec. 24, 1910): 899–908 (quote on 899). He also used these words in several speeches. See, for example, TR to Minnesota legislature, St. Paul, April 4, 1903, Theodore Roosevelt, Papers (Washington, DC: Library of Congress), hereafter, TR Papers (LC).

24. TR, *Realizable Ideals*, 32; TR, *Autobiography*, 89, 91–93.

25. TR's Annual Message to Congress, Dec. 7, 1903, *Papers Relating to the Foreign Relations of the United States, with the Annual Message of the President Transmitted to Congress* (hereafter *FRUS*), Washington, DC: U.S. GPO, 1903.

26. Roosevelt's quote at the gravesite differs from his wording in a commencement address he gave to the Young Women of the National Cathedral School in Washington, DC on June 6, 1906. In his advice to the students, he urged them to serve their neighbors, develop personal character, and "Keep your eyes on the stars, but your feet on the ground." TR, "President to Girls," *Washington Post*, June 7, 1906, 5; Roosevelt used similar words on a number of occasions. For example, on the campaign trail in Chicago in 1900, he offered the directive to "Keep your eyes on the stars, but don't forget that your feet are necessarily on the earth." See "Roosevelt Says No," *The Daily Inter Ocean* (Chicago), April 27, 1900, 1.

27. For a discussion of the various challenges to Roosevelt's record of events, see "The Question of Credibility," in Marks, *Velvet on Iron*, 37–88. After scrutinizing Roosevelt's accounts of the most significant foreign policy events of his presidency, Marks concludes that "On balance . . . the circumstantial evidence is heavily on his [TR's] side whenever he made a statement of fact." It "is fair to say," Marks continues, "that, as far as one can judge from the diplomatic record, his original reputation for honesty stands upon solid ground." Ibid., 70.

28. Bishop, *TR and his Times*, 1: vii, ix; Morris, *Rise of TR*, 393–94; TRC online at https://www.theodorerooseveltcenter.org/Research/Collections.aspx.

29. TR, *Autobiography*, 398–99.

30. All quoted in Morris, *Rise of TR*, 743. In 1917, Roosevelt and his wife Edith began giving his papers to the Library of Congress, a vast collection, since augmented by contributions from relatives and others. The papers cover 1878 to 1919, from his entry into Harvard College through his death. The bulk of these papers appeared on 485 reels of microfilm, many of which are also in the indispensable eight-volume collection of Theodore Roosevelt's *Letters* published in 1954 and cited in full above (see Morison, et al., eds., *Letters of TR*). Now, all his papers are digitized (including additions after the microfilm edition) and available online. In addition, the Theodore Roosevelt Center at Dickinson State University in North Dakota is working with the Library of Congress and other holders of archival collections to produce an even more

complete digital collection available online to researchers. Sara Aridi, "Thousands of Theodore Roosevelt's Papers Are Now Online," *New York Times*, Oct. 17, 2018.

31. TR to Schurman, Sept. 10, 1903, Morison, et al., eds., *Letters of TR*, 3: 595–96.
32. TR, *Autobiography*, 86.
33. TR to Kermit Roosevelt, Jan. 27, 1915, TR Papers (LC).
34. TR, *Autobiography*, 346–47.
35. TR to Sternburg, July 19, 1902, Morison, et al., eds., *Letters of TR*, 3: 298.
36. TR, *Autobiography*, 404–05.

PROLOGUE

1. TR, *Autobiography*, 572.
2. For a concise analysis of the diverse perspectives on America's war in the Philippines, see Richard E. Welch, Jr., *Response to Imperialism: The United States and the Philippine-American War, 1899–1902* (Chapel Hill: University of North Carolina Press, 1979); Clay Risen, *The Crowded Hour: Theodore Roosevelt, the Rough Riders, and the Dawn of the American Century* (New York: Scribner, 2019), 275; Morris, *Theodore Rex*, 24–25, 97–101, 104, 110; see also Gregg Jones, *Honor in the Dust: Theodore Roosevelt, War in the Philippines, and the Rise and Fall of America's Imperial Dream* (New York: New American Library, 2012). The Philippines became independent in 1946.
3. Morris, *Theodore Rex*, 179.
4. TR, *Autobiography*, chap. 2, *passim*; Wagenknecht, *Seven Worlds of TR*, 24; Patricia O'Toole, "Teddy Roosevelt, Health Care Visionary," *NYT*, Jan. 8, 1919, A23; Lewis L. Gould, *Edith Kermit Roosevelt: Creating the Modern First Lady* (Lawrence: University Press of Kansas, 2013), 17–18; Risen, *Crowded Hour*, 114–15; Carleton Putnam, *Theodore Roosevelt: The Formative Years, 1858–1886* (New York: Charles Scribner's Sons, 1958), 72, 232–33. Putnam's work was the first of a projected multivolume biography that he never finished—a "neglected masterpiece," according to one historian. See Morris, *Rise of TR*, 781. The thieves had stolen a boat from Roosevelt's ranch. Gould, *TR*, 13. The focus of this study is Roosevelt's foreign policy and does not address the multitude of domestic problems he faced alongside global concerns while in the White House.
5. TR, *Autobiography*, 14, 19, 30, 43; Putnam, *TR*, 23, 75; TR to Kermit Roosevelt, March 5, 1904; Joseph B. Bishop, ed., *Theodore Roosevelt's Letters to His Children* (New York: Charles Scribner's Sons, 1919), 93; Goodwin, *Leadership*, 27.
6. Putnam, *TR*, 41–48; TR, *Autobiography*, 7–8, 11.
7. Hagedorn, *Roosevelt Family of Sagamore Hill*, 47; TR to Edward S. Martin, Nov. 26, 1900, Morison, et al., eds., *Letters of TR*, 2: 1443. Martin wrote for *Harper's Weekly* and *Life Magazine*, the latter of which he founded in 1883.
8. TR to Garland, July 19, 1903, TR Papers (LC).
9. Putnam, *TR*, 53; TR, *Autobiography*, 11; TR to unidentified newspaper correspondent in Albany, May 1, 1884, Morison, et al., eds., *Letters of TR*, 1: 67; Dalton, *TR*, 35.

10. Roosevelt's feelings perhaps showed in February 1907, when he declared in an address at Harvard University focusing on civic responsibilities, "I did not intend to have to hire somebody else to do my shooting for me." *Almanac of Theodore Roosevelt, The Complete Speeches and Addresses of Theodore Roosevelt,* online at http://www.theodore-Roosevelt.com/trspeechescomplete.htm.

11. Morris, *Rise of TR,* 8–10; Putnam, *TR,* 47; Dalton, *TR,* 536 n.65; David McCullough, *Mornings on Horseback* (New York: Simon and Schuster, 1981), 44; TR, *Autobiography,* 12–13.

12. McCullough, *Mornings on Horseback,* 74–76.

13. TR, *Autobiography,* 28, 164–66; TR, "National Life and Character," *The Sewanee Review,* 2, no. 3 (May 1894): 353–76 (quote on 372).

14. TR to father, Sept. 18, 1872, Morison, et al., eds., *Letters of TR,* 1: 6.

15. TR, *Autobiography,* 20–21; TR to Aunt Annie Bulloch Gracie, Jan. 26, 1873, Morison, et al., eds., *Letters of TR,* 1: 6–7; Goodwin, *Leadership,* 26.

16. James R. Holmes, *Theodore Roosevelt and World Order: Police Power in International Relations* (Washington, DC: Potomac Books, 2006), 13–14; TR, *Autobiography,* 25; TR to father, April 15, 1877, Morison, et al., eds., *Letters of TR,* 1: 27.

17. TR, *Autobiography,* 17, 27; Putnam, *TR,* 28–29.

18. TR's diary, April 18, Dec. 11, 1878, Feb. 8, 10, 1880, TR Papers (LC); Putnam, *TR,* 141.

19. TR to father, June 15, 1873, Morison, et al., eds., *Letters of TR,* 1: 8–9; TR to father and mother, Feb. 11, 1877, ibid., 24; TR, *Autobiography,* 25; Putnam, *TR,* 184. Phi Beta Kappa is an honor society that originated at the College of William and Mary in 1776 to promote academic freedom and liberal arts in accordance with its motto: "Love of wisdom is the guide of life."

20. TR, *Autobiography,* 24; Morris, *Rise of TR,* xxxii; Dalton, *TR,* 413.

21. TR to Old Hal (Henry Davis Minot), Feb. 20, 1878, Morison et al., eds., *Letters of TR,* 1: 31; TR's diary, March 5, 1878, TR Papers (LC).

22. Ibid., Feb. 12, April 2, June 30, Sept. 1, 1878; Putnam, *TR,* 149–51.

23. TR's diary, March 9, June 19, 1878, TR Papers (LC); TR to Old Hal, Feb. 20, 1878, Morison et al., eds., *Letters of TR,* 1: 31; TR quoted in Putnam, *TR,* 150.

24. TR's diary, Feb. 12, July 11, 14, Sept. 1, 1878, TR Papers (LC); TR quoted in Putnam, *TR,* 148, 151.

25. TR's diary, April 18, 1878, TR Papers (LC).

26. Putnam, *TR,* 173; Dalton, *TR,* 71; Morris, *Rise of TR,* 78, 80, TR quote on 80.

27. TR's diary, Jan. 30, 1880, TR Papers (LC).

28. TR's diary, Dec. 21, 22, 1878, Jan. 26, 1879, July 29, 1880, TR Papers (LC); Morris, *Rise of TR,* 86; Putnam, *TR,* 167–68, 175; McCullough, *Mornings on Horseback,* 220.

29. Morris, *Rise of TR,* 90–92; Putnam, *TR,* 166, 179–80; Henry F. Pringle, *Theodore Roosevelt: A Biography* (New York: Harcourt, Brace and World, 1931), 30; Ellen Steese (staff writer), "'My Purest Queen . . .' Teddy Roosevelt's Love Letters to Alice Lee Show the Rough Rider's Softer Side," *Christian Science Monitor,* July 3, 1986, 37, 41. "Only the Lee family called him Teddy or Teddykins," according to Wallace Dailey, curator at Harvard's Pusey Library.

30. Henry F. Pringle, " . . . Especially Pretty Alice," *American Heritage*, 9, issue 2 (Feb. 1958); Pringle, *TR*, 28–38; Putnam, *TR*, 171; Dalton, *TR*, 75; Morris, *Rise of TR*, 80 ff., 101. The Hasty Pudding Club is the oldest social club at Harvard (established in 1795) and counts among its membership five presidents: John and John Quincy Adams, Theodore and Franklin D. Roosevelt, and John F. Kennedy.

31. Quoted in Morris, *Rise of TR*, 83.

32. TR quoted in Goodwin, *Leadership*, 31; TR's diary, Jan. 25, March 11, 1880, TR Papers (LC). See also Morris, *Rise of TR*, 101–02.

33. Dalton, *TR*, 73; Morris, *Rise of TR*, 104.

34. TR's diary, Dec. 31, 1880, TR Papers (LC).

35. Ibid., Oct. 6, 1880; Dalton, *TR*, 77; Morris, *Rise of TR*, 49, 116.

36. Morris, *Rise of TR*, 116, 130–37.

37. Putnam, *TR*, 383–85.

38. Ibid., 386.

39. Ibid.

40. Ibid.

41. Ibid., 386–87; Dalton, *TR*, 88–89.

42. TR's diary, Feb. 14, 1884, TR Papers (LC); Putnam, *TR*, 388; Goodwin, *Leadership*, 125; Morris, *Rise of TR*, 230.

43. TR's diary, Feb. 16, 1884, TR Papers (LC); Putnam, *TR*, 387–88; Morris, *Rise of TR*, 232.

44. TR, "In Memory of My Darling Wife Alice Hathaway Roosevelt and of My Beloved Mother Martha Bulloch Roosevelt" (New York: G. P. Putnam's Sons, 1884), 4–5 (TRC).

45. Roosevelt's stubborn resistance to speaking his wife's name is evidenced by his adoption of the nickname Baby Lee for the child Alice. See Morris, *Rise of TR*, 232; Putnam, *TR*, 391.

46. Ibid., 389; Morris, *Rise of TR*, 237; TR to Andrew Dickson White (first friend), Feb. 18, 1884, Morison, et al., eds., *Letters of TR*, 1: 65–66; TR to Carl Schurz, Feb. 21, 1884, ibid., 66; William W. Sewall (second friend), *Bill Sewall's Story of Theodore Roosevelt* (New York: Harper and Bros., 1919), 160, 172. White was the first president of Cornell University and later a diplomat. Schurz was a German revolutionary who came to the United States in the late 1840s and became a journalist and a reformer in the Republican Party. Roosevelt had met Sewall in the Dakotas.

47. Sewall, *Bill Sewall's Story of TR*, 47; Hermann Hagedorn, *Roosevelt in the Badlands* (Boston and New York: Houghton Mifflin and Co., 1921), 149; Merrifield and TR exchange in Putnam, *TR*, 555–56; Dalton, *TR*, 97. Shortly after the conversation with Merrifield, Roosevelt returned home, where he had a soon-to-be famous encounter with Edith Kermit Carow, the second Mrs. Theodore Roosevelt.

48. Putnam, *TR*, 456–57; Herman Hagedorn, ed., *The Works of Theodore Roosevelt*, 20 vols. (New York: Scribner's Sons, 1926), 1: 149–52.

49. Putnam, *TR*, 456–57.

50. Morris, *Rise of TR*, 231–33; Dalton, *TR*, 90. Roosevelt mentioned Alice a few times in conversations with close friends. Ibid., 89.

51. TR, *Autobiography*, 362–63.

52. TR quoting father in Dalton, *TR*, 89. Hagedorn, *Roosevelt Family of Saga-more Hill*, 6, 11–12; Putnam, *TR*, 118, 385; Morris, *Rise of TR*, 237, 298; TR, *Auto-biography*, 328; tract on "Sagamore Hill" (TRC).

53. Morris, *Rise of TR*, xxix, 22, 77–82; Dalton, *TR*, 85; TR to Bamie, Sept. 20, 1886, Harvard College Library (TRC); Sylvia Jukes Morris, *Edith Kermit Roosevelt: Portrait of a First Lady* (New York: Coward, McCann and Geoghegan, Inc., 1980), 58, 91.

54. Putnam, *TR*, 555; Morris, *Rise of TR*, 307–09; Hagedorn, *Roosevelt Family of Sagamore Hill*, 13; TR's diary, April 3, 1879, TR Papers (LC); TR to Bamie, Sept. 20, 1886, Harvard College Library (TRC); Morris, *Edith Kermit Roos-evelt*, 91.

55. Morris, *Rise of TR*, 307–09; Hagedorn, *Roosevelt Family of Sagamore Hill*, 9–11, 13–14, 426.

56. TR, *Autobiography*, 164.

57. Ibid., 552; Bishop, *TR*, 1: 4–5.

58. Dalton, *TR*, 89; Putnam, *TR*, 198–99.

59. Dalton, *TR*, 89; Gould, *Edith Kermit Roosevelt*, 16; TR to Parkman, July 13, 1889, Morison, et al., eds., *Letters of TR*, 1: 173. According to Corinne, when Elliott died, "Theodore was more overcome than I have ever seen him—cried like a little child for a long time." Quoted in Morris, *Rise of TR*, 488, and Dalton, *TR*, 141.

60. TR to Merrifield, Sept. 25, 1889, Morison, et al., eds., *Letters of TR*, 1: 187–88.

61. TR, *Ranch Life and the Hunting Trail*, 100; TR on religion in Corinne Robin-son Roosevelt, *My Brother Theodore Roosevelt* (New York: Charles Scribner's Sons, 1921), 235, 336; Darrin Grinder and Steve Shaw, *The Presidents and Their Faiths: From George Washington to Barack Obama* (Boise: Elevate Publishing Co., second ed., 2016), 129–31; TR, *Autobiography*, 29.

62. Putnam, *TR*, 311–12; Sewall, *Bill Sewall's Story of TR*, 41; Wister, *Roosevelt*, 43; James E. Amos, *Theodore Roosevelt: Hero to His Valet* (New York: John Day Co., 1927), 58. North Dakota was admitted to the Union as a state in 1889.

63. TR address at Carnegie Library, Fargo College, North Dakota, Sept. 5, 1910, quoted in Dalton, *TR*, 101; TR speech at Sioux Falls, South Dakota, Sept. 3, 1910, quoted in Hagedorn, *Roosevelt in Badlands*, 10–11, 27.

64. Dalton, *TR*, 62; Morris, *Theodore Rex*, 101–02; For an insightful analysis of Roosevelt's views on the application of Darwinism to America's international role see David H. Burton, "Theodore Roosevelt's Social Darwinism and Views on Impe-rialism," *Journal of the History of Ideas* 26 (Jan.–March 1965): 103–18.

65. Ibid., 179; TR to Kipling, Jan. 5, 1898, Morison, et al., eds., *Letters of TR*, 1: 753–54; Howard K. Beale, *Theodore Roosevelt and the Rise of America to World Power* (Baltimore: The Johns Hopkins Press, 1956), 31–33; TR quoted ibid., 32.

66. The term "the Orient" was in common usage at the time, but going forward—excluding quotations (of course) and incidents where "the Orient" best suits the con-text—the region will be referred to by its modern designation as East Asia.

67. Turner quoted in Morris, *Rise of TR*, 479. For the full address, see Frederick Jackson Turner, "The Significance of the Frontier in American History," *American*

Historical Association, *Annual Report for the Year 1893* (Washington, DC: GPO, 1894), 199–227.

68. TR to Turner, Feb. 10, 1894, Morison, et al., eds., *Letters of TR*, 1: 363.

69. TR to Edward Oliver Wolcott (Republican senator of Colorado), Sept. 15, 1900, ibid., 2: 1403; Morris, *Rise of TR*, 478–79; Holmes, *TR and World Order*, 65.

70. Alice Roosevelt Longworth, *Crowded Hours: Reminiscences of Alice Roosevelt Longworth* (New York: Charles Scribner's Sons, 1933), 29; Finley Peter Dunne, "On War Preparations," in *Mr. Dooley in Peace and in War* (Boston: Small, Maynard and Co., 1899), 9.

71. Morris, *Theodore Rex*, 23; TR to George Putnam, editor at the publishing house, Jan. 21, 1898, Morison, et al., eds., *Letters of TR*, 1: 766; Gerstle, "TR and American Nationalism," 10; The front cover of the paperback version of *The Rise of Theodore Roosevelt* by Edmund Morris brings this image to mind. Photo from TR Collection, Harvard College Library.

72. Risen, *Crowded Hour*, 216; TR, *Autobiography*, 247–48; Gould, *TR*, 21–22. TR to Robinson (married to Roosevelt's sister Corinne), July 27, 1898, H. W. Brands, ed., *The Selected Letters of Theodore Roosevelt* (New York: Cooper Square Press, 2001), 205. In response to claims that Roosevelt exaggerated his role in this battle, Major-General Samuel S. Sumner of the U.S. Army wrote a letter to President Roosevelt on May 11, 1905, defending his summary of the fighting at San Juan Hill on the basis of having been there to order Roosevelt's forces to assault the area. Encl. in Appendix A, TR, *Autobiography*, 277–78.

73. Secretary of State Hay produced two circular notes articulating the Open Door Policy. The first in 1899 proposed that nations engaged in China respect the rights of all nations to trade freely with China. The second note in 1900 committed the United States to safeguarding the territorial and administrative integrity of China. For a detailed examination of the Roosevelt administration's approach to the Open Door, see Gregory Moore, *Defining and Defending the Open Door Policy: Theodore Roosevelt and China, 1901–1909* (Lanham: Lexington Books, 2015).

74. Edith quoted in Gould, *Edith Kermit Roosevelt*, 22; TR quoted in Wagenknecht, *Seven Worlds of TR*, 169.

75. TR to Platt, Feb. 1, 1900, Morison, et al., eds., *Letters of TR*, 2: 1157; TR to Platt, Feb. 7, 1900, ibid., 1174; Bishop, *TR*, 1: 134; TR to Lodge, June 25, 1900, Henry Cabot Lodge, ed., *Selections from the Correspondence of Theodore Roosevelt and Henry Cabot Lodge, 1884–1918*, 2 vols. (New York: Charles Scribner's Sons, 1925), 1: 486; Morris, *Rise of TR*, 755–57. Roosevelt was an undergraduate at Harvard when he first met Lodge, then a beginning professor of history. They became close friends during the 1884 presidential campaign. Beale, *TR and Rise of America*, 20.

76. Dalton, *TR*, 191; Morris, *Rise of TR*, 741, 747, 755, 765; TR to Lodge, July 1, 1899, Morison, et al., eds., *Letters of TR*, 2: 1023. Morris claims that Roosevelt was "the most famous man in America" when he returned from the Spanish-American War in 1898. Morris, *Rise of TR*, 698.

77. Morris, *Rise of TR*, 762–63; Hanna quoted ibid., 763, 767. See also Arthur Wallace Dunn, *From Harrison to Harding: A Personal Narrative, Covering a Third of a Century, 1888–1921*, 2 vols. (New York: G. P. Putnam's Sons, 1922), 1: 331–39.

78. Draft notes of Address of Vice President Roosevelt, Minnesota State Fair in Minneapolis, Sept. 2, 1901, Harvard College Library (TRC); "Col. Roosevelt Sees the People: Minneapolis Doffs Her Hat and Gives the Vice President a Right Royal Welcome," *Minneapolis Journal*, Sept. 2, 1901, 1.

79. TR to Lodge, Feb. 3, 1900 ("strictly secret"), Lodge, ed., *Correspondence of TR and Lodge*, 1: 449; TR to Lodge, April 9, 1900, ibid., 456; Aida D. Donald, *Lion in the White House: A Life of Theodore Roosevelt* (New York: Basic Books, 2007), xiii–xiv.

80. Hagedorn, *Roosevelt Family of Sagamore Hill*, 117; Morris, *Theodore Rex*, 3.

81. Dalton, *TR*, 199–201; Morris, *Theodore Rex*, 3–7; Hagedorn, *Roosevelt Family of Sagamore Hill*, 116–19.

82. Ibid., 120–22.

83. Dalton, *TR*, 199–201.

84. Henry Adams to Elizabeth Cameron, Sept. 16, 1901, Worthington C. Ford., ed., *The Letters of Henry Adams, 1838–1918*, 2 vols. (Boston and New York: Houghton Mifflin, 1930–38), 2: 354.

85. Buffalo Bill quoted in TR to TR, Jr., Feb. 19, 1904, Bishop, ed., *TR's Letters to His Children*, 91–92; Hanna quoted in Morris, *Theodore Rex*, 30.

86. Hanna quoted in Herman H. Kohlsaat, *From McKinley to Harding: Personal Recollections of Our Presidents* (New York: Charles Scribner's Sons, 1923), 100–01. Kohlsaat was a publisher of the *Chicago Times Herald* (later the *Record General*), who was on the train and heard Hanna's criticism. He soon became a confidant of President Roosevelt. Morris, *Theodore Rex*, 18, 256.

87. For these exchanges, see Kohlsaat, *From McKinley to Harding*, 101–03.

88. TR to Spring Rice, April 14, 1889, Morison, et al., eds., *Letters of TR*, 1: 157; TR quoted in Beale, *TR and Rise of America*, 37.

89. Pringle, *TR*, 126; Beale, *TR and Rise of America*, 36–37; Henry Cabot Lodge and Theodore Roosevelt, *Hero Tales from American History* (New York: Century Co., 1895).

90. Theodore Roosevelt, *The Winning of the West*, 4 vols. (New York: G. P. Putnam's Sons, 1889–96), 3: "The Founding of the Trans-Alleghany Commonwealths, 1784–1790," and 4: "The Indian Wars, 1784–1787."

91. Spring Rice to Valentine Chirol (British historian, journalist, and diplomat), early Dec. 1904, Stephen Gwynn, ed., *The Letters and Friendships of Sir Cecil Spring Rice: A Record*, 2 vols. (Boston: Houghton Mifflin Co., 1929), 1: 437; Dunne quoted in Roosevelt, *My Brother TR*, 207.

92. Lewis L. Gould, *The Presidency of Theodore Roosevelt* (Lawrence: University Press of Kansas, 1991), 22–23, 118–19; Robert J. Norrell, *Up from History: The Life of Booker T. Washington* (Cambridge, MA: The Belknap Press, 2009), 1–5.

93. Thomas G. Dyer, *Theodore Roosevelt and the Idea of Race* (Baton Rouge: Louisiana State University Press, 1980), 89–90, 102; TR to John Strachey, Nov. 20, 1901, TR Papers (LC); TR to Carl Schurz, Dec. 24, 1903, ibid.

94. Ibid., 223; H. W. Brands, *T.R. The Last Romantic* (New York: Basic Books, 1997), 421–22; Washington to TR, Oct. 1, 4, 16, 1901, TR Papers (LC); R. J. Belzer

to TR, Oct. 18, 1901, ibid.; TR to Lodge, Oct. 28, 1901, Lodge, ed., *Correspondence of TR and Lodge*, 2: 510.

95. TR to Strachey, Nov. 20, 1901, TR Papers (LC); TR to Tourgée, Nov. 8, 1901, Morison, et al., eds., *Letters of TR*, 3: 190.

96. TR to Tourgée, Nov. 8, 1901, Morison, et al., eds., *Letters of TR*, 3: 190–91.

97. Dyer, *TR and Idea of Race*, chap. 1; ibid., 45–48, 112, 127–40; Beale, *TR and Rise of America*, 29–30; Dalton, *TR*, 126; TR to Rice, June 16, 1905, Morison et al., eds., *Letters of TR*, 4: 1233.

98. Roosevelt, *My Brother TR*, 206.

99. TR quoted ibid., 206–07; Dalton, *TR*, 206–07.

100. First TR quote in Dalton, *TR*, 206; TR's second quote in Roosevelt, *My Brother TR*, 106.

101. Wister, *Roosevelt*, 225. In Federalist Paper No. 10, James Madison wrote in 1787 that a faction was "a number of citizens, whether amounting to a majority or a minority of the whole, who are united and actuated by some common impulse of passion, or of interest, adverse to the rights of other citizens, or to the permanent and aggregate interests of the community." Avalon Project: Documents on Law, History and Diplomacy, Yale Law School, https://avalon.law.yale.edu/.

102. Richard H. Collin, *Theodore Roosevelt's Caribbean: The Panama Canal, the Monroe Doctrine, and the Latin American Context* (Baton Rouge: Louisiana State University Press, 1990), 250; TR quoted in Wister, *Roosevelt*, 225; Hay and Root quoted in Wagenknecht, *Seven Worlds of TR*, 162.

103. "Address of Hon. Theodore Roosevelt before the Naval War College," June 2, 1897, 12, TR Center.

104. Alfred T. Mahan, *The Influence of Sea Power upon History, 1660–1783* (Boston: Little, Brown and Co., 1890).

105. Kenneth A. Kagan, "Alfred Thayer Mahan: Turning America to the Sea," in Frank J. Merli and Theodore A. Wilson, eds., *Makers of American Diplomacy: From Benjamin Franklin to Alfred Thayer Mahan* (New York: Charles Scribner's Sons, 1974), 279–304. This is the first of two volumes, the second volume subtitled *From Theodore Roosevelt to Henry Kissinger*.

CHAPTER 1

1. Theodore Roosevelt, "How the United States Acquired the Right to Dig the Panama Canal," *Outlook*, Oct. 7, 1911, 314–18 (quotes on 314), http://www.theodore-Roosevelt.com/trspeechescomplete.htm; Philippe Bunau-Varilla, *Panama: The Creation, Destruction and Resurrection* (New York: McBride, Nast and Co., 1914), 93.

2. Collin, *TR's Caribbean*, 134, 137–38.

3. Ibid., 135–36; Walter LaFeber, *The Panama Canal: The Crisis in Historical Perspective,* updated ed. (New York: Oxford University Press, 1989. Originally published in 1978 and expanded in 1979), 9.

4. Collin, *TR's Caribbean*, 170; TR to Mahan, Feb. 14, 1900, Morison, et al., eds., *Letters of TR*, 2: 1185; TR, "Roosevelt Wants This Country to Control the Nicaragua Canal," *Indianapolis Journal*, Feb. 12, 1900, 1.

5. TR to Hay, Feb. 18, 1900, Morison, et al., eds., *Letters of TR*, 2: 1192; TR to Spring Rice, March 2, 1900, ibid., 1209.

6. TR to Lee, March 18, 1901, ibid., 3: 19. Roosevelt had met Lee in Cuba during the Spanish-American War. At that time a military attaché, Lee became a member of Parliament and was a lifelong correspondent with Roosevelt. See numerous references to their correspondence in Hagedorn, *Roosevelt Family of Sagamore Hill*.

7. TR to Lodge, March 27, 1901, Lodge, ed., *Correspondence of TR and Lodge*, 1: 484–85.

8. Ibid., 485.

9. TR to Lodge, March 27, 1901, Morison, et al., eds., *Letters of TR*, 3: 32.

10. Lodge to TR, March 30, 1901, Lodge, ed., *Correspondence of TR and Lodge*, 1: 487.

11. Ibid., 488.

12. TR to Lodge, June 19, 1901, ibid., 1: 494.

13. TR to Lee, April 24, 1901, Morison, et al., eds., *Letters of TR*, 3: 65.

14. TR to Coudert, July 3, 1901, ibid., 105–06. Coudert was a member of President Grover Cleveland's Venezuela Boundary Commission of the late 1890s; TR (warning Holleben against violating the Monroe Doctrine) to Spring Rice, July 3, 1901, ibid., 109.

15. TR to Key, July 6, 1901, ibid., 111.

16. TR to Hay, Oct. 8, 1901, ibid., 166–67; TR to Sternburg, Oct. 11, 1901, ibid., 172.

17. See Bradford Perkins, *The Great Rapprochement: England and the United States, 1895–1914* (New York: Atheneum, 1968).

18. Collin, *TR's Caribbean*, 142; Miles P. DuVal, Jr., *Cadiz to Cathay: The Story of the Long Diplomatic Struggle for the Panama Canal* (New York: Greenwood Press, 1968), 102–08; McCullough, *Path Between the Seas*, 45–69, 102.

19. President Hayes to U.S. Senate, James D. Richardson, ed., *A Compilation of the Messages and Papers of the Presidents*, 20 vols. (New York: Bureau of National Literature, 1917), 10: 4537–38; LaFeber, *Panama Canal*, 8–11; Collin, *TR's Caribbean*, 143–44. Benjamin Bidlack was the U.S. chargé to New Granada (later Colombia). Ibid., 133.

20. For the problems in building a canal, see the following works: Collin, *TR's Caribbean*, 145–46; McCullough, *Path Between the Seas*; DuVal, *Cadiz to Cathay*; Dwight C. Miner, *The Fight for the Panama Route: The Story of the Spooner Act and the Hay-Herrán Treaty* (New York: Columbia University Press, 1940. Reprint: New York: Octagon Books, 1966); Matthew Parker, *Panama Fever: The Epic Story of One of the Greatest Human Achievements of All Time—the Building of the Panama Canal* (New York: Doubleday, 2007).

21. For the magnitude of the canal project, see McCullough, *Path Between the Seas*, 529–31.

22. Quoted in LaFeber, *Panama Canal*, 11.

23. McCullough, *Path Between the Seas*, 273–74.

24. Collin, *TR's Caribbean*, 161; McCullough, *Path Between the Seas*, 264–65, 274–76.

25. Collin, *TR's Caribbean*, 169, 172, 195–96; LaFeber, *Panama Canal*, 15; William H. Harbaugh, *The Life and Times of Theodore Roosevelt* (New York: Oxford University Press, 1975. Revised ed. Originally published as *Power and Responsibility* by Farrar, Straus and Cudahy, Inc., 1961), 197; Morris, *Theodore Rex*, 112–13; Harbaugh, *Life and Times of TR*, 197.

26. McCullough, *Path Between the Seas*, 265–66; LaFeber, *Panama Canal*, 16.

27. Miner, *Fight for Panama Route*, 119–20, 120 n.16; Collin, *TR's Caribbean*, 177–78; McCullough, *Path Between the Seas*, 266, 325–27.

28. Collin, *TR's Caribbean*, 177; McCullough, *Path Between the Seas*, 266.

29. Collin, *TR's Caribbean*, 152–53.

30. These exchanges quoted in Morris, *Theodore Rex*, 84, cited in *New York Herald*, Jan. 17, 1902.

31. Collin, *TR's Caribbean*, 152–53: Morris, *Theodore Rex*, 83–84.

32. Morris, *Theodore Rex*, 84.

33. Ibid., 598 n.84; Earl Harding, *The Untold Story of Panama* (New York: Athene Press, Inc., 1959), 12; Collin, *TR's Caribbean*, 177–78, 199; Miner, *Fight for Panama Route*, 120–21; McCullough, *Path Between the Seas*, 274, 325–27.

34. U.S. Congress, House Committee on Foreign Affairs, *The Story of Panama: Hearings on the Rainey Resolution Before the Committee on Foreign Affairs of the House of Representatives* (Washington, DC: GPO, 1913), 166 (hereafter HR, *Story of Panama*).

35. Haupt meeting with Roosevelt, told by Haupt to Harding. See Harding, *Untold Story of Panama*, v, 13. Henry Hall from the *New York World* presented evidence to the Rainey Committee that Walker called Haupt out of a commission meeting to plead with him to sign the report—that the president "demanded" a unanimous vote. See HR, *Story of Panama*, 166 (Insert 41, n.47). Haupt's account seems more convincing. Hall was a former editor of the English section of the Panama newspaper owned by members of the government. Harding, *Untold Story of Panama*, 76–77.

36. Lewis M. Haupt, "Why Is An Isthmian Canal Not Built?" *North American Review*, 175 (July 1902): 128–35 (quotes on 129). Congressional testimony in 1912 claimed that Haupt explained his switch from Nicaragua to Panama to a correspondent of the *New York World* and that the explanation appeared in his article in the *North American Review* (cited above). Despite Haupt's request that the minutes of the Walker Commission include his reasons, no one involved in the congressional investigation years afterward could find a printing of the minutes in the public record. HR, *Story of Panama*, 166.

37. Morris, *Theodore Rex*, 84.

38. *NY Herald*, Jan. 19, 1902, 1, quoted in Morris, *Theodore Rex*, 84; ibid., 598 n.84; McCullough, *Path Between the Seas*, 266–67; Harbaugh, *Life and Times of TR*, 197.

39. Morris, *Theodore Rex*, 85; DuVal, *Cadiz to Cathay*, 158; Morgan quoted in *NYT*, Jan. 21, 1902, 1.

40. *NYT*, Jan. 21, 1902, 1–2.

41. Morris, *Theodore Rex*, 85.

42. Collin, *TR's Caribbean*, 146, 154; McCullough, *Path Between the Seas*, 289–91; Charles D. Ameringer, "The Panama Canal Lobby of Philippe Bunau-Varilla and William Nelson Cromwell," *American Historical Review*, 68 (June 1963): 346–63.

43. McCullough, *Path Between the Seas*, 290–91.

44. Collin, *TR's Caribbean*, 154; HR, *Story of Panama*, 70–71; LaFeber, *Panama Canal*, 15–16.

45. HR, *Story of Panama*, 61–62; quote from *NY World*, Oct. 4, 1908, cited in Miner, *Fight for Panama Route*, 76–77.

46. Miner, *Fight for Panama Route*, 76–77; Morris, *Theodore Rex*, 85; Hall's testimony, Feb. 15, 1912, HR, *Story of Panama*, 460.

47. LaFeber, *Panama Canal*, 16–17; McCullough, *Path Between the Seas*, 162; Collin, *TR's Caribbean*, 150–52; David Howarth, *Panama: Four Hundred Years of Dreams and Cruelty* (New York: McGraw-Hill Book Co., 1966), 198; Morris, *Theodore Rex*, 85–86; HR, *Story of Panama*, 6.

48. Bunau-Varilla, *Panama*, 177. See also McCullough, *Path Between the Seas*, 277. Newsman Edward Mitchell quoted ibid., 278.

49. Collin, *TR's Caribbean*, 151; LaFeber, *Panama Canal*, 17.

50. Proclamation by TR, Feb. 22, 1902, *FRUS*, Dec. 2, 1902, 517–19; McCullough, *Path Between the Seas*, 259.

51. LaFeber, *Panama Canal*, 17; Harbaugh, *Life and Times of TR*, 197.

52. Collin, *TR's Caribbean*, 196–97; Morris, *Theodore Rex*, 116; McCullough, *Path Between the Seas*, 328; Harbaugh, *Life and Times of TR*, 197.

53. Morris, *Theodore Rex*, 111–12; Collin, *TR's Caribbean*, 196–98; Miner, *Fight for Panama Route*, 123–24; LaFeber, *Panama Canal*, 17–18; Harbaugh, *Life and Times of TR*, 197; McCullough, *Path Between the Seas*, 269, 328; DuVal, *Cadiz to Cathay*, 167.

54. Collin, *TR's Caribbean*, 217. The full text of the Spooner Act of June 28, 1902, is in DuVal, *Cadiz to Cathay*, 497–501.

55. TR to Hay, March 12, 1903, Morison, et al., eds., *Letters of TR*, 3: 445; Collin, *TR's Caribbean*, 218–19. Roosevelt had also shown great concern over another treaty at the time, that with Cuba—which likewise passed the Senate.

56. Miner, *Fight for Panama Route*, 264; Collin, *TR's Caribbean*, 222.

57. McCullough, *Path Between the Seas*, 333; Collin, *TR's Caribbean*, 222–24.

58. Collin, *TR's Caribbean*, 158, 165–68; Miner, *Fight for Panama Route*, 52–54; McCullough, *Path Between the Seas*, 335–36; Beaupré to Hay, March 30, 1903, *FRUS*, Dec. 7, 1903, 133–34.

59. Miner, *Fight for Panama Route*, 264; Beaupré to Hay, April 15, 1903, *FRUS*, Dec. 7, 1903, 134–35; Collin, *TR's Caribbean*, 224–25. The Colombian minister of finance was General Julio Fernández.

60. Beaupré to Hay, May 4, 1903, *FRUS*, Dec. 7, 1903, 142–43 (quote on 142). Collin, *TR's Caribbean*, 215, 221, 226.

61. Hay to Beaupré, June 9, 1903, *FRUS*, Dec. 7, 1903, 146. Beaupré was under directives to keep this note confidential, but he could summarize its essence verbally or provide Colombia a copy in the form of a memorandum. Ibid.

62. HR, *Story of Panama*, 348, 357; McCullough, *Path Between the Seas*, 342–43; Harding, *Untold Story of Panama*, 23–24, 26; Collin, *TR's Caribbean*, 246–47; Parker, *Panama Fever*, 221, 228; HR, *Story of Panama*, 694.

63. HR, *Story of Panama*, 357. Quote by Henry Hall of *New York World*.

64. Ibid., 344; Morris, *Theodore Rex*, 241–42; McCullough, *Path Between the Seas*, 336–37.

65. HR, *Story of Panama*, 344.

66. Ibid., 344–45; Morris, *Theodore Rex*, 242–43.

67. HR, *Story of Panama*, 345.

68. Ibid.

69. Ibid.; Morris, *Theodore Rex*, 242.

70. "An Ultimatum to Colombia," *New York Sun*, June 14, 1903, 1. According to one writer, Roosevelt never told reporters anything "on the record," but he authorized them to paraphrase what he said without attributing the words to him. John M. Thompson, *Great Power Rising: Theodore Roosevelt and the Politics of U.S. Foreign Policy* (New York: Oxford University Press, 2019), 14–15.

71. Beaupré to Hay, June 17, 1903, *FRUS*, Dec. 7, 1903, ibid., 151; Marroquin quoted in Beaupré to Hay, June 20, 1903, ibid., 154; ibid., encl. in "Counter Memorandum" from Minister Luis Rico, Department of Foreign Affairs, Bogotá, June 18, 1903, ibid., 151–52.

72. "Counter Memorandum," June 18, 1903, encl. in Beaupré to Hay, June 20, 1903, ibid., 153.

73. Beaupré to Hay, June 20, 1903, ibid., 154–55.

74. Beaupré to Hay, July 2, 1903, ibid., 157.

75. Beaupré to Hay, July 5, 1903, ibid., 158; Joseph B. Bishop, *The Panama Gateway* (New York: Charles Scribner's Sons, 1913), 123–24.

76. Beaupré to Hay, July 9, 1903 (received July 12), *FRUS*, Dec. 7, 1903, 163; LaFeber, *Panama Canal*, 28; Collin, *TR's Caribbean*, 230–31, 595.

77. Hay to Beaupré, July 13, 1903, *FRUS*, Dec. 7, 1903, 164.

78. Beaupré to Hay, July 11, 1903, ibid., 163–64.

79. TR to Hay, July 14, 1903, TR Papers (LC).

80. Collin, *TR's Caribbean*, 249–50; Beaupré to Hay, July 21, 1903, *FRUS*, Dec. 7, 1903, 165.

81. Beaupré to Hay, Aug. 5, 1903, TR Papers (LC).

82. Hay to Beaupré, July 31, 1903, *FRUS*, Dec. 7, 1903, 168; Beaupré to Rico, Aug. 5, 1903, encl. in Beaupré to Hay, Aug. 7, 1903, ibid., 176–77; HR, *Story of Panama*, 351.

83. Beaupré to Hay, Aug. 15, 1903, *FRUS*, Dec. 7, 1903, 182.

84. Ibid.

85. Beaupré to Hay, Aug. 12, 1903, ibid., 179 (7 p.m.); Beaupré to Hay, Aug. 15, 1903, ibid., 184.

86. Beaupré to Hay, Aug. 12, 1903 (three messages), ibid., 179 (7 p.m.), 180 (10 p.m.).
87. Beaupré to Hay, Aug. 15, 1903, ibid.
88. Ibid., 183; Collin, *TR's Caribbean*, 235.
89. McCullough, *Path Between the Seas*, 266–67, 333; LaFeber, *Panama Canal*, 21–22.
90. TR, *Autobiography*, 536, 538; TR to Hay, Aug. 19, 1903, TR Papers (LC).
91. Beaupré to Hay, Aug. 15, 1903, *FRUS*, 184.

CHAPTER 2

1. TR quoted in Morris, *Theodore Rex*, 255; TR to Spring Rice, Jan. 18, 1904, Bishop, *TR*, 1, 297.
2. TR, *Autobiography*, 544–46; Virginian quoted in a letter encl. in Senator John Tyler Morgan to Hay, Sept. 27, 1902, cited in William R. Thayer, *The Life and Letters of John Hay*, 2 vols. (Boston: Houghton Mifflin, 1915), 2: 304.
3. Morris, *Theodore Rex*, 4, 240. In late September 1901, Hay's closest friend, John George Nicolay, died in Washington from a lingering illness. As President Lincoln's two secretaries, they roomed across the hall from his office in the White House and later co-wrote a multi-volume work, *Abraham Lincoln: A History*. See John Taliaferro, *All the Great Prizes: The Life of John Hay, from Lincoln to Roosevelt* (New York: Simon and Schuster, 2013), 411.
4. Bishop, *TR*, 1:279.
5. HR, *Story of Panama*, 353–54; Cullom quoted in *New York Herald*, Aug. 15, 1903, cited in McCullough, *Path Between the Seas*, 339.
6. Hay to TR, Aug. 16, 1903, TR Papers (LC); TR to Hay, Aug. 17, 1903, ibid.; Morris, *Theodore Rex*, 263–64; HR, *Story of Panama*, 354.
7. Collin, *TR's Caribbean*, 239–40.
8. Ibid., 240–41; Cass to Mirabeau Lamar, minister to Central America, July 25, 1858, reference in Moore memo reprinted in DuVal, *Cadiz to Cathay*, 502–07 (quote on 503).
9. Moore memo in DuVal, *Cadiz to Cathay*, 503, 505; TR's special message to Congress, Jan. 4, 1904, *FRUS*, Dec. 7, 1903, 264, 273; Morris, *Theodore Rex*, 264–65 (emphasis in original); Harbaugh, *Life and Times of TR*, 202; Collin, *TR's Caribbean*, 241–42.
10. Moore memo in DuVal, *Cadiz to Cathay*, 503, 507.
11. TR to Hay, Aug. 19, 1903, TR Papers (LC); Editors' note, Morison, et al., eds., *Letters of TR*, 3: 567, n.2; McCullough, *Path Between the Seas*, 326–27; Collin, *TR's Caribbean*, 242–43; TR, *Autobiography*, 527.
12. Hay to TR, Aug. 22, 1903, cited in Morris, *Theodore Rex*, 265.
13. Beaupré to Hay, Aug. 24, 1903, *FRUS*, Dec. 7, 1903, 188; Hay to Beaupré, Aug. 24, 1903, ibid.; Hay to Beaupré, Aug. 29, 1903, ibid., 189; McCullough, *Path Between the Seas*, 341.

14. Hay to Beaupré, Aug. 29, 1903, *FRUS*, Dec. 7, 1903, 189; Beaupré to Hay, Aug. 31, 1903, ibid., 190; Beaupré to Hay, Sept. 5, 1903, ibid., 191–92.

15. TR to Hay, Sept. 15, 1903, Morison, et al., eds., *Letters of TR*, 3: 599.

16. Beaupré to Hay, Sept. 25, 1903, *FRUS*, Dec. 7, 1903, 202–04; Miner, *Fight for Panama Route*, 301–05.

17. Morris, *Theodore Rex*, 273; TR to Hanna, Oct. 5, 1903, Morison, et al., eds., *Letters of TR*, 3: 625; TR to Shaw, Oct. 7, 1903, TR Papers (LC).

18. Quoted in Majority Report of the Panama Canal Committee of the Colombian Senate, Oct. 14, 1903, encl. in Beaupré to Hay, Oct. 16, 1903, *FRUS*, Dec. 7, 1903, 212–13.

19. HR, *Story of Panama*, 352; Beaupré to Hay, Sept. 30, 1903, *FRUS*, Dec. 7, 1903, 204; Majority Report of Panama Canal Committee, Oct. 14, 1903, encl. in Beaupré to Hay, Oct. 16, 1903, ibid., 212–13.

20. McCullough, *Path Between the Seas*, 342–43. Working with Black were Lieutenant Mark Brooke and Austin C. Harper from Pennsylvania. HR, *Story of Panama*, 349.

21. HR, *Story of Panama*, 349, 357–58.

22. Ibid., 349–50.

23. Ibid., 357; McCullough, *Path Between the Seas*, 343.

24. HR, *Story of Panama*, 382; McCullough, *Path Between the Seas*, 104, 106, 345–46.

25. HR, *Story of Panama*, 359; Harding, *Untold Story of Panama*, 25; Parker, *Panama Fever*, 228–29.

26. HR, *Story of Panama*, 690; McCullough, *Path Between the Seas*, 345–46; Parker, *Panama Fever*, 229; Collin, *TR's Caribbean*, 321; Harding, *Untold Story of Panama*, 26.

27. HR, *Story of Panama*, 359, 362, 693; Harding, *Untold Story of Panama*, 26; McCullough, *Path Between the Seas*, 346; Parker, *Panama Fever*, 229.

28. McCullough, *Path Between the Seas*, 345; HR, *Story of Panama*, 359–60, 691.

29. McCullough, *Path Between the Seas*, 345; HR, *Story of Panama*, 360; Parker, *Panama Fever*, 229.

30. HR, *Story of Panama*, 360.

31. Ibid.

32. Congressional testimony by Henry Hall of *New York World*'s staff before Rainey committee, Feb. 12, 1912, ibid., 360–61; McCullough, *Path Between the Seas*, 345–46.

33. HR, *Story of Panama*, 361–62; Harding, *Untold Story of Panama*, 26–27; Collin, *TR's Caribbean*, 248–49.

34. Herrán to Rico, Sept. 5, 1903; Rico to Herrán, Sept. 10, 1903; Herrán to Rico, Sept. 11, 1903; Herrán to Rico, Sept. 15, 1903, all cited in HR, *Story of Panama*, 361–62.

35. HR, *Story of Panama*, 362, 694; McCullough, *Path Between the Seas*, 346.

36. HR, *Story of Panama*, 362, 694, 695, 702.

37. Hall testimony, Feb. 13, 1912, HR, *Story of Panama*, 7, 42, 365–66; Bunau-Varilla, *Panama*, 288–89; Collin, *TR's Caribbean*, 253. No one has found a copy of

a Cromwell telegram to Bunau-Varilla, but McCullough is dubious about calling the timely arrival of Bunau-Varilla a coincidence. Matthew Parker takes the same position, supporting his claim by calculating the time needed to make the trip if Cromwell had cabled him immediately after Herrán issued his warning. Parker's calculations fit with Bunau-Varilla's arrival time in New York. See McCullough, *Path Between the Seas*, 349; Parker, *Panama Fever*, 230.

38. McCullough, *Path Between the Seas*, 347; Bunau-Varilla, *Panama*, 289.

39. Bunau-Varilla, *Panama*, 289; McCullough, *Path Between the Seas*, 347; Harding, *Untold Story of Panama*, 29.

40. HR, *Story of Panama*, 697. Bunau-Varilla, *Panama*, 289–90.

41. Ibid., 290–91.

42. Ibid., 291.

43. Ibid., 290–91.

44. Ibid., 292–93; HR, *Story of Panama*, 366; Bishop, *Panama Gateway*, 38, McCullough, *Path Between the Seas*, 136, 349–50; Collin, *TR's Caribbean*, 134; Philippe Bunau-Varilla, *The Great Adventure of Panama* (New York: Doubleday, Page and Co., 1920); LaFeber, *Panama Canal*, 24–25.

45. HR, *Story of Panama*, 697.

46. Bunau-Varilla, *Panama*, 288–89; Harding, *Untold Story of Panama*, 28.

47. Bunau-Varilla, *Panama*, 294–95.

48. Ibid., 295.

49. Ibid.

50. Ibid., 295–96. It is unclear whether Bunau-Varilla revealed his partial ownership of *Le Matin*.

51. Ibid.

52. Ibid., 296–97.

53. Ibid., 297.

54. Bunau-Varilla to Moore, Oct. 3, 1903, ibid., 305–09.

55. Ibid., 305–06.

56. Ibid., 310.

57. Duque to Hay, Sept. 21, 1903, TR Papers (LC).

58. Adee to TR, Sept. 30, 1903, ibid.

59. Cromwell quoted in a telegram from the *New York Herald*'s correspondent in Washington to the home office, Oct. 7, 1903, cited in HR, *Story of Panama*, 366; *New York Daily Tribune*, Oct. 8, 1903, 6.

60. Bunau-Varilla, *Panama*, 310.

61. Ibid., 177; Henry Hall of the *New York World*'s staff provided evidence of this meeting between Cromwell and Roosevelt to the Rainey Committee hearings of 1912. HR, *Story of Panama*, 366.

62. This account of Bunau-Varilla's meeting with the president rests on several sources: Bunau-Varilla, *Panama*, 310–12; Thomas Schoonover, "Research Note: Max Farrand's Memorandum on the U.S. Role in the Panamanian Revolution of 1903," *Diplomatic History*, 12 (Fall 1988): 501–06; Morris, *Theodore Rex*, 274–75, 666–67 n.275; McCullough, *Path Between the Seas*, 350–51; DuVal, *Cadiz to Cathay*, 298–300; Miner, *Fight for Panama Route*, 356; Collin, *TR's Caribbean*, 256;

Gustave Anguizola, *Philippe Bunau-Varilla: The Man Behind the Panama Canal* (Chicago: Nelson Hall, 1980), 238.

63. Schoonover, "Research Note," 505; Morris, *Theodore Rex*, 274–75.

64. Bunau-Varilla, *Panama*, 312.

65. Ibid., 312–14.

66. Schoonover, "Research Note," 505.

67. TR to Shaw, Oct. 10, 1903, TR Papers (LC); McCullough, *Path Between the Seas*, 351.

68. Bunau-Varilla, *Panama*, 313–16, 361.

69. Ibid., 316.

70. Ibid., 316–17.

71. Ibid., 317–18.

72. Ibid., 318; Morris, *Theodore Rex*, 277; McCullough, *Path Between the Seas*, 354–55.

73. Bunau-Varilla, *Panama*, 316–19.

74. Root to Jessup, July 16, 1931, in Philip C. Jessup, *Elihu Root*, 2 vols. (New York: Dodd, Mead and Co., 1938; reprinted by Archon Books, 1964), vol. 1: 403–04.

75. Bunau-Varilla got the appointment at the insistence of Arango, one of the provisional government leaders established after the revolution. HR, *Story of Panama*, 368–69. The *New York World* later accused Bunau-Varilla of pledging $100,000 of his own funds to facilitate his interest in becoming Panama's first minister. Ibid., 713–14. Despite Bunau-Varilla's claim that he advanced the full amount promised, evidence suggests that he gave no more than $25,000. Ibid., 714; Morris, *Theodore Rex*, 291. As shown earlier in this chapter, Bunau-Varilla asserted that the $100,000 was to pay troops after the revolution.

76. Harding, *Untold Story of Panama*, 85–86.

77. HR, *Story of Panama*, 699–700.

78. Ibid., 688, 699–700. Earlier that same day of October 16, two secret agents from the army reported to the president that their travels through Panama revealed information essential to launching a U.S. military campaign on the Isthmus (discussed later in this chapter). Ibid., 710.

79. Ibid., 699–700; Harding, *Untold Story of Panama*, 85.

80. HR, *Story of Panama*, 71–72; Roosevelt quoted by Raoul, in Harding, *Untold Story of Panama*, 86. Harding was in Panama gathering materials for the *New York World*'s defense against the libel suit filed by former President Roosevelt.

81. Harding, *Untold Story of Panama*, 66–67, 86–87; quote from Dr. Phillip Embury, cited in a *New York World* reporter's memorandum of conversation, ibid., 87.

82. HR, *Story of Panama*, 693.

83. Collin, *TR's Caribbean*, 324; HR, *Story of Panama*, 71–72, 105, 693. McCullough asserts that "no solid evidence, no evidence of any kind" supports the claim that Amador talked with Hay and the president. *Path Between the Seas*, 384. For a disparaging view of Amador, see Howarth, *Panama*, 226–27, 234.

84. Pringle, *TR*, 224.

85. Bunau-Varilla, *Panama*, 320–23; McCullough, *Path Between the Seas*, 356–57; Collin, *TR's Caribbean*, 150–51; Harding, *Untold Story of Panama*, 31. The narrowly conscripted zone infuriated Panamanians holding property outside, but Amador assured them the United States would block Colombian retaliation. Ibid., 31–32.

86. Bunau-Varilla, *Panama*, 323.

87. Telegram in ibid., 323–24.

88. HR, *Story of Panama*, 700, 713–14; Harding, *Untold Story of Panama*, 86.

89. Morris, *Rise of TR*, 658, 661, 664; McCullough, *Path Between the Seas*, 357–62; HR, *Story of Panama*, 372, 716.

90. Ibid., 372, 377–79.

91. Ibid., 378–79.

92. Ibid., 583–84, 703, 707; Theodore Roosevelt, *Addresses and Presidential Messages of TR, 1902–1904* (New York: G. P. Putnam's Sons, 1904), 438–39.

93. HR, *Story of Panama*, 583–84, 704, 710.

94. "Bought Arms in America," Nov. 5, 1903, *NYT*, 2.

95. HR, *Story of Panama*, 710.

96. Beaupré to Hay, Nov. 2, 1903, *FRUS*, Dec. 7, 1903, 221–22.

97. Collin, *TR's Caribbean*, 315, 331, 333; Miner, *Fight for Panama Route*, 360; McCullough, *Path Between the Seas*, 350, 352, 360; Schoonover, "Research Note," 503–04.

98. *NYT*, Nov. 1, 1903, 4; "Revolution on Isthmus: Colombian Government Alarmed by Secession News from Panama," *Washington Post*, Oct. 30, 1903, 1; Schoonover, "Research Note," 504; Bunau-Varilla, *Panama*, 333; McCullough, *Path Between the Seas*, 360.

99. *NYT*, Nov. 5, 1903, 1; Bunau-Varilla, *Panama*, 330–31; McCullough, *Path Between the Seas*, 359–60.

100. Bishop, TR, 1:296; Bunau-Varilla, *Panama*, 332–33.

101. Beaupré to Hay, Nov. 2, 1903, *FRUS*, Dec. 7, 1903, 222.

102. Quote from memo cited in Schoonover, "Research Note," 504.

103. Harding, *Untold Story of Panama*, 33.

104. Hubbard to secretary of navy, Nov. 8, 1903, *FRUS*, Dec. 7, 1903, 269; Hubbard's Nov. 8 missive is also included in TR's special message to Congress, Jan. 4, 1904, *FRUS*, Dec. 7, 1903, Charles Darling, acting secretary of navy, to U.S. consul in Colón, Nov. 2, 1903, ibid., 247; LaFeber, *Panama Canal*, 26.

105. Darling to cruiser commanders, Nov. 2, 3, 1903, *FRUS*, Dec. 1903, 247; Morris, *Theodore Rex*, 283, 288; McCullough, *Path Between the Seas*, 358, 364–66; Collin, *TR's Caribbean*, 262; Harding, *Untold Story of Panama*, 33–34; Bishop, *Panama Gateway*, 126. In addition to the *Nashville* and the *Dixie*, the U.S. Navy sent the *Atlanta* (400 forces), the *Boston* (400), the *Concord* (250), the *Marblehead* (300), and the *Wyoming* (400). Darling mentioned the vessels' names in his instructions of November 2 and 3 cited above. Troop estimates in *NYT*, Nov. 5, 1903, 1.

106. Ibid., Nov. 4, 1903, 1; Hubbard to secretary of navy, Nov. 8, 1903, *FRUS*, Dec. 1903, 269; Morris, *Theodore Rex*, 283; McCullough, *Path Between the Seas*, 364–66. McCullough estimates that about a dozen wives accompanied their husbands to Panama. Ibid., 365–66.

107. "*Nashville* Orders Held by Bogotá: Colombian Government's Trick with Navy Dispatches," *NYT*, Nov. 5, 1903, 1.

108. McCullough, *Path Between the Seas*, 365–67; DuVal, *Cadiz to Cathay*, 324; Hubbard to secretary of navy, Nov. 3, 1903, *FRUS*, Dec. 7, 1903, 249; Hubbard to secretary of navy, Nov. 8, 1903, ibid., 269–70; Collin, *TR's Caribbean*, 235; Miner, *Fight for Panama Route*, 329, 333; Harding, *Untold Story of Panama*, 33–34. After Shaler's death in 1910, the Panama assembly unanimously passed a resolution giving him the title of *Hero of the Republic.* Ibid., 65. Marroquin had appointed Obaldia to the office in an ill-advised effort to mollify the separatists. Obaldia was a friend of Amador. Obaldia later agreed to cooperate in the election of General Rafael Reyes as Marroquin's successor and assure that Congress would pass the canal treaty at the next session. HR, *Story of Panama*, 354.

109. McCullough, *Path Between the Seas*, 366.

110. Ehrman to Hay, Nov. 3, 1903, *FRUS*, Dec. 7, 1903, 231.

111. HR, *Story of Panama*, 394–95; Miner, *Fight for Panama Route*, 360.

112. HR, *Story of Panama*, 395.

113. Ibid., 396–97 (Hall testimony on 397); Loomis to Ehrman, Nov. 4, 1903, Richardson, ed., *Messages and Papers of Presidents*, 15: 6788–89; Ehrman to Hay, Nov. 4, 1903, *FRUS*, Dec. 7, 1903, 232; Ehrman to Loomis, Nov. 9, 1903, ibid., 254–55; Harding, *Untold Story of Panama*, 34; McCullough, *Path Between the Seas*, 371; Collin, *TR's Caribbean*, 266; Miner, *Fight for Panama Route*, 364.

114. *NYT*, Nov. 4, 1903, 1.

115. Ehrman to Hay, Nov. 5, 1903, *FRUS*, Dec. 7, 1903, 233; Ehrman to Hay, Nov. 10, 1903, ibid., 235.

116. Acting Secretary of Navy Charles Darling to commander of *Nashville*, Nov. 3, 1903, ibid., 248; Hubbard to secretary of navy, Nov. 8, 1903, ibid., 270; Loomis to Malmros in Colón, sent at 8:45 PM, Nov. 3, 1903, ibid., 236; Loomis to Ehrman (sent at 11:18 PM), Nov. 3, 1903, ibid., 231.

117. Hubbard to secretary of navy (William H. Moody), Nov. 4, 1903, U. S. Senate, *Diplomatic History of the Panama Canal* (Sen. Doc. 474, 63rd Congress, 2nd Sess. (Washington: GPO, 1914), 579.

118. McCullough, *Path Between the Seas*, 372–73.

119. Hubbard to secretary of navy, Nov. 5, 1903, Richardson, ed., *Messages and Papers of Presidents*, 15: 6912–13.

120. Ibid., 6913; Miner, *Fight for Panama Route*, 366–67, 369.

121. Hubbard to secretary of the navy, Nov. 5, 1903, Richardson, ed., *Messages and Papers of Presidents*, 15: 6912.

122. Hubbard to secretary of navy, Nov. 5, 1903, *FRUS*, Dec. 7, 1903, 250–51; Hubbard to secretary of navy, Nov. 8, 1903, Richardson, ed., *Messages and Papers of Presidents*, 15: 6915–16.

123. U.S. consul Oscar Malmros to Hay, Nov. 5, 1903, *FRUS*, Dec. 7, 1903, 237–38; *NYT*, Nov. 1, 1903, 1.

124. Hubbard to secretary of navy, Nov. 8, 1903, *FRUS*, Dec. 7, 1903, 270.

125. Hubbard to secretary of navy, Nov. 8, 1903, Richardson, ed., *Messages and Papers of Presidents*, 15: 6916.

126. Ibid., 6917.

127. Hubbard to secretary of navy, Nov. 8, 1903, *FRUS*, Dec. 7, 1903, 270–71; Ehrman to Hay, Nov. 5, 1903, ibid., 232–33.

128. McCullough, *Path Between the Seas*, 375–76.

129. Ibid., 376.

130. *NY Herald*, Nov. 4, 1903, 1, cited in Harding, *Untold Story of Panama*, 35; *NY Sun*, Nov. 4, 1903, 1; *Washington Post*, Nov. 4, 1903, 1. "MARINES LANDED AT COLON," proclaimed the *New York Tribune* on November 5.

131. *NYT*, Nov. 4, 1903, 1.

132. "The Panama Danger," *NYT*, Nov. 5, 1903, 8; *Times* (of London), Nov. 5, 1903, quoted ibid., 1.

133. Amador speech, Nov. 4, 1903, HR, *Story of Panama*, 446–47.

134. Miner, *Fight for Panama Route*, 360; DuVal, *Cadiz to Cathay* 320–21; Malmros to Hay, Nov. 5, 1903, *FRUS*, Dec. 7, 1903, 237–38; Ehrman to Loomis, Nov. 9, 1903, ibid., 255; Malmros to Hay, Nov. 4, 1903, Richardson, ed., *Messages and Papers of Presidents*, 15: 6794.

135. HR, *Story of Panama*, 447, 453; McCullough, *Path Between the Seas*, 376; Collin, *TR's Caribbean*, 266; DuVal, *Cadiz to Cathay*, 333; Harding, *Untold Story of Panama*, 35.

136. HR, *Story of Panama*, 372, 446–47; Harding, *Untold Story of Panama*, 35; Miner, *Fight for Panama Route*, 362–63; Collin, *TR's Caribbean*, 260–61. McCullough argues that there is "no evidence of any kind" that American money helped finance the revolution. McCullough, *Path Between the Seas*, 384.

137. Miner, *Fight for Panama Route*, 364; DuVal, *Cadiz to Cathay*, 226, 329; Ehrman to Hay, Nov. 4, 1903, Richardson, ed., *Messages and Papers of Presidents*, 15: 6789 (two telegrams); Committee of the provisional government to Hay, Nov. 4, 1903, *FRUS*, Dec. 7, 1903, 238; Arango, Boyd, and Arias to Hay, Nov. 4, 1903, ibid., 689; Brid to Hay, Nov. 4, 1903, ibid., 239. *FRUS* refers to Demetro Brida, but Demetrio Brid is probably the correct rendition, as used in HR, *Story of Panama*, 397.

138. TR to Kermit Roosevelt, Nov. 4, 1903, Morison, et al., eds., *Letters of TR*, 3: 644; McCullough, *Path Between the Seas*, 380.

139. Arango, Boyd, and Arias to Hay, Nov. 6, 1903, *FRUS*, Dec. 7, 1903, 689; Ehrman to Loomis, Nov. 9, 1903, ibid., 255; Malmros to Hay, Nov. 6, 1903, ibid., 238; HR, *Story of Panama*, 52, 378, 458; Hay to Beaupré, Nov. 6, 1903, Richardson, ed., *Messages and Papers of Presidents*, 15: 6798; Beaupré to Hay, Nov. 7, 1903, ibid., 6799–6800; Bishop, *Panama Gateway*, 133–34; DuVal, *Cadiz to Cathay*, 335, 358; McCullough, *Path Between the Seas*, 376–77.

140. Provisional government to Hay, Nov. 5, 6, 1903, *FRUS*, Dec. 7, 1903, 239; Ehrman to Hay, Nov. 6, 1903, ibid., 233–34; Arango, Boyd, and Arias to Hay, Nov. 5, 6, 1903, Richardson, ed., *Messages and Papers of Presidents*, 15: 6796–97.

CHAPTER 3

1. Provisional government to Hay, Nov. 5, 6, 1903, *FRUS*, Dec. 7, 1903, 239; Ehrman to Hay, Nov. 6, 1903, ibid., 233–34; Arango, Boyd, and Arias to Hay, Nov. 5, 6, 1903, Richardson, ed., *Messages and Papers of Presidents*, 15: 6796–97; McCullough, *Path Between the Seas*, 387.

2. Hay to Beaupré, Nov. 6, 1903, *FRUS*, Dec. 7, 1903, 225–26, 240–41; To Whom It May Concern, Nov. 6, 1903, Morison, et al., eds., *Letters of TR*, 3: 649.

3. TR to Hay, Nov. 6, 1903, Morison, et al., eds., *Letters of TR*, 3: 648; Straus memo to TR, Nov. 6, 1903, encl. ibid., 648–49 n.1.

4. TR, *Autobiography*, 538; Jessup, *Root*, 1: 403–05, 453; Knox and Root quotes in Richard W. Leopold, *Elihu Root and the Conservative Tradition* (Boston: Little Brown, 1954), 178; Brands, *T. R. The Last Romantic*, 488; Schoonover, "Research Note," 505–06; LaFeber, *Panama Canal*, 45; Collin, *TR's Caribbean*, 293. Root was one of a small number of Americans who could make a comment like this without drawing the president's anger. Roosevelt publicly hailed him as "the greatest man that has arisen on either side of the Atlantic in my lifetime." In a convention speech in Chicago in June 1904, Roosevelt called him "the brutal friend to whom I pay the most attention." Jessup, *Root*, 1: 422, 423.

5. TR to Shaw, Nov. 6, 1903, Morison, et al., eds., *Letters of TR*, 3: 649. Roosevelt used a similar phrase in an October 10 note to Shaw. See TR to Shaw, Oct. 10, 1903, ibid., 628.

6. Beaupré to Hay, Nov. 6, 1903, *FRUS*, Dec. 7, 1903, 225, 241; Beaupré to Hay, Nov. 7, 1903, ibid., 226, 241–42.

7. Hay to Herrán, Nov. 6, 1903, encl. in Hay to Beaupré, Nov 6, 1903, ibid., 243; Herrán to Hay, Nov. 7, 1903, ibid., 243–44.

8. Beaupré to Hay, Nov. 9, 1903, *FRUS*, Dec. 7, 1903, 227, 242; Collin, *TR's Caribbean*, 208, 234, 272.

9. Beaupré to Hay, Nov. 11, 1903, *FRUS*, Dec. 7, 1903, 227–28.

10. Hay to Beaupré, Nov. 11, 1903, ibid., 228, 243.

11. TR to Spring Rice, Nov. 9, 1903, Morison, et al., eds., *Letters of TR*, 3: 651.

12. Tower to Hay, Nov. 10, 1903, *FRUS*, Dec. 7, 1903, 244; Porter to Hay, Nov. 11, 1903, ibid., 244–45. Tower was ambassador to Germany from December 1902 to June 1908.

13. Bunau-Varilla, *Panama*, 353, 354, 358.

14. Provisional government to Hay, Nov. 5, 6, 1903, *FRUS*, Dec. 7, 1903, 239; Ehrman to Hay, Nov. 6, 1903, ibid., 233–34; Arango, Boyd, and Arias to Hay, Nov. 5, 6, 1903, Richardson, ed., *Messages and Papers of Presidents*, 15: 6796–97; Bunau-Varilla, *Panama*, 355, 358; McCullough, *Path Between the Seas*, 387–88.

15. Three days before this meeting, Hay learned of Bunau-Varilla's appointment from the new government in Panama City. See Arango, Arias, and Boyd to Hay, Nov. 6, 1903, *FRUS*, Dec. 7, 1903, 239; Bunau-Varilla, *Panama*, 358; McCullough, *Path Between the Seas*, 388.

16. Bunau-Varilla, *Panama*, 355, 358.

17. Ibid., 358.

18. Ibid., 359; Ehrman to Hay, Nov. 11, 1903, *FRUS*, Dec. 7, 1903, 235.

19. Bunau-Varilla, *Panama*, 360–61; Bunau-Varilla to Hay, Nov. 11, 1903, *FRUS*, Dec. 7, 1903, 245; Loomis to Bunau-Varilla, Nov. 12, 1903, ibid.

20. Exchange of remarks between Bunau-Varilla and TR, Nov. 13, 1903, *FRUS*, Dec. 7, 1903, 246; Bunau-Varilla, *Panama*, 366; Morris, *Theodore Rex*, 297.

21. McCullough, *Path Between the Seas*, 391; Harding, *Untold Story of Panama*, 15; LaFeber, *Panama Canal*, 29.

22. Bunau-Varilla, *Panama*, 368.

23. Ibid., 221, 367–68; John Major, "Who Wrote the Hay-Bunau-Varilla Convention?" *Diplomatic History*, 8 (April 1984): 115–23; Collin, *TR's Caribbean*, 280–81.

24. Major, "Hay-Bunau-Varilla Convention," 120–21.

25. Bunau-Varilla, *Panama*, 371–72.

26. HR, *Story of Panama*, 282; Ameringer, "Panama Canal Lobby," 362.

27. HR, *Story of Panama*, 283.

28. Ibid., 282.

29. Ibid., 30, 284; Bunau-Varilla, *Panama*, 371–72.

30. Ameringer, "Panama Canal Lobby," 347, 351. The Sullivan-Cromwell law firm charged the New Panama Canal Company $833,449 in fees covering 1896–1904. Ibid., 347 n.6. For "Cromwell's Brief," see Appendix A, "General Statement of the Services Rendered by Messrs. Sullivan and Cromwell as General Counsel in America of La Compagnie Nouvelle Du Canal De Panama," HR, *Story of Panama*, 197–203 (Contents), 205–98 (text).

31. Bunau-Varilla, *Panama*, 3, 372; Collin, *TR's Caribbean*, 283.

32. Bunau-Varilla to Hay, Nov. 17, 1903, Bunau-Varilla, *Panama*, 372–73.

33. Hay to Bunau-Varilla, Nov. 17, 1903, ibid., 373.

34. Bunau-Varilla quoted ibid., 374.

35. Ibid., 368–70; Bunau-Varilla to Hay, Nov. 18, 1903, ibid.; 374; Major, "Hay-Bunau-Varilla Convention," 118, 121–22; Collin, *TR's Caribbean*, 281; quote from Article 3 of the final treaty. See the full text of the Hay-Bunau-Varilla Treaty, Nov. 18, 1903, online at the Avalon Project, https://avalon.law.yale.edu/20th_century/pan001.asp#art1.

36. LaFeber, *Panama Canal*, 29–30.

37. Major, "Hay-Bunau-Varilla Convention," 122–23.

38. Bunau-Varilla, *Panama*, 375–76.

39. Ibid., 376; Major, "Hay-Bunau-Varilla Convention," 122–23.

40. Bunau-Varilla, *Panama*, 376–77.

41. Ibid., 429.

42. Harding, *Untold Story of Panama*, 41.

43. Collin, *TR's Caribbean*, 281, 283; Isthmian Canal Convention, Nov. 18, 1903, Richardson, ed., *Messages and Papers of Presidents*, 15: 6890–97; DuVal, *Cadiz to Cathay*, 498; LaFeber, *Panama Canal*, 29–30.

44. Bunau-Varilla, *Panama*, 377–78; McCullough, *Path Between the Seas*, 395.

45. Bunau-Varilla, *Panama*, 358, 360.

46. Ibid., 378; Morris, *Theodore Rex*, 297–98; McCullough, *Path Between the Seas*, 395; Collin, *TR's Caribbean*, 283; Miner, *Fight for Panama Route*, 378; LaFeber, *Panama Canal*, 30.

47. Bunau-Varilla, *Panama*, 383–85.

48. Ibid., 393, 398. The White House encouraged the meeting and offered use of the American ship *Mayflower*. Collin, *TR's Caribbean*, 284, 284–85 n.27.

49. Bunau-Varilla, *Panama*, 398–99.

50. Ibid., 400; Collin, *TR's Caribbean*, 285.

51. Ibid., 289. Two years earlier, in December 1901, Roosevelt and Reyes briefly discussed a canal through Panama. Ibid., 229–30.

52. Reyes to Hay, Dec. 8, 1903, Richardson, ed., *Messages and Papers of Presidents*, 15: 6926–27; Hay to Reyes, Dec. 11, 1903, ibid., 6927–28. See their correspondence in *FRUS*, Dec. 7, 1903, 279–81, 283–313.

53. Collin, *TR's Caribbean*, 229–30, 285, 289; Reyes quoted ibid., 289.

54. TR to Spooner, Jan. 20, 1904, Morison, et al., eds., *Letters of TR*, 3: 700.

55. *Public Opinion*, XXV, Nov. 19, 1903, 643, quoted in LaFeber, *Panama Canal*, 31; TR to Gresham, Nov. 30, 1903, Morison, et al., eds., *Letters of TR*, 3: 662–63.

56. TR to Gresham, Nov. 30, 1903, Morison, et al., eds., *Letters of TR*, 3: 662–63.

57. TR to Osborn, Dec. 9, 1903, in Bishop, *TR*, 1: 293.

58. President Roosevelt's Third Annual Message to Congress, Dec. 7, 1903, *FRUS*, Dec. 7, 1903, 37–38; Collin, *TR's Caribbean*, 134, 139–40; McCullough, *Path Between the Seas*, 32–33, 136; Morris, *Theodore Rex*, 112, 264–65.

59. TR's Third Annual Message, *FRUS*, Dec. 7, 1903, 38–39. The "eminent Colombian" was certainly General Reyes.

60. Ibid., 40, 42.

61. Root to Porter, Dec. 15, 1903, in Jessup, *Root*, 1: 402.

62. Thompson to TR, Dec. 18, 1903, TR Papers (LC).

63. TR to Thompson, Dec. 22, 1903, Morison, et al., eds., *Letters of TR*, 3: 675.

64. Francis Loomis, acting secretary of state, to William I. Buchanan, Dec. 12, 1903, *FRUS*, Dec. 7, 1903, 689; Buchanan to Hay, Dec. 25, 1903, ibid., 314, 690; "Envoy to Panama Named," *NYT*, Dec. 13, 1903, 2. The two officials were Doctor Gonzales Guill, sub-secretary for foreign affairs, and Doctor Juan Mendez, private secretary to the junta.

65. Buchanan to Hay, Dec. 25, 1903, *FRUS*, Dec. 7, 1903, 314–16, 690–91; Buchanan's remarks, encl. 2: ibid., 315, 691; Encl. 3: Junta's response to Buchanan's arrival, ibid., 315–16; "Mr. Buchanan in Panama: New United States Minister Presents His Credentials," *NYT*, Dec. 26, 1903, 3.

66. J. R. Taylor, "Credit Given to Mr. Hay: Panamanians Think Panama Owes Her Independence to Him," *NYT*, Dec. 28, 1903, 3.

67. Message from the President (to Congress) of the United States Transmitting a Statement of Action in Executing the Act Entitled "An Act to Provide for the Construction of a Canal Connecting the Waters of the Atlantic and Pacific Oceans" (approved June 28, 1902), Jan. 4, 1904, *FRUS*, Dec. 7, 1903, 261–63; TR,

Autobiography, 540. See full address in Richardson, ed., *Messages and Papers of Presidents*, 15: 6901–26.

68. Message from President to Congress, Jan. 4, 1904, *FRUS*, Dec. 7, 1903, 264–65.

69. Ibid., 275–76. Other countries extending recognition were Argentina, Brazil, Chile, Nicaragua, Costa Rica, Peru, Cuba, China, Austria-Hungary, Denmark, Sweden, Norway, Belgium, Italy, Japan, and Switzerland. DuVal, *Cadiz to Cathay*, 354; Collin, *TR's Caribbean*, 286–87.

70. Message from President to Congress, Jan. 4, 1904, *FRUS*, Dec. 7, 1903, 271.

71. Ibid., 272.

72. Ibid., 277.

73. Ibid., 274, 278.

74. *Congressional Record, Senate*, 37 Congress, Nov. 23–24, 1903, 426–27. Thanks to a former student of mine, Patrick Rickert, for calling my attention to Morgan's charges in the Senate.

75. Story in Bishop, *TR*, 1: 305.

76. Editors' note, Morison, et al., eds., *Letters of TR*, 3: 689 n.2. Professor John Bassett Moore helped the president write his special message. Ibid.

77. Loomis to TR, Jan. 5, 1904, quoted in DuVal, *Cadiz to Cathay*, 299; Hay to Reyes, Jan. 5, 1904, cited in Bishop, *Panama Gateway*, 136.

78. For these three meetings, see Chap. Two of this book.

79. TR to Bigelow, Jan. 6, 1904, Morison, et al., eds., *Letters of TR*, 3: 689.

80. TR to Lodge, Jan. 6, 1904, Lodge, ed., *Correspondence of TR and Lodge*, 2: 73–74.

81. TR to Moore, Jan. 6, 1904, Morison, et al., eds., *Letters of TR*, 3: 690.

82. Moore to TR, Jan. 7, 1904, TR Papers (LC).

83. Bunau-Varilla, *Panama*, 417.

84. Ibid.

85. TR to Spring Rice, Jan. 18, 1904, Morison, et al., eds., *Letters of TR*, 3: 699.

86. LaFeber, *Panama Canal*, 39–41. For the text of the Hay-Bunau-Varilla Treaty, see *FRUS*, Dec. 6, 1904, 543–51.

87. TR to William Hale, Episcopal clergyman and managing editor of the *Philadelphia Public Ledger*, Feb. 26, 1904, Morison, et al., eds., *Letters of TR*, 4: 740.

88. Alban G. Snyder, U.S. minister to Colombia, to Hay, Jan. 2, 1904, *FRUS*, Dec. 6, 1904, 204; Snyder to Hay, Feb. 28, 1904, ibid., 205; Snyder to Hay, March 26, 1906, ibid., 206; Hay to Snyder, April 28, 1904, ibid., 224; Snyder to Hay, July 4, 1904, ibid., 225.

89. Hay to Rhodes, Dec. 8, 1903, in Bishop, *TR*, 1: 298; Hay to Fisher, Jan. 30, 1904, ibid., 300; Hay's address, July 6, 1904, ibid., 300–01.

90. Bunau-Varilla, *Panama*, 336, 410.

91. TR, *Autobiography*, 539–40.

92. "I'm Off for the Ditch," *NYT*, Nov. 9, 1906, 1; "Roosevelt As Stoker in Hold of Warship," *NYT*, Nov. 14, 1906, 1; Editors' note, Morison, et al., eds., *Letters of TR*, 5: 495 n.1; TR to Kermit Roosevelt, Nov. 11 (?), 1906, ibid., 495.

93. TR to Kermit Roosevelt, Nov. 14, 1906, ibid., 495.

94. McCullough, *Path Between the Seas*, 496; TR, *Autobiography*, 543; Bishop, *Panama Gateway*, 234–35, 238, 251; "President at Panama," *NYT*, Nov. 15, 1906, 1; "The President Climbs a Canal Steam Shovel," *NYT*, Nov. 17, 1906, 1; "Rides Along Canal—President Boards Work Train to Inspect a Cut," *Washington Post*, Nov. 17, 1906, 1.

95. "Roosevelt Delivers Warning to Panama—Tells the Country to Beware of Revolutions," *NYT*, Nov. 16, 1906, 1–2; "Roosevelt As Stoker," 1. For a superb account of Gorgas's struggles against malaria and yellow fever, see McCullough, *Path Between the Seas*, chap. 15.

96. H. G. Squiers, U.S. minister to Panama, to Elihu Root, secretary of state, Nov. 20, 1906, *FRUS*, Dec. 3, 1906, part 2, 1194, 1196. Encl. 1: Amador's speech, Nov. 17, 1906, 1195–96; Encl. 2: TR's speech, Nov. 17, 1906, ibid., 1196–97; "Canal Visit Is Ended," *Washington Post*, Nov. 18, 1906, 1; "President on the Sea," *Washington Post*, Nov. 19, 1906, 1; TR to Kermit Roosevelt, Nov. 20, 1906, Morison, et al., eds., *Letters of TR*, 5: 496–98.

97. McCullough, *Path Between the Seas*, 508–10, 533–34; Bishop, *Panama Gateway*, 176, 287; TR, *Autobiography*, 543.

98. Bunau-Varilla, *Panama*, 428.

99. TR to aide, conversation of that day summarized in Archibald to Clara, Jan. 30, 1909, Archibald W. Butt, *The Letters of Archie Butt: Personal Aide to President Roosevelt*, ed. by Lawrence F. Abbott (Garden City: Doubleday, Page and Co., 1924), 314. "Dear Clara" was Mrs. Lewis F. Butt, sister-in-law of Archibald Butt.

CHAPTER 4

1. TR to Anna Roosevelt Cowles, March 30, 1896, Morison, et al., eds., *Letters of TR*, 1: 522; TR to William S. Cowles (Anna's husband), April 5, 1896, ibid., 524.

2. TR to McCalla, April 19, 1897, ibid., 599; TR to McCalla, Aug. 3, 1897, ibid., 636; Address of Honorable Theodore Roosevelt before the Naval War College, June 2, 1897, 16, 18, Washington, DC, Navy Branch: GPO, 1897 (TRC).

3. TR's address before Naval War College, June 2, 1897, 18–20 (TRC).

4. TR to Spring Rice, Aug. 13, 1897, Morison, et al., eds., *Letters of TR*, 1: 644–45.

5. Ibid., 645–46.

6. Dexter Perkins, *A History of the Monroe Doctrine* (Boston: Little, Brown and Company, 1963. Revision of *Hands Off: A History of the Monroe Doctrine*, 1941), 151, 194–95.

7. TR to Lodge, Aug. 3, 1897, Morison, et al., eds., *Letters of TR*, 1: 638; TR to Hay, Nov. 4, 1897, ibid., 707; TR to Kimball, Dec. 17, 1897, ibid., 743.

8. TR to Chandler, Dec. 23, 1897, ibid., 746.

9. TR to Francis Moore, Feb. 5, 1898, ibid., 768–69; TR to Francis Moore, Feb. 9, 1898, ibid., 772. Moore was an underwriter for fire insurance in New York.

10. TR to Charles Arthur Moore, Feb. 14, 1898, ibid., 772. Moore was a New York businessman.

11. Treaty of Peace Between the United States and Spain, Dec. 10, 1898, http://avalon.law.yale.edu/19th_century/sp1898.asp.

12. TR to Lodge, Aug. 28, 1899, Morison, et al., eds., *Letters of TR*, 2: 1063; TR to Sternburg, Nov. 27, 1899, ibid., 1097–98; Morris, *Rise of TR*, 624.

13. TR to Kimball, Jan. 9, 1900, Morison, et al., eds., *Letters of TR*, 2: 1130–31; TR to Cowles, March 2, 1900, ibid., 1208; TR to Root, April 30, 1900, ibid., 1275; Morris, *Rise of TR*, 615; Perkins, *History of Monroe Doctrine*, 210–11.

14. TR to Lodge, June 19, 1901, Morison, et al., eds., *Letters of TR*, 3: 97–98; TR to Sternburg, July 12, 1901, ibid., 115–16; Morris, *Theodore Rex*, 178.

15. TR's First Annual Message to Congress, Dec. 3, 1901, *FRUS*, Dec. 3, 1901, 36–37.

16. Morris, *Theodore Rex*, 179; Perkins, *History of Monroe Doctrine*, 210–13; Collin, *TR's Caribbean*, 111–12.

17. "Difficulty of Germany with Venezuela," Dec. 11, 1901, *FRUS*, Dec. 3, 1901, 192–94. For these events, see Edward B. Parsons, "The German and American Crisis of 1902–1903," *The Historian*, 33, no. 3 (May 1971): 436–52.

18. Perkins, *History of Monroe Doctrine*, 226; Dept. of State Memo, Dec. 16, 1901, encl. in Hay to Holleben, Dec. 16, 1901, *FRUS*, Dec. 3, 1901, 195. Hay served as secretary of state from September 1898 to his death in July 1905.

19. Imperial German Embassy to Hay, Dec. 20, 1901, *FRUS*, Dec. 3, 1901, 196.

20. TR to White, Dec. 17, 1901, Morison, et al., eds., *Letters of TR*, 3: 208; TR to Sternburg, Dec. 24, 1901, TR Papers (LC). White was a historian and co-founder of Cornell University and its first president.

21. White to TR, Jan. 4, 1902, TR Papers (LC). Sternburg became ambassador to the United States in July 1903. TR to Sternburg, July 30, 1903, ibid.

22. Taylor to TR, ca. late Nov. 1902, TR Papers, cited in Morris, *Theodore Rex*, 178, 629 n.178.

23. Morris, *Theodore Rex*, 180; H. Percival Dodge of the U.S. Embassy in Berlin to Hay, Nov. 28, 1902, *FRUS*, Dec. 7, 1903, 417.

24. Hill to Bowen, Nov. 29, 1902, *FRUS*, Dec. 7, 1903, 788. A host of countries other than Germany and Britain had claims against Venezuela, including Italy. Hill to Bowen, Dec. 1, 1902, ibid.; Bowen to Hay, Dec. 2, 1902, ibid.

25. See Perkins, *History of Monroe Doctrine*, 218, 224–25; Beale, *TR and Rise of America*, 398–99.

26. Hay to White, Dec. 5, 1902, *FRUS*, Dec. 7, 1903, 452.

27. "Ultimatum to Venezuela," *Times* of London, Dec. 8, 1902, encl. in Dodge to Hay, Dec. 10, 1902, ibid., 419; "Grounds for the Action," *NYT*, Dec. 9, 1902, 1–2.

28. "Ultimatum to Venezuela," 419.

29. Ibid., 419–20; Castro press statement quoted in Brian S. McBeth, *Gunboats, Corruption, and Claims: Foreign Intervention in Venezuela, 1899–1908* (Westport: Greenwood Press, 2001), 88. The *Agencia Pumar* published foreign news twice a day.

30. "Ultimatum to Venezuela," 420, 430; McBeth, *Gunboats, Corruption, and Claims*, 81–82, 88.

31. W. H. D. Haggard of British legation in Caracas to Bowen, Dec. 8, 1902, encl. in Bowen to Hay, Dec. 13, 1902, *FRUS*, Dec. 7, 1903, 795; Pilgrim-Baltazzi of

German legation in Caracas to Bowen, Dec. 8, 1902, ibid.; Bowen to Hay, Dec. 8, 1902, ibid., 789.

32. "Envoys Leave Caracas," *NYT*, Dec. 9, 1902, 1; Collin, *TR's Caribbean*, 93–94; Morris, *Theodore Rex*, 181–82, 185; Parsons, "German and American Crisis," 436–37, 442; Beale, *TR and Rise of America*, 400; Harbaugh, *Life and Times of TR*, 187–88.

33. TR warning quoted in TR to Henry White, Aug. 14, 1906, Morison, et al., eds., *Letters of TR*, 5: 358–59; TR's second warning quoted in Morris, *Theodore Rex*, 187.

34. Kaiser quoted in Morris, *Theodore Rex*, 189.

35. TR to William R. Thayer (historian), Aug. 21, 1916, Morison, et al., eds., *Letters of TR*, 8: 1104; Morris, *Theodore Rex*, 189. Years later, Roosevelt remarked that Bünz was "the one man who sized me up right." TR quoted ibid., 633 n.189.

36. Perkins, *History of Monroe Doctrine*, 194–95, 207, 220.

37. Bowen to Hay, Dec. 9, 1902, *FRUS, Dec.*, 7, 1903, 790; McBeth, *Gunboats, Corruption, and Claims*, 89; Morris, *Theodore Rex*, 185, 187–88; Collin, *TR's Caribbean*, 89.

38. Ibid., 93–94; Bowen to Hay, Dec. 9, 10, 1902, *FRUS*, Dec. 7, 1903, 790–91.

39. Hay to Bowen, Dec. 10, 1902, ibid., 791; Bowen to Hay, Dec. 11, 1902, ibid., 791–92; Baralt to Bowen, Dec. 9, 1902 and Bowen to Baralt, Dec. 11, 1902, encl. Bowen to Hay, Dec. 13, 1902, ibid., 793.

40. Hay to White, Dec. 12, 1902, *FRUS*, Dec. 7, 1903, 452; Promemoria, Imperial German Embassy in Washington, DC, Dec. 20, 1901, *FRUS*, Dec. 3, 1901, 196. On the Crete blockade, the United States was not a signatory of the Berlin Treaty of 1897 involving Britain, France, Italy, Germany, Austria-Hungary, and Russia, which approved the naval blockade around the island, nor did it acquiesce to any act that violated international rights or "the commerce or interests of the United States." Secretary of State John Sherman to Sir Julian Pauncefote, British ambassador in Washington, March 26, 1897, *FRUS*, Dec. 6, 1897, 255. White to Lord Lansdowne (British foreign secretary), Dec. 13, 1902, encl. in White to Hay, Dec. 17, 1902, *FRUS*, Dec. 7, 1903, 454–55.

41. Parsons, "German and American Crisis," 443; Beale, *TR and Rise of America*, 421.

42. Sternburg to TR, Dec. 15, 1902, TR Papers (LC).

43. Morris, *Theodore Rex*, 188–89; Marks, *Velvet on Iron*, 42; Beale, *TR and Rise of America*, 413; U.S. ambassador Charlemagne Tower Jr. in Berlin to Hay, Dec. 14, 1902, *FRUS*, Dec. 7, 1903, 421; Tower to Hay, Dec. 17, 1902, ibid., 421–22. Tower was a lawyer, businessman, and professor of history at the University of Pennsylvania who served as U.S. ambassador to Russia from 1899 to late November 1902, before becoming ambassador to Germany in December and remaining at that post until mid-1908.

44. Hay to Tower, Dec. 16, 1902, ibid., 421; Hay to White, Dec. 16, 1902, ibid., 453.

45. Tower to Hay, Dec. 17, 1902, ibid., 421–22; White to Hay, Dec. 16, 1902, ibid., 453; McBeth, *Gunboats, Corruption, and Claims*, 92; Nancy Mitchell, "The Height of the German Challenge: The Venezuela Blockade, 1902–3," *Diplomatic History*, 20, Issue 2 (Spring 1996): 195.

46. White to Hay, Dec. 17, 1902, *FRUS*, Dec. 7, 1903, 454.

47. White to Hay, Dec. 18, 1902, ibid., 455; Beale, *TR and Rise of America*, 414–15; Collin, *TR's Caribbean*, 105–06, 108.

48. Beale, *TR and Rise of America*, 414; Holleben quoted in Morris, *Theodore Rex*, 191.

49. Morris, *Theodore Rex*, 191.

50. Parsons, "German and American Crisis," 444–45; Seward W. Livermore, "Theodore Roosevelt, the American Navy, and the Venezuelan Crisis of 1902–1903," *American Historical Review*, 5 (April 1946): 452–71 (see 464–65); Paul S. Holbo, "Perilous Diplomacy: Public Diplomacy and the Press in the Venezuelan Crisis, 1902–1903," *The Historian*, 32 (May 1970): 428–48 (see 436).

51. Livermore, "TR, American Navy, and Venezuelan Crisis," 464; Hay to Tower, Dec. 16, 1902, *FRUS*, Dec. 7, 1903, 421; Tower to Hay, Dec. 19, 1902, ibid., 423–24; White (in London) to Hay, Dec. 18, 19, 1902, ibid., 455, 456; Beale, *TR and Rise of America*, 414–16, 420; Parsons, "German and American Crisis," 446.

52. Beale, *TR and Rise of America*, 416; White to Hay, Dec. 20, 1902, *FRUS*, Dec. 7, 1903, 458; Bowen to Hay, Dec. 22, 1902, ibid., 801; Tower to Hay, Dec. 22, 1902, ibid., 425. La Guaira and Puerto Cabello were Venezuela's two major ports. Collin, *TR's Caribbean*, 112.

53. Hay to White, Dec. 19, 1902, *FRUS*, Dec. 7, 1903, 456–57.

54. See Perkins, *History of Monroe Doctrine*, 234; McBeth, *Gunboats, Corruption, and Claims*, 92; Hay to Tower, Dec. 26, 1902, *FRUS*, Dec. 7, 1903, 428.

55. TR to Shaw, Dec. 26, 1902, Morison, et al., eds., *Letters of TR*, 3: 396–97; TR to Cleveland, Dec. 26, 1902, ibid., 398; TR to Crawford, June 12, 1911, ibid., 7: 283; TR to Lee, June 27, 1911, ibid., 297.

56. There are a number of works addressing the variables contributing to the Alaska boundary dispute. Among them are Beale, *TR and Rise of America*; Thomas A. Bailey, "Theodore Roosevelt and the Alaska Boundary Settlement," *Canadian Historical Review*, 18 (June 1937): 123–30; Charles S. Campbell, Jr., *Anglo-American Understanding, 1898–1903* (Baltimore: The Johns Hopkins Press, 1957), 65–78; Gould, *Presidency of TR*; David G. Haglund, "The TR Problem in Canadian History," *London Journal of Canadian Studies* 23 (2008): 31–44; Marks, *Velvet on Iron*, 61–64, 105–11; John A. Munro, ed., *The Alaska Boundary Dispute* (Toronto: Copp-Clark, 1970); Norman Penlington, *The Alaska Boundary Dispute: A Critical Reappraisal* (Toronto: McGraw-Hill, 1972); and Perkins, *Great Rapprochement*, 162–75. For an excellent examination of the boundary dispute that draws heavily on British sources see Cory L. Andrews, "Gold, Land, and the Big Stick: Theodore Roosevelt and the Alaska Boundary Crisis," masters thesis, (Georgia Southern University, 1997).

57. For a discussion of the complex issues (geographic and political) resulting from the gold rush, see Campbell, *Anglo-American Understanding*, 65–67, 134–37, 142–46, 330–36; With Canada part of the British Empire, it is no surprise that an Anglo-American Joint High Commission included the boundary issue on its agenda. It, however, failed to find a solution before disbanding in February of 1899. For the deliberations and struggles of this body, see ibid., 88–147; Hay to Choate, June 15, 1899, Thayer, ed., *The Life and Letters of John Hay*, 207.

58. Beale, *TR and Rise of America*, 111–12.

59. Edward Parliament Kohn, *This Kindred People: Canadian-American Relations and the Anglo-Saxon Idea, 1895–1903* (Montreal: McGill-Queen's Press, 2004), 174; Hay to TR July 7, 1902, TR Papers, LC; Hay to TR July 14, 1902, ibid.

60. Beale, *TR and Rise of America*, 114–15; Kohn, *This Kindred People*, 175; Hay notified Herbert of the Senate's approval of the agreement in mid-February. Hay to Herbert, Feb. 13, 1903, *FRUS*, Dec. 7, 1903, 493–94.

61. Beale, *TR and Rise of America*, 114–15; Kohn, *This Kindred People*, 176–77.

62. William N. Tilchin, *Theodore Roosevelt and the British Empire: A Study in Presidential Statecraft* (New York: St. Martin's, 1997), 30–34; *Brooklyn Eagle* reference in Thomas A. Bailey, *A Diplomatic History of the American People*, Seventh Ed. (New York: Appleton-Century-Crofts, 1964), 509; *Times* quoted in Marks, *Velvet on Iron*, 108. It should be noted that Roosevelt did, indeed, approach Supreme Court justices for service on the commission, but they declined. Campbell has noted that the selections would have been men equally inflexible on the boundary. See Campbell, *Anglo-American Understanding*, 311–12; Choate to Hay, April 1, 1903, *FRUS*, Dec. 7, 1903, 494.

63. Marks, *Velvet on Iron*, 107; Beale, *TR and Rise of America*, 115.

64. Campbell, *Anglo-American Understanding*, 323–24; Beale, *TR and Rise of America*, 122–23; Concerning the press by Canada for a delay in talks, Herbert had made it clear to Hay in late March that his government did intend to pursue postponement. Herbert to Hay, March 23, 1903, *FRUS*, Dec. 7, 1903, 496.

65. Quoted in Marks, *Velvet on Iron*, 62.

66. Hay quoted in Campbell, *Anglo-American Understanding*, 333; ibid., 333–35.

67. Choate quoted ibid., 339; Lodge to TR, Oct. 12, 1903, Lodge, ed., *Correspondence of TR and Lodge*, two: 69.

68. To get the unbroken coastline he required, Roosevelt had, in fact, been willing to yield all four islands in the Portland Canal. See Campbell, *Anglo-American Understanding*, 339. Recent scholarship has portrayed Roosevelt's willingness to yield the Portland Canal islands and a small piece of the panhandle as indicative of a more nuanced diplomacy—one that understood the geopolitical import of "honour" among Anglo-Saxon peer nations. For a full discussion, see David G. Haglund and Tudor Onea, "Victory without Triumph: Theodore Roosevelt, Honour, and the Alaska Panhandle Boundary Dispute," *Diplomacy and Statecraft*, 19 (2008): 20–41.

69. TR to Lodge, June 29, 1903, Lodge, ed., *Correspondence of TR and Lodge*, 2: 37; For a details on the commission's deliberations see Campbell, *Anglo-American Understanding*, 330–45.

70. TR to White, Nov. 26, 1903, TR Papers, LC; Roosevelt had struggled with a recalcitrant U.S. Congress to make good on McKinley and Root's "implied promises of trade concessions" with the Cubans that would, it was hoped, stabilize their economy. Considering it a "moral question," Roosevelt was determined to win reciprocity between American commercial interests and Cuban sugar. Only after the cohesion of American opponents dissipated with the fragmenting of the American sugar trust would he be able to push the agreement through Congress. This he would do by the end of the year. See Collin, *TR's Caribbean*, 525–27.

71. For documents on the commission's settlement, see "Decision of the Alaskan Boundary Tribunal under the Treaty of January 24, 1903, between the United States and Great Britain," *FRUS*, Dec. 7, 1903, 543–45.

72. Herbert quoted in Gould, *Presidency of TR*, 83.

73. Bowen to Hay, Jan. 7, 1903, *FRUS*, Dec. 7, 1903, 803; Castro to Bowen, Jan. 8, 1903 encl. in Hay to White, Jan. 8, 1903, ibid., 468.

74. McBeth, *Gunboats, Corruption, and Claims*, 91; Collin, *TR's Caribbean*, 108–11.

75. TR quoted ibid., 111.

76. Herbert quoted ibid.

77. White to Hay, Feb. 10, 14, 1903, *FRUS*, Dec. 7, 1903, 475–76. Germany formally lifted the blockade of Puerto Cabello and Maracaibo on February 16, 1903. German notice from Chancellor Bülow on lifting the blockade, Feb. 16, 1903, encl. in Tower to Hay, Feb. 19, 1903, ibid., 437; Tower to Hay, Feb. 21, 1903, ibid.

78. Drago to Martin Garcia Méron, minister of the Argentine Republic to the United States, Dec. 29, 1902, *FRUS*, Dec. 7, 1903, 2–3 (note transmitted to Hay); Perkins, *History of Monroe Doctrine*, 247–48; Collin, *TR's Caribbean*, 87, 493–96.

79. Hay to Méron, Feb. 17, 1903, *FRUS*, Dec. 7, 1903, 5–6; Collin, *TR's Caribbean*, 87, 493, 497–99.

80. TR to Hay, March 13, 1903, TR Papers (LC).

81. Perkins, *History of Monroe Doctrine*, 234–35; TR to Hay, March 13, 1903, Morison, et al., eds., *Letters of TR*, 3: 446; Theodore Roosevelt, *American Ideals*, in Hagedorn, ed., *Works of TR*, 13: 168.

82. Collin, *TR's Caribbean*, 116–19; Raymond A. Esthus, *Theodore Roosevelt and the International Rivalries* (Claremont: Regina Books, 1970), 416; Jay Sexton, *The Monroe Doctrine: Empire and Nation in Nineteenth-Century America* (New York: Hill and Wang, 2011), 228.

83. Award of the Tribunal of Arbitrators Constituted in Virtue of the Protocols Signed at Washington on May 7, 1903 . . . Done at The Hague, in the Permanent Court of Arbitration, Feb. 22, 1904, The Venezuelan Preferential Case, *Report of International Arbitral Awards* (United Nations, 2006), 9: 99–110; Collin, *TR's Caribbean*, 117; "Hague Tribunal Decides for Blockading Powers," *San Francisco Call*, Feb. 23, 1904.

84. Bowen to Hay, June 25, 1904, *FRUS*, Dec. 5, 1905, 919–20; Bowen to Hay, July 22, 1904, ibid., 920; Acting Secretary of State Alvey Adee to Bowen, July 26, 1904, ibid., 925; Bowen to secretary of state, July 30, 1904, ibid.; Bowen to Hay, Aug. 5, 7, 1904, ibid., 927, 928; Editors' note, Morison et al., eds., *Letters of TR*, 4: 914 n.2.

85. TR to Hay, Aug. 30, 1904, Morison, et al., eds., *Letters of TR*, 4: 914; TR to Hay, Sept. 2, 1904, ibid., 917; TR to Hay, April 2, 1905, ibid., 1156. Roosevelt told Hay that turning over the customs house to the Belgians would illustrate the policy he had authorized Elihu Root to announce by reading from a letter at the Cuban dinner (discussed below). TR to Hay, Sept. 2, 1904, ibid., 917.

86. See Morris, *Theodore Rex*, 177; Beale, *TR and Rise of America*, 403; Livermore, "TR, American Navy, and Venezuelan Crisis," 463; Parsons, "German and American Crisis," 436, 443–48, 451–52; Marks, *Velvet on Iron*, 47–50, 52–54.

87. Marks, *Velvet on Iron*, 42–47. Morris added to Marks's list a series of missing dispatches of the French ambassador in Paris, as well as the gaps in the usually heavy correspondence between Hay and his assistant secretary of state, Alvey Adee. Morris, *Theodore Rex*, 628 n.177.

88. TR, *Autobiography*, 100; Adams quoted in Livermore, "TR, American Navy, and Venezuelan Crisis," 470 n.94; Moody quoted ibid., 466.

89. TR to Hay, Jan. 13, 1905 (reference to term "kitchen ambassadors" and its comparison to the "kitchen cabinet" during Andrew Jackson's presidency), Morison, et al., eds., *Letters of TR*, 4: 1102; TR to Spring Rice, Nov. 1, 1905, ibid., 5: 63; TR to Reid, June 27, 1906, ibid., 319.

90. TR to White, Aug. 14, 1906, ibid., 5: 58–59.

91. Ibid., 359; Esthus, *TR and International Rivalries*, 42; Parsons, "German-American Crisis," 451–52.

92. Beale, *TR and Rise of America*, 412–13; TR quoted in Morris, *Theodore Rex*, 177; E. Alexander Powell, *Yonder Lies Adventure* (New York: Macmillan, 1932), 312. Powell was a consular official in Syria and Egypt from 1906–1909 and later war correspondent during World War I.

93. TR to Thayer, Aug. 21, 1916, Morison, et al., eds., *Letters of TR*, 8: 1101–02. See Thayer, *Hay*, 2: 411–17.

94. TR to Thayer, Aug. 21, 1916, Morison, et al., eds., *Letters of TR*, 8: 1102.

95. Ibid., 1102–03.

96. Ibid., 1103. Roosevelt shared this story with Sternburg four days later. Parsons, "German and American Crisis," 451.

97. TR to Thayer, Aug. 21, 1916, Morison, et al., eds., *Letters of TR*, 8: 1103; Editors' note, ibid., 5: 319 n.2; Morris, *Theodore Rex*, 189. The Oval Office came into being in 1909 during the presidency of William Howard Taft.

98. Editors' note, Morison et al., eds., *Letters of TR*, 5: 319 n.2; TR to Thayer, Aug. 21, 1916, ibid., 8: 1103.

99. Ibid., 1103–04.

100. Ibid. Roosevelt informed Lodge of the warning sent to the emperor through his consul general in New York. TR to Lodge, June 19, 1901, ibid., 3: 98; TR to Thayer, Aug. 21, 1916, ibid., 8: 1104.

101. Ibid.

102. Ibid.; Morris, *Theodore Rex*, 191; Harbaugh, *Life and Times of TR*, 188; Morison, et al., eds., *Letters of TR*, 8: 1104.

103. TR to Thayer, Aug. 21, 1916, Morison, et al., eds., *Letters of TR*, 8: 1104; Dewey to Wood, May 23, 1916, encl. ibid., 1104–05.

104. TR to Thayer, Aug. 23, 1916, ibid., 1107; TR to Thayer, Aug. 27, 1916, ibid., 1107–08.

105. TR to Taylor, March 28, 1903, Bishop, *TR*, 1: 239.

106. Morris, *Theodore Rex*, 210; Beale, *TR and Rise of America*, 418.

107. TR to Dewey, March 30, 1903, ibid.; Morris, *Theodore Rex*, 210.

108. Ibid., 645 n.210; Frederick Palmer, *With My Own Eyes: A Personal Story of Battle Years* (Indianapolis: The Bobbs-Merrill Co., 1932), 128–29.

109. Mitchell, "The Height of the German Challenge," 185–210.

110. Livermore, "TR, American Navy, and Venezuelan Crisis," 452–71.

111. The Teller Amendment was the congressional reply to President McKinley's war message of that same day.

112. TR to Congress, March 27, 1902, *FRUS*, Dec. 2, 1902, 320–21.

113. Perkins, *History of Monroe Doctrine*, 196, 230–31.

114. Platt Amendment, Feb. 25, 1901, *Congressional Record*, 56th Congress, 2nd session, 1901, 2954; Herbert G. Squiers of U.S. legation in Havana to Hay, April 11, 1903, FRUS, Dec. 7, 1903, 356–57; Stephen Irving Max Schwab, *Guantánamo, USA: The Untold History of America's Cuban Outpost* (Lawrence: University Press of Kansas, 2009), 88.

115. Michael J. Strauss, *The Leasing of Guantánamo Bay* (Westport: Greenwood Press, 2009), 35; Schwab, *Guantánamo*, 3–4, 87–94.

116. Palma's address to Cuban Congress, Nov. 2, 1903, encl. in Squiers to Hay, Nov. 7, 1903, *FRUS*, Dec. 7, 1903, 356, 361, 365; Commercial Convention Between the United States and Cuba, Dec. 17, 1903, ibid., 375–81; Schwab, *Guantánamo*, 94.

117. William F. Powell (chargé) to Hay, April 10, 1903, *FRUS*, Dec. 7, 1903, 390.

118. Ibid., 390–91; DuVal, *Cadiz to Cathay*, 368.

119. Powell to Hay, April 10, 1903, *FRUS*, Dec. 7, 1903, 390.

120. Despradele to Powell, April 22, 1903, *FRUS*, Dec. 7, 1903, 393–94; Powell to Hay, May 12, 1903, ibid., 393; Powell to Despradele, April 22, 1903, ibid., 394.

121. Editors' note, Morison et al., eds., *Letters of TR*, 4: 724 n.1; Harbaugh, *Life and Times of TR*, 189; Collin, *TR's Caribbean*, 392.

122. TR to TR Jr., Feb. 10, 1904, Morison, et al., eds., *Letters of TR*, 4: 724.

123. TR to Joseph Bishop (friend and journalist), Feb. 23, 1904, ibid., 734. Edmund Morris cites John Hay's diary entry of March 18, 1904, in observing that Roosevelt made the same denial to his cabinet except that he used the image of an anaconda. Morris, *Theodore Rex*, 681 n.319.

124. TR to Bishop, Feb. 23, 1904, Morison, et al., eds., *Letters of TR*, 4: 734–35; Morris, *Theodore Rex*, 318–19; Perkins, *History of Monroe Doctrine*, 238–39.

125. TR to Burton, Feb. 23, 1904, Morison, et al., eds., *Letters of TR*, 4: 736–37.

126. TR to Root, May 20, 1904, ibid., 801. Root served as secretary of war from Aug. 1, 1899 to Jan. 31, 1904, and as secretary of state from July 19, 1905 to Jan. 27, 1909.

127. Editors' note, Morison et al., eds., *Letters of TR*, 4: 801–02 n.2.

128. TR to Nicholas M. Butler (president of Columbia University), June 3, 1904, ibid., 819; TR to Root, June 7, 1904, ibid., 821–22.

129. TR to Harry S. Edwards (journalist and author), June 8, 1904, ibid., 824. Edwards would give the seconding speech for Roosevelt's Republican nomination for the presidency on July 26, 1904. Ibid.; TR to Schurman, July 25, 1904, ibid., 865. Schurman would advise Roosevelt in writing his acceptance speech for the Republican nomination for the presidency on July 26, 1904. Ibid.

130. Root had done most of the work on the text before becoming secretary of state after Hay died of ill health in early 1905. Jessup, *Root*, 1: 470; Arthur P. Whitaker, *The Western Hemisphere Idea: Its Rise and Decline* (Ithaca: Cornell University Press, 1954), 99; President's Fourth Annual Message to Congress, Dec. 6, 1904,

Richardson, ed., *Messages and Papers of Presidents*, 16: 7052–53; TR quoted in Harbaugh, *Life and Times of TR*, 190.

131. TR, Fourth Annual Message to Congress, Dec. 6, 1904, Richardson, ed., *Messages and Papers of Presidents*, 16: 7053; Harbaugh, *Life and Times of TR*, 190.

132. TR's Fourth Annual Message to Congress, Dec. 6, 1904, Richardson, ed., *Messages and Papers of Presidents*, 16: 7054.

133. Ibid., 7054–55; Harbaugh, *Life and Times of TR*, 190.

134. Collin, *TR's Caribbean*, 393.

135. TR to Senate, March 6, 1905, Richardson, ed., *Messages and Papers of Presidents*, 16: 7080–81.

136. TR to Adee, March 28, 1905, Morison, et al., eds., *Letters of TR*, 4: 1148; Cable from U.S. minister in Dominican Republic, Thomas C. Dawson, encl. ibid.; Harbaugh, *Life and Times of TR*, 190–91.

137. Ibid., 191.

138. Ibid.; Cable from U.S. minister in Dominican Republic, Thomas C. Dawson, encl. Morison, et al., eds., *Letters of TR*, 4: 1148–49; TR to Bishop (friend), March 23, 1905, ibid., 1144–45.

139. Editors' note, ibid., 1148 n.1; TR to Adee, March 28, 1905, ibid., 1149; Perkins, *History of Monroe Doctrine*, 241–42 (Roosevelt's quote on 242). See Howard C. Hill, *Roosevelt and the Caribbean* (Chicago: University of Chicago Press, 1927), 160–69, and Bishop, *TR*, 1: 430–35.

140. TR to Spring Rice, July 24, 1905, Morison, et al., eds., *Letters of TR*, 4: 1283–86.

141. TR's Fifth Annual Address to Congress, Dec. 5, 1903, Richardson, ed., *Messages and Papers of Presidents*, 16: 7374–76.

142. Perkins, *History of Monroe Doctrine*, 243–44; TR to Lodge, April 30, 1906, Morison, et al., eds., *Letters of TR*, 5: 252, 257. Roosevelt had responded to Adams's request by reading and commenting on an article he had written about Egypt: "Reflex Light from Africa," *Century Illustrated Monthly* (May–Oct. 1906), 72: 101–11.

143. TR's Fourth Annual Message to Congress, Dec. 6, 1904, Richardson, ed., *Messages and Papers of Presidents*, 16: 7053; Collin, *TR's Caribbean*, 498–99; Perkins, *History of Monroe Doctrine*, 247–48. For Roosevelt's ideas on arbitration, see Hay to Tower, Dec. 26, 1902, *FRUS*, Dec. 7, 1903, 428.

144. TR to Trevelyan, Sept. 9, 1906, Morison, et al., eds., *Letters of TR*, 5: 401; TR quoted in Morris, *Theodore Rex*, 456.

145. TR to Taft, Sept. 28, 1906, Morison, et al., eds., *Letters of TR*, 5: 434; TR to Taft, Sept. 30, 1906, 435; Lodge to TR, Sept. 29, 1906, Lodge, ed., *Correspondence of TR and Lodge*, 2: 237.

146. TR to Taft, Jan. 22, 1907, Morison, et al., eds., *Letters of TR*, 5: 560; TR to Sydney Brooks (writer), Dec. 28, 1908, ibid., 6: 1445.

147. TR to Carnegie, Feb. 26, 1909, in Jessup, *Root*, 1: 560; Root, *Addresses on International Subjects (1916)*, 123, cited ibid., 560–61.

148. TR to Chicago audience, April 2, 1903, quoted in Bishop, *TR*, 1: 239–40.

149. TR to Hale, Dec. 3, 1908, Morison, et al., eds., *Letters of TR*, 6: 1408.

150. Ibid.

151. TR to Reid, Dec. 4, 1908, ibid., 1410.

152. The lack of respect extended to a Canada that was gaining footing as a consequential actor left a lasting residue of resentment toward the United States, with its ire clearly directed at Theodore Roosevelt. For a discussion of the tension between the North American neighbors created by the Alaska settlement and the differing views on Roosevelt's role, see Haglund, "TR Problem in Canada-U.S. Relations," 31–44; see also Tony McCulloch, "Theodore Roosevelt and Canada: Alaska, The "Big Stick' and the North Atlantic Triangle, 1901–1909," in Serge Ricard, ed., *A Companion to Theodore Roosevelt* (Malden: Wiley-Blackwell Publishing, 2011), 293–313.

CHAPTER 5

1. Beale, *TR and Rise of America*, 154, 154 n*; That John Hay's seat at the cabinet table would, after a brief interim appointment, be ably filled by Elihu Root should not diminish the significance of the loss of one of America's most loyal and capable statesmen. On July 3, Roosevelt issued a proclamation lauding Hay's half century of service to the nation "crowned" by his efforts as secretary of state. Roosevelt noted that he pursued those efforts "with such farsighted reading of the future and such loyalty to lofty ideals as to confer lasting benefits not only upon our own country but upon all the nations of the earth." The president knew he had been fortunate to have Hay at the table, but must have been relieved that Hay's absence would be tempered by the continued counsel and statesmanship of Root. See Theodore Roosevelt, *Proclamation 578*, July 3, 1905, https://www.presidency.ucsb.edu/documents/proclamation-578-announcing-the-death-john-hay.

2. TR's Inaugural Address, March 4, 1905, TR Center; see Greg Russell, "Theodore Roosevelt, Geopolitics, and Cosmopolitan Ideals," *Review of International Studies*, 32, no. 3 (July 2006): 541–59.

3. TR to Spring Rice, Aug. 5, 1896, Morison, et al., eds., *Letters of TR*, 1: 555; TR to Spring Rice, Aug. 13, 1897, ibid., 646.

4. TR to Spring Rice, Aug. 11, 1899, ibid., 2: 1051–52.

5. TR, "Address at Mechanics' Pavilion," San Francisco, CA, May 13, 1903, TR Papers (LC).

6. Ibid.; TR quoted Morris, *Theodore Rex*, 229.

7. Alexis de Tocqueville, *Democracy in America*, 2 vols. (New York: Vintage Books, 1945. Originally published in Paris in 1835 and 1840), 2: 37–38; TR to James Bryce (British writer), Jan. 6, 1888, Morison, et al., eds., *Letters of TR*, 1: 134; Morris, *Rise of TR*, 392. De Tocqueville was a political theorist and historian who later became the French minister of foreign affairs.

8. TR, *Address of President Roosevelt at Mechanics' Pavilion*, San Francisco, California, May 13, 1903. TR Center.

9. Beale, *TR and Rise of America*, 20–21.

10. Raymond A. Esthus, *Theodore Roosevelt and Japan* (Seattle: University of Washington Press, 1966), 9–11; Morris, *Theodore Rex*, 229.

11. TR to Sternburg, Oct. 11, 1901, Morison, et al., eds., *Letters of TR*, 3: 172; For a comprehensive treatment of the "Open Door" policy that focuses on the Theodore Roosevelt administration, see Moore, *TR and China*.

12. Edwin H. Conger, U.S. minister in China, to Hay, Dec. 3, 1901, *FRUS*, Dec. 2, 1902, 271; Hay to Conger, Dec. 6, 1901, ibid.; For the back and forth between China and Russia as they worked toward the 1901 agreement, see Moore, *TR and China*, 57–60.

13. Hay to Mr. Wu, Feb. 3, 1902, ibid., 275 (enclosed memo, Feb. 1, 1902, ibid., 275–76); Hay to Conger, Feb. 1, 1902, ibid.; Tower to Count Vladimir Lamsdorff, Russian minister for foreign affairs, Feb. 3, 1902, 928 encl. in Tower, U.S. ambassador to Russia, to Hay, ibid., 928; The United States also sent the memo to Austria, Belgium, France, Germany, Great Britain, Italy, Japan, the Netherlands, and Spain. Ibid., 275.

14. Conger to Hay, Feb. 4, 1902, ibid., 276; Lamsdorff to Tower, Feb. 9, 1902, ibid., 929 encl. in Tower to Hay, Feb. 12, 1902, ibid., 928–29.

15. Conger to Hay, Sept. 26, 1902, ibid., 281; Gregory Moore cautions that Russia's assurances should be viewed skeptically as St. Petersburg only accepted the "principles of the Open Door as understood by Russia." Moore, *TR and China*, 61.

16. Conger to Hay, April 23, 1903, *FRUS*, Dec. 7, 1903, 253–54; TR to Albert Shaw (editor of *Review of Reviews*), June 22, 1903, Morison, et al., eds., *Letters of TR*, 3: 497–98. For these issues, see Tyler Dennett, *Roosevelt and the Russo-Japanese War* (Garden City: Doubleday, Page and Co., 1925), chap. 6.

17. TR to Abbott, June 22, 1903, Morison, et al., eds., *Letters of TR*, 3: 500–01.

18. TR to Hay, May 22, 1903, ibid., 478.

19. Griscom to Hay, July 14, 1903, *FRUS*, Dec. 7, 1903, 615.

20. Griscom to Hay, July 20, 1903, ibid., 616; Griscom to Hay, July 22, 1903, ibid., 617.

21. Russian demands given to Second Assistant Secretary of State Alvey Adee, Sept. 12, 1903, ibid., 617–18.

22. Moore, *TR and China*, 68–78.

23. Griscom to Hay, Sept. 21, 1903, ibid., 618; Komura to Hay, Dec. 21, 1903, ibid., 619; Griscom to Hay, Dec. 18, 1903, ibid.

24. Griscom to Hay, Dec. 24, 1903, ibid., 621–22.

25. Griscom to Hay, Dec. 31, 1903, ibid., 622.

26. Griscom to Hay, Jan. 13, 1904, *FRUS*, Dec. 6, 1904, 410–11; For a detailed discussion of the intricacies and international ramifications of the war, see John Albert White, *The Diplomacy of the Russo-Japanese War* (Princeton: Princeton University Press, 1964); Bernard Pares, *A History of Russia* (New York: Vintage Books, 1965. Original publication, 1926), 445.

27. Griscom to Hay, Jan. 8, 1904, *FRUS*, Dec. 6, 1904, 410; Griscom to Hay, Jan. 13, 1904, ibid., 410–11; Griscom to Hay, Jan. 27, 1904, ibid., 411; Griscom to Hay, Feb. 5, 1904, ibid., 411; Memo from Japan to Russia, Feb. 6, 1904, encl. in Griscom to Hay, Feb. 6, 1904, ibid., 412.

28. Griscom to Hay, Feb. 7, 1904, ibid., 413.

29. Griscom to Hay, Feb. 9, 1904, ibid., 413; *NYT*, Feb. 10, 1904, 1. Edmund Morris claims that the Japanese sank Russia's two largest battleships, severely disabled

another, and crippled or destroyed four cruisers. Morris, *Theodore Rex*, 311. Not until the Second Hague Peace Conference in October 1907 did it become a violation of international law to begin hostilities without first declaring war. "Laws of War: Opening of Hostilities" (Hague III), Oct. 18, 1907, Convention Relative to the Opening of Hostilities, Article I—Lillian Goldman Law Library, Yale Law School (Avalon Project).

30. Japanese Declaration of War, Feb. 10, 1904, quoted in *The Japan Times* of Tokyo, Feb. 11, 1904, encl. in Griscom to Hay, Feb. 18, 1904, *FRUS*, Dec. 6, 1904, 414.

31. Griscom to Hay, Feb. 11, 1904, *FRUS*, Dec. 6, 1904, 413.

32. TR to Oscar Straus (lawyer with expertise in international law and diplomacy), Feb. 9, 1904, Morison, et al., eds., *Letters of TR*, 4: 721; Hay to Griscom, Feb. 10, 1904, *FRUS*, Dec. 6, 1904, 418; Takahira to Hay, Feb. 11, 1904, ibid., 419; Griscom to Hay, Feb. 15, 1904, ibid.; See editors' note, Morison, et al., eds., *Letters of TR*, 4: 721 n.1. See also A. Whitney Griswold, *The Far Eastern Policy of the United States* (New York: Harcourt, Brace and Co., Inc., 1938).

33. TR to Root, Feb. 16, 1904, Morison, et al., eds., *Letters of TR*, 4: 731; TR to TR Jr., Feb. 10, 1904, ibid., 724. Root was in between cabinet positions at this time, leaving the war department on Jan. 31, 1904, and becoming secretary of state on July 19, 1905, following Hay's death on July 1.

34. TR to Theodore Burton (Inland Waterways Commission), Feb. 23, 1904, ibid., 736–37.

35. Dennett, *Roosevelt and Russo-Japanese War*, 34–35.

36. TR to Kermit Roosevelt, March 5, 1904, Morison, et al., eds., *Letters of TR*, 4: 744.

37. TR to James Roche, March 16, 1904, Morison, et al., eds., *Letters of TR*, 4: 755; TR to Spring Rice, March 19, 1904, ibid., 759–60.

38. TR to Henry White, Feb. 17, 1904, Morison, et al., eds., *Letters of TR*, 4: 732; TR to Spring Rice, June 13, 1904, ibid., 829.

39. TR to Kaneko, April 23, 1904, ibid., 777; Charles E. Neu, *The Troubled Encounter: The United States and Japan* (New York: John Wiley and Sons, 1975), 42–43.

40. TR to Spring Rice, June 13, 1904, Morison, et al., eds., *Letters of TR*, 4: 829–30.

41. Ibid., 830–31.

42. Ibid., 829, 831–32.

43. Ibid., 832–33.

44. TR to Spring Rice, June 13, 1904, ibid., 832.

45. TR to Hay, July 26, 1904, ibid., 865.

46. TR to Sternburg, Aug. 15, 1904, ibid., 4: 896; Editors' note, ibid., 896 n.1. For the kaiser's position, see John Hay's memorandum of late 1904 in Alfred L. P. Dennis, *Adventures in American Diplomacy, 1896–1906* (New York: E. P. Dutton and Co., 1928), 387–88.

47. TR to Alvey Adee, Aug. 24, 1904, Morison, et al., eds., *Letters of TR*, 4: 904; TR to Hay, Sept. 2, 1904, ibid., 917; TR to Hay, Aug. 29, 1904, ibid., 913; Hay to Conger, Aug. 26, 1904, *FRUS*, Dec. 6, 1904, 137.

48. TR to Cannon, Sept. 12, 1904, Morison, et al., eds., *Letters of TR*, 4: 923, 929; Dalton, *TR*, 230–31, 243, 246; Morris, *Theodore Rex*, 114.

49. TR to Cannon, Sept. 12, 1904, Morison, et al., eds., *Letters of TR*, 4: 929, 939–40.

50. TR to Hay, Sept. 19, 1904, ibid., 946. Roosevelt had returned a letter to Hay from Spring Rice, which led to his comment about so many people thinking Russia would win the war. See Spring Rice to Hay, Aug. 31, 1904, Gwynn, ed., *Letters and Friendships of Sir Cecil Spring Rice*, 1: 424–26.

51. TR quoted in Morris, *Theodore Rex*, 356.

52. TR to Dunne, Nov. 23, 1904, Morison, et al., eds., *Letters of TR*, 4: 1042.

53. TR to Meyer, Dec. 26, 1904, ibid., 1079–80; Meyer diary, Jan. 7, 1905, in M. A. DeWolfe Howe, *George von Lengerke Meyer: His Life and Public Service* (New York: Dodd, Mead, 1920), 108–09; Wayne A. Wiegand, *Patrician in the Progressive Era: A Biography of George Von Lengerke Meyer* (New York: Garland Publishing Co., 1988), 61–62; Lodge to Meyer, Feb. 16, 1905, quoted ibid., 63; Dennett, *Roosevelt and Russo-Japanese War*, 33. Lodge was an instructor at Harvard in 1884 when meeting Roosevelt, who was then an undergraduate student.

54. TR to Meyer, Dec. 26, 1904, Morison, et al., eds., *Letters of TR*, 4: 1079–80; Esthus, *TR and Japan*, 61.

55. TR to Spring Rice, Dec. 27, 1904, Morison, et al., eds., *Letters of TR*, 4: 1085–86.

56. Ibid., 1087–88.

57. TR to Cannon, Dec. 27, 1904, ibid., 1080.

58. Editors' note, ibid., 1081 n.1; Roosevelt's Fourth Annual Message, Dec. 6, 1904, Richardson, ed., *Messages and Papers of Presidents*, 16: 7055.

59. Kaiser's cable to TR, Jan. 5, 1905, Morison, et al., eds., *Letters of TR*, 4: 1099 n.1; TR to Sternburg, Jan. 10, 1905, ibid., 1099; TR to Sternburg, Jan. 12, 1905, ibid., 1100–01.

60. TR to Meyer, Feb. 6, 1905, Morison, et al., eds., *Letters of TR*, 4: 1115.

61. TR to Hay, Jan. 28, 1905, ibid., 1112; TR to Meyer, Feb. 6, 1905, ibid., 1116. Japan established a protectorate over Korea in November 1905. Editors' note, ibid., 1112 n.2. Five years later, in 1910, Japan annexed Korea, an action Roosevelt declared "inevitable." Theodore Roosevelt, *Fear God and Take Your Own Part* (New York: George H. Doran and Co., 1916), 294.

62. See Roger J. Spiller's introductory essay to Tadayoshi Sakurai, *Human Bullets: A Soldier's Story of the Russo-Japanese War* (Lincoln: University of Nebraska Press, 1999. Originally titled *Human Bullets: A Soldier's Story of Port Arthur* and published by Houghton, Mifflin and Company in Boston, 1907), xiii. See also Raymond A. Esthus, *Double Eagle and Rising Sun: The Russians and Japanese at Portsmouth in 1905* (Durham: Duke University Press, 1988), 23–25.

63. TR to King Edward VII of England, March 9, 1905, Morison, et al., eds., *Letters of TR*, 4: 1136; TR to Trevelyan, March 9, 1905, ibid., 1134. Roosevelt claimed he unofficially warned Russia through the French government. Ibid.

64. TR to Hull, March 16, 1905, ibid., 1141.

65. TR to Hay, March 30, 1905, ibid., 1150; TR to Sternburg, March 31, 1905, ibid., 1155.

66. TR to Hay, April 2, 1905, ibid., 1157.

67. Ibid.

68. Morris, *Theodore Rex*, 245.

69. TR to Hay, April 2, 1905, Morison, et al., eds., *Letters of TR*, 4: 1157–58.

70. Morris, *Theodore Rex*, 385.

71. TR to Taft, April 8, 1905, Morison, et al., eds., *Letters of TR*, 4: 1158–59; TR to Hay, April 2, 1905, ibid., 1158; TR to Taft, April 20, 1905, ibid., 1162–63.

72. Barbara W. Tuchman, *The Zimmermann Telegram* (New York: Macmillan Publishing Co., 1958), 25–26.

73. Ibid., 26.

74. Editors' note, Morison, et al., eds., *Letters of TR*, 4: 1169 n.2. For this issue, see Thomas A. Bailey, *Theodore Roosevelt and the Japanese-American Crises: an Account of the International Complications arising from the Race Problem on the Pacific Coast* (Stanford: Stanford University Press, 1934).

75. TR to Kennan, May 6, 1905, Morison, et al., eds., *Letters of TR*, 4: 1168–69.

76. Ibid., 1169–70; Dennett, *Roosevelt and Russo-Japanese War*, 115–16.

77. TR to Kennan, May 6, 1905, Morison, et al., eds., *Letters of TR*, 4: 1169.

78. TR to Lodge, May 15, 1905, ibid., 1180–81.

79. TR to Trevelyan, May 13, 1905, ibid., 1174.

80. TR to Spring Rice, May 13, 1905, ibid., 1179; TR to Lodge, May 15, 1905, ibid., 1180.

81. TR to Lodge, May 15, 1905, Lodge, ed., *Correspondence of TR and Lodge*, 2: 121–22.

82. Ibid., 123.

83. Lodge to TR, June 3, 1905, ibid., 128.

84. TR to Rockhill, May 18, 1905, Morison, et al., eds., *Letters of TR*, 4: 1184, Editors' note, ibid., n. 1. The United States had gained the railway concession in 1898, but in the summer of 1905, China was upset about America's immigration policy and gave in to British arguments for canceling the concession to the United States. Editors' note, ibid., 1109 n. 2; Dennett, *Roosevelt and Russo-Japanese War*, 155.

85. TR to Lodge, May 24, 1905, Lodge, ed., *Correspondence of TR and Lodge*, 2: 124.

86. Esthus, *TR and Japan*, 102–07; Morris, *Theodore Rex*, 399–400.

87. Harbaugh, *Life and Times of TR*, 265.

88. Root to Jessup, Sept. 5, 1930, in Jessup, *Root*, 2: 62. One cannot resist noting the historical parallels between the U.S.-Japanese policies toward Korea and the U.S.-Soviet policies toward Eastern Europe at the World War II conference at Yalta in February 1945.

89. Dennett, *Roosevelt and Russo-Japanese War*, 111–16.

90. Morris, *Theodore Rex*, 377–78.

91. TR to Hay, April 2, 1905, Morison, et al., eds., *Letters of TR*, 4: 1157–58.

92. Esthus, *Double Eagle and Rising Sun*, 37–38; Harbaugh, *Life and Times of TR*, 268; Morris, *Theodore Rex*, 387; Howe, *Meyer*, 152.

93. TR to Kaneko, May 31, 1905, Morison, et al., eds., *Letters of TR*, 4: 1198.

CHAPTER 6

1. TR to Lodge, June 16, 1905, Morison, et al., eds., *Letters of TR*, 4: 1221–22; Esthus, *TR and Japan,* continues to be a useful source for the Portsmouth Conference. See Chapter Five, *passim.*

2. TR to Andrew Dickson White, June 1, 1905, ibid., 1200. White was a historian and a diplomat who co-founded Cornell University and served as its first president for nearly twenty years.

3. Lodge to TR, June 3, 1905, Lodge, ed., *Correspondence of TR and Lodge*, 2: 128; TR to Lodge, June 5, 1905, ibid., 130–31.

4. TR to Lodge, June 5, 1905, Morison, et al., eds., *Letters of TR*, 4: 1202–04.

5. TR to Meyer, June 5, 1905, TR Collection, Harvard College Library (HCL), at TRC.

6. TR to Lodge, June 5, 1905, Morison, et al., eds., *Letters of TR*, 4: 1204–05.

7. Wiegand, *Patrician in Progressive Era*, 75–76; TR to Lodge, June 16, 1905, Lodge, ed., *Correspondence of TR and Lodge*, 2: 140.

8. Tower to TR, n.d., encl. in TR to Lodge, June 5, 1905, *ibid.*: 131–32; DS memo to Meyer, June 5, 1905, TR Papers (LC).

9. TR to Lodge, June 5, 1905, Morison, et al., eds., *Letters of TR*, 4: 204; TR to Lodge, June 16, 1905, ibid., 1222–23; TR to Meyer, June 5, 1905, TR Papers (LC); TR to Meyer, n.d., encl. in TR to Lodge, June 5, 1905, Lodge, ed., *Correspondence of TR and Lodge*, 2: 132–33; Esthus, *Double Eagle and Rising Sun*, 42.

10. TR to Lodge, June 5, 1905, Lodge, ed., *Correspondence of TR and Lodge*, 2: 130–31.

11. Meyer to TR, June 5, 1905, TR Papers (LC).

12. TR to Lodge, June 5, 1905, Morison, et al., eds., *Letters of TR*, 4: 1204.

13. Ibid., 1204–05; TR to Taft, May 31, 1905, ibid., 1198.

14. TR to Lodge, June 5, 1905, Lodge, ed., *Correspondence of TR and Lodge*, 2: 134–35.

15. Ibid.

16. Meyer to Hay, June 7, 1905, TR Papers (LC); Meyer to TR, June 9, 1905, ibid.; Howe, *Meyer*, 146 (empress mentioned in Meyer's diary entry for April 12, 1905), 157–62; Wiegand, *Patrician in Progressive Era*, 68; Dennett, *Roosevelt and Russo-Japanese War*, 193.

17. Meyer to Hay, June 7, 1905, TR Papers (LC); Meyer to TR, Howe, *Meyer*, 160–61; Wiegand, *Patrician in Progressive Era*, 72–74; Dennett, *Roosevelt and Russo-Japanese War*, 194.

18. Meyer to Hay, June 7, 1905, encl. in TR to Lodge, June 16, 1905, Morison, et al., eds., *Letters of TR*, 4: 1222–23; Meyer to Hay, June 7, 1905, TR Papers (LC); Meyer to TR, June 9, 1905, ibid.; Howe, *Meyer*, 165.

19. TR to Lodge, June 16, 1905, Morison, et al., eds., *Letters of TR*, 4: 1223.

20. Ibid. Roosevelt termed Cassini "very indignant" in expressing his third protest. Ibid.

21. Ibid.

22. TR to Lodge, June 16, 1905, Lodge, ed., *Correspondence of TR and Lodge*, 2: 141; Beale, *TR and Rise of America*, 283–87; Harbaugh, *Life and Times of TR*, 268–69.

23. TR to Lodge, June 16, 1905, Lodge, ed., *Correspondence of TR and Lodge*, 2: 140.

24. Ibid., 142–43.

25. Loomis to Meyer, June 8, 1905, *FRUS*, Dec. 5, 1905, 807; Loomis to Griscom, ibid., 808; Griscom to secretary of state, June 10, 1905, ibid., 809; TR to Lodge, June 16, 1905, Lodge, ed., *Correspondence of TR and Lodge*, 2: 143.

26. TR to Lodge, June 16, 1905, Morison, et al., eds., *Letters of TR*, 4: 1225.

27. Ibid., 1229–30.

28. TR to Griscom, June 16, 1905, encl. in TR to Lodge, June 16, 1905, Lodge, ed., *Correspondence of TR and Lodge*, 2: 150, 152; TR to Lodge, June 16, 1905, ibid., 152.

29. Ibid., 152–53.

30. Ibid., 152. Mikado was a title used by non-Japanese in referring to the Japanese emperor.

31. Ibid., 144–45.

32. TR to Takahira, June 15, 1905, encl. in TR to Lodge, June 16, 1905, ibid., 146; ibid., 144–46; Howe, *Meyer*, 161, 165.

33. TR to Meyer, June 8, 1905, Morison, et al., eds., *Letters of TR*, 4: 1224; Meyer to TR, June 9, 1905, TR Papers (LC).

34. TR to Oscar Straus, June 15, 1905, Morison, et al., eds., *Letters of TR*, 4: 1220; TR to Cassini, June 15, 1905, ibid., 1221; Meyer to secretary of state, June 12, 1905, *FRUS*, Dec. 5, 1905, 810; TR to Lodge, June 16, 1905, Lodge, ed., *Correspondence of TR and Lodge*, 2: 144–46. Straus was a diplomat who became the first Jewish cabinet member when he served as Secretary of Commerce and Labor from December 1906 to March 1909.

35. Lodge to TR, May 12, 1905, Morison, et al., eds., *Letters of TR*, 4: 1192 n.1; TR to Lodge, May 24, 1905, ibid., 1192; Lodge to TR, June 10, 1905, Lodge, ed., *Correspondence of TR and Lodge*, 2: 135–36. The Danish government had rejected a U.S. attempt to purchase the West Indies in 1902, a decision that Washington attributed to German influence—which Denmark denied. The United States purchased the Danish West Indies (St. Thomas, St. John, and St. Croix) from Denmark on March 31, 1917, for $25 million and changed their name to the Virgin Islands. Dennis, *Adventures in American Diplomacy*, 271–75.

36. Memo from Sternburg to TR, June 11, 1905, Morison, et al., eds., *Letters of TR*, 5: 235–36. Roosevelt added a note at the bottom of Sternburg's memorandum that "Russia has lately been using the Morocco question as a means to bring Russia, France, and Germany together; undoubtedly for her policy in the Far East." Editors' note, ibid., 235 n.2.

37. TR to Reid, April 28, 1906, ibid., 236. Reid was owner of the *New York Tribune,* and he served as minister to France from 1889 to 1892 and as ambassador to Britain from 1905 until his death in December 1912.

38. TR to Lodge, June 16, 1905, Lodge, ed., *Correspondence of TR and Lodge*, 2: 155.

39. Takahira to TR, mid-June 1905, encl. in TR to Lodge, June 16, 1905, ibid., 151; TR to Lodge, June 16, 1905, ibid., 156.

40. TR to Spring Rice, June 16, 1905, Morison, et al., eds., *Letters of TR*, 4: 1233–34.

41. Ibid., 1233; TR to Lodge, June 16, 1905, Lodge, ed., *Correspondence of TR and Lodge*, 2: 153.

42. Bishop, *TR*, 394; TR to Spring Rice, June 16, 1905, Morison, et al., eds., *Letters of TR*, 4: 1234.

43. Meyer to TR, June 16, 18, 1905, *FRUS*, Dec. 5, 1905, 811.

44. Lodge to TR, June 18, 1905, Lodge, ed., *Correspondence of TR and Lodge*, 2: 157.

45. TR to David Schneider, June 19, 1905, Morison, et al., eds., *Letters of TR*, 4: 1240–41. Schneider was the missionary and president of North Japan College. Ibid., 1240 n.1.

46. TR to Meyer, June 19, 1905, ibid., 1241–42.

47. Dennett, *Roosevelt and Russo-Japanese War*, 236–37; Hay to Meyer, June 23, 1905, *FRUS*, Dec. 5, 1905, 812.

48. TR to Tower, June 24, 1905, Morison, et al., eds., *Letters of TR*, 4: 1253.

49. TR to Sternburg, June 23, 1905, ibid., 1251; TR to Sternburg, June 25, 1905, ibid., 1256–57.

50. Acting Secretary of State Herbert Peirce to Meyer, June 26, 1905, *FRUS*, Dec. 5, 1905, 813; Count Lamsdorff, Russian foreign minister, to Meyer, June 17/30, 1905, ibid., 815; Griscom to Acting Secretary of State Alvey Adee, July 7, 1905, ibid., 817.

51. TR to Meyer, July 7, 1905, TR Papers (LC); TR to Lodge, July 11, 1905, Lodge, ed., *Correspondence of TR and Lodge*, 2: 165–66.

52. Rockhill to Peirce, July 5, 1905, *FRUS*, Dec. 5, 1905, 816; Peirce to Rockhill, July 6, 1905, ibid., 817; Rockhill to Adee, July 8, 1905, ibid., 818; Prince Ch'ing to Rockhill, July 6, 1905, encl. ibid.; Chinese minister in Washington, Chentung Liang-Cheng, to Adee, July 10, 1905, ibid., 818–19.

53. TR to Reid, June 30, 1905, Morison, et al., eds., *Letters of TR*, 4: 1258; TR to Lodge, July 18, 1905, Lodge, ed., *Correspondence of TR and Lodge*, 2: 169.

54. TR to Meyer, July 18, 1905, Morison, et al., eds., *Letters of TR*, 4: 1276.

55. Loomis to Reid, June 15, 1905, TRC; TR to Reid, July 7, 1905, ibid., 1265; TR to Spring Rice, July 24, 1905, ibid., 1284–85.

56. TR to Spring Rice, July 24, 1905, ibid., 1284–85.

57. TR to Reid, July 29, 1905, ibid., 1292.

58. Ibid., 1293.

59. Meyer to Acting Secretary of State Adee, July 13, 1905, *FRUS*, Dec. 5, 1905, 819; Meyer to Acting Secretary of State Peirce, July 3, 1905, ibid., 816; Meyer to Acting Secretary of State Adee, July 20, 1905, ibid., 819. John Hay had died on July 1, 1905.

60. Taft to Elihu Root, secretary of state, July 29, 1905, TR Papers (LC); TR to Taft, Oct. 7, 1905, Morison, et al., eds., *Letters of TR*, 5: 49; Morris, *Theodore Rex*, 399–400; Griswold, *Far Eastern Policy*, 110–16, 125–26; Charles E. Neu, *An Uncertain Friendship: Theodore Roosevelt and Japan, 1906–1909* (Cambridge, MA: Harvard University Press, 1967), 102, 104. Historian Tyler Dennett first made the

memorandum public in a conference in 1924 by calling it a "secret pact." He then published his finding in an article titled, "President Roosevelt's Secret Pact with Japan," *Current History*, 21 (1924–25): 15–21.

61. TR to Taft, July 31, 1905, Morison, et al., eds., *Letters of TR*, 4: 1293.

62. Henry Hendrix, *Theodore Roosevelt's Naval Diplomacy: The U.S. Navy and the Birth of the American Century* (Annapolis: Naval Institute Press, 2009), 107, 113–15.

63. Esthus, *Double Eagle and Rising Sun*, 71–72, 74 (Witte quote); Sydney Harcave, *Count Sergei Witte and the Twilight of Imperial Russia: A Biography* (Armonk: M. E. Sharpe, 2004), 147–48; White, *Diplomacy of Russo-Japanese War*, 240.

64. TR to Lodge, Aug. 4, 1905, Lodge, ed., *Correspondence of TR and Lodge*, 2: 171–72; Abraham Yarmolinsky, translator and ed., *The Memoirs of Count Witte* (Garden City and Toronto: Doubleday and Co., 1921; New York: Howard Fertig, 1967. Originally published in 1920), 144–45, 152; TR to Spring Rice, Nov. 1, 1905, Gwynn, ed., *Letters and Friendships of Spring Rice*, 2: 8; Eugene A. Trani, *The Treaty of Portsmouth: An Adventure in American Diplomacy* (Lexington: University of Kentucky Press, 1969), 118–21. The day after his meeting with the Japanese emissaries, Roosevelt urged them not to make any reference to indemnity in a note to his Harvard friend Baron Kentaro Kaneko, who was in Oyster Bay and working with Komura. TR to Kaneko, July 29, 1905, Morison, et al., eds., *Letters of TR*, 4: 1293.

65. Trani, *Treaty of Portsmouth*, 121; Morris, *Theodore Rex*, 406–07.

66. This account is derived from Morris, *Theodore Rex*, 407–08; Howe, *Meyer*, 191–92; Bishop, *TR*, 1: 404–05; Trani, *Treaty of Portsmouth*, 121; Harbaugh, *Life and Times of TR*, 269; Hendrix, *TR's Naval Diplomacy*, 115, 117–18.

67. Bishop, *TR*, 1: 405.

68. For wartime diplomacy and peace negotiations, see Trani, *Treaty of Portsmouth*; Esthus, *Double Eagle and Rising Sun*; White, *Diplomacy of the Russo-Japanese War*.

69. TR to Reid, Aug. 3, 1905, Morison, et al., eds., *Letters of TR*, 4: 1298.

70. Ibid.

71. Ibid.; TR to Sternburg, Aug. 21, 1905, ibid., 1306.

72. Ibid., 1306–07; TR to Jusserand, Aug. 21, 1905, ibid., 1307–08; TR to Meyer, Aug. 21, 1905, TR Papers (LC).

73. TR to Kaneko, Aug. 22, 1905, Morison, et al., eds., *Letters of TR*, 4: 1308–09.

74. TR to Assistant Secretary of State Peirce, Aug. 23, 1905, ibid., 1311–12.

75. TR to Meyer, Aug. 21, 1905, TR Papers (LC).

76. TR to Meyer, Aug. 23, 1905, ibid.; Dennett, *Roosevelt and Russo-Japanese War*, 251–54.

77. Meyer to TR, Aug. 23, 1905, TR Papers (LC); Wiegand, *Patrician in Progressive Era*, 86–87.

78. Meyer to TR, Aug. 23, 25, 1905, TR Papers (LC); Wiegand, *Patrician in Progressive Era*, 87–88; Trani, *Treaty of Portsmouth*, 144–46; Dennett, *Roosevelt and Russo-Japanese War*, 270–71; Esthus, *Double Eagle and Rising Sun*, 141–43. Meyer's 1842 reference was to the Webster-Ashburton Treaty. See Howard Jones and Donald A. Rakestraw, *Prologue to Manifest Destiny: Anglo-American Relations in the 1840s* (Lanham: Rowman & Littlefield, 1997).

79. TR to Kaneko, Aug. 22, 1905, Morison, et al., eds., *Letters of TR*, 4: 1308–10; TR to Kaneko, Aug. 23, 1905, ibid., 1312–13.

80. TR to White, Aug. 23, 1905, ibid., 1313.

81. Meyer to TR, Aug. 24, 1905, encl. in TR to Lodge, Sept. 2, 1905, ibid., 5: 6; Hendrix, *TR's Naval Diplomacy*, 126. Meyer asked Roosevelt for the approximate amount of money Japan had on deposit inside the United States from the last war loan. About $50 million, Roosevelt replied. TR to Meyer, Aug. 25, 1905, encl. in TR to Lodge, Sept. 2, 1905, Morison, et al., eds., *Letters of TR*, 5: 6. I want to thank a former graduate student of mine at the University of Alabama, Paul Grass, for allowing me to draw from his research paper emphasizing the impact of Meyer's diplomacy in resolving the Sakhalin issue.

82. TR to Meyer, Aug. 25, 1905, Morison, et al., eds., *Letters of TR*, 4: 1314–15.

83. TR to Kermit Roosevelt, Aug. 25, 1905, ibid., 1316–17.

84. Telegram from Komura to Kaneko, Aug. 27, 1905, encl. in Kaneko to TR, Aug. 27, 1905, TR Papers (LC).

85. TR to Wilhelm II, Aug. 27, 1905, Morison, et al., eds., *Letters of TR*, 4: 1317.

86. Komura to Kaneko, Aug. 28, 1905, TR Papers (LC); Kaneko to TR, Aug. 28, 1905, ibid.

87. TR quoted in Beale, *TR and Rise of America*, 304.

88. Kaneko to TR, Aug. 29, 1905, Bishop, *TR,* 1: 412.

89. TR to Peirce, Aug. 29, 1905, Morison, et al., eds., *Letters of* TR, 4: 1326.

90. Meyer to TR, Aug. 29, 1905, Howe, *Meyer*, 205; TR to Meyer, Sept. 1, 1905, Meyer Papers, Massachusetts Historical Society, cited in TRC; Harbaugh, *Life and Times of TR*, 270.

91. Yarmolinsky, translator and ed., *Memoirs of Count Witte*, 159, 161.

92. Ratification of Treaty of Portsmouth, Sept. 5, 1905, *FRUS*, Dec. 5, 1905, 824–26. The Mongols invaded Europe in the thirteenth century. Richard Connaughton, *Rising Sun and Tumbling Bear: Russia's War with Japan* (London: Cassell, revised ed., 2003), 10. Originally published by Routledge Press in 1988 as *The War of the Rising Sun and Tumbling Bear: A Military History of the Russo-Japanese War, 1904–1905.*

93. TR to Trevelyan, Sept. 12, 1905, Morison, et al., eds., *Letters of TR*, 5: 22–23.

94. Witte quoted in Bishop, *TR,* 1: 419–20.

95. Rosen quoted ibid., 420.

96. Martens quoted ibid., 421–22.

97. TR to Sternburg, Sept. 6, 1905, Morison, et al., eds., *Letters of TR*, 5: 15; TR to Trevelyan, Sept. 12, 1905, ibid., 22.

98. See notes of gratitude from Wilhelm, Nicolas, and Makido to TR all dated Aug. 29, 1905, in Bishop, *TR,* 1: 413; "Nobel Peace Prize Acceptance Speech," May 5, 1910, in "Articles and Speeches of Theodore Roosevelt," TR, *Almanac of Theodore Roosevelt, The Complete Speeches and Addresses of Theodore Roosevelt.* Online at http://www.theodore-Roosevelt.com/trspeechescomplete.html; Roosevelt received $45,482.83 for the prize, which he donated to the American Red Cross and numerous other people and organizations helping soldiers and their families of the Great War. TR to Congressman James Gallivan of Massachusetts, July 2, 1918,

Morison, et al., eds., *Letters of TR*, 8: 1344–45; TR to Gallivan, Aug. 22, 1918, ibid., 1363–66.

99. TR to Alice Roosevelt, Sept. 2, 1905, Morison, et al., eds., *Letters of TR*, 5: 2.
100. TR quoted in Bishop, *TR*, 1: 405.

CHAPTER 7

1. TR's Fifth Annual Message to Congress, Dec. 5, 1905, Richardson, ed., *Messages and Papers of Presidents*, 16: 7371–72.
2. Ibid., 7372–74; Joshua David Hawley explores Roosevelt's commitment to a high moral standard in *Theodore Roosevelt: Preacher of Righteousness* (New Haven: Yale University Press, 2008).
3. TR to Spring Rice, Nov. 1, 1905, Morison, et al., eds., *Letters of TR*, 5: 63–64.
4. Ibid., 61.
5. TR to Spring Rice, June 16, 1905, ibid., 4: 1233–34.
6. Acting Secretary of State Robert Bacon to Japanese chargé in Washington, Feb. 10, 1906, *FRUS*, Dec. 3, 1906, 1089; Wilson to Root, April 5, 1906, ibid., 177; Wilson to Root, April 12, 1906, ibid., 178; Saionji to Wilson, April 11, 1906, encl. in Japanese chargé Eki Hioki in Washington to Root, April 12, 1906, ibid., 179–80; Esthus, *TR and Japan*, 1966, 117-21. Saionji was twice prime minister—from 1906 to 1908 and 1911 to 1912.
7. Root to Hioki, April 13, 1906, *FRUS*, Dec. 3, 1906, 182; TR to Reid, June 27, 1906, Morison, et al., eds., *Letters of TR*, 5: 320.
8. TR to Henry White, Aug. 14, 1906, ibid., 359.
9. Esthus, *TR and Japan*, 106.
10. Bailey, *TR and the Japanese-American Crises*, 1; Esthus, *TR and Japan*, 128–29.
11. Ibid., 129.
12. See Gunther Barth, *Bitter Strength: A History of the Chinese in the United States, 1850–1870* (Cambridge: Harvard University Press, 1964).
13. Esthus, *TR and Japan*, 134–35; Bailey, *TR, and Japanese-American Crises*, chaps. 2–8; Aoki interaction with Root, ibid., 60–66; Aoki quoted ibid., 66. The titles for Japan's representatives to the U.S. had changed from minister to ambassador beginning with Aoki at the end of 1905. When Takahira returned to Washington after Aoki's resignation in December 1907, he returned with the title of ambassador. Esthus, *TR and Japan*, 123.
14. TR to Hale, Oct. 27, 1906, Morison, et al., eds., *Letters of TR*, 5: 473–74.
15. Ibid., 474; Esthus, *TR and Japan*, 142.
16. Ibid.
17. Ibid., 474–75.
18. TR to Kermit Roosevelt, Oct. 27, 1906, ibid., 475–76.
19. Morris, *Theodore Rex*, 493; Dewey quoted ibid., 494.
20. Bailey, *TR and Japanese-American Crises,* 88–89. *Chronicle* quoted ibid., 88 n.13.

21. Metcalf to TR, Nov. 2, 1906, TR Papers (LC); Bailey, *TR and Japanese-American Crises*, 87–88; Root quoted in Esthus, *TR and Japan*, 144.

22. TR to Metcalf, Nov. 27, 1906, TR Papers (LC); Editors' notes, Morison, et al., eds., *Letters of TR*, 5: 510 ns.1, 3.

23. TR's Sixth Annual Message, Dec. 3, 1906, in *FRUS*, Dec. 3, 1906, XLII–XLIII, or in Richardson, ed., *Messages and Papers of Presidents*, 16: 7434–35; Esthus, *TR and Japan*, 147, 148, 150; Neu, *Uncertain Friendship*, 46–50. The president's message went to Congress on December 4, 1906. The California delegation denounced his stand on Japan. "Californians Bitter at Roosevelt's Attack," *NYT*, Dec. 5, 1906, 1.

24. TR to John St. Loe Strachey, Dec. 21, 1906, quoted in Bailey, *TR and Japanese-American Crises*, 92–93; ibid., 101.

25. TR to Sir Edward Grey, Dec. 18, 1906, Morison, et al., eds., *Letters of TR*, 5: 528–29; Bailey, *TR and Japanese-American Crises*, 79; Esthus, *TR and Japan*, 149; Neu, *Uncertain Friendship*, 96, 310–12.

26. Editors' note, Morison, et al., eds., *Letters of TR*, 5: 521 n.1; TR to Wheeler, Dec. 20, 1906, ibid., 530; TR to Strachey, Dec. 21, 1906, ibid., 532.

27. Bigelow quoted in Morris, *Theodore Rex*, 483; Esthus, *TR and Japan*, 146.

28. Bailey, *TR and Japanese-American Crises*, 86, 86–87 n.6, 94–96; quotes by consul and minister for foreign affairs, ibid., 95; Neu, *Uncertain Friendship*, 29.

29. TR to Otis, Jan. 8, 1907, Morison, et al., eds., *Letters of TR*, 5, 541; *Metcalf Report*, cited in Esthus, *TR and Japan*, 142–43; Bailey, *TR and Japanese-American Crises*, 35, 37.

30. Esthus, *TR and Japan*, 154–55.

31. Ibid., 155; Bailey, *TR and Japanese-American Crises*, 37, 131; Benjamin Wheeler to TR, Nov. 4, 1902, TR Papers (LC). Roosevelt's friend and journalist, George Kennan, had sent him copies of two articles he had written for *McClure* magazine, warning him of the widespread corruption in the city. Kennan to TR, Feb. 2, 1907, TR Papers (LC). Schmitz, or "Handsome Gene," as the popular musician turned politician was known, was later convicted of what he called "trumped-up charges" of extortion by his "political enemies" but went free on appeal. Ibid., 175 n.23; Esthus, *TR and Japan*, 170; Neu, *Uncertain Friendship*, 79. See "MAYOR SCHMITZ BACK; SAYS HE IS NO GRAFTER Detectives Will Trail Him All the Way to San Francisco," *New York Times*, Nov. 24, 1906, 6. Schmitz and his wife were on six weeks of vacation in Europe when learning of the charges and encountered the press on arriving in New York before continuing on to San Francisco.

32. Morris, *Theodore Rex*, 484; Bailey, *TR and Japanese-American Crises*, 144; Esthus, *TR and Japan*, 164.

33. Morris, *Theodore Rex*, 484; Bailey, *TR and Japanese-American Crises*, 170 n.12; TR to Gillett, March 9, 1907, TR Papers (LC).

34. ibid.

35. TR to Gillett, March 11, 1907, ibid.

36. Ibid.; Bailey, *TR and Japanese-American Crises*, 143–44.

37. TR to Gillett, March 11, 1907, TR Papers (LC); Bailey, *TR and Japanese-American Crises*, 145; see also, Robert DeC. Ward, "The New Immigration Act," *The North American Review*, 185, no. 619 (July 19, 1907): 587–93.

38. TR to Schmitz, March 12, 1907, TR Papers (LC); Neu, *Uncertain Friendship*,76.

39. Bailey, *TR and Japanese-American Crises*, 143-44,175-76,189–91. Shortly after the decision was made to withdraw the Root case, a private case was filed on behalf of ten-year-old Keikichi Aoki by his father Michitsugu in *Aoki v. M.A. Deane* (1907) to also test the California law on the basis of the 1894 treaty. The case was settled out of court. See David Brudnoy, "Race and the San Francisco School Board Incident: Contemporary Evaluations," *California Historical Quarterly*, 50, no. 3 (Sep. 1971): 300–01.

40. Editors' note, Morison, et al., eds., *Letters of TR*, 5: 510 n.3; Esthus, *TR and Japan*, 150.

41. TR to Kaneko, May 23, 1907, Morison, et al., eds., *Letters of TR*, 5: 671.

42. For 1907 anti-immigrant violence on the West Coast, see Erika Lee, "Hemispheric Orientalism and the 1907 Pacific Coast Race Riots," *Amerasia Journal* 33, no. 2 (2007): 19–47.

43. TR, *Autobiography*, 564–65; TR to Henry White (friend), July 30, 1907, quoted in Esthus, *TR and Japan*, 193; Thomas A. Bailey, "The World Cruise of the American Battleship Fleet, 1907–1909," *Pacific Historical Review*, 1 (December 1932): 398.

44. TR to John Strachey, Feb. 22, 1907, Morison, et al., eds., *Letters of TR*, 5: 596–97.

45. TR to Lodge, July 10, 1907, ibid., 709; Editors' note, ibid., 709 n.1; TR's Fourth Annual Message, Dec. 6, 1904, Richardson, ed., *Messages and Papers of Presidents*, 16: 7056; Bailey, *TR and Japanese-American Crises*, chap. 10.

46. TR to Lodge, July 10, 1907, Morison, et al., eds., *Letters of TR*, 5: 710.

47. TR to Root, July 13, 1907, ibid., 717–18. Congress passed the Chinese Exclusion Act in 1882, renewed it ten years later, and made it permanent in 1902. Congress repealed it in December 1943.

48. TR to Sternburg, July 16, 1907, Morison, et al., eds., *Letters of TR*, 5: 720–21. Roosevelt shared his interest in a world cruise with several correspondents, including Lodge, Root, and Newberry. Bailey, "World Cruise," 393, 393 n.21.

49. Bailey, *TR and Japanese-American Crises*, 214–15, 224–25, 228, 230, 244; "Admiral Predicts War," *NYT*, July 5, 1907, 1; ibid. (no title to article).

50. Editors' note, Morison, et al., eds., *Letters of TR*, 5: 724 n.1; Esthus, *TR and Japan*, 187–88; Bailey, *TR and Japanese-American Crises*, 235–36, 239–42. For historians who have discerned a war scare during this period, see ibid., 227–28; Esthus, *TR and Japan*, 155–56; Morris, *Theodore Rex*, 484–85; and Neu, *Uncertain Friendship*, 97, 101–03.

51. TR to Sternburg, July 16, 1907, Morison, et al., eds., *Letters of TR*, 5: 720–21; TR to Root, July 23, 1907, ibid., 725.

52. TR to Newberry, July 24, 1907, ibid., 726; TR to Newberry, Aug. 6, 1907, ibid., 743–44.

53. TR to Root, July 26, 1907, ibid., 730.

54. Hendrix, *TR's Naval Diplomacy*, 155; Kenneth Wimmel, *Theodore Roosevelt and the Great White Fleet: American Sea Power Comes of Age* (Dulles: Brassey's, 1998), xii; Editors' note, Morison, et al., eds., *Letters of TR*, 5: 738 n.1; Esthus, *TR and Japan*, 141; Bailey, *TR and Japanese-American Crises*, 225–27.

55. TR, *Autobiography*, 568.

56. TR quoted in Wimmel, *TR and Great White Fleet,* 223 (congressional member not identified); Morris, *Theodore Rex,* 502.

57. TR to Abbott, Sept. 13, 1907, Morison, et al., eds., *Letters of TR,* 5: 791–92.

58. Wimmel, *TR and Great White Fleet,* 194–97, 243, 247; Neu, *Uncertain Friendship,* 94, 114; Matthew M. Oyos, "Theodore Roosevelt and the Implements of War," *Journal of Military History,* 60 (Oct. 1996): 631–55; Robert A. Hart, *The Great White Fleet: Its Voyage Around the World, 1907–1909* (Boston: Little, Brown and Co., 1965), 54.

59. Evans quoted in Bailey, *TR and Japanese-American Crises,* 261. Evans became known as "Fighting Bob" after warning Chile in 1891 that he would sink all its ships in Valparaiso if its authorities continued to insult the United States. Hart, *Great White Fleet,* 45. For the most detailed account of the voyage, see two volumes by Franklin Matthews, *With the Battle Fleet: Cruise of the Sixteen Battleships of the United States Atlantic Fleet from Hampton Roads to the Golden Gate, December, 1907-May, 1908* (New York: B. W. Huebsch, 1909. First printing, Oct. 1908), and *Back to Hampton Roads, Cruise of the United States Atlantic Fleet from San Francisco to Hampton Roads, July 7, 1908-February 22, 1909. Supplementary to "With the Battle Fleet"* (New York: B. W. Huebsch, 1909). Matthews traveled with the fleet and was a nationally syndicated columnist with millions of readers. James R. Reckner, *Teddy Roosevelt's Great White Fleet* (Annapolis: Naval Institute Press, 1988), 94–95.

60. TR quoted in Wimmel, *TR and Great White Fleet,* xv; Reckner, *TR's Great White Fleet,* 24.

61. Wimmel, *TR and Great White Fleet,* 226; Reckner, *TR's Great White Fleet,* 27; Hendrix, *TR's Naval Diplomacy,* 155–56, 158–59.

62. Bailey, *TR and Japanese-American Crises,* 263, 274, 281, 281 n.68.

63. TR to Sperry, March 21, 1908, Morison, et al., eds., *Letters of TR,* 6: 979; Esthus, *TR and Japan,* 264.

64. Ibid.; Hart, *Great White Fleet,* 220–29.

65. TR address to Naval War College, Newport, RI, July 22, 1908. Text and story in "President Demands Hard-Hitting Navy," *NYT,* July 23, 1908, 1–2.

66. "Great White Fleet," essay (TRC); Wimmel, *TR and Great White Fleet,* 243; Bailey, *TR and Japanese-American Crises,* 294; Hart, *Great White Fleet,* 299.

67. "Home Welcome Greets Returning Battle Fleet," *Washington Evening Star,* Feb. 22, 1909, https://chroniclingamerica.loc.gov/lccn/sn83045462/1909-02-22/ed-1 /seq-1/; TR quote in Archibald Butt to Clara (his sister-in-law, Mrs. Lewis F. Butt), Feb. 24, 1909, in Abbott, ed., *Letters of Archie Butt,* 353–54; Hendrix, *TR's Naval Diplomacy,* 162; Reckner, *TR's Great White Fleet,* 155; Morris, *Theodore Rex,* 549. The day before the fleet's return, the president received word that his sister Corinne had lost her son Stewart from a fall out of his sixth-floor dormitory window at Harvard. Roosevelt expressed his grief in a telegram and joined her after the ceremonial welcome to the fleet. Hendrix, *TR's Naval Diplomacy,* 162; TR to Douglas and Corinne Robinson, Feb. 21, 1909, Morison, et al., eds., *Letters of TR,* 6: 1533.

68. TR, *Autobiography,* 563.

69. Ibid., 282; Reckner, *TR's Great White Fleet*, 107–08, 118; Hart, *Great White Fleet*, 157. In the original version of this agreement, the signatories pledged support for the "territorial integrity of China." But over the course of the discussions, the final draft did not include the word "territorial," leaving China unprotected because of this omission combined with the mutual U.S.-Japanese approval of the status quo. Ibid., 232–33.

70. Hart, *Great White Fleet*, 235–36; TR to Taft, Dec. 8, 1910, Morison, et al., eds., *Letters of TR*, 7: 180; TR to Taft, Dec. 22, 1910, ibid., 189–92. The June 21, 1909 edition of *The Sydney Morning Herald* published "The annual return of the strength of the world's navies" as of "May 14." The report sets the comparative battleship inventory at 53 British, 32 German, 26 American, 18 French, and 14 Japanese.

71. Quoted in Hart, *Great White Fleet*, 235–36.

72. Esthus, *TR and Japan*, 249; Reckner, *TR's Great White Fleet*, 160; Bailey, "World Cruise," 418–20; Bailey, *TR and Japanese-American Crises*, 295–98, 301; TR to Henry White, April 27, 1908, TR Papers (LC).

73. Editors' note, Morison, et al., eds., *Letters of TR*, 6: 1018 n.2; Editors' note, ibid., 1515 n.1.

74. TR to Root, April 17, 1908, TR Papers (LC); TR to Kermit Roosevelt, April 19, 1908, ibid.; Reckner, *TR's Great White Fleet*, 157–58, 160, 162.

75. TR to Cortelyou, April 19, 1908, TR Papers (LC).

76. TR to Taft, March 3, 1909, Morison, et al., eds., *Letters of TR*, 6: 1543. Roosevelt had earlier warned Newberry that dividing the U.S. fleet would "leave in one ocean a considerable fragment of the fleet, not enough to stand by itself, but enough to greatly weaken by its absence the remainder of the fleet." TR to Newberry, Aug. 6, 1907, ibid., 5: 743–44.

77. Editors' note, ibid., 6: 1543 n.1.

78. TR to FDR, May 10, 1913, ibid., 7: 729.

CHAPTER 8

1. Bülow's words were, "we do not want to put anyone in our shadow, but we also demand our place in the sun." See http://germanhistorydocs.ghi-dc.org/pdf/eng/607_Buelow_Place%20in%20the%20Sun_111.pdf.

2. Esthus, *TR and International Rivalries*, 58–61.

3. Robert Kagan, *The Ghost at the Feast: America and the Collapse of World Order, 1900–1941* (New York: Alfred A. Knopf, 2023), 86–95.

4. While "open door" essentially suggests the same concept and policy pursuit, the upper-case Open Door, as tradition dictates, has been reserved for China.

5. Esthus, *TR and International Rivalries,* 70; TR to Reid, April 28, 1906, Morison et al., eds., *Letters of TR,* 5: 230; Beale, *TR and Rise of America*, 358; Hay quoted in Peter Larsen, "Theodore Roosevelt and the Moroccan Crisis, 1904-06" (doctoral dissertation, Princeton University, 1984), 105.

6. Beale, *TR and Rise of America*, 355–57.

7. Eugene N. Anderson, *The First Moroccan Crisis, 1904–1906* (Chicago: University of Chicago Press, 1930); Beale, *TR and Rise of America*, 356; Dennett, *Roosevelt and Russo-Japanese War*; Dennis, *Adventures in American Diplomacy*, chap. 19; Sidney B. Fay, *The Origins of the World War*, 2 vols. (New York: Macmillan Co., 1928), 1: 168–92; Gwynn, ed., *Letters and Friendships of Spring Rice*, 1: chap. 13, and 2: chap. 14; Pringle, *TR*, 274–76; Editors' note, Morison, et al., eds., *Letters of TR*, 4: 1161 n.1.

8. Esthus, *TR and International Rivalries*, 71; TR to Reid, April 28, 1906, Morison et al., eds., *Letters of TR*, 5: 230–31.

9. Ibid., 231–32; Beale, *TR and Rise of America*, 360.

10. TR to Taft, April 8, 1905, Morison, et al., eds., *Letters of TR*, 4: 1159.

11. TR to Taft, April 20, 1905, ibid., 1161–62.

12. Ibid., 1162.

13. Durand quoted in Larsen, "TR and Moroccan Crisis," 116.

14. TR to Taft, April 20, 1905, Morison, et al., eds., *Letters of TR*, 4: 1165.

15. TR to Francis Loomis, April 20, 1905, ibid., 1165; TR to Sternburg, April 20, 1905, ibid., 1166. In his note to Sternburg, Roosevelt explained that the U.S. involvement in China, the Japanese-Russian war, Santo Domingo, Venezuela, and Panama made it impossible to focus on Morocco.

16. Sternburg to TR, May 13, 1905, encl. in TR to Reid, April 28, 1906, ibid., 5: 231; Esthus, *TR and International Rivalries*, 71–72.

17. TR to Spring Rice, May 13, 1905, Morrison, et al., eds., *Letters of TR*, 4: 1177.

18. Ibid., 1178.

19. Ibid.

20. Ibid., 1178–79.

21. TR to Lodge, May 15, 1905, ibid., 1181.

22. TR to Spring Rice, May 26, 1905, ibid., 1194.

23. Roosevelt's summation of the kaiser's views expressed in Sternburg's memo to TR, May 29, 1905, enclosed in TR to Reid, April 28, 1906, Morison et al., eds., *Letters of TR*, 5: 232.

24. Esthus, *TR and International Rivalries*, 74; TR to Reid, April 28, 1906, Morison et al., eds., *Letters of TR*, 5: 232. It is worth noting that the American legation in Morocco was well aware of the 1880 treaty and continued to consult it. For example, during the period of the Moroccan crisis, the United States successfully adjudicated a grievance in Tangier on the basis of the treaty. See U.S. Minister to Morocco Gummeré to Root, Sept. 26 and Oct. 20, 1905, *FRUS*, Dec. 5, 1905, 685–86.

25. TR to Reid, April 28, 1906, Morison et al., eds., *Letters of TR*, 5: 234; TR to Sternburg, April 20, 1905, encl. ibid., 233–34; For a discussion of the relative military strength of Britain, France, and Germany at the time of the Moroccan crisis in 1905, see David G. Herrmann, *The Arming of Europe and the Making of the First World War* (Princeton: Princeton University Press, 1996), 40–47.

26. Beale, *TR and Rise of America*, 364 n. a., 364–67; Herrmann, *The Arming of Europe*, 38.

27. TR to Reid, April 28, 1906, Morison et al., eds., *Letters of TR*, 5: 232; Kaiser's thoughts in Sternburg to TR, June 11, 1905, encl. ibid., 234–35; TR to Reid, April 28, 1906, ibid., 232.

28. Sternburg to TR, June 11, 1905, encl. ibid., 235–36. Roosevelt noted at the bottom of the page that "Russia has lately been using the Morocco question as a means to bring Russia, France and Germany together; undoubtedly for her policy in the Far East." Editors' note, ibid., 235 n.2.

29. Russell, "Theodore Roosevelt, Geopolitics, and Cosmopolitan Ideals," 541–59; TR to Reid, April 28, 1906, Morison et al., eds., *Letters of TR*, 5: 236; TR to Jusserand, in Bishop, *TR*, 1: 77.

30. TR to Jusserand, in Bishop, *TR*, 1: 478.

31. TR to Reid, April 28, 1906, Morison et al., eds., *Letters of TR*, 5: 236; TR to Jusserand, in Bishop, *TR*, 1: 477–78; TR quoted in Esthus, *TR and International Rivalries*, 80.

32. Jusserand quoted in Harbaugh, *Life and Times of TR*, 278.

33. Sternburg to TR, June 18, 1905, encl. in TR to Reid, April 28, 1906, Morison et al., eds., *Letters of TR*, 5: 238.

34. Beale, *TR and Rise of America*, 364 n.a., 364–67.

35. TR to Sternburg of June 20, 23, and 25, 1905, encl. in TR to Reid, April 28, 1906, Morison et al., eds., *Letters of TR*, 5:238–40. The two letters of June 23 and 25 are also in ibid 4: 1250–51, 1256–57.

36. TR to Sternburg, June 25, 1905, Morison, et al., eds., *Letters of TR*, 4: 1256–57.

37. Rouvier to Jusserand, June 23, 1905, in Bishop, *TR*, 1: 478–80; Jusserand to TR, June 25, 1905, TR Papers (LC).

38. TR to Sternburg, June 23, 1905, Morison, et al., eds., *Letters of TR*, 4: 1251; TR to Sternburg, June 25, 1905, ibid., 1256–57.

39. Beale, *TR and Rise of America*, 368.

40. TR to Sternburg, June 25, 1905, Morison, et al., eds., *Letters of TR*, 4: 1257; Bishop, *TR*, 1: 485; Esthus, *TR and International Rivalries*, 80.

41. Sternburg to TR, June 28, 1905, TR Papers (LC); Bishop, *TR*, 1: 487.

42. TR to Jusserand, June 30, 1905, ibid.; Beale, *TR and Rise of America*, 369.

43. Esthus, *TR and International Rivalries*, 81–82.

44. Sternburg to TR, June 28, 1905, TR Papers (LC); TR to Lodge, July 11, 1905, Morison, *Letters of TR*, 4: 1272–73; Esthus, *TR and International Rivalries*, 82.

45. Jusserand to TR, June 25, 1905, TR Papers (LC).

46. TR to Jusserand, June 30, 1905, ibid.

47. Bishop, *TR*, 1: 485–88; Esthus, *TR and International Rivalries*, 82.

48. Arrangement signed by Germany and France in Paris, July 8, 1905, encl. in U.S. ambassador Robert McCormick in Paris to Acting Secretary of State Adee, July 12, 1905, *FRUS*, Dec. 5, 1905, 669; McCormick to Adee, July 10, 1905 (France and England); U.S. ambassador Charlemagne Tower in Berlin to Adee, July 10, 1905, both ibid., 668; Anderson, *First Moroccan Crisis*, 254–55.

49. Lodge to TR, July 8, 1905, TR Papers (LC).

50. TR to Lodge, July 11, 1905, Lodge, ed., *Correspondence of TR and Lodge*, 2: 166; TR to Reid, April 28, 1906, Morison et al., eds., *Letters of TR*, 5: 230.

51. TR to Lodge, July 11, 1905, Morison, et al., eds., *Letters of TR*, 4: 1272–73.

52. TR to Reid, April 28, 1906, ibid., 5: 242.

53. Jusserand to Root, Sept. 28, 1905, *FRUS*, Dec. 5, 1905, 672; Gummeré to Root, Oct. 27, 1905, ibid., 675; German Chargé Bussche to Root, Oct. 28, 1905, ibid., 676; Esthus, *TR and International Rivalries*, 83.

54. Ibid., 83–84.

55. Root to Jusserand, Nov. 2, 1905, *FRUS*, Dec. 5, 1905, 675; Root to German chargé, Nov. 2, 1905, ibid., 676; Root to Gummeré, Nov. 17, 1905, ibid., 676. Root later told White that the United States also based its participation on a treaty with Morocco in 1836, which awarded the United States special privileges, including most-favored-nation treatment. Root to White, Nov. 28, 1905, ibid., 677–78. The third secretary of the embassy in London, Lewis Einstein, served as the delegation's secretary. White had a three-decades-long diplomatic career, marred only by President Taft's later decision to remove him from the service and thereby alienate Roosevelt in doing so. Esthus, *TR and International Rivalries*, 17–18.

56. Root to White, Nov. 28, 1905, *FRUS*, Dec. 5, 1905, 678–79. According to Root, the Moroccan government should support commercial opportunities for all natives, put an end to religious, racial, and class discrimination against "non-Mohammedans", and protect justice in the courts. It was also vital for France and Morocco to suppress arms smuggling in the border area between Morocco and Algeria, and to stop all contraband traffic, both inland and along the coast. Other changes were needed, including financial reforms, revenue collections and taxes, and restrictions against private monopolies of public services. Ibid., 679.

57. Esthus, *TR and International Rivalries*, 83.

58. TR quoted in Dalton, *TR*, 281; TR to Bishop, March 23, 1905, Morison, et al., eds., *Letters of TR*, 4: 1144–45. The Senate approved the Dominican treaty in 1907.

59. TR to Reid, April 28, 1906, Morison et al., eds., *Letters of TR*, 5: 242; Esthus, *TR and International Rivalries*, 11–14; Wagenknecht, *Seven Worlds of TR*, 119.

60. Esthus, *TR and International Rivalries*, 113; TR to Reid, April 28, 1906, Morison et al., eds., *Letters of TR*, 5: 242.

61. Esthus, *TR and International Rivalries*, 91; TR to Reid, April 28, 1906, Morison et al., eds., *Letters of TR*, 5: 242–43.

62. Kaiser to TR, Jan. 29, 1906, cited in Root to Kaiser, Feb. 19, 1906, encl. in TR to Reid, April 28, 1906, Morison et al., eds., *Letters of TR*, 5: 243; Esthus, *TR and International Rivalries*, 91–92, Root quoted, 92.

63. White quoted ibid., 94.

64. Ibid., 95.

65. Ibid., 96–97; TR's message to kaiser in Root to Sternburg, Feb. 19, 1906, encl. in TR to Reid, April 28, 1906, Morison et al., eds., *Letters of TR*, 5: 243; Sternburg to TR, Feb. 22, 1906, encl. ibid., 244.

66. Sternburg to TR, Feb. 22, 1906, ibid.; Esthus, *TR and International Rivalries*, 97–98.

67. Quoted ibid., 98.

68. Root to Sternburg, March 7, 1906, encl. in TR to Reid, April 28, 1906, Morison et al., eds., *Letters of TR*, 5: 245–46; Esthus, *TR and International Rivalries*, 99.

69. Chancellor quoted in Beale, *TR and Rise of America*, 379 n.a.

70. Ibid., 379.

71. White and Gummeré to Root, March 27, 1906, *FRUS*, Dec. 3, 1906, 1483–84. The French government had changed hands the day before and delayed the conference until a new delegate arrived. Ibid., 1484; Esthus, *TR and International Rivalries*, 101.

72. Root to Sternburg, March 17, 1906, encl. in TR to Reid, April 28, 1906, Morison et al., eds., *Letters of TR*, 5: 247–48.

73. Sternburg to TR, March 19, 1906, encl. in TR to Reid, April 28, 1906, ibid., 249; White and Gummeré to Root, March 27, 1906, *FRUS*, Dec. 3, 1906, 1486.

74. TR to Reid, April 28, 1906, Morison et al., eds., *Letters of TR*, 5: 249.

75. Ibid., 249–50.

76. Ibid., 250; Bishop, *TR*, 1: 503. The lengthy April 28, 1906, letter to Whitelaw Reid consulted throughout this discussion of Algeciras was not made public until 1920 when it appeared in its entirety in Bishop, *TR*, 1: 467–505. In it, Roosevelt offered his account of the story behind the Moroccan negotiations. He confessed that he would have done anything he could "legitimately" do for the French, because he believed their position to be sound. But, he added, "I did not intend to take any position which I would not be willing at all costs to maintain." The president claimed to be on "close terms" with Sternburg, but "with Jusserand, who is one of the best men I have ever met, and whose country was in the right on this issue, I was even on closer terms." Roosevelt asserted that he was able "to do anything at all in so difficult and delicate a matter," solely because Jusserand and Sternburg were "such excellent men." The letter, with its substantive enclosures, has been the subject of considerable debate among historians. Did Roosevelt tailor his reflection on events to his liking and, perhaps, to elevate his role, or was his reporting accurate? For a brief outline on this debate, see Beale, *TR and Rise of America*, 388–89 n.a. Beale notes that Roosevelt's critics staged their attack without having consulted the evidence, which establishes "Roosevelt an amazingly accurate reporter in this instance." See also Marks's assessment in *Velvet on Iron,* 67–69.

77. White and Gummeré to Root, April 3, 1906, *FRUS*, Dec. 3, 1906, 1487–91.

78. Root to White, April 5, 1906, ibid., 1491–92; White and Gummeré to Root, April 7, 1906, ibid., 1492. The most difficult issue in the act related to the organization of a police force at the ports in Morocco. The force would come under the sultan's sovereignty, with the police recruited by his government (the maghzen) from Moorish Mohammedans, commanded by Moorish leaders (kaids), and distributed among the eight ports open for trade. The French would have police officers at four ports, the Spanish at two, and a mix of French and Spanish officers at the remaining two. Finally, an inspector-general from the Swiss government would be at Tangier and conduct at least one inspection a year of the police force and submit his report to the maghzen. General Act of the International Conference of Algeciras, April 7, 1906, ibid., 1497–98.

79. TR to Jusserand, April 25, 1906, Morison, et al., eds., *Letters of TR*, 5: 220–21; Root to White, June 2, 1906, *FRUS*, Dec. 3, 1906, 1495.

80. TR's Sixth Annual Message to Congress, Dec. 3, 1906, Richardson, ed., *Compilation of Messages and Papers of Presidents*, 17: 7445–46.

81. TR to Strachey, Feb. 22, 1907, Morison, et al., eds., *Letters of TR*, 5: 596. For the classic explanation of how war came to Europe in the fall of 1914, see Barbara W. Tuchman, *The Guns of August* (New York: Dell Publishing Co., 1962). Mutual fear and distrust—much of which was unfounded—lay at the base, as Roosevelt had emphasized almost a decade earlier.

82. Moltke quoted in Morris, *Theodore Rex*, 714 n.441; ibid., 440–42; Allan Nevins, *Henry White: Thirty Years of American Diplomacy* (New York: Harper Bros., 1930), 271; Esthus, *TR and International Rivalries*, 109.

83. TR to Sternburg, quoted in Harbaugh, *Life and Times of TR*, 280; TR to Reid, June 27, 1906, Morison, et al., eds., *Letters of TR*, 5: 319; TR's account of Algeciras in TR to Reid, April 28, 1906, ibid., 230–51.

84. Quoted in Morris, *Theodore Rex*, 714 n.441. Arthur Lee was the friend. Ibid.

85. TR to Jusserand quoted in Harbaugh, *Life and Times of TR*, 279–80; Beale, *TR and Rise of America*, 388 n.28.

86. Nevins, *White*, 266; White quoted ibid., 281.

87. Italy was aligned with Germany and Austria-Hungary in the Triple Alliance before the war but joined the fighting on the side of the Triple Entente in the spring of 1915.

EPILOGUE

1. *NYT*, Feb. 14, 1905, 5.

2. Inaugural Address of President TR, March 4, 1905, in Inaugural Addresses of Presidents of the United States, Avalon Project, http://avalon.law.yale.edu.

3. Fifth Annual Message of the President, TR, Dec. 5, 1905, *FRUS*, Dec. 5, 1905, 32.

4. HR, *Story of Panama*, 301–02, 311; Harding, *Untold Story of Panama*, 48–49, 97–98; No. 541, *US v. Press Publishing Company* (Jan. 3, 1911), 31 Supreme Court 212 (Oct. Term, 1910): 7, 9. For the libel account, see Clyde R. Peirce, *The Roosevelt Panama Libel Cases: A Factual Study of a Controversial Career of Teddy Roosevelt, Father of the Panama Canal* (New York: Greenwich Book Publishers, 1959).

5. Harding, *Untold Story of Panama*, 99–100.

6. Ibid., 100.

7. Ibid.

8. Ibid. Raoul died in Paris on March 23, 1934. Ibid. Roosevelt died on Jan. 6, 1919.

9. TR to Rhodes, Nov. 29, 1904, Morison, et al., eds., *Letters of TR*, 4: 1049. TR to Sydney Brooks, Dec. 28, 1908, ibid., 6: 1444; TR to Lodge, Jan. 28, 1909, ibid., 1491.

10. TR's Charter Day Address at the University of California at Berkeley, March 23, 1911, in *NYT*, March 24, 1911, 1; Morris, *Colonel Roosevelt*, 134.

11. Roosevelt, "How the United States Acquired the Right to Dig the Panama Canal," 314–18 (quotes on 314–15).

12. TR, *Autobiography*, 526.

13. TR to Thayer, July 2, 1915, Morison, et al., eds., *Letters of TR*, 8: 944.

14. Ibid., 944–45.

15. HR, *Story of Panama*, 305.

16. Collin, *TR's Caribbean*, 324–25; TR quoted in McCullough, *Path Between the Seas*, 617.

17. Watt Stewart, "The Ratification of the Thomson-Urrithia Treaty," *The Southwestern Political and Social Science Quarterly* 10 (March 1930): 416–28. See 418, 420, 425–27; quote in Parker, *Panama Fever*, 466—from Terence Graham, "The 'Interests of Civilization'? Reaction in United States against the 'Seizure' of the Panama Canal Zone, 1903–1904" (Doctoral thesis at University of Lund, Sweden: Esselte Studium, 1983, 1983), 158.

18. "President Demands Hard-Hitting Navy," *NYT*, July 23, 1908, 1–2.

19. TR to Lodge, May 24, 1905, Morison, et al., eds., *Letters of TR*, 4: 1191; TR to William E. Dodd, Feb. 13, 1912, ibid., 7: 501. Roosevelt had written a letter praising Dodd's book, *Statesmen of the Old South; or, From Radicalism to Conservative Revolt* (New York: Macmillan Co., 1911). Ibid., 500.

20. TR's speech quoted in TR to Lodge, Sept. 30, 1903, Morison, et al., eds., *Letters of TR*, 3: 607; Gould, *Presidency of TR*, 19–20, 300–01.

21. Dyer, *TR and Idea of Race*, 1–10, 28–30. Dyer credits *Our Young Folks* with reinforcing "racial stereotypes and mythology" for the impressionable young Theodore, ibid., 3–4; Dalton, *TR*, 126.

22. Gould, *Presidency of TR*, 237–38 (TR speech); TR to Wister, April 27, 1906, Morison, et al., eds., *Letters of TR*, 5: 226; Morris, *Theodore Rex*, 52–55; Dyer, *TR and Idea of Race*, 105.

23. TR to Tourgée, Nov. 8, 1901, Morison, et al., eds., *Letters of TR*, 3: 190–91; Bishop, *TR*, 1: 165–66. Among several positions, Tourgée was the U.S. consul in Bordeaux, France, and a judge during the Reconstruction era. Ibid., 165.

24. Morris, *Theodore Rex*, 58.

25. Dalton, *TR*, 321; Gould, *Presidency of TR*, 236–37.

26. Ibid., 237–43; Morris, *Theodore Rex*, 453–54.

27. "Army clears 167 Black Soldiers Disciplined in a Shooting in 1906," *NYT*, Sept. 29, 1972, 1; See John D. Weaver, *The Brownsville Raid* (New York: Norton, 1973).

28. "Editorial: Theodore Roosevelt," *The Crisis*, 17, no. 4 (Feb. 1919): 163.

29. *Roosevelt in the Kansas City Star; War-Time Editorials* (Boston: Houghton Mifflin Co., 1921), "Sedition, A Free Press, and Personal Rule," May 7, 1918, 149, online at: https://archive.org/details/rooseveltkan00roosrich/page/, 148–49.

30. Gould, *Presidency of TR*, 297, 300; Hagedorn, *Roosevelt Family of Sagamore Hill*, 167.

31. Hagedorn, *Roosevelt Family of Sagamore Hill*, 193–95. For a fascinating look at the impact of the inner circle of women in Roosevelt's life on his development into the iconic president he became see Edward F. O'Keefe, *The Loves of Theodore*

Roosevelt: The Women Who Created a President, (New York: Simon & Schuster, 2024).

32. TR, *Autobiography*, 547; Elihu Root, "Roosevelt's Conduct Of Foreign Affairs," in Herman Hagedorn, ed., *The Works of Theodore Roosevelt* 17 (New York: Scribners', 1926), xiii.

33. TR, *Autobiography*, 212.

34. Ibid., 553; TR to Mrs. John Graham of Kentucky, March 5, 1915, Morison, et al., eds., *Letters of TR*, 8: 908. While the assertion that "Not one American soldier or sailor died in action against a foreign power during his presidency" is technically accurate, the loss of American soldiers in suppressing the rebellion in the Philippines should not be overlooked. By the time Roosevelt declared an end to the U.S.-Filipino War (1898–1902) on July 4, 1902, about nine months into his presidency, over 4,200 American soldiers had died either in battle or from disease. The cost to the Filipinos was exponentially higher, with an estimated loss of 16,000–20,000 soldiers and ten times that number in civilian deaths. See H. W. Brands, *Bound to Empire: The United States and the Philippines* (New York: Oxford University Press, 1992); Welch, *Response to Imperialism*; Stephen Wertheim, "Reluctant Liberator: Theodore Roosevelt's Philosophy of Self-Government and Preparation for Philippine Independence," *Presidential Studies Quarterly* 39, no. 3 (September 2009): 500–03.

35. TR to Friedrich von Stumm, Dec. 2, 1914, Morison, et al., eds., *Letters of TR*, 8: 857. Stumm was a longtime diplomat and head of the political division of the Foreign Ministry of Germany.

36. On Theodore Jr., in World War II, see https://valor.militarytimes.com/hero /2922. For TR in the Spanish-American War, see https://www.c-span.org/video/ ?c4709169/roosevelt-medal-honor.

37. Morris, *Colonel Roosevelt*, 230, 243–45; Morris, *Edith Kermit Roosevelt*, 385–89; Dalton, *TR*, 404.

38. Morris, *Colonel Roosevelt*, 230, 244.

39. Ibid., 244; Wagenknecht, *Seven Worlds of TR*, 150–51.

40. TR's speech in Milwaukee, in Joseph B. Bishop, ed., *TR: The Ultimate Collection* (Prague: Madison & Adams Publishing, 2017), Location 61105, 61111. Kindle ed.

41. Wagenknecht, *Seven Worlds of TR*, 22, 151; Morris, *Colonel Roosevelt*, 243–48; Dalton, *TR*, 404–05; "A Speech at Milwaukee, Wisconsin, 14 October 1812," Lewis L. Gould, ed., *Bull Moose on the Stump: The 1912 Campaign Speeches of Theodore Roosevelt* (Lawrence: University Press of Kansas, 2008), 175; Candice Millard, *Theodore Roosevelt's Darkest Journey: The River of Doubt* (New York: Random House, Inc., 2005), 10–11. Roosevelt was moved by train from Milwaukee to Mercy Hospital in Chicago soon afterward. Longworth, *Crowded Hours*, 216–17.

42. TR, "The Right of the People to Rule," Carnegie Hall Address, March 20, 1912. For recorded excerpts of this speech, see https://www.loc.gov/item/99391599/ or https://www.americanrhetoric.com/speeches/teddyrooseveltrightpeoplerule.htm. The latter reference contains the text of the speech.

43. Millard, *River of Doubt*; Morris, *Colonel Roosevelt*, 1–3, 305–48. In addition to family, Roosevelt lost his personal aide, Major Archibald W. Butt, who went down with the *Titanic* in April 1912. Ibid., 182; Abbott, ed., *The Letters of Archie Butt*, xxvii–xxviii.

44. Millard, *River of Doubt*, 1–3, 305–48; Morris, *Theodore Rex*, 423–24; Morris, *Colonel Roosevelt*, 451–52; Hagedorn, *Roosevelt Family of Sagamore Hill*, 262; Wagenknecht, *Seven Worlds of TR*, 60–61, 153; George Monteiro, "'The President and the Poet': Robinson, Roosevelt, and The Touchstone," *Colby Quarterly* 10, no. 8, article 8 (1974): 512–14. Online at: https://digitalcommons.colby.edu/cq/vol10/iss8/8.

45. Ethel quoted in Eric Burns, *The Golden Lad: The Haunting Story of Quentin and Theodore Roosevelt* (New York: Pegasus Books, 2016), 155–56; Dalton, *TR*, 503; Geoffrey C. Ward, *A First-Class Temperament: The Emergence of Franklin Roosevelt* (New York: Harper and Row, 1989), 388–89; Hagedorn, *Roosevelt Family of Sagamore Hill*, 412–14.

46. Wagenknecht, *Seven Worlds of TR*, 11; TR quoted ibid.; Hagedorn quoted in Morris, *Colonel Roosevelt*, 530.

47. TR to Mary L. Brown, July 26, 1918, Morison, et al., eds., *Letters of TR*, 8: 1355; Morris, *Colonel Roosevelt*, 538. Roosevelt expressed his sorrow to his longtime friend and fellow soldier, Bob Ferguson, over what war had done to his four sons. "Quentin killed, dying as a war hawk should . . . over the enemy's lines; Archie crippled, and given the French war cross for gallantry; Ted gassed once . . . wounded seriously, and cited for 'conspicuous gallantry'; Kermit with the British military cross, and now under [General John J.] Pershing [commander of American Expeditionary Force in Europe]." TR letter quoted in Ward, *First-Class Temperament*, 389. Years after Roosevelt's death, Kermit committed suicide.

48. Wister, *Roosevelt*, 371.

49. TR quoted in Goodwin, *Leadership*, 354; Wagenknecht, *Seven Worlds of TR*, 24 (quote on TR), 29 (quote by TR); Amos, *TR*, 152; Hagedorn, *Roosevelt Family of Sagamore Hill*, 422–23; Morris, *Theodore Rex*, 377, 452; Morris, *Colonel Roosevelt*, 725 n.553.

50. Theodore Roosevelt, *The Great Adventure: Present-Day Studies in American Nationalism* (New York: Charles Scribner's Sons, 1918), 1, 8.

51. Bishop, *TR*, 2: 458.

52. Corinne and TR quotes in Morris, *Colonel Roosevelt*, 549.

53. Amos, *TR*, 156–58; TR quoted in Morris, *Colonel Roosevelt*, 550–53; Morris, *Edith Kermit Roosevelt*, 433–37; Dalton, *TR*, 513; Hagedorn, *Roosevelt Family of Sagamore Hill*, 424. Edith died in 1948.

54. Ethel Roosevelt to Kermit Roosevelt, Jan. 6, 1919, quoted in Morris, *Colonel Roosevelt*, 725 n.553.

55. Amos, *TR*, 158–62.

56. Morris, *Colonel Roosevelt*, 553–54; Marshall quoted in Doris Kearns Goodwin, *The Bully Pulpit: Theodore Roosevelt, William Howard Taft, and the Golden Age of Journalism* (New York: Simon and Schuster, 2013), 746.

57. TR, *Autobiography*, 572.

58. Among a small number of writers who have assessed the whole of Roosevelt's diplomacy, the most outspoken critic has been historian Howard K. Beale in his study, *TR and the Rise of America*. Several historians have focused on Roosevelt's presidential foreign policy and generally approve of the results. See, for example, Morris, *Theodore Rex*; Gould, *Presidency of TR*; and Holmes, *TR and World Order*, the last arguing that Roosevelt wanted the United States to act as "an international police power" in establishing "constitutional republics" where possible. See 70, 74; Frederick Marks, III's collection of essays, *Velvet on Iron*, offers a positive assessment of Roosevelt's foreign policy, stressing that he cannot be reduced to the "colorful character, full of fire and fury," or the "Rough Rider" who simply benefited from "good luck and good advice." Instead, he was a complex and capable diplomat fully responsible for his successes in foreign affairs. Quotes on page xi; For a discussion of Roosevelt historiography, see Richard H. Collin, "Symbiosis versus Hegemony: New Directions in the Foreign Relations Historiography of Theodore Roosevelt and William Howard Taft," *Diplomatic History* 19, no. 3 (Summer 1995): 473–97.

59. Beale, *TR and Rise of America*, 456.

60. Ibid., 454.

61. Marks, *Velvet on Iron*, 12–13.

62. Ibid., 171.

63. Joseph B. Bishop, ed., *Complete Works of TR* (Prague: Madison & Adams Publishing, 2017), Locations 56450, 56489, 56505, 56538, 56544, Kindle ed.

64. TR's First Annual Message to Congress, Dec. 3, 1901, Richardson, ed., *Messages and Papers of Presidents* 15: 6662.

65. TR to Knox, July 24, 1903, Morison, et al., eds., *Letters of TR*, 3: 528.

66. When Roosevelt did speak on lynching, his condemnation was clear and acknowledged as such. See the reprint of article "The President and Lynching" from the *New York Commercial Advertiser* of May 1902, defending Roosevelt's comments on lynching in a recent speech at Arlington Cemetery. The article notes that Roosevelt is "the first President to mention lynching in a public address anywhere," https://www.theodorerooseveltcenter.org/Research/Digital-Library/Record?libID=o282696. TRC; Beale, *TR and Rise of America*, 32, 34–35. Pringle called Roosevelt an "ardent imperialist" who, like the British, sought to discourage nationalism and keep the order necessary for civilization to develop. Pringle, *TR*, 360–61.

67. The irony of Roosevelt's dilemma was not missed by the press. A simple but glaring example can be seen in *"If bronze could change!" Puck Magazine*, September 1908. https://www.theodorerooseveltcenter.org/Research/Digital-Library/Record?libID=o287252. TRC.

68. Beale, *TR and Rise of America*, 169–70; *Nation* quote, ibid., 169.

69. Marks, *Velvet on Iron*, 191–92; Beale, *TR and Rise of America*, 169–70. Shortly after his presidency, Roosevelt applied this belief to a chastising speech at the Guildhall in London that was prompted by his firsthand observation of unrest in Egypt, punctuated by the assassination of a prime minister by Egyptian nationalists. You are not just the guardians of an Empire, he told his British audience, "you are also the guardians of the interests of civilization; and the present condition of affairs

in Egypt is a grave menace to both your Empire and the entire civilized world." See ibid., 165–68, TR quoted 168.

70. Marks, *Velvet on Iron*, 140.

71. William Williamson, "Mount Rushmore," 1975, 3. https://www.theodoroo seveltcenter.org/Research/Digital-Library/Record?libID=o274520. TRC.

72. Michael Patrick Cullinane, *Theodore Roosevelt's Ghost: The History and Memory of an American Icon* (Baton Rouge: Louisiana State University Press), 219.

Bibliography

PRIMARY SOURCES

Adams, Henry. *The Education of Henry Adams.* Boston: Houghton Mifflin, 1918.

Amos, James E. *Theodore Roosevelt: Hero to His Valet.* New York: John Day Co., 1927.

Aridi, Sara. "Thousands of Theodore Roosevelt's Papers Are Now Online." *New York Times*, October 17, 1918. Online at https://www.nytimes.com/2018/10/17/arts/theodore-roosevelt-papers-online.html.

Avalon Project: Documents on Law, History and Diplomacy, Yale Law School. Online at https://avalon.law.yale.edu/.

Dunne, Finley Peter. *Mr. Dooley Says.* New York: Charles Scribner's Sons, 1919. Copyright 1910.

Dunne, Finley Peter. "On War Preparations." In *Mr. Dooley in Peace and in War.* Boston: Small, Maynard and Co., 1899.

The Hague. Permanent Court of Arbitration, February 22, 1904. The Venezuelan Preferential Case. *Report of International Arbitral Awards.* United Nations, 2006.

Heaton, John L. *The Story of a Page: Thirty Years of Public Service and Public Discussion in the Editorial Columns of The New York World.* New York: Harper and Brothers Publishers, 1913.

Lodge, Henry Cabot and Theodore Roosevelt. *Hero Tales from American History.* New York: Century Co., 1895.

Longworth, Alice Roosevelt. *Crowded Hours: Reminiscences of Alice Roosevelt Longworth.* New York: Charles Scribner's Sons, 1933.

Matthews, Franklin. *Back to Hampton Roads, Cruise of the United States Atlantic Fleet from San Francisco to Hampton Roads, July 7, 1908. February 22, 1909.* Supplementary to *With the Battle Fleet.* New York: B. W. Huebsch, 1909.

Matthews, Franklin. *With the Battle Fleet: Cruise of the Sixteen Battleships of the United States Atlantic Fleet from Hampton Roads to the Golden Gate, December, 1907-May, 1908.* New York: B. W. Huebsch, 1909. First printing, October 1908.

Robinson, Corinne Roosevelt. *My Brother Theodore Roosevelt.* New York: Charles Scribner's Sons, 1921.

Root, Elihu. "Roosevelt's Conduct Of Foreign Affairs." In *The Works of Theodore Roosevelt*, edited by Herman Hagedorn, 17: xiii. New York: Scribner's 1926.

Turner, Frederick Jackson. "The Significance of the Frontier in American History." American Historical Association, *Annual Report for the Year 1893*, 199–227. Washington, DC: GPO, 1894.

University of California, Riverside, Center for Bibliographical Studies and Research, *California Digital Newspapers.* Online at https://cdnc.ucr.edu.

Theodore Roosevelt's Publications, Articles, Collections, Speeches

Roosevelt, Theodore. "Address of Honorable Theodore Roosevelt before the Naval War College, June 2, 1897." Washington, DC: U.S. Navy, GPO, 1897. Online at Theodore Roosevelt Center.

Roosevelt, Theodore. *Addresses and Presidential Messages of TR, 1902-1904.* New York: G. P. Putnam's Sons, 1904.

Roosevelt, Theodore. *Almanac of Theodore Roosevelt, The Complete Speeches and Addresses of Theodore Roosevelt.* Online at http://www.theodore-Roosevelt.com/trspeechescomplete.html.

Roosevelt, Theodore. "American Ideals." In *The Works of Theodore Roosevelt*, edited by Hermann Hagedorn, 13: 168. New York: Charles, Scribner's Sons, 1926.

Roosevelt, Theodore. *An Autobiography.* New York: Macmillan, 1913. Unabridged paperback ed. New York: DaCapo Press, 1985. Introduction by Elting E. Morison.

Roosevelt, Theodore. "The Coal Miner at Home." *Outlook*, December 24, 1910, 899–908.

Roosevelt, Theodore. *Fear God and Take Your Own Part.* New York: George H. Doran and Co., 1916.

Roosevelt, Theodore. *The Great Adventure: Present-Day Studies in American Nationalism.* New York: Charles Scribner's Sons, 1918.

Roosevelt, Theodore. "How the United States Acquired the Right to Dig the Panama Canal." *Outlook* (October 7, 1911): 314–18. Online at: https://play.google.com/books/reader?id=68AnAAAAYAAJ&hl=en&pg=GBS.PA291.

Roosevelt, Theodore. "In Memory of My Darling Wife Alice Hathaway Roosevelt and of My Beloved Mother Martha Bulloch Roosevelt." New York: G. P. Putnam's Sons, 1884. Online at: https://www.theodorerooseveltcenter.org/Research/Digital-Library/Record?libID=o286490.

Roosevelt, Theodore. "National Life and Character." *The Sewanee Review*, 2 (May 1894): 353–76.

Roosevelt, Theodore. Papers. Library of Congress, Washington, DC.

Roosevelt, Theodore. Personal Diary. Theodore Papers. Library of Congress, Washington, DC.

Roosevelt, Theodore. Photographs. Theodore Roosevelt Collection. Harvard College Library. Online at https://library.harvard.edu/collections/theodore-roosevelt
-collection.
Roosevelt, Theodore. *Proclamation 578*, July 3, 1905. Online at: https://www.presi-
dency.ucsb.edu/documents/proclamation-578-announcing-the-death-john-hay.
Roosevelt, Theodore. *Ranch Life and the Hunting Trail*. New York: Century Co.,
1885.
Roosevelt, Theodore. *Realizable Ideals* [The Earl Lecture Series at Pacific Theologi-
cal Seminary in Berkeley, California in 1911]. San Francisco: Whitaker and Ray-
Wiggin Co., 1912.
Roosevelt, Theodore. "Roosevelt Wants This Country to Control the Nicaragua
Canal." *Indianapolis Journal*, February 12, 1900.
Roosevelt, Theodore. "Sedition, A Free Press, and Personal Rule." In *Roosevelt in
the Kansas City Star; War-Time Editorials* (May 7, 1918), 148. Boston: Houghton
Mifflin Co., 1921. Online at https://archive.org/details/rooseveltkan00roosrich/
page/1921.
Roosevelt, Theodore. *The Winning of the West*, 6 vols. New York: G. P. Putnam's
Sons, 1889–1903.

Published Sources

Abbott, Lawrence F., ed. *The Letters of Archie Butt: Personal Aide to President Roo-
sevelt*. Garden City: Doubleday, Page and Co., 1924.
Adams, Henry. *The Education of Henry Adams*. Boston: Houghton Mifflin, 1918.
Bishop, Joseph B. *The Panama Gateway*. New York: Charles Scribner's Sons, 1913.
Bishop, Joseph B. *Theodore Roosevelt and His Time*, 2 vols. New York: Charles
Scribner's Sons, 1920.
Bishop, Joseph B., ed. *Theodore Roosevelt's Letters to His Children*. New York:
Charles Scribner's Sons, 1919.
Bishop, Joseph B., ed. Theodore Roosevelt, Henry Cabot Lodge. *The Complete Works
of Theodore Roosevelt*. Prague: Madison & Adams Publishing, 2017. Kindle.
Bishop, Joseph B., ed. Theodore Roosevelt, Henry Cabot Lodge. *Theodore Roosevelt,
The Ultimate Collection*. Prague: Madison & Adams Publishing, 2017. Kindle.
Brands, H. W., ed. *The Selected Letters of Theodore Roosevelt*. New York: Cooper
Square Press, 2001.
Bunau-Varilla, Philippe. *The Great Adventure of Panama*. New York: Doubleday,
Page and Co., 1920.
Bunau-Varilla, Philippe. *Panama: The Creation, Destruction and Resurrection*. New
York: McBride, Nast and Co., 1914.
de Tocqueville, Alexis. *Democracy in America*, 2 vols. New York: Vintage Books,
1945. Originally published in Paris in 1835 and 1840.
Dunn, Arthur Wallace. *From Harrison to Harding: A Personal Narrative, Covering
a Third of a Century, 1888-1921*, 2 vols. New York: G. P. Putnam's Sons, 1922.
Ford, Worthington C., ed. *The Letters of Henry Adams, 1838-1918*, 2 vols. Boston
and New York: Houghton Mifflin, 1930–1938.

Gould, Lewis L., ed. *Bull Moose on the Stump: The 1912 Campaign Speeches of Theodore Roosevelt.* Lawrence: University Press of Kansas, 2008.

Gwynn, Stephen, ed. *The Letters and Friendships of Sir Cecil Spring Rice: A Record,* 2 vols. Boston: Houghton Mifflin Co., 1929.

Hagedorn, Hermann. *Roosevelt in the Bad Lands.* Boston and New York: Houghton Mifflin and Co., 1921.

Hagedorn, Hermann. *The Roosevelt Family of Sagamore Hill.* New York: Macmillan, 1954.

Hagedorn, Hermann, ed. *The Works of Theodore Roosevelt,* 20 vols., National ed. New York: Charles Scribner's Sons, 1926.

Harding, Earl. *The Untold Story of Panama.* New York: Athene Press, Inc., 1959.

Haupt, Lewis M. "Why Is An Isthmian Canal Not Built?" *North American Review,* 175 (July 1902): 128–35.

Kohlsaat, Herman H. *From McKinley to Harding: Personal Recollections of Our Presidents.* New York: Charles Scribner's Sons, 1923.

Lodge, Henry Cabot, ed. *Selections from the Correspondence of Theodore Roosevelt and Henry Cabot Lodge, 1884-1918,* 2 vols. New York: Charles Scribner's Sons, 1925.

Mahan, Alfred T. *The Influence of Sea Power upon History, 1660-1783.* Boston: Little, Brown and Co., 1890.

Morison, Elting E., John M. Blum, and Alfred Chandler, eds. *The Letters of Theodore Roosevelt,* 8 vols. Cambridge: Harvard University Press, 1951–54.

Munro, John, ed. *The Alaska Boundary Dispute.* Toronto: Copp-Clark, 1970.

Nicolay, John George and John Hay. *Abraham Lincoln: A History,* 10 vols. New York: The Century Co., 1890.

Palmer, Frederick Palmer. *With My Own Eyes: A Personal Story of Battle Years.* Indianapolis: The Bobbs-Merrill Co., 1932.

Richardson, James D., ed. *A Compilation of the Messages and Papers of the Presidents,* 20 vols. New York: Bureau of National Literature, 1917.

Roscoe, Thayer William, ed. *The Life and Letters of John Hay.* Boston: Houghton Mifflin, 1915.

Sakurai, Tadayoshi. *Human Bullets: A Soldier's Story of the Russo-Japanese War.* Lincoln: University of Nebraska Press, 1999. Originally titled *Human Bullets: A Soldier's Story of Port Arthur* and published by Houghton, Mifflin and Company in Boston, 1907.

Sewall, William W. *Bill Sewall's Story of Theodore Roosevelt.* New York: Harper and Bros., 1919.

Thayer, William R. "John Hay and the Panama Republic." *Harper's Monthly* (July 1915): 131, 165–75.

Thayer, William R. *The Life and Letters of John Hay,* 2 vols. Boston: Houghton Mifflin, 1915.

Video of Roosevelt's flight. Online at https://www.airspacemag.com/videos/category /history-of-flight/teddy-roosevelt-goes-flying_1/ (LC). Or, https://www.youtube .com/watch?v=yIlpDwMKzJo.

Wister, Owen. *Roosevelt: The Story of a Friendship, 1880-1919.* New York: Macmillan Co., 1930.

Yarmolinsky, Abraham, trans. and ed. *The Memoirs of Count Witte.* Garden City and Toronto: Doubleday and Co., 1921.

Newspapers and Magazines

Century Illustrated Monthly
Christian Science Monitor
Daily Inter Ocean
Harper's Monthly
Indianapolis Journal
Indianapolis News
Minneapolis Journal
New York Commercial Advisor
New York Herald
New York Sun
New York Times
New York Tribune
New York World
Newsweek
Puck Magazine
San Francisco Call
Smithsonian Magazine
Sydney Morning News
Washington Evening Star
Washington Post

U.S. Congress

U.S. House of Representatives. House Committee on Foreign Affairs. *The Story of Panama: Hearings on the Rainey Resolution Before the Committee on Foreign Affairs of the House of Representatives.* Washington, DC: GPO, 1913.

U.S. Senate. *Congressional Record, Senate*, 37 Congress.

U. S. Senate. *Diplomatic History of the Panama Canal.* Senate Document 474, 63rd Congress, 2nd Session. Washington, DC: GPO, 1914.

U.S. Department of State

Papers Relating to the Foreign Relations of the United States, with the Annual Message of the President Transmitted to Congress, December 3, 1901. Washington, DC: U.S. GPO, 1901.

Papers Relating to the Foreign Relations of the United States, with the Annual Message of the President Transmitted to Congress, December 2, 1902. Washington, DC: U.S. GPO, 1902.

Papers Relating to the Foreign Relations of the United States, with the Annual Message of the President Transmitted to Congress, December 7, 1903. Washington, DC: U.S. GPO, 1903.

Papers Relating to the Foreign Relations of the United States, with the Annual Message of the President Transmitted to Congress, December 6, 1904. Washington, DC: U.S. GPO, 1904.

Papers Relating to the Foreign Relations of the United States, with the Annual Message of the President Transmitted to Congress, December 5, 1905 Washington, DC: U.S. GPO, 1905.

Papers Relating to the Foreign Relations of the United States, with the Annual Message of the President Transmitted to Congress, December 3, 1906. Washington, DC: U.S. GPO, 1906.

Papers Relating to the Foreign Relations of the United States, with the Annual Message of the President Transmitted to Congress, December 3, 1907. Washington, DC: U.S. GPO, 1907.

SECONDARY SOURCES

Books

Anderson, Eugene N. *The First Moroccan Crisis, 1904-1906.* Chicago: University of Chicago Press, 1930.

Anguizola, Gustave. *Philippe Bunau-Varilla: The Man Behind the Panama Canal.* Chicago: Nelson Hall, 1980.

Bailey, Thomas A. *A Diplomatic History of the American People*, 7th ed. New York: Appleton-Century-Crofts, 1964.

Bailey, Thomas A. *Theodore Roosevelt and the Japanese-American Crises: An Account of the International Complications Arising from the Race Problem on the Pacific Coast.* Stanford: Stanford University Press, 1934.

Barth, Gunther. *Bitter Strength: A History of the Chinese in the United States, 1850-1870.* Cambridge: Harvard University Press, 1964.

Beale, Howard K. *Theodore Roosevelt and the Rise of America to World Power.* Baltimore: The Johns Hopkins Press, 1956.

Brands, H. W. *Bound to Empire: The United States and the Philippines.* New York: Oxford University Press, 1992.

Brands, H. W. *T. R. The Last Romantic.* New York: Basic Books, 1997.

Burns, Eric. *The Golden Lad: The Haunting Story of Quentin and Theodore Roosevelt.* New York: Pegasus Books, 2016.

Campbell, Jr., Charles S. *Anglo-American Understanding, 1898-1903.* Baltimore: The Johns Hopkins Press, 1957.

Classen, Mikel B. *Teddy Roosevelt and the Marquette Libel Trial.* Charleston: History Press, 2015.

Collin, Richard H. *Theodore Roosevelt's Caribbean: The Panama Canal, the Monroe Doctrine, and the Latin American Context.* Baton Rouge: Louisiana State University Press, 1990.

Connaughton, Richard. *Rising Sun and Tumbling Bear: Russia's War with Japan.* London: Cassell, revised ed., 2003. Originally published as *The War of the Rising*

Sun and Tumbling Bear: A Military History of the Russo-Japanese War, 1904-1905. Boca Raton: Routledge Press, 1988.

Cullinane, Michael Patrick. *Remembering Theodore Roosevelt: Reminiscences of his Contemporaries.* New York: Palgrave McMillan, 2021.

Cullinane, Michael Patrick. *Theodore Roosevelt's Ghost: The History and Memory of an American Icon.* Baton Rouge: Louisiana State University Press, 2017.

Dalton, Kathleen. *Theodore Roosevelt: A Strenuous Life.* New York: Random House, Inc., 2002.

Dennett, Tyler. *Roosevelt and the Russo-Japanese War.* Garden City: Doubleday, Page and Co., 1925.

Dennis, Alfred L. P. *Adventures in American Diplomacy, 1896-1906.* New York: E. P. Dutton and Co., 1928.

Donald, Aida D. *Lion in the White House: A Life of Theodore Roosevelt.* New York: Basic Books, 2007.

DuVal, Jr., Miles P. *Cadiz to Cathay: The Story of the Long Diplomatic Struggle for the Panama Canal.* New York: Greenwood Press, 1968.

Dyer, Thomas G. *Theodore Roosevelt and the Idea of Race.* Baton Rouge: Louisiana State University Press, 1980.

Esthus, Raymond A. *Double Eagle and Rising Sun: The Russians and Japanese at Portsmouth in 1905.* Durham: Duke University Press, 1988.

Esthus, Raymond A. *Theodore Roosevelt and the International Rivalries.* Claremont: Regina Books, 1970.

Esthus, Raymond A. *Theodore Roosevelt and Japan.* Seattle: University of Washington Press, 1966.

Fay, Sidney B. *The Origins of the World War,* 2 vols. New York: Macmillan Co., 1928.

Fite, Gilbert. *Mount Rushmore.* Norman: University of Oklahoma Press, 1952.

Goodwin, Doris Kearns. *The Bully Pulpit: Theodore Roosevelt, William Howard Taft, and the Golden Age of Journalism.* New York: Simon and Schuster, 2013.

Goodwin, Doris Kearns. *Leadership in Turbulent Times.* New York: Simon and Schuster, 2018.

Gould, Lewis L. *Edith Kermit Roosevelt: Creating the Modern First Lady.* Lawrence: University Press of Kansas, 2013.

Gould, Lewis L. *The Presidency of Theodore Roosevelt.* Lawrence: University Press of Kansas, 1991.

Gould, Lewis L. *Theodore Roosevelt.* New York: Oxford University Press, 2012.

Grinder, Darrin and Steve Shaw. *The Presidents and Their Faiths: From George Washington to Barack Obama,* 2nd ed. Boise: Elevate Publishing Co., 2016.

Griswold, A. Whitney. *The Far Eastern Policy of the United States.* New York: Harcourt, Brace and Co., 1938.

Harbaugh, William H. *The Life and Times of Theodore Roosevelt.* New York: Oxford University Press, 1975. Revised ed. Originally published as *Power and Responsibility: The Life and Times of Theodore Roosevelt.* New York: Farrar, Straus and Cudahy, Inc., 1961.

Harcave, Sydney. *Count Sergei Witte and the Twilight of Imperial Russia: A Biography.* Armonk: M. E. Sharpe, 2004.

Hart, Robert A. *The Great White Fleet: Its Voyage Around the World, 1907-1909.* Boston: Little, Brown and Co., 1965.

Hendrix, Henry. *Theodore Roosevelt's Naval Diplomacy: The U.S. Navy and the Birth of the American Century.* Annapolis: Naval Institute Press, 2009.

Herring, George C. *From Colony to Superpower: U.S. Foreign Relations Since 1776.* New York: Oxford University Press, 2008.

Herrmann, David G. *The Arming of Europe and the Making of the First World War.* Princeton: Princeton University Press, 1996.

Hill, Howard C. *Roosevelt and the Caribbean.* Chicago: University of Chicago Press, 1927.

Holmes, James R. *Theodore Roosevelt and World Order: Police Power in International Relations.* Washington: Potomac Books, 2006.

Howarth, David. *Panama: Four Hundred Years of Dreams and Cruelty.* New York: McGraw-Hill Book Co., 1966.

Howe, M. A. DeWolfe. *George von Lengerke Meyer: His Life and Public Service.* New York: Dodd, Mead, 1920.

Jessup, Philip C. *Elihu Root,* 2 vols. New York: Dodd, Mead and Co., 1938; Reprint: Hamden: Archon Books, 1964.

Jones, Howard and Donald A. Rakestraw. *Prologue to Manifest Destiny: Anglo-American Relations in the 1840s.* Lanham: Rowman & Littlefield, 1997.

Kagan, Robert. *The Ghost at the Feast: America and the Collapse of World Order, 1900-1941.* New York: Alfred A. Knopf, 2023.

Kohn, Edward Parliament. *This Kindred People: Canadian-American Relations and the Anglo-Saxon Idea, 1895-1903.* Montreal: McGill-Queen's Press, 2004.

LaFeber, Walter. *The Panama Canal: The Crisis in Historical Perspective,* updated ed. New York: Oxford University Press, 1989. Originally published in 1978 and expanded in 1979.

Leopold, Richard W. *Elihu Root and the Conservative Tradition.* Boston: Little, Brown and Co., 1954.

Marks III, Frederick W. *Velvet on Iron: The Diplomacy of Theodore Roosevelt.* Lincoln: University of Nebraska, 1979.

McBeth, Brian S. *Gunboats, Corruption, and Claims: Foreign Intervention in Venezuela, 1899-1908.* Westport: Greenwood Press, 2001.

McCullough, David. *Mornings on Horseback.* New York: Simon and Schuster, 1981.

McCullough, David. *The Path Between the Seas.* New York: Simon and Schuster, 1977.

Millard, Candice. *Theodore Roosevelt's Darkest Journey: The River of Doubt.* New York: Random House, Inc., 2005.

Miner, Dwight C. *The Fight for the Panama Route: The Story of the Spooner Act and the Hay-Herrán Treaty.* New York: Colombia University Press, 1940. Reprint: New York: Octagon Books, 1966.

Moore, Gregory. *Defining and Defending the Open Door Policy: Theodore Roosevelt and China, 1901-1909.* Lanham: Lexington Books, 2015.

Morris, Edmund. *Colonel Roosevelt.* New York: Random House, 2010.

Morris, Edmund. *The Rise of Theodore Roosevelt.* New York: Coward, McCann and Geoghegan, 1979 (revised paperback ed., New York: Modern Library, 2001).

Morris, Edmund. *Theodore Rex.* New York: Random House, 2001.

Morris, Sylvia Jukes. *Edith Kermit Roosevelt: Portrait of a First Lady.* New York: Coward, McCann and Geoghegan, 1980.

Nester, William R. *Theodore Roosevelt and the Art of American Power: An American for All Time.* Lanham: Lexington Books, 2021.

Neu, Charles E. *An Uncertain Friendship: Theodore Roosevelt and Japan, 1906-1909.* Cambridge: Harvard University Press, 1967.

Neu, Charles E. *The Troubled Encounter: The United States and Japan.* New York: John Wiley and Sons, 1975.

Nevins, Allan. *Henry White: Thirty Years of American Diplomacy.* New York: Harper Bros., 1930.

Niemeier, Jean Gilbreath. *The Panama Story.* Portland: Metropolitan Press, 1968.

Norrell, Robert J. *Up from History: The Life of Booker T. Washington.* Cambridge: The Belknap Press, 2009.

O'Keefe, Edward F., *The Loves of Theodore Roosevelt: The Women Who Created a President.* New York: Simon & Schuster, 2024.

Pares, Bernard. *A History of Russia.* New York: Vintage Books, 1965. Original publication, 1926.

Parker, Matthew. *Panama Fever: The Epic Story of One of the Greatest Human Achievements of All Time—the Building of the Panama Canal.* New York: Doubleday, 2007.

Peirce, Clyde R. *The Roosevelt Panama Libel Cases: A Factual Study of the Controversial Career of Teddy Roosevelt, Father of the Panama Canal.* New York: Greenwich Book Publishers, 1959.

Penlington, Norman. *The Alaska Boundary Dispute: A Critical Reappraisal.* Toronto: McGraw-Hill, 1972.

Perkins, Bradford. *The Great Rapprochement: England and the United States, 1895-1914.* New York: Atheneum, 1968.

Perkins, Dexter. *A History of the Monroe Doctrine.* Boston: Little, Brown and Co., 1963. Revision of *Hands Off: A History of the Monroe Doctrine,* 1941.

Powell, E. Alexander. *Yonder Lies Adventure.* New York: Macmillan, 1932.

Pringle, Henry F. *Theodore Roosevelt: A Biography.* New York: Harcourt, Brace and World, 1931.

Putnam, Carleton. *Theodore Roosevelt: The Formative Years, 1858-1886.* New York: Charles Scribner's Sons, 1958.

Reckner, James R. *Teddy Roosevelt's Great White Fleet.* Annapolis: Naval Institute Press, 1988.

Risen, Clay. *The Crowded Hour: Theodore Roosevelt, the Rough Riders, and the Dawn of the American Century.* New York: Scribner, 2019.

Schwab, Stephen Irving Max. *Guantánamo, USA: The Untold History of America's Cuban Outpost.* Lawrence: University Press of Kansas, 2009,

Sexton, Jay. *The Monroe Doctrine: Empire and Nation in Nineteenth-Century America.* New York: Hill and Wang, 2011.

Strauss, Michael J. *The Leasing of Guantánamo Bay.* Westport: Greenwood Press, 2009.

Taliaferro, John. *All the Great Prizes: The Life of John Hay, from Lincoln to Roosevelt.* New York: Simon and Schuster, 2013.

Thompson, John M. *Great Power Rising: Theodore Roosevelt and the Politics of U.S. Foreign Policy.* New York: Oxford University Press, 2019.

Tilchin, William N. *Theodore Roosevelt and the British Empire: A Study in Presidential Statecraft.* New York: St. Martin's, 1997.

Trani, Eugene A. *The Treaty of Portsmouth: An Adventure in American Diplomacy.* Lexington: University of Kentucky Press, 1969.

Tuchman, Barbara W. *The Guns of August.* New York: Dell Publishing Co., 1962.

Tuchman, Barbara W. *The Zimmermann Telegram.* New York: Macmillan Publishing Co., 1958.

Tyrrell, Ian. *American Exceptionalism: A New History of an Old Idea.* Chicago: University of Chicago Press, 2022.

Wagenknecht, Edward. *The Seven Worlds of Theodore Roosevelt.* New York: Longman's, Green and Co., 1958.

Ward, Geoffrey C. *A First-Class Temperament: The Emergence of Franklin Roosevelt.* New York: Harper and Row, 1989.

Weaver, John D. *The Brownsville Raid.* New York: Norton, 1973.

Welch, Jr., Richard E. *Response to Imperialism: The United States and the Philippine-American War, 1899-1902.* Chapel Hill: University of North Carolina Press, 1979.

Whitaker, Arthur P. *The Western Hemisphere Idea: Its Rise and Decline.* Ithaca: Cornell University Press, 1954.

White, John Albert. *The Diplomacy of the Russo-Japanese War.* Princeton: Princeton University Press, 1964.

Wiegand, Wayne A. *Patrician in the Progressive Era: A Biography of George Von Lengerke Meyer.* New York: Garland Publishing Co., 1988.

Wimmel, Kenneth. *Theodore Roosevelt and the Great White Fleet: American Sea Power Comes of Age.* Dulles: Brassey's, 1998.

Articles and Essays

Ameringer, Charles D. "The Panama Canal Lobby of Philippe Bunau-Varilla and William Nelson Cromwell." *American Historical Review,* 68 (June 1963): 346–63.

Bailey, Thomas A. "Theodore Roosevelt and the Alaska Boundary Settlement." *Canadian Historical Review,* 18 (June 1937): 123–30.

Bailey, Thomas A. "The World Cruise of the American Battleship Fleet, 1907-1909." *Pacific Historical Review,* 1 (December 1932): 389–423.

Beschloss, Michael. "When T.R. Saw Lincoln." *New York Times,* May 21, 2014.

Brudnoy, David. "Race and the San Francisco School Board Incident: Contemporary Evaluations." *California Historical Quarterly,* 50, no. 3 (September 1971): 300–01.

Burton, David H. "Theodore Roosevelt's Social Darwinism and Views on Imperialism." *Journal of the History of Ideas*, 26 (January–March 1965): 103–18.

Collin, Richard H. "Symbiosis versus Hegemony: New Directions in the Foreign Relations Historiography of Theodore Roosevelt and William Howard Taft." *Diplomatic History*, 19, no. 3 (Summer 1995): 473–97.

Dennett, Tyler. "President Roosevelt's Secret Pact with Japan." *Current History*, 21 (1924–25): 15–21.

Gerstle, Gary. "Theodore Roosevelt and the Divided Character of American Nationalism." *History Cooperative*. https://historycooperative.org/journal/theodore-roosevelt-and-american-nationalism/#more-5834.

Haglund, David G. "The TR Problem in Canadian History." *London Journal of Canadian Studies*, 23 (2008): 31–44.

Haglund, David G. and Tudor Onea. "Victory without Triumph: Theodore Roosevelt, Honour, and the Alaska Panhandle Boundary Dispute." *Diplomacy and Statecraft*, 19 (2008): 20–41.

Holbo, Paul S. "Perilous Diplomacy: Public Diplomacy and the Press in the Venezuelan Crisis, 1902-1903." *The Historian*, 32 (May 1970): 428–48.

Kagan, Kenneth A. "Alfred Thayer Mahan: Turning America to the Sea." In *Makers of American Diplomacy: From Benjamin Franklin to Alfred Thayer Mahan*, edited by Frank J. Merli and Theodore A. Wilson, 279–304. New York: Charles Scribner's Sons, 1974.

Lee, Erika. "Hemispheric Orientalism and the 1907 Pacific Coast Race Riots." *Amerasia Journal* 33, no. 2 (2007): 19–47.

Livermore, Seward W. "Theodore Roosevelt, the American Navy, and the Venezuelan Crisis of 1902-1903." *American Historical Review*, 5 (April 1946): 452–71.

Lorant, Stefan. "The Boy in the Window." *American Heritage*, 6 (June 1955): 24–25.

Major, John. "Who Wrote the Hay-Bunau-Varilla Convention?" *Diplomatic History*, 8 (April 1984): 115–23.

McCulloch, Tony. "Theodore Roosevelt and Canada: Alaska, The 'Big Stick' and the North Atlantic Triangle, 1901-1909." In *A Companion to Theodore Roosevelt*, edited by Serge Richard, 293–313. Malden: Wiley-Blackwell Publishing, 2011.

Mitchell, Nancy. "The Height of the German Challenge: The Venezuela Blockade, 1902-03." *Diplomatic History*, 20 (April 1996): 185–210.

Monteiro, George. "'The President and the Poet': Robinson, Roosevelt, and *The Touchstone*." *Colby Library Quarterly* 10, no. 8, article 8 (December 1974): 512–14. Online at https://digitalcommons.colby.edu/cgi/viewcontent.cgi?referer=https://www.google.com/&httpsredir=1&article=2167&context=cq.

Oyos, Matthew M. "Theodore Roosevelt and the Implements of War." *Journal of Military History*, 60 (October 1996): 631–55.

Parsons, Edward B. "The German and American Crisis of 1902-1903." *The Historian*, 33, no. 3 (May 1971): 436–52.

Peirce, Clyde R. "The Panama Libel Cases." *Indiana Magazine of History*, 33 (June 1937): 171–86.

Pringle, Henry F. " ... Especially Pretty Alice." *American Heritage*, 9 (February 1958): 62–105.

Ricard, Serge. "The State of Theodore Roosevelt Studies." H-Diplo State of the Field Essay (October 24, 2014). Online at http://tiny.cc/E116.

Russell, Greg. "Theodore Roosevelt, Geopolitics, and Cosmopolitan Ideals." *Review of International Studies*, 32 (July 2006): 541–59.

Schoonover, Thomas. "Research Note: Max Farrand's Memorandum on the U.S. Role in the Panamanian Revolution of 1903." *Diplomatic History*, 12 (Fall 1988): 501–06.

Stewart, Watt. "The Ratification of the Thomson-Urrlutia Treaty." *The Southwestern Political and Social Science Quarterly*, 10 (March 1930): 416–28.

Tilchin, William N. "Setting the Foundation: Theodore Roosevelt and the Construction of an Anglo-American Special Relationship." In *Artists of Power: Theodore Roosevelt, Woodrow Wilson and Their Enduring Impact on U.S. Foreign Policy*, edited by William N. Tilchin and Charles E. Neu, 45–65. Westport: Praeger Security International, 2005.

Wade, Eric and Mary Rambaran-Olm. "The Many Myths of the Term 'Anglo-Saxon.'" *Smithsonian Magazine*, July 14, 2021 (online).

Ward, Robert DeC. "The New Immigration Act." *The North American Review*, 185, no. 619 (July 19, 1907): 587–93.

Wertheim, Stephen. "Reluctant Liberator: Theodore Roosevelt's Philosophy of Self-Government and Preparation for Philippine Independence." *Presidential Studies Quarterly*, 39, no. 3 (September 2009): 500–03.

Williamson, William. "Mount Rushmore." 1975. Theodore Roosevelt Center. https://www.theodorerooseveltcenter.org/Research/Digital-Library/Record?libID =o274520. Theodore Roosevelt Digital Library. Dickinson State University.

Doctoral Dissertations and MA Theses

Andrews, Cory L. "Gold, land, and the Big Stick: Theodore Roosevelt and the Alaskan Boundary Crisis." Georgia Southern University, 1997.

Graham, Terence. "The 'Interests of Civilization'? Reaction in United States against the 'Seizure' of the Panama Canal Zone, 1903-1904." University of Lund, Sweden, 1983.

Larsen, Peter. "Theodore Roosevelt and the Moroccan Crisis, 1904-06." Princeton University, 1984.

Index

131–40, 211, 246; Great White
Fleet and, 211, 246; malaria in,
104; Monroe Doctrine (Roosevelt
Corollary) and, 132, 139; Moore
and, 63; Panama revolution and, 74;
Permanent Treaty with, 133; U.S.
intervention in, 131–33, 139–41. *See
also* Spanish-American War
Culebra Cut, 35, 103
Cullinane, Michael Patrick, 255–56
Cullom, Shelby, 53–54
Curacao, 114
Czolgosz, Leon, 19

Danish Asiatic Company, 176
Darwin, Charles, 15
"Data for a History of the
Independence" (Cromwell), 45
Davis, Jefferson, 96
Davis, Richard Harding, 68
Dawson, Thomas C., 138
Delcassé, Théophile, 155, 223
Democracy in America (Tocqueville),
145
Denby, Charles, 208
Denmark, 176
Dennett, Tyler, 165
Despradele, Fidelio, 134
Dewey, George: Japan and, 200; Russo-
Japanese War and, 183; in Spanish-
American War, 28; Venezuela/
Germany and, 113, 116, 127, 128,
129–30
Dickson, Andrew, 111
Dickinson State University, 255
Dixie, USS, 74–75, 79
Dodd, William E., 241
Dominican Republic, 105, 131, 133–34,
135, 137–40, 205, 230
Drago Doctrine, 123, 139
Drago, Luis, 123, 139. *See also* Drago
Doctrine
Drake, E. A., 58
Dreadnought, HMS, 209, 252
Dual Alliance, 166, 217

Dulles, John Foster, 40
Dunne, Finley Peter, 16, 23, 156
Duque, J. Gabriel: Hay and, 64, 70, 76,
100; Panama revolution and, 56, 57,
58–59, 64, 70, 76, 100
Durand, Mortimer, 220, 230
Dutch Reformed Church, 3

Eastern Siberia, 175, 179, 186, 187, 191
Edward VII, King of England, 159, 193
Egypt: Britain and, 217; Entente
Cordiale and, 219. *See also* Suez
Canal
Ehrman, Felix, 76, 81–82, 85, 87
Embury, Philip, 70
Entente Cordiale, 166, 217–20, 223,
235–36
Espriella, Francisco V. de la, 87
Esthus, Raymond, 235
Estrada Palma, Tomás, 133
Evans, Robley D. "Fighting Bob," 209,
210
Exclusion Acts, 172

Falke (German gunboat), 123
Farnham, Roger, 45, 46, 58; Bunau-
Varilla, and, 89; Panama revolution
and, 59
Fifth Avenue Presbyterian Church (New
York), 10
Finland: Germany and, 144; Russia and,
170
Fisher, George W., 102
Formosa, 212
France, 4, 9, 17, 60–61, 111, 248;
Britain and, 217–19, 222–23, 224,
230, 235; China and, 147, 197;
Dominican Republic and, 137; in
Dual Alliance, 166, 217; Germany
and, 166, 176–77, 179, 196, 215,
216, 218–22, 225–28, 231, 232,
234; Japan and, 208; Mexico and,
110; Morocco and, 176–77, 196,
217, 218–33; Open Door and, 147;
Panama Canal and, 31, 34–37, 51,

169–93, 201–2; Jews and, 24, 146,
170; Manchuria and, 146–47, 148,
149–51, 153, 154, 157–59, 161,
163, 166, 174, 180–81, 188–89,
191, 196–97; Morocco and, 230–31;
Panama Canal and, 41; Sino-
Japanese War and, 217; in Triple
Entente, 236
Russo-Japanese War, 143–68; armistice
in, 180; Britain and, 118, 144–45,
149, 156–57, 158, 166, 218; China
and, 148–49, 150–52, 154, 155,
157–58, 159, 161, 165, 176, 178,
180; France and, 159, 165, 166,
218; Japanese naval victory in,
166–67; Korea and, 150–51, 153,
158, 164–65, 174, 181–82, 197,
212; in Manchuria, 146, 147–49,
150–51, 153, 154, 158, 159, 165,
166; negotiations of, 169–91;
plenipotentiaries for, 173, 175–76,
179, 182, 189; Portsmouth Treaty
of, 191–93, 196, 245, 255; problems
from, 196; Sakhalin Island and,
173–74, 176, 178–81, 185–90;
Siberia and, 147, 150, 170, 175, 179,
181, 185

Sagamore Hill, 2, 12, 13, 25, 55, 101,
193, 239; Sternburg at, 109; Wister
at, 248–49
Saionji, Kimmochi, 196
Sakhalin Island, 173–74, 176, 177,
178–81, 185–90, 191, 224
Saltonstall, Dick, 7; and wife (Rose), 7
Sanchez, Juan Franco, 134
Sanclemente, Manuel Antonio, 44
San Francisco: gold reserve in, 213;
Oriental Public School in, 198–206
San Francisco Chronicle, 200,
202
San Francisco School Board, 198–200,
203–5
San Juan Hill, 17, 246
Santiago (Cuba), 17, 103, 132

Santo Domingo (Dominican Republic),
133–34, 138–39, 176
Schmitz, Eugene, 203, 205
Schrank, John, 246
Schurman, Jacob, 136
Schurz, Carl, 11
*The Secret Service of the Confederate
States in Europe* (Bulloch, J.), 4
"separate but equal," 198
Sewall, William, 11, 14
The Sewanee Review, 4–5
Seward, William H., 110
Shaler, James, 60, 76; Torres and,
77–78, 79
Shaw, Albert, 55–56, 67, 84, 117
Shaw, Leslie, 91
Sherman, William T., 68
Siberia: Chinese Eastern Railway in,
150; Portsmouth peace negotiations
and, 170, 175, 179, 181, 185–87,
189, 191; Russo-Japanese War and,
147, 150; Trans-Siberian Railroad
and, 146
Sino-Japanese War, 146, 150–51, 161,
191, 217
Smalley, George, 118
Social Darwinism: in Germany, 216;
Roosevelt, T., and, 15, 242
Socrates, 5, 164, 241
South Manchurian Railway, 191
Spain: Mexico and, 16, 17, 22, 27,
28, 30, 31, 41, 103, 106, 107, 108,
110, 112, 155, 218, 228, 231, 233,
246; Morocco and, 218, 228–36;
Venezuela and, 112
Spanish-American War, 27–28, 30,
98–99, 106, 107–8, 131, 144, 209,
246; Dewey in, 113; Rough Riders
in, 3, 16–17
Spencer, Herbert, 15
Sperry, Charles S., 210–11
Spooner, John (Spooner Act), 42, 47, 54–
55; Hay-Bunau-Varilla Treaty and, 94
Spring Rice, Cecil: Anglo-Japanese
Alliance and, 196; as best man

About the Author and Editor

Howard Jones, University of Alabama Research Professor of History Emeritus, was the author of numerous books and articles on the history of U.S. foreign relations. Among his works are the award-winning *To the Webster-Ashburton Treaty*; *Mutiny on the Amistad*, which contributed to Steven Spielberg's major motion picture *Amistad*; *Union in Peril* and *Blue and Gray Diplomacy*, both essential reading on the international dimensions of the Civil War; *The Bay of Pigs*; *Death of a Generation: How the Assassinations of Diem and JFK Prolonged the Vietnam War*; and, most recently, *New York Times* "Editors' Choice" title *My Lai: Vietnam, 1968, and the Descent into Darkness*.

Donald A. Rakestraw is Georgia Southern University and Winthrop University Professor of History Emeritus. Among his publications are *For Honor or Destiny: The Anglo-American Crisis over the Oregon Territory*; *Prologue to Manifest Destiny: Anglo-American Relations in the 1840s* (with Howard Jones), a *Choice* Academic Book of the Year for 1997; and, most recently, *Daniel Webster: Defender of Peace*.